1993

"THESE SAD BUT GLORIOUS DAYS"

Margaret Fuller during the siege of Rome, by Thomas Hicks. By permission of the Houghton Library, Harvard University.

MARGARET FULLER

"These Sad But Glorious Days"

DISPATCHES FROM
EUROPE, 1846–1850

EDITED BY
LARRY J. REYNOLDS
AND
SUSAN BELASCO SMITH

Yale University Press
New Haven & London

Published with assistance from the Kingsley Trust Association Publication
Fund established by the Scroll and Key Society of Yale College.

Designed by Nancy Ovedovitz. Set in Garamond No. 3 type by Tseng
Information Systems, Inc. Printed in the United States of America by
Vail-Ballou Press, Binghamton, New York.

Library of Congress Cataloging-in-Publication Data
Fuller, Margaret, 1810–1850.
These sad but glorious days : dispatches from Europe, 1846–1850 /
Margaret Fuller ; edited by Larry J. Reynolds and Susan Belasco Smith.
p.   cm.
Includes bibliographical references and index.
ISBN 0-300-05038-0
1. Europe—Description and travel—1800–1918.   2. Europe—History—
1848–1849.   3. Fuller, Margaret, 1810–1850—Journeys—Europe.
I. Reynolds, Larry Joe, 1942–   .   II. Smith, Susan Belasco, 1950–
III. Title.
D919.F963   1992
914.04'83—dc20   91-13159
                                                                   CIP

The paper in this book meets the guidelines for permanence and durability
of the Committee on Production Guidelines for Book Longevity of the
Council on Library Resources.

10   9   8   7   6   5   4   3   2   1

CONTENTS

EDITORIAL NOTE

The texts of the dispatches reprinted in this volume are based on the *Tribune* texts, yet they are certainly far different from the originals. The words are un-altered, but pieces that appeared weeks apart in separate issues of a daily news-paper are now placed side by side; they are also separated from their original contexts, that is, from the other items surrounding them in print—reports on the revolutionary scene, news of political elections, local events, poetry, edi-torials, advertisements, and so on. We have enlarged the type, put it on better paper, and added scholarly footnotes. In short, we have privileged these texts and made them into something they never were.

We believe it is important to acknowledge this transformation. As Jerome J. McGann has pointed out, there is a need to distinguish, much more than schol-ars have in the past, between a literary work and a material text. The work, as McGann has explained, is not a static, closed, finished abstract verbal creation, but an ongoing series of specific textual (re)productions, each a material social product, embedded in a different time and place for different uses and ends.[1] Although the linguistic text we are presenting here is indeed Fuller's, at least as it appeared in the *Tribune,* the material text is obviously new and designed for current as opposed to past needs—unavoidably so. There exists, of course (Gatsby notwithstanding), no way to repeat the past, no way to reproduce a text that will recreate the original experience of reading these dispatches as they first appeared in the *Tribune.* A modern reader can, of course, travel to one of the few research libraries in this country that house volumes of the original *Tribune,* but reading the yellowed, brittle pages in the hushed confines of a rare book room means confronting the dispatches as old and valuable documents, which they certainly were not when first published. If one turns instead to microfilm copies of the *Tribune,* one encounters dim, hard-to-read projections of light very much linked to alienating modern machinery. Even if facsimile reproductions of the dispatches existed, there would be a newness about them linking them more closely to the present than to the past. Like it or not, we can only reconstruct the past as an expression of our own era; the challenge is to treat it fairly in the process of representing it. What we have constructed here, then, is a modern text that conforms as closely as possible to Fuller's intentions yet responds to the needs and interests of contemporary readers.

[1] See especially McGann's "The Text, the Poem, and the Problem of Historical Method" in his *The Beauty of Inflections: Literary Investigations in Historical Method and Theory* (Oxford: Oxford University Press, 1988), 111–32.

Fuller, perhaps due to her editorship of the *Dial,* came very close to sharing the views of modern textual editors. McGann has argued that "an experience of the objectivity of 'the text' in all its rich and various determinations—is fundamental to the *experience* of literary texts (or works) as well," [2] and Fuller would have agreed. Although she had no control over the material production of the dispatches in the *Tribune* and often never saw them in print, she thought of "texts" as materialized in specific ways by specific people for specific purposes. She subscribed to a dominant cultural ideology that privileged book production over newspaper production, and for her, as for us today, the latter was a lowly subgenre, ephemeral in nature. In fact, one of her main frustrations with newspaper writing was the impermanence and devaluation it implied; she recognized that typeface, formatting, paper quality, and cost all affect the reception of a work, diminishing or elevating its importance in the eyes of author and readers. When she said she would elaborate upon the socialism she subscribed to, but not "in the small print of *The Tribune,*" she was indicating that she understood all that the actuality of "small print" implied—lack of attention, value, respect. Similarly, when she wrote Mrs. Cranch that she had published one but not another of Christopher Pearse Cranch's poems in the *Tribune,* she explained her decision thus: "Pearse's Colonna poem was incorporated into one of my letters with mention of the picture, and, no doubt, printed, though I never read the number of the Tribune which contained it. The poem from Naples I never sent. That needs the clear type and margins of a magazine, or perhaps he will publish a vol on his return." [3] In other words, Cranch's best work deserved better textual production than the *Tribune* could provide. The same was true of her own work, at least so it seems today, and we believe the "clear type and margins" of the present volume would please Fuller if she could see them. Though not the "History" she hoped would bring her fame, this book is nevertheless hers and a fitting substitute for the one she never saw published.

We are not the first editors, of course, to recognize the historical and literary value of the dispatches and to reprint them in a book. The most complete edition, however, the one used by scholars for 134 years, her brother Arthur's *At Home and Abroad* (1856), is out of print, incomplete, and, by modern standards, quite corrupt. When Greeley provided Arthur with copies of the original dispatches from the *Tribune* files, he told him, "Of course, so far as we *do* print, we must print what she wrote, correcting any errors of expression which may have escaped her in the loveless haste of letter writing." [4] Their "correcting" in-

---

[2] Ibid., 96.

[3] Hudspeth 5:204.

[4] Manuscript letter, 4 March 1855, Fuller Correspondence, Houghton Library, Harvard University.

volved altering Fuller's word choice, phrasing, sentences, and punctuation, and removing (without any indication they had done so) material they considered inappropriate. They also left out four of the dispatches entirely, as well as large portions of her translations from contemporary newspapers, translations which provide a sense of historical context and reveal Fuller's ties to a larger political movement. By fashioning this new and complete collection of the dispatches, we have tried to allow Fuller to speak once again in her own words to a new audience.

The only emendations made to the texts of the dispatches as they first appeared in the *Tribune* have been corrections of obvious typographical errors or misspellings. (Fuller's manuscript dispatches are not extant.) No attempt has been made to modernize archaic spellings (such as "hight" and "visiter," which were acceptable in Fuller's day) or to regularize punctuation. (A list of emendations appears in the appendix.) Compound words hyphenated at the ends of lines in the *Tribune* are here reprinted with or without hyphens according to the practice in Fuller's day. The dispatches are reprinted in the chronological order of their composition, which corresponds to the order of their publication, with two exceptions.[5] Fuller signed her dispatches with a star (★), at times incorporating it into her last sentence, so we have reproduced it in this edition. She did not give her dispatches titles; those given to most of them in the *Tribune*— "Things and Thoughts in Europe," plus a Roman numeral—are Greeley's and lack authority. We have supplied new titles and numbers for the information and convenience of the reader.[6] In our notes we have made every effort to identify all of the references to unfamiliar people, places, events, and artifacts; in reluctant silence, we have let go those that eluded us.

During the time we have worked together on this edition, we have been fortunate in the help we have received from a number of people and institutions. Our first and greatest debt is to Robert Hudspeth, not only for his personal generosity and encouragement, but also for his *The Letters of Margaret Fuller*, an invaluable resource for anyone interested in Fuller's life and works. We have also benefited from the helpful suggestions and information given us by Charles Capper, Joel Myerson, and Rosella Zorzi.

[5] Dispatch 17 was published before dispatch 16, though written after it; similarly, dispatch 33 was written after dispatch 32, though published before it. Apparently in these two cases the later dispatch overtook the earlier one in the mail (see Joel Myerson, *Margaret Fuller: A Descriptive Bibliography* [Pittsburgh: University of Pittsburgh Press, 1978], 141, 143).

[6] Because Greeley entitled dispatch 30 "Undaunted Rome" and did not assign it a Roman numeral in the "Things and Thoughts" series, our dispatches 31 through 36 correspond to his XXX through XXXV. The last dispatch, number 37, he entitled merely "Italy."

Friends and colleagues in the English departments at Texas A&M University and Allegheny College were kind enough to read parts of the manuscript and to help us track down elusive nineteenth-century persons, places, and references; we wish to thank David Anderson, Stanley Archer, Judith Bean, Jeffrey Cox, Donald Dickson, Margaret Ezell, James Harner, Terence Hoagwood, Craig Kallendorf, Lisa Lovelace, Janet McCann, Katherine O'Keeffe, Kenneth Price, Diane D'Amico, Frederick Frank, Diane Goodman, Lloyd Michaels, David Miller, Brian Rosenberg, and Susan Walsh. Anthony LoBello, professor of mathematics at Allegheny College, translated several Italian sources and identified a number of references that had eluded us.

The Interdisciplinary Group for Historical Literary Study at Texas A&M supported the project in a variety of ways. A number of libraries and their staffs also assisted in our work. We are indebted to the Houghton Library, Harvard University; the American Antiquarian Society; the Fruitlands Museum; the New-York Historical Society; the New Jersey Historical Society; Indiana University Library; the Hillman Library, University of Pittsburgh; the Moody Library, Baylor University; and Cynthia Burton, Don Vrabel, and Jane Westenfield of the Pelletier Library, Allegheny College.

Ellen Graham and Harry Haskell of Yale University Press provided us with expert editorial assistance, for which we are grateful. Finally, Carol Reynolds and Joel M. Smith helped at every stage—in all of the most important ways.

AHA Fuller, Arthur B., ed. *At Home and Abroad, or Things and Thoughts in Europe*. By Margaret Fuller. Boston: Cosby, Nichols, 1856.

Baedeker Baedeker, Karl. *Italy: Handbook for Travellers*. 11th ed. 3 vols. Leipzig: Baedeker, 1899.

Berkeley Berkeley, G. F. H., and J. Berkeley. *Italy in the Making: January 1st 1848 to November 16th 1848*. 1940; rpt. London: Cambridge University Press, 1968.

Bondanella Bondanella, Peter, and Julia Conway Bondanella, eds. *Dictionary of Italian Literature*. Westport, Conn.: Greenwood Press, 1977.

Cambridge Modern History Ward, A. W., G. W. Prothero, and Stanley Leathes, eds. *Cambridge Modern History*. 14 vols. New York: Macmillan, 1902–1910.

Chambers's Biographical Dictionary Thorne, J. D., ed. *Chambers's Biographical Dictionary*. New York: St. Martin's, 1968.

Chevigny Chevigny, Bell Gale. *The Woman and the Myth: Margaret Fuller's Life and Writings*. Old Westbury, N.Y.: Feminist Press, 1976.

DAB Johnson, Allen, and Dumas Malone, eds. *The Dictionary of American Biography*. 20 vols. New York: Scribner's, 1928–36.

DNB Stephen, Leslie, and Sidney Lee, eds. *The Dictionary of National Biography*. 22 vols. London: Oxford University Press, 1937–38.

Deiss Deiss, Joseph Jay. *The Roman Years of Margaret Fuller*. New York: Crowell, 1969.

Eagle Eagle, Dorothy, and Hilary Carnell. *The Oxford Literary Guide to the British Isles*. Oxford: Oxford University Press, 1977.

Fejtö Fejtö, François, ed. *The Opening of an Era: 1848*. New York: Howard Fertig, 1966.

Great Britain Baedeker, Karl. *Handbook for Travellers to Great Britain*. 7th ed. London: T. Fisher Unwin, 1910.

Groce Groce, George C., and David H. Wallace. *The New-York Historical Society's Dictionary of Artists in America, 1564–1860*. New Haven: Yale University Press, 1957.

Grove Sadie, Stanley, ed. *The New Grove Dictionary of Music and Musicians*. 20 vols. London: Macmillan, 1980.

Hearder Hearder, Harry. *Italy in the Age of the Risorgimento, 1790–1870*. New York: Longman, 1983.

Hudspeth Hudspeth, Robert N., ed. *The Letters of Margaret Fuller*. 5 vols. to date. Ithaca: Cornell University Press, 1983–.

Kobbé Kobbé, Gustave. *Kobbé's Complete Opera Book*. London: Bodley Head, 1987.

London Encyclopedia Weinreb, Ben, and Christopher Hibbert. *The London Encyclopedia*. Bethesda, Md.: Adler and Adler, 1986.

Marraro Marraro, Howard R. *American Opinion on the Unification of Italy*. New York: Columbia University Press, 1932.

Masson Masson, Georgina. *The Companion Guide to Rome*. 6th ed. New York: Prentice-Hall, 1986.

Maurice Maurice, C. Edmund. *The Revolutionary Movement of 1848–49 in Italy, Austria-Hungary, and Germany*. New York: Putnam, 1887.

Memoirs *Memoirs of Margaret Fuller Ossoli*. Ed. R. W. Emerson, W. H. Channing, and J. F. Clarke. 2 vols. 1884; rpt. New York: Burt Franklin, 1972.

Mitchell Mitchell, Sally. *Victorian Britain: An Encyclopedia*. New York: Garland, 1988.

NCE *The New Catholic Encyclopedia*. 18 vols. Washington, D.C.: Catholic University of America, 1967.

New Cambridge Modern History *The New Cambridge Modern History*. 14 vols. New York: Cambridge University Press, 1957–1970.

Newman Newman, Edgar Leon, ed. *Historical Dictionary of France from the 1815 Restoration to the Second Empire*. New York: Greenwood, 1987.

OCA Osborne, Harold, ed. *The Oxford Companion to Art*. Oxford: Oxford University Press, 1970.

OCAL Hart, James D. *The Oxford Companion to American Literature*. 5th ed. New York: Oxford University Press, 1983.

OCEL Drabble, Margaret, ed. *The Oxford Companion to English Literature*. 5th ed. New York: Oxford University Press, 1985.

OCFL Harvey, Paul, and J. E. Heseltine. *The Oxford Companion to French Literature*. Oxford: Oxford University Press, 1959.

OCGL Garland, Henry, and Mary Garland. *The Oxford Companion to German Literature*. Oxford: Oxford University Press, 1976.

OCM Scholes, Percy A. *The Oxford Companion to Music*. Oxford: Oxford University Press, 1970.

ODA Chilvers, Ian, and Harold Osborne, eds. *The Oxford Dictionary of Art*. New York: Oxford University Press, 1988.

Reynolds Reynolds, Larry J. *European Revolutions and the American Literary Renaissance*. New Haven: Yale University Press, 1988.

Robertson Robertson, Priscilla. *Revolutions of 1848: A Social History*. Princeton: Princeton University Press, 1952.

Rostenberg Rostenberg, Leona. "Margaret Fuller's Roman Diary." *Journal of Modern History* 12 (1940):209–20.

Stern Stern, Madeleine B. *The Life of Margaret Fuller*. New York: Dutton, 1942.

Story Story, William Wetmore. *Roba di Roma*. 8th ed. 2 vols. Boston: Houghton Mifflin, 1887.

Treasures Treasures of Britain and Treasures of Ireland. 3d ed. New York: Norton, 1976.

Trevelyan Trevelyan, George Macaulay. *Garibaldi's Defense of the Roman Republic, 1848–49*. London: Longmans, Green, 1941.

Zorzi Zorzi, Rosella Mamoli. *Margaret Fuller: Un'americana a Roma, 1847–1849*. Pordenone: Studio Tesi, 1986.

Things and Thoughts in Europe.

Special correspondence of The Tribune.   [No. XXXII

The French Treason at Rome....Oudinot....Lesseps....
Letter of the Triumvirate....Reply of Lesseps....
Course of Oudinot....The Wounded Italians....Gari-
baldi....Italian Young Men....Military Funeral....
Havoc of the Siege....Courage of Mazzini....False-
ness of the London Times.

ROME, June 10, 1849.

Messrs. Greeley & McElrath :

What shall I write of Rome in these sad but glorious days? Plain facts are the best; for my feelings I could not find fit words.

When I last wrote the second act of the French comedy was being played.

In the first, the French Government affected to consult the Assembly. The Assembly, or a majority of the Assembly, affect to believe the pretext it gave and voted funds for 12,000 men to go to Civita Vecchia. Arriving there, Oudinot proclaimed that he had come as a friend and brother. He was received as such. Immediately he took possession of the town, disarmed the Roman troops, and published a manifesto in direct opposition to his first.

He sends to Rome that he is coming there as a friend; receives the answer that he is not wanted and cannot be trusted. This answer he chooses to consider as coming from a minority and advances on Rome. The pretended majority on which he counts never shows itself by a single motion within the walls. He makes an assault and is defeated. On this subject his dispatches to his Government are full of falsehoods that would disgrace the lowest pick-pocket-falsehoods which it is impossible he should not know to be such.

The Assembly passes a vote of blame. M. Louis Bonaparte writes a letter of compliment and assurance that this course of violence shall be sustained. In conformity with this promise, 12,000 more troops are sent. This time it is not thought necessary to consult the Assembly.

SECOND ACT

Now appears in Rome M. Ferdinand Lesseps, Envoy, &c. of the French Government. He declares himself clothed with full powers to treat with Rome. He cannot conceal his surprise at all he sees there, at the ability with which preparations have been made for defense, at the patriotic enthusiasm which pervaded the population. Nevertheless, in beginning his game of treaty-making, he was not ashamed to insist on the French occupying the city. Again and again repulsed, he again and again returned to the charge on this point. And here I shall translate the letter addressed to him by the Triumvirate, both for its perfect candor of statement and to give an idea of the sweet and noble temper with which these treacherous aggressions have been met. :

terventions with which it is hoped to overwhelm us, that of the French has been the most perilous. Against the soldiers of Austria and the King of Naples we can fight, for God protects a good cause. But we *do not wish to fight* against the French. We are toward them in a state not of war but of simple defense. But this position, the only one we wish to take wherever we meet France, has for us all the inconveniences without any of the favorable chances of war.

The French expedition has, from the first, forced us to concentrate our troops, thus leaving our frontier open to Austrian invasion, Bologna and the cities of Romagna unsustained. The Austrians have profited by this. After eight days of heroic resistance by the population Bologna was forced to yield. We had bought in France arms for our defense. Of these ten thousand fusils have been detained between Marseilles and Civita Vecchia. These are in your hands. Thus with a single blow you deprive us of ten thousand soldiers. In every armed man is a soldier against the Austrians.

Your forces are disposed around our walls as if for a siege. They remain there without avowed aim or programme. They have forced us to keep the city in a state of defense which weighs upon our finances. They force us to keep here a body of troops who might be saving our cities from the occupation and ravages of the Austrians. They hinder our circulation, our provisions, our couriers. They keep minds in a state of excitement and distrust which might, if our population were less good and devoted, lead to sinister results. They do *not* engender anarchy nor reaction, for both are impossible at Rome, but they sow the seed of irritation against France and it is a misfortune for us who were accustomed to love and hope in her.

We are besieged, Monsieur, besieged by France, in the name of a protective mission, while some leagues off the King of Naples, flying, carries off our hostages, and the Austrian slays our brothers.

You have presented propositions. Those propositions have been declared inadmissible by the Assembly. To-day you add a fourth to the three already rejected.— This says that France will protect from foreign invasion all that part of our territory that may be occupied by her troops. You must yourself feel that this changes nothing in our position.

The parts of the territory occupied by your troops are in fact protected; but if only for the present, to what are they reduced? and if it is for the future, have we no other way to protect our territory than by giving it up entirely to you?

The root of the question is not there. It is in the occupation of Rome. This demand has constantly stood first in your list of propositions. Now we have had the honor to say to you, Monsieur, that is impossible. The people will never consent to it. If the occupation of Rome has for its aim only to protect it, the people thank you, but tell you at the same time that, able to defend Rome by its own forces, it would be dishonored even in your eyes by declaring itself insufficient, and needing the aid of some regiments of French soldiers. If the occupation has otherwise a political object, which God forbid, the people, which has given itself freely these institutions, cannot suffer it. Rome is its Capital,

INTRODUCTION

Margaret Fuller's dispatches from Europe, written between 23 August 1846 and 6 January 1850, began as a series of engaging travel letters to the *New-York Tribune* by America's most prominent female intellectual. They eventually became a moving account of the most widespread political upheaval in modern history as seen through the eyes of a would-be revolutionary in the midst of the turmoil. Fuller became a radical in her social and political thought at almost the same time that a wave of revolutions swept the Continent, and she soon found herself not only reporting upon them, but thoroughly committed to them.

In the spring of 1848, while Fuller was living in Rome, more than fifty revolutions erupted in Austria, Prussia, Italy, and the lesser German states, with peripheral uprisings in Spain, Ireland, Denmark, and Rumania. In the months that followed, the unrest persisted, especially in Italy and Hungary, where the revolutions became wars of national liberation. Throughout the Western world, attention focused on this "great, last QUESTION of the age," as Harriet Beecher Stowe called it, "the great controversy now going on in the world between the despotic and the republican principle."[1] By the end of the summer of 1849, with the fall of the republics of Rome and Venice and the defeat of the Hungarian armies by the combined forces of Austria and Russia, the despotic principle had prevailed.

Despite the failure of the revolutions of 1848–49, they evoked an unprecedented outpouring of support from Americans, who attributed them to America's democratic example. Sympathy meetings, banquets, toasts, poems, songs, marches, speeches, and resolutions in favor of the revolutions became signs of the times. News from abroad was a precious commodity. Whenever word came by telegraph that a ship had been sighted off Boston Harbor or had arrived in New York City, anticipation swelled. "All flock to the newspaper offices," one Norwegian visitor reported, "and there is great competition among the various papers as to which one shall reap the profits of satisfying the public. An army of little boys waits impatiently outside the newspaper offices. As soon as the papers are out they rush off in every direction noisily crying their wares."[2] "God 'twas delicious!" Walt Whitman later recalled, "That brief, tight, glori-

---

[1] *The Key to Uncle Tom's Cabin; Presenting the Original Facts and Documents upon which the Story Is Founded* (1854; rpt. New York: Arno Press and the New York Times, 1968), 238, 237.

[2] *America in the Forties: The Letters of Ole Munch Raeder*, translated and edited by Gunnar J. Malmin (Minneapolis: University of Minnesota Press, 1929), 169.

ous grip / Upon the throats of kings."[3] The inspiration for his sentiments, and for those of thousands of Americans, was Fuller's dispatches.[4]

As a foreign correspondent for Horace Greeley's *New-York Tribune*, Fuller supplied her American readers not only with the news they so eagerly sought, but also with informed analyses supporting the republican cause. Though other reporters often witnessed events that Fuller missed, her classical education, her comprehensive study of Jefferson's writings, and her acute historical consciousness gave her coverage exceptional richness and depth. Among her contemporaries, only Charles A. Dana and George William Curtis, both former Brook Farmers writing for the *Tribune* from Paris and Berlin, respectively, approached her in education and intellect, but even they lacked her extensive knowledge of Europe and its dis-ease.

In her travels throughout England, France, and Italy during 1846–47, Fuller had met those who became leaders in the revolutionary movement, and as a resident of Italy from 1848 to 1850, she actively allied herself with the republican cause. From her apartment on the Piazza Barberini in Rome, she witnessed the attack of 16 November 1848 on the Quirinal Palace, which precipitated the pope's flight from the city and the establishment of the Roman Republic headed by her friend Joseph Mazzini; with her lover, Giovanni Ossoli, a captain in the Civic Guard, she suffered through the June 1849 siege and bombardment of Rome by the French army sent to restore the pope; and, as director of Fata Bene Fratelli, a hospital on Tiber Island, she nursed the wounded and dying who fell in the defense of the city. These unique circumstances combined with Fuller's abilities and commitment to make her dispatches a stirring account of the struggle for liberty in Europe.[5]

Collected here in their entirety for the first time, the dispatches are arguably Fuller's finest literary achievement. Their engaging contents, their vital, organic form, their supple, powerful prose, and their use of a memorable romantic persona raise them far above the level of ordinary journalism.[6] Those written from Italy especially, numbers 13 through 37 in the series, can be viewed as a rare kind of historical narrative, almost postmodern in its revelation of the

[3] *The Early Poems and the Fiction*, ed. Thomas L. Brasher (New York: New York University Press, 1963), 38.

[4] For Fuller's influence upon Whitman, see Reynolds 137–39.

[5] The most thorough and reliable accounts to date of Fuller's years in Europe can be found in Stern, Deiss, and Chevigny. Charles Capper is writing what promises to be the new standard biography of Fuller, the first volume of which is forthcoming from Oxford University Press. Primary materials dealing with Fuller's life in Europe can be found in Hudspeth and *Memoirs*, but the latter is unreliable and must be used with care.

[6] For a discussion of the art of the dispatches, see Reynolds 62–78.

reversals and ruptures attending history as lived, yet thoroughly romantic in its search for great ideas and heroes shaping history as written. In her private letters as well as the dispatches, Fuller alluded to the "great history" her anguish and suffering entitled her to write. Her manuscript "History of the Late Revolutionary Movements in Italy"[7] disappeared in the June 1850 shipwreck of the *Elizabeth,* which took her life and those of Ossoli and their child. Fortunately, however, the pages of the *Tribune* preserved this valuable substitute. Though probably less certain and full than Fuller's more ambitious post facto history, the dispatches have an immediacy, intensity, and suspense that her book surely would have lacked. These qualities, along with Fuller's astute analyses of people and events, give the dispatches an enduring interest and power. As Bell Gale Chevigny has observed, "In these dispatches, all her values are intact and so focused and actualized that they make her accounts of hopefulness, restlessness, political suspense, and battle riveting even now."[8]

As she was about to leave for Europe in 1846, Fuller told her friends that her trip, the dream of a lifetime, had been too long delayed to have much effect on her intellectual or emotional development. Thirty-six, she implied, was too old to expect new personal growth. She was wrong, of course, in part because Europe erupted in revolution, in part because she was prepared for a conversion experience, a feeling of being reborn. In her private mythology, Fuller always imagined Europe her true home, a place where she would flourish. As a child growing up in Cambridgeport, Massachusetts, she pretended she was a European princess being raised among commoners, and later she spoke of herself as an exotic flower planted in the wrong soil. The tutelage of her father focused her thoughts upon Europe, especially Rome, at an early age, and from him she learned to read the classics in Latin at the age of six. In her 1840 autobiographical sketch, she acknowledged "the influence of the great Romans, whose thoughts and lives were my daily food during those plastic years. . . . ROME! it stands by itself, a clear Word. The power of will, the dignity of a fixed purpose

---

[7] An announcement in the *New-York Weekly Tribune* for 23 January 1850 (p. 5:3) states: "S. MARGARET FULLER (now Marchioness Ossoli, but we like the old name best) has nearly completed, says the Boston Republican, an elaborate History of the late Revolutionary Movements in Italy, in which will be included extended observations upon the Social, Political, Religious and Aesthetical condition of the country, notices of its most eminent persons, &c. &c. It will probably be published before the close of the Winter both in New-York and London. This work, or rather the survey and study of Italy on which it is based, has engrossed the attention of the authoress through several years past. We have some reason to expect her return to this country next Summer, accompanied by her husband and child."

[8] Chevigny 371.

is what it utters."[9] Not surprisingly, she would later describe contemporary Rome in similar terms.[10]

As an adult in her twenties, Fuller continued to regard Europe with deep admiration because of its artistic and intellectual achievements. In the 1830s, she, like others in her Boston-Cambridge-Concord circle of friends, responded enthusiastically to Italian art and to the new ideas emanating from Europe, especially the spirit of romanticism generated by Carlyle, Coleridge, Cousin, Kant, Hegel, de Staël, and her beloved Goethe. She longed to imbibe this spirit near its source, thinking it would spur her intellectual growth. "I find how true was the lure that always drew me towards Europe," she wrote Emerson from Rome in December 1847. "It was no false instinct that said I might there find an atmosphere to develop me in ways I need. Had I only come ten years earlier." [11]

In 1836 Fuller had planned to go abroad with her friend Eliza Farrar and the writer Harriet Martineau, who was returning to England. The death of Fuller's father in October 1835, however, left her responsible for her family's welfare and changed her plans. "If I am not to go with you," she wrote Mrs. Farrar in the spring of 1836, "I shall be obliged to tear my heart, by a violent effort, from its present objects and natural desires. But I shall feel the necessity, and will do it if the life-blood follows through the rent." When she realized that her sense of responsibility would indeed prevent her from leaving, she declared that she would "try to forget" herself and "act for others' sakes." [12] From 1836 to 1846, Fuller functioned as head of her family, advising her brothers Eugene and William Henry in their businesses, financing the educations of her brothers Arthur and Richard, arranging for the care of her retarded brother, Lloyd, and providing financial and emotional support to her mother and her sister Ellen (wife of the poet Ellery Channing, who deserted her and their child).

During these years, Fuller also earned distinction as a teacher, editor, and author. She taught at Bronson Alcott's progressive and controversial Temple School in Boston, and then at the new Greene Street School in Providence, Rhode Island. After moving back to Boston in December 1838, she gave private language lessons, worked on a biography of Goethe, and became an active member of the Transcendental Club. During the winters of 1839–44, she held her series of "Conversations" at Elizabeth Peabody's bookshop on West Street in Boston, and from January 1840 to March 1842 she edited the transcendentalist journal *The Dial* with energy and skill. In the summers of 1842 and 1844

[9] *Memoirs* 1:18–19.

[10] See especially her "Recollections of the Vatican," *United States Magazine and Democratic Review* 27 (July 1850): 64–71.

[11] Hudspeth 4:315.

she vacationed in Concord, becoming better friends with Emerson and Hawthorne, who were captivated by her. During the summer of 1843 she traveled in the Midwest with her friend Sarah Clarke, a trip that she later wrote about in *Summer on the Lakes, in 1843* (1844). This book caught the attention of Greeley, editor of the *Tribune,* who asked her to become literary critic for his paper and offered to publish her next book, an expansion of her *Dial* essay "The Great Lawsuit," which appeared as *Woman in the Nineteenth Century* in February 1845.

With encouragement from her friends, including Emerson and Hawthorne,[13] Fuller accepted Greeley's offer and began work on the *Tribune* in December 1844. Her assignment was to write three articles a week on literary and social topics. Fuller's literary criticism, almost all scholars agree, excels through its astuteness and rigor; only Poe among her American contemporaries equaled her in this genre. Her social criticism, dealing with prisoners, prostitutes, immigrants, the mentally ill, and the poor and outcast in general, was similarly thoughtful and pointed. Though often dismissive of her newspaper writing, Fuller enjoyed it because it gave her a sense of purpose and financial independence, as well as a larger audience than she had ever known. "As to the public part," she wrote her brother Eugene in March 1845, "this is entirely satisfactory. I do just as I please, and as much or little as I please, and the Editors express themselves perfectly satisfied, and others say that my pieces *tell* to a degree, I could not expect. I think, too, I shall do better and better. I am truly interested in this great field which opens before me and it is pleasant to be sure of a chance at half a hundred thousand readers." [14]

The public-spirited, homespun Greeley admired Fuller greatly and took both a personal and a professional interest in her career. The working relationship between editor and correspondent did much to shape Fuller's European dispatches, and the understandings and misunderstandings between the two explain much about the emphasis and timing of her letters. Their relationship, which began in the winter of 1844 when Fuller came to live with Greeley and his wife, was uneasy at first, because her work habits conflicted with his.[15] Greeley

---

[12] Hudspeth 1:247, 254.

[13] See Fuller's 1844 Journal, on deposit by Mrs. Lewis F. Perry at the Massachusetts Historical Society. Fuller's entry for 22 September 1844 relates that she spent "some hours with Waldo," and adds, "Tea at the Hawthornes & walk home with H. Very bright cold moonlight. Both W. and H. think the N.Y. plan one of great promise, which I did not expect."

[14] Hudspeth 4:56. In her essay "American Literature," Fuller would celebrate American journalism. See S. Margaret Fuller, *Papers on Literature and Art,* 2 vols. (New York: Wiley & Putnam, 1846), 2:140–41.

[15] A good account of Fuller's life with the Greeleys in New York City can be found in

practically lived at the *Tribune* offices, and he kept up a whirlwind pace of editorial writing, traveling, and lecturing, all on behalf of the workingman and the Whig party. Fuller, who preferred to work at home, had difficulty with deadlines owing to her poor health (especially her debilitating migraine headaches), which made Greeley impatient; nevertheless, he extended excellent advice about writing more clearly and quickly, and she came to appreciate his help and friendship. "He teaches me things, which my own influence on those who have hitherto approached me, has prevented me from learning," [16] she wrote a correspondent. In the spring of 1845 she told her brother Eugene, "Mr Greeley I like, nay more, love. He is, in his habits, a slattern and plebeian, and in his heart, a nobleman. His abilities, in his own way, are great. He believes in mine to a surprising extent. We are true friends." [17] For his part, Greeley became fond as well as admiring of Fuller and praised her publicly as "one of the most independent, free-spoken and large-souled of the [female] sex . . . a gifted, earnest and thoroughly informed woman—an embodied Intellect." [18] Her letters from abroad he came to value quite highly, for their own sake and for their positive effect on circulation.

Fuller became interested in the role of foreign correspondent to the *Tribune* when James Nathan assumed it a year before she did. Nathan, a German businessman with whom she was in love, had gone abroad in June 1845 with his "English maiden," a young woman who was apparently his mistress.[19] At some point after leaving, he decided not to see Fuller again (though he lacked the courage to tell her this, and later the decency to return her love letters). Yet he used her to secure letters of introduction from George Bancroft (then secretary of the navy) and to arrange for the *Tribune* to publish his letters from abroad. As Fuller edited his submissions, she gave him professional advice that reveals the theory behind her own practice.

The travel-writing genre had become so popular and overworked that Fuller believed the first quality to strive for was originality. This she thought could best be achieved by focusing on the personal.[20] After reading Nathan's first

---

Constance Penta, "Fuller's Folly: The Eccentric World of Margaret Fuller and the Greeleys," master's thesis, Columbia University, 1960. See also Greeley's recollection in *Memoirs* 2: 152–63.

[16] Hudspeth 4:40.

[17] Hudspeth 4:56.

[18] *Graham's Magazine* 27 (March 1845): 143.

[19] See Hudspeth 5:8.

[20] For an excellent discussion of the vogue of travel writing in America, see Lawrence Buell, *Literary Transcendentalism: Style and Vision in the American Renaissance* (Ithaca: Cornell University Press), 188–202. Buell points out that for the Transcendentalists, including Fuller, the center of literary interest in such writing "is not what the traveler sees or the

pieces, she told him, "They are very good. I shall, however, remodel them I have now a little leaving out some particulars that are better known than you suppose. . . . Give, next, letters from Paris (in full) from Switzerland, beautiful as that on the moon at sea. Rome is an all hacknied theme and by the most accomplished pens, but you will find somewhat of your own, no doubt. Do not describe outward objects there in detail we know every nook of St Peters, every statue, every villa, by heart almost. But what you see and your own thoughts will interest." [21] A week later, having received more of his disappointing efforts, she told him, "If you could mix in them personal life still more; it would improve them. Send these too as often as you can that the interest may be kept alive." [22]

Fuller's idea that continuity mattered to readers informed her own travel letters, although she finally gave up trying to maintain it because sickness and depression created large gaps between her submissions. She had more success putting into practice her notion that the unfamiliar present should take precedence over the familiar past. "The last describing ancient Rome I did not publish," she wrote Nathan on 28 February 1846. "Every object in the eternal City is too familiar to the reading public. I wish you had sent, instead, the letter on Modern Rome, for your observations on what you personally meet are always original and interesting." [23] Though her advice was wasted on Nathan, Fuller soon followed it herself, and "Modern Rome" became her great topic.

Although Fuller thrived in New York City, she never gave up her dream of going to Europe, and in the spring of 1846 she was saving money to this end when her friends Marcus and Rebecca Spring offered to take her abroad with them. They would pay for her lodging and travel expenses in exchange for her being a companion to Rebecca and a tutor to their twelve-year-old son, Edward. According to Rebecca, Fuller was so moved by the offer that "she cried for joy." [24] Since meeting the Springs in February 1845, Fuller had come to appreciate their humanity and warmth. "They are people of whom any one would

---

adventures he experiences, but the self-portrayal of the traveller himself" (196).

In a forthcoming essay in *Resources for American Literary Study,* Susan Belasço Smith points out that with *Summer on the Lakes,* Fuller wrote a travel book possessing an external narrative that counters the idea about America promoted by early Victorians, and an internal narrative in which Fuller grapples with clarifying her own world view. In the European dispatches, Fuller evidences a new historical understanding of herself in the world.

[21] Hudspeth 4:156.

[22] Hudspeth 4:159.

[23] Hudspeth 4:190.

[24] "Friendships of Rebecca Buffum Spring," arranged by her granddaughter, Beatrice Buffum-Spring Borchardt (from original manuscript), Raritan Bay Union Collection, New Jersey Historical Society, p. 6.

say 'To know them is to love them,' " she wrote a friend.[25] Marcus was a wealthy, philanthropic, self-made merchant who divided his time between business and social causes. Rebecca, the daughter of one of the founders of the New England Anti-Slavery Society, was a bright, bold, charming Quaker who shared her husband's interest in social reform. Both were friends with Greeley, who helped Fuller achieve some financial independence from the Springs on the trip by paying in advance for fifteen of her dispatches.

On 6 August 1846 Greeley, his wife, and their young son "Pickie" saw Fuller off on her voyage to Europe. She took with her $120 for the fifteen letters. The agreement with the *Tribune* was a mixed blessing, for though it provided money and independence, it meant the expenditure of her time and energy, resources better spent, she often thought, on observation and self-culture. Though she spoke slightingly of the dispatches in her private correspondence and implied she dashed them off with little thought, she actually worked hours and sometimes days on each, often exhausting herself in the process.[26] When she had filed a dispatch, she would mention it in letters to friends, calling their attention to what she had written, thus revealing the satisfaction she took in her efforts.

Because her readership included thousands of strangers, Fuller felt it necessary to focus on the "external" part of her life in her dispatches. However, repressing her private experiences became more difficult as her "inner" life became more intense and stressful. In fact, her later dispatches are remarkably personal, especially when compared to other material appearing in the columns of the *Tribune*. Fuller eventually revealed her joys, fears, anger, sorrow, and despair in ways no other journalist of the day was willing to. This became one of the features of the new eclectic genre represented by the dispatches, a genre overfull, excessive, extravagant in the original sense of the term. That is, the dispatches wander far outside the boundaries of conventional travel writing and take on the qualities of the history, the sermon, the political manifesto, the historical romance, and especially the diary.[27]

[25] Hudspeth 4:49.

[26] For example, in a letter to Marcus Spring written on 9 August 1847, Fuller writes, "I have nearly killed myself finishing a letter for the Tribune" (Hudspeth 4:286). Similarly, on 1 January 1848 she informs her brother Richard that she had previously felt well, "but now 16 days of rain, unhappily preceded by three or four of writing have quite destroyed me for the present. My health will never be good for any thing to sustain me in any work of value. I must content myself with doing very little and by and by comes Death to reorganize perhaps for a fuller freer life" (Hudspeth 5:40). The work Fuller had been engaged in sixteen days before writing to Richard was her long dispatch 19 for the *Tribune*. She completed it on 17 December 1847.

[27] In this sense, Fuller was a typical Transcendentalist. As Lawrence Buell has pointed

Ralph Cohen, in an account of the generation of new literary genres, has argued that "genres are open categories. Each member alters the genre by adding, contradicting, or changing constituents, especially those members most closely related to it." [28] Fuller, by adding historical, political, and deeply personal components to her dispatches, revealed her originality, her boldness, and perhaps her sense of isolation. Months of living abroad, with little news from home, eventually caused her to lose touch with the American public and to imagine and address them as she did intimate friends with whom she maintained a regular correspondence. A refrain of her early private letters from abroad is that the *Tribune* contained "slight and public sketches," which she would later write out in another, "more interesting" form for her "intimates." With the exception of several letters to Caroline Sturgis Tappan (the first of which, apparently destroyed, told about the birth of Fuller's child), she never followed through on this plan. The *Tribune* itself became the recipient of the "more interesting" account of her life.

Tappan, Fuller's nearest and dearest friend, was the one person to whom she wrote complaining about the Springs. Though Fuller got along remarkably well with the Springs during the twelve months she traveled with them, she later faulted them for being oblivious to her unexpressed feelings. After parting with them, she wrote Tappan, "I was very weary of the good friends who were with me, because they never knew what I was feeling, and always brought forward what I wanted to leave behind." [29] Nevertheless, the Springs freed Fuller from financial worries and exposed her to an external world she might easily have missed if traveling alone. Not only did they visit celebrated sights and people; they also investigated the living and working conditions of the poor. As the dispatches reveal, the party toured mechanics' institutes in Manchester and Liverpool, descended into a coal mine at Newcastle, saw "sooty servitors tending their furnaces" (dispatch 7) in Sheffield, visited a model prison in London, and did more of the same in France and Italy. One of the Springs' purposes on the trip was to learn about recent social improvements that they could introduce into American society, either through Marcus's business or by means of a utopian community.

---

out, "On the whole, the Transcendentalists were exceedingly weak in the genres most in favor today (poetry, drama, prose fiction); but they had strong affinities with other genres and subgenres about which less is known . . ." (*Literary Transcendentalism,* 16). Also relevant is Buell's observation that the leading characteristics of Transcendental rhetoric are "inchoate structure, prodigal imagery, wit, paradox, symbolism, aphoristic statement, paratactic syntax, and a manifesto-like tone" (ibid., 18).

[28] "History and Genre," *New Literary History* 17 (1986):204.

[29] Hudspeth 5:42.

The Springs had purchased shares in Brook Farm; later they would invest heavily in the North American Phalanx and found the Raritan Bay Union in 1852.[30] Though they believed in the ownership of personal property, they were attracted to socialism and actively supported abolitionism. In fact, they probably deserve credit for the abrupt change in Fuller's attitude toward abolitionists while she was abroad, a change biographers have attributed to the distance and perspective Europe provided.[31] Rebecca Spring consistently spoke out against slavery, even to slave holders, and her unpublished journal reveals that Fuller saw her in action at least once, during a visit from Thomas Carlyle and Joseph Mazzini in London. As Carlyle held forth in his best reactionary mode, Rebecca recalled,

> Margaret was standing before the open fire, looking amused; Massini [sic] was walking, with his hands behind him, looking annoyed; others grouped about. I heard Carlyle say, "If people consent to be slaves, they deserve to be slaves! I have no pity for them!" As I started towards him, Margaret laughed, "I have been wondering how long Rebecca would bear it!" I told him of the severe slave laws against teaching slaves to read, and yet they contrived to learn. What wit and skill they used in escaping, often running a long way on the railroad track until they saw a train approaching, which passing over would obliterate the scent, and thus they would escape the bloodhounds. I told him of many things. Carlyle listened, frequently commenting, "I am glad to hear it! I am glad to hear it!"

After Rebecca's reprimand, Carlyle became gentle, kissed Eddie good night and for the rest of the evening "was charming, and we all sat around him, the delighted listeners to his picture talk."[32] A year later, Fuller wrote in dispatch

---

[30] See Beatrice E. Borchardt, "Lady of Utopia: The Story of Marcus and Rebecca Buffum Spring of Eagleswood," 1973, Raritan Bay Union Collection, New Jersey Historical Society.

[31] See, for example, Francis E. Kearns, "Margaret Fuller and the Abolition Movement," *Journal of the History of Ideas* 25 (1964): 120–27.

[32] "Friendships of Rebecca Buffum Spring," arranged by Beatrice Buffum-Spring Borchardt, Raritan Bay Union Collection, New Jersey Historical Society, pp. 14–15.

Carlyle, in a letter of 18 December 1846 to Emerson, wrote, "Miss Fuller came duly as you announced; was welcomed for your sake and her own. A high-soaring, clear, enthusiast soul; in whose speech there is much of all that one wants to find in speech. A sharp subtle intellect too; and less of that shoreless Asiatic dreaminess than I have sometimes met with in her writings. We like one another very well, I think, and the Springs too were favourites" (*The Correspondence of Emerson and Carlyle,* ed. Joseph Slater [New York and London: Columbia University Press, 1964], 410).

18 from Rome, "How it pleases me here to think of the Abolitionists! I could never endure to be with them at home, they were so tedious, often so narrow, always so rabid and exaggerated in their tone. But after all, they had a high motive, something eternal in their desire and life; and, if it was not the only thing worth thinking of it was really something worth living and dying for to free a great nation from such a terrible blot, such a threatening plague." Fuller is certainly expressing a new opinion,[33] but she is also conveying a tribute to a beloved friend, as Rebecca, then back in America, would have known when she read it.

The Springs' example of social engagement accounted in part, it seems, for Fuller's eventual involvement in the Italian revolutionary movement; but while she traveled with them, a romantic reflexiveness and self-concern remained the dominant quality of her temperament. "I was always out of the body," she later confessed, "and they, good friends, were *in.*"[34] One of the feelings Fuller first had to deal with in Europe was the hurt caused by James Nathan's rejection of her. Soon after her arrival in England, she received a letter from him announcing his engagement to a German friend. This news apparently devastated her for a while. The first two dispatches she sent to the *Tribune,* before she heard from him, offer unsurprising reflections upon the voyage over, the sights in Liverpool and Chester, and a visit to the elderly Wordsworth. Her third dispatch, from Edinburgh, on the other hand, is unusually brief and wooden, a result undoubtedly of the news she has just received and the psychological pain she is suffering. Dispatch 4, written several days later and discussing Robert Burns, Dr. Andrew Combe, and Thomas De Quincey, shows slightly more energy. It is in dispatch 5, however, that her writing takes on a new power and originality as she describes a night she spent lost in the fog on Ben Lomond—, an exciting and dangerous adventure that may have originated in thoughts of suicide.[35]

On 8 October 1846, Carlyle wrote his brother John, "Yesternight there came a bevy of Americans from Emerson; one Margaret Fuller the chief figure of them: a strange *lilting* lean old maid, not nearly such a bore as I expected: we are to see them again." A month later he wrote, "Last night, a weary tea with the American Margt Fuller and Mazzini,—not to be repeated!" Ibid., n. 6.

[33] Though long opposed to slavery, Fuller had a strained relationship with abolitionists. See Kearns, "Margaret Fuller and the Abolition Movement."

[34] Hudspeth 4:291.

[35] Robert N. Hudspeth has made the conjecture about Fuller's suicidal state of mind, basing it on Rebecca's journal observation that Margaret, after receiving Nathan's letter, became sad and restless and rode on top of the stagecoach in the pouring rain as the party journeyed to Loch Katrine and Ben Lomond. See Hudspeth 4:10 and Borchardt, "Lady of Utopia," n.p.

(The article is a classic set piece, which Whitman clipped and saved among his papers.)

Whatever the depth of Fuller's despair, this experience apparently contributed to her growing concern for suffering humanity, especially women. Her next dispatch, for example, tells of the misery and degradation of the poor of Glasgow: "I saw here in Glasgow persons, especially women, dressed in dirty, wretched tatters, worse than none, and with an expression of listless, unexpecting woe upon their faces, far more tragic than the inscription over the gate of Dante's *Inferno*" (dispatch 6). In dispatch 10, her account of the tragic actress Rachel, whom she went to see seven or eight times in Paris, reveals similar interest in "grief in its most desolate aspects," as does her description, in dispatch 13, of the victimized young silk weavers of Lyons. "To themselves be woe," she exclaims, "who have eyes and see not, ears and hear not, the convulsions and sobs of injured Humanity!"

Fuller had never been a particularly contented person, but in Europe she began to perceive her life more in tragic terms than she ever had before, not just because of Nathan, but also because of a multitude of disappointments. In her correspondence she dwelt more and more on the poor and oppressed of Europe, and though she experienced several months of great happiness with Ossoli in the fall of 1848, she eventually represented social conditions, especially the failed Italian revolutions, as a dark backdrop to the tragedy she imagined herself living. Because Fuller had devoted so much of her life to literature— as reader, editor, and author—she thought instinctively in terms of literary forms, often conflating art and life.[36] This habit of perception shaped her experiences and endowed them—and her writings—with a richness and luxuriance uncommon to New England.

The European revolutionary movement, which Fuller embraced and then saw crushed, emerged out of very real and widespread social misery. The industrial revolution had brought with it crowding, smoke, grime, poverty, and vice, all recently aggravated by the potato blight, poor wheat harvests, the dramatic rise in the price of bread, and a slump in manufacturing. The Europe Fuller encountered on her travels during 1846 and 1847 teemed with unemployment, famine, and social unrest, as well as corrupt and despotic governments unable or unwilling to fashion solutions to these problems. Meanwhile, socialists and communists were calling more and more persuasively for radical social and political change. *The Communist Manifesto,* which appeared in February 1848,

---

[36] Albert J. Von Frank discusses Fuller's sense of life as art in *The Sacred Game: Provincialism and Frontier Consciousness in American Literature, 1630–1860* (London: Cambridge University Press, 1985), 114–35.

was but one of many radical critiques of the times. The revolutions of 1848–49 came as no surprise to the observant.

In Britain, Fuller quickly perceived, as she says in dispatch 6, that "need indeed is flaring throughout Scotland and England for the devoutest application of intellect and love to the cure of ills that cry aloud, and, without such application, *must* ere very long seek help by other means than words." She alludes to revolution here obliquely, for though she anticipated it, she hoped social change could be brought about peacefully though the efforts of England's reform leaders, including George Dawson, James Martineau, William J. Fox, and William and Mary Howitt, all of whom she discusses in dispatches 7 and 8. (England successfully avoided revolution in 1848, but more through massive emigration and the force of arms than any alleviation of the suffering and starvation of the poor.)

The first person Fuller met on her travels who was devoted to revolution rather than reform was Joseph Mazzini, the Italian patriot and exile who had founded "Young Italy" and would assume the leadership of the Roman Republic after Pope Pius IX fled the Papal States. Obsessed with the idea of establishing a unified and republican Italy, and willing to shed blood and wage war to achieve this end, Mazzini was nevertheless a gentle, religious ascetic who impressed Fuller with his commitment and holiness. Fuller met him in London at the Carlyles', and in dispatch 9 she credits him with being "not only one of the heroic, the courageous, and the faithful—Italy boasts many such—but . . . also one of the wise." Two years later Mazzini became the hero of the historical tragedy she fashioned about the rise and fall of the Roman Republic. In dispatch 21 Fuller translates and quotes in full his eloquent and presumptuous letter to Pope Pius IX, and in dispatch 30 she describes his triumphant entry into Rome, as a Roman citizen and imminent head of the Republic.

In mid-November 1846, Fuller and the Springs left London and went to Paris, where they remained until 25 February 1847. Near the end of their stay, Fuller met another revolutionary who affected her profoundly: Adam Mickiewicz, political exile and Poland's great national poet. Handsome, charismatic, dedicated to freeing his country from the domination of Austria, Prussia, and Russia, Mickiewicz was also an ardent advocate of women's rights who presumed to tell Fuller what role she should play in the coming era. After their first meeting, he sent her a letter which she later regarded "with great reverence as one of the very few addresses to me to which I could respond."[37] In it he called her:

[37] Hudspeth 5:175.

The only one among women genuinely initiated into the antique world, the only one to whom it has been given to touch that which is decisive in today's world and to comprehend in advance the world to come.

Your spirit is bound to the history of Poland, of France, and begins to bind itself to the history of America.

You belong to the second generation of minds.

Your mission is to contribute to the deliverance of the Polish, French, and American woman.

You have acquired the right to know and maintain the rights and obligations, the hopes and exigencies of virginity.

For you, the first step in your deliverance and in the deliverance of your sex (of a certain class) is to know if it is permitted to you to remain virgin.[38]

Fuller's political commitment in Italy and the prophetic tone that found its way into her *Tribune* dispatches may have been inspired by this encouragement from Mickiewicz, as may have her decision to take a lover and lose her virginity. We say "may," for though Fuller made a habit of granting certain men influence over her (perhaps because of the dominant presence of her father during her youth), she maintained her independence in the process, often evoking and shaping the counsel they gave.

The attraction Fuller felt toward Mickiewicz was considerable.[39] She wrote Emerson, "I found in him the man I had long wished to see, with the intellect and passions in due proportion for a full and healthy human being, with a soul constantly inspiring."[40] Emerson, whose lack of passion had prevented full intimacy between Fuller and himself in the summer of 1840, would have understood the implied comparison. To Rebecca Spring, who worried about Fuller's attraction to Mickiewicz, Fuller wrote, "You ask me if I love M. I answer he affected me like music or the richest landscape, my heart beat with joy that he at once felt beauty in me also. When I was with him I was happy; and thus far the attraction is so strong that all the way from Paris I felt as if I had left my life behind, and if I followed my inclination I should return at this moment and leave Italy unseen."[41] Fuller did not return, though, nor did she discuss Mickiewicz in her *Tribune* dispatches, at least not until he came to Rome thirteen months later to raise troops to fight for Polish independence. Like Ossoli and then her son, Mickiewicz meant too much to her to write publicly about him. He remained in her thoughts, however, and she corresponded with him, spent time

---

[38] Hudspeth 5:176.

[39] The fullest account of the relationship is to be found in Leopold Wellisz, *The Friendship of Margaret Fuller D'Ossoli and Adam Mickiewicz* (New York: Leopold Wellisz, 1947).

[40] Hudspeth 4:261.

[41] Hudspeth 4:263.

with him in Rome (he stayed in her rooms), confided in him, and, when her son was born, chose him to be the boy's godfather.[42]

Although Mazzini and Mickiewicz were the two major revolutionaries Fuller became intimate with in Europe,[43] a number of other intellectuals she met in Paris in the winter of 1846–47 contributed to her radicalization.[44] Writing about social problems at home before her voyage, Fuller focused on the need for reform but did not advocate any "ism." Her outlook was liberal, not radical, and as Margaret V. Allen has said, "her columns show that she implicitly believed that knowledge of wrongs or evils led to their correction: her readers had only to be told of injustice and suffering, and inevitably these ills would be eradicated."[45] Her association with the Springs surely enhanced her social awareness in Europe, just as her friendships with Greeley and William H. Channing had done in New York City; however, it was the critical need for sociopolitical change in Europe, along with the plans and ideas of European intellectuals, that stimulated Fuller to begin thinking of herself as a radical.

When she arrived in London, she expressed regret that her essays "of a radical stamp" had not been included in her just-published book *Papers on Literature and Art,* for "now is just the time for them to make their mark here."[46] Greeley, who had long been committed to Associationism (or Fourierism, as it was also called), asked Fuller in February 1847 to send him a portrait of Fourier and to write a dispatch on the Associationists she had met and would meet. In her dispatch of 30 September 1846 detailing the appalling poverty in Glasgow, she had defended the Associationists "for their attempt to find prevention against such misery and wickedness in our land" (dispatch 5), and in March 1847, having received Greeley's letter, she wrote about "the need of some radical measures of reform" in Europe and discussed Fourier's "large and noble" views. "I should

[42] Soon after the birth of her child, Fuller wrote Giovanni Ossoli, "I am not very competent to give advice about baptism, which I do not understand well, but the godfather whom I would like to have for the baby is my friend the Pole. He knows about the existence of the baby[;] he is a devout Catholic, he is a distinguished man who could be a help to him in his future life, and I want him to have some friend in case something happens to us" (Hudspeth 5:125).

[43] In a letter of ca. May 1848, she wrote Emerson that Mickiewicz and Mazzini were "the persons who have been most to me in Europe" (Hudspeth 5:63).

[44] Excellent accounts of Fuller's radicalization can be found in Margaret V. Allen, "The Political and Social Criticism of Margaret Fuller," *South Atlantic Quarterly* 72 (Autumn 1973): 560–73; Ann Douglas, *The Feminization of American Culture* (New York: Knopf, 1977), 313–48; and Chevigny 282–303 and 366–401. See also Chevigny's more recent "To the Edges of Ideology: Margaret Fuller's Centrifugal Evolution," *American Quarterly* 38 (Summer 1986): 173–201.

[45] "The Political and Social Criticism of Margaret Fuller," 564.

[46] Hudspeth 4:235.

pity," she writes, "the person who, after the briefest sojourns in Manchester and Lyons,—the most superficial acquaintance with the population of London and Paris,—could seek to hinder a study of his thoughts or be wanting in reverence for his purposes" (dispatch 12). In her next dispatch, after discussing the silk weavers of Lyons, she lauds the establishment of crèches, day-care centers where children of working parents are cared for by wet nurses, and she proclaims, "Here, again, how is one reminded of Fourier's observations and plans."

The definitive study of Margaret Fuller's radicalization remains to be written, but when it is, Greeley, the Springs, and the Parisian socialists Fuller encountered in the winter of 1846–47 will certainly figure as major formative influences. At the time of her visit, Paris was the center of European intellectual life and a remarkable coherence characterized the thinking of its leading leftists. "There I found every topic intensified, clarified, reduced to portable dimensions,"[47] Fuller wrote her friend Mary Rotch. Perhaps the most important socialist Fuller met was George Sand (Madame Dudevant), the popular novelist and political activist whose love affairs with a series of men, including Chopin, many Americans found scandalous. Fuller, who had written favorably of Sand's fiction, responded enthusiastically to the woman.[48] "She personally inspired me with warm admiration and esteem," Fuller wrote a friend. "I never liked a woman better."[49] In Paris, Fuller also met and was impressed by Clarisse Vigoureux, an early follower of Fourier; Félicité Robert de Lamennais, the French abbé and highly influential socialist philosopher; Pauline Roland, socialist and radical feminist; Victor Considérant, the well-known disciple of Fourier and editor of *La Démocratie pacifique* (which became "my paper" for Fuller during her residence in Italy); and Pierre Leroux, a leading socialist and a founder of *La Revue indépendente* (which published a translation of Fuller's "American Literature" and arranged for her to become a regular contributor when she returned to America).[50]

---

[47] Hudspeth 4:273.

[48] For Fuller's commentary on Sand's writings, see Chevigny 57–58, 205–07.

[49] Well aware of American disapproval of Sand's personal life, Fuller declared, "She needs no defence, but only to be understood, for she has bravely acted out her nature, and always with good intentions" (Hudspeth 5:13). Three years later, after Fuller herself took Marchese Giovanni Ossoli as her lover and had a baby out of wedlock, she declared, "For bad or for good, I acted out my character," and, as Chevigny has pointed out, "the echo is strong proof of the sanction Sand's extraordinary influence provided for the younger woman" (301).

[50] Hudspeth 5:242, 4:253. When Fuller met Leroux and Considérant, both were committed utopianists. Leroux had established a commune at Boussac, France, and many years later, in 1881, would help his brother Jules found the Cloverdale colony in the Sonoma Valley of California. In 1855 Considérant founded a short-lived colony at Reunion, Texas (near Dallas), after escaping from France following his conviction for treason. (He led an armed

Although Fuller spoke often about her newly formed "radicalism" in letters to friends, much remains mysterious about it, for while she promised to elaborate (and perhaps did in her lost "History"), all that we have are her cryptic allusions. Utopian socialism of a Fourieristic kind, though, rather than revolutionary socialism, seems to have been the type of new sociopolitical thought she had acquired. In Europe Fuller came to believe that republicanism and socialism could somehow be *practically* linked, as they were not in America. Moreover, the romantic religious messianism that had long informed her thought gave her a framework for understanding and interpreting the socialist-republican ideas at work in the upheavals she was soon to witness.[51]

Though Fuller had been attracted to utopian schemes in the past, she had been too much the self-reliant individualist to commit herself to them. (In the early 1840s, for example, she had a room at Brook Farm and visited there several times but would not join the community.) Now she seemed convinced that such utopianism held the only hope for the future, and she was ready to commit herself to it. Soon after she arrived in Italy, she wrote William H. Channing, "Art is not important to me now. . . . I take interest in the state of the people, their manners, the state of the race in them. I see the future dawning; it is in important aspects Fourier's future." [52] Six months later, she addressed the problem of America's avoiding "the evils that have grown out of the commercial system in the old world" and declared, "I do, indeed, say what I believe, that voluntary association for improvement in these particulars will be the grand means for my nation to grow and give a nobler harmony to the coming age" (dispatch 18). Later, after becoming an unwed mother, Fuller probably felt even more sensitive to social forms and conventions and more attracted by the prospect of a new kind of society, one free from the institution of marriage.[53] Though she

---

rebellion against the government of Louis-Napoleon when the latter sent French troops to Italy in the summer of 1849.) See *Socialism and American Life*, ed. Donald Drew Egbert and Stow Persons, vol. 1 (Princeton: Princeton University Press, 1952), 636, 188–90, and Rondel V. Davidson, Introduction to *Au Texas* by Victor Considérant (1854; rpt. Philadelphia: Porcupine Press, 1975), n.p.

[51] We are indebted to Charles Capper for several of the observations in this paragraph.

[52] Hudspeth 4:271.

[53] Chevigny has pointed out that "Fourier was a pioneering radical feminist, not only advocating sexual equality but also criticizing in detail the institutions of marriage and the family. Fuller's reiterated mention of his name in public and private writing suggests he was in possession of a scheme of values she wanted and increasingly needed to accept" (383).

Whether Fuller and Ossoli ever married remains uncertain. One obstacle for them was that Fuller was a Protestant and Ossoli a Catholic, and in order to marry in a church ceremony, they needed a papal dispensation. Ossoli's and Fuller's commitment to the republican cause and Ossoli's estrangement from his brothers who were in the papal service made such an arrangement difficult at best. For them to marry secretly outside the church meant

admired Mazzini and his plan to unite and republicanize Italy, she faulted him for not appreciating the promise of utopian socialism. Mazzini "aims at political emancipation," she wrote in dispatch 24, "but he sees not, perhaps would deny, the bearing of some events, which even now begin to work their way. . . . I allude to that of which the cry of Communism, the systems of Fourier, &c. are but forerunners."

When Fuller arrived in Italy in early March 1847, her radicalism was still a state of mind rather than a course of action. For four more months she remained the American tourist and concentrated on observing the stimulating scenes around her. She and the Springs first visited Genoa, where they met Mazzini's mother, then went to Naples and Rome. In dispatch 14 from Rome, she gave her readers obligatory accounts of Italian art and scenery, but as a result of her new interests she also described the popular enthusiasm for Pope Pius IX ("Pio Nono"), whose reforms were inspiring hope and unrest throughout Italy. Less than a year earlier, on 16 July 1846, Pius IX had begun his reign by pardoning almost a thousand political prisoners, an act that thundered across Europe and in essence began the Italian revolutions.[54] His other reforms, such as putting weapons in the hands of citizens by establishing the Civic Guard, sparked an enthusiasm for reform and national independence that soon proved revolutionary. Looking back on recent history at the beginning of 1850, Carlyle observed, "Not long ago, the world saw, with thoughtless joy which might have been very thoughtful joy, a real miracle not heretofore considered possible or conceivable in the world,—a Reforming Pope." This "simple pious creature," Carlyle went on, awakened, "as no other man could do, the sleeping elements; mothers of the whirlwinds, conflagrations, earthquakes. . . . All Europe exploded, boundless, uncontrollable; and we had the year 1848, one of the most singular, disastrous, amazing, and on the whole humiliating years the European world ever saw."[55] Such was a reactionary's view; for Fuller and other liberals, the pope at first seemed to embody the hope of the age.

For decades the Italians had been suffering from foreign oppression and reactionary government, especially that of the regressive Pope Gregory XVI, who died on 1 June 1846. In 1847, when Fuller arrived, Italy was not a nation, but a collection of small states. The Congress of Vienna in 1815 had tried to root

Ossoli's risking a total break with his family. Stern speculates the marriage took place on 4 April 1848 in a town outside Rome. Deiss believes they were married at Florence in the fall of 1849. Chevigny provides a good summary of opinion on the marriage issue (4n).

[54] See *Cambridge Modern History* 11:74.

[55] *Latter-Day Pamphlets* (1853; rpt. Freeport, N.Y.: Books for Libraries Press, 1972), 30–32.

out the spirit of democracy and nationalism that the French Revolution had loosed upon the world by dividing up the spoils of Napoleon's empire. Thus, in the south of the peninsula, the Spanish Bourbon Ferdinand II ruled despotically over the degraded citizens of Naples and Sicily; Austrian troops occupied rich Lombardy and Venetia in the north; in the northwest the vacillating King Charles Albert of Piedmont-Sardinia suppressed dissent among his citizens and dreamed of expanding his kingdom by means of a national war. Grand Duke Leopold II of Tuscany ruled benevolently, but his alliance through marriage with the Austrian empire limited his tolerance for reform. The small duchies of Parma and Modena were likewise under Austrian influence, and the ruler of Lucca was a madman.[56] The Papal States, which cut across the middle of the peninsula, had religious ties to Austria, which was a Catholic nation, yet the de facto ruler of Austria, the powerful Prince Metternich, soon came to distrust the new pope's reform measures, which he correctly perceived as a threat to Austrian hegemony.

To her credit, Fuller immediately understood that Pius IX, whatever his good intentions, would eventually face political realities that would limit his commitment to a free and united Italy. On her first visit to Rome, in May 1847, she delighted in his "magnetic sweetness" (dispatch 19) of expression and praised his setting "his heart upon doing something solid for the benefit of man" (dispatch 19); however, her Protestant upbringing, and the anti-Catholic prejudices it inculcated, made her skeptical. For the pope to lead an anti-Austrian movement, he would have to place his allegiance to his country over that to his church, and this, Fuller saw, he could not do. In dispatch 21 she wrote, "Whenever there shall be collision between the Priest and the Reformer, the Priest shall triumph," and her prediction proved true. In the spring of 1848, Pius won acclaim from his people by sending troops to support King Charles Albert's war against Austria, but he quickly recalled the troops when Catholic Austria protested, leading Fuller to call his action "base and treacherous." The pope further alienated Fuller and his people by appointing as his new minister in the fall of 1848 Count Pellegrino Rossi, an aloof and provocative aristocrat. When Rossi was assassinated and the pope fled Rome in disguise, Fuller declared, "These are the acts either of a fool or a foe. No more of him! His day is over" (dispatch 26). By the summer of 1849, Pius had become Fuller's hated enemy, for to regain his temporal power, he allowed the French to bombard Rome and kill hundreds of its defenders. The irony of his position as father to his people did not escape Fuller, nor would she let her readers overlook it.

It was during her first visit to Rome that Fuller saw not only the pope, but

[56] *Cambridge Modern History* 11:69–70.

also, at St. Peter's, the handsome, twenty-six-year-old Catholic Italian who would become the father of her child. Before her relationship with Marchese Giovanni Ossoli could develop, however, she and the Springs proceeded northward to Florence and then to Bologna, Ravenna, and Venice, arriving the first week in July 1847. In Venice, Fuller parted with the Springs; she wanted to see more of Italy, especially Rome, while their plans were to tour Germany and Austria and then return to the United States. After the Springs left in mid-July, Fuller spent the summer in Milan and on the lakes in northern Italy and Switzerland. She met a number of Milanese radicals, including Constanza Arconati Visconti, Christina Trivulzio Belgiojoso, Pietro Maestri, and Anselmo Guerrieri-Gonzaga, all of whom were committed to the struggle against Austrian oppression. From them Fuller learned why the Italians felt such deep-seated hatred toward the Austrians. As Joseph Deiss has said, "For the first time in her experience she met men to whom instruments of torture had been applied—the red-hot brand, the 'Spanish shoes' of iron, the iron glove to squeeze and break the fingers. One such was Gaetano De Castillia, who had been condemned to death by the Austrians. After vigorous protests by leading Italians, the sentence had been commuted to twenty years in the Spielberg—considered by everyone worse than death."[57] A number of the Milanese radicals Fuller met would head the revolutionary government in 1848.

During the summer of 1847 the tension between Austrians and Italians nearly erupted in violence, ironically because the Austrians wished to provoke revolution and war. Prince Metternich controlled a military force far superior to any the Italians could muster and felt the time was right to create an excuse for armed intervention and the suppression of reform. In July 1847 Austrian troops, on the pretence that one of their countrymen had been assassinated in Ferrara, marched on the town, which was located in the Papal States. The reaction of Pius IX was a mere protest. A month later Austria repeated the provocation, but again Pius IX chose protest over a declaration of war. The Austrians then withdrew from the town. Meanwhile, a series of popular demonstrations occurred in August in the Kingdom of Naples and Sicily, which Ferdinand II quickly suppressed.

During this troubled summer, Fuller wrote only one dispatch to the *Tribune*. From Milan on August 9, she told her readers that "some important change is inevitable here," but she claimed, "I am yet too much a stranger to speak with assurance of impressions I have received" (dispatch 15). Her minimal correspondence at this time and her reluctance to comment on imminent events resulted from her belief that her fifteenth dispatch would be her last. In actu-

[57] Deiss 76.

ality this was a misunderstanding, the first of a series between her and Greeley which would interrupt the dispatches, color her letters, and make her life difficult. In the cover letter accompanying her fourteenth dispatch, she apparently mentioned her disappointment at terminating her correspondence, for Greeley wrote back in amazement on July 29:

> How you imbibed the mistaken notion that I wished you to write us only fifteen letters for The Tribune, I cannot imagine. All I ever heard about fifteen in the premises was your own proposition to write so many letters for $120 in consideration of advance payment—a proposition not necessary to secure the advance, which could have been more considerable had you asked it. . . . I do not wish to urge you to write, but be it understood, once for all, that so many letters as you choose to write will be paid for, in such time and manner as shall to you be most agreeable. I do not deal in compliments, and shall not solicit contributions from you or others unless I desire to receive them. All the letters you see fit to send us at $10 each will be more than welcome.[58]

Thus reassured, she continued with the dispatches, writing ten during the next ten months.

As her sixteenth dispatch indicates, Fuller enjoyed her vacation on the Italian lakes in 1847. Returning to Rome in mid-October, she renewed her acquaintance with Ossoli and experienced some of the happiest weeks of her life, as dispatches 18 and 19 reveal by their tone. "My life at Rome is thus far all I hoped," she wrote her mother. "I have not been so well since I was a child, nor so happy ever as during the last six weeks."[59] When she learned that she was pregnant, apparently near the end of December 1847, her mood altered considerably. Dispatch 20 contains an account of the incessant rain and her depression. ("I find myself without strength, without appetite, almost without spirits," she tells her *Tribune* readers.) During the first months of 1848, Fuller experienced a wide range of emotions. On the one hand, like almost everyone in the Western world, she felt tremendous excitement about the revolutionary events of that year. In dispatch 18, she had predicted revolution throughout Europe, and in dispatch 22, written on 27 January 1848, she reported that indeed revolution "has now broken out in Naples." In the weeks that followed, King Louis-Philippe was toppled in Paris and the French Republic proclaimed; Metternich, the most powerful despot in Europe, fled Vienna; King Frederick William IV of Prussia was forced to withdraw from Berlin and agree to the election of a con-

---

[58] Manuscript letter, Fuller Correspondence, Houghton Library, Harvard University.
[59] Hudspeth 4:312.

stituent assembly; the Austrians were driven from Milan during "Five Glorious Days" of revolution; and in Venice the Austrians were also ejected, and the Republic of St. Mark proclaimed. Meanwhile, King Charles Albert declared war on Austria, and volunteer troops from Naples and the Papal States marched to Lombardy to help the Milanese fight the Austrian army. In dispatch 23, Fuller describes the rapturous response of the Romans to these events, and in her private correspondence she reveals her own euphoria. "I have been engrossed, stunned almost, by the public events that have succeeded one another with such rapidity and grandeur," she wrote William Channing. "It is a time such as I always dreamed of, and for long secretly hoped to see. I rejoice to be in Europe at this time, and shall return possessed of a great history." [60]

Despite her joy and excitement, Fuller felt unhappy about her pregnancy and feared she would die in childbirth—not an unlikely prospect at the time for a woman of thirty-seven with a history of lingering illnesses. To keep her pregnancy a secret from friends and acquaintances, Fuller left Rome and went to the Abruzzi mountains; the explanation she offered was that she wished to go to the quiet countryside to write a book about her impressions of Europe. Given the unsettled state of European affairs, however, this project must have struck others as premature. Greeley, whom she informed that her twenty-fourth dispatch would be the last she would write for the *Tribune,* felt especially perplexed.

Fuller completed dispatch 24 on 13 May and left Rome several weeks later. This removal was exceptionally painful for her, not only because she missed Ossoli and her friends but also because she felt isolated from the rich flow of news about current events, a flow that had become intensely important to her. In her twenty-fourth dispatch, she had declared, "Here things are before my eyes worth recording, and, if I cannot help this work, I would gladly be its historian"; and yet, while maintaining her desire to write the history of the times, she gave up the opportunity to observe and record. She may have tried to write in Aquila, where she went on 29 May, and later in Rieti at the end of July. However, it seems likely she got little done, for she suffered much from loneliness and poor health throughout the summer. On 22 June she told Costanza Visconti, "I am here, in a lonely mountain home, writing the narrative of my European experience. To this I devote great part of the day. Three or four hours I pass in the open air, on donkey or on foot. When I have exhausted this spot, perhaps I shall try another. Apply as I may, it will take three months, at least, to finish my book. It grows upon me." [61] But it was the baby, not the book, that

[60] Hudspeth 5:58.
[61] Hudspeth 5:73.

was developing within her, and without companions, without access to news or reference books, Fuller seems to have made little progress on her narrative. While she was in Aquila, the delays in the mail from Ossoli upset her, and on 27 June she wrote him, "Now for two weeks I have not received any papers, nor have I heard from you in reply to my last two letters. I know nothing about the things that I am interested in; I feel lonely, imprisoned, too unhappy." [62]

Contributing to Fuller's discontent was the knowledge that whatever she might write about her "European experience" would soon seem trivial when viewed in light of such recent events as the "Bloody June Days" in Paris, the horrible slaughter of some forty-five hundred rebelling workers by government troops and the national guard. When she told Emelyn Story that she was writing every day on her book and making rapid progress, she added, "It is true that as I write, it don't seem worth making such a fuss about, but one must persist to get anything done in this dissipated world." [63] And when Fuller did hear about political events after the fact, the news often dampened her spirits. On May 18, for example, Ferdinand II withdrew his troops from the war against Austria in the north in order to put down insurrection in his own kingdom. (In four months, he would bomb his own people at Messina and earn the nickname "King Bomba.") The pope too withdrew the papal forces from the north, declaring he had no intention of waging war against Austria. On 25 July the Austrian general Radetzky overwhelmed Charles Albert's Piedmontese army at Custoza, and Albert then abandoned Milan to the Austrians after promising to defend the city. On 9 August an armistice was signed and the Austrians marched south and attacked Bologna in the Papal States. Everyone wondered whether the pope would send troops to Bologna, and though Fuller wished he would, she worried that the Civic Guard and thus Ossoli would be among them. On 16 August she lamented in a letter to her brother Richard, "I do not say anything of public affairs, but all goes wrong. My dearest friends are losing all, and the Demon with his cohort of traitors, prepares to rule anew these heavenly fields and mountains. But I do not quite despair yet. France may aid." [64] On 5 September Fuller gave birth to her son, Angelo Eugene Philip, and returned to Rome in early November without him. Desiring to rejoin Ossoli while keeping their child a secret from others, she resigned herself to leaving the baby in Rieti in the care of a nurse.

The psychological and physical pain Fuller suffered during the summer and fall of 1848 was aggravated by her poverty, which was severe, and she blamed Greeley (unfairly) for her plight. In May 1847 she had asked him to send her

[62] Hudspeth 5:79.
[63] Hudspeth 5:74–75.
[64] Hudspeth 5:105.

six hundred dollars to live on. Though strapped for funds, he sent the money after selling part of his interest in the *Tribune*; on 4 April 1848 he wrote her, "I have . . . been hard at work to raise the money for you to go by the steamship from Boston to-morrow. I have just accomplished it, but it has nearly broken my back. . . . I obtained $100 from the office (all I could get) on your account; the other $500 is between you and myself personally." [65] Unfortunately, Fuller's Paris bankers did not notify her that they had received the funds, and when she checked with Barings of London, who had sent the money on to Paris, they said they had no money for her, so she thought Greeley had lied. "As to Mr Greeley he shows no disposition to further my plans," she wrote her brother Richard on 16 August. "Liberality on the part of the Tribune would have made my path easy. . . . But people rarely think one like me worth serving or saving." [66]

Fuller's self-pity, caused in great part by the anxiety accompanying her pregnancy, strained her friendship with Greeley to its limit. When he learned about her complaint, he became irritated, especially because Fuller had already let him down by stopping her correspondence at a time when his readers were desperate for news and commentary. Her stated reasons for stopping—her poor health and a desire to write about her travels—struck him as weak, as indeed they were. At first, though, he suppressed his feelings in the hopes of changing her mind. On 27 June 1848 he wrote her,

> I regret the resolution announced in your last not to write farther for The Tribune, but I do not complain of it. I can very well understand that an implied obligation to write periodically to a distant journal must be irksome, especially to one in ill health; but I thought in this case the fact that you were to write when you pleased and as you pleased would deprive the engagement of any character of constraint or task-work. I still think you will do well to write us occasionally, when you have any thing to communicate to your American friends generally; and it seems to me that your letters have of late so generally referred to matters of the passing moment (all the more valuable to us) that their publication could not interfere with any idea you may have of a book to be issued after your return. But do exactly what seems most agreeable, and don't make your life a drudgery for the sake of a few dollars. [67]

In this same letter, Greeley tried to coax Fuller into further correspondence by telling her to make out a bill to the *Tribune* for the postage of her recent,

[65] Manuscript letter, Fuller Correspondence, Houghton Library, Harvard University.
[66] Hudspeth 5:104.
[67] Manuscript letter, Fuller Correspondence, Houghton Library, Harvard University.

longer letters, "far longer than we had a right to expect," and for their extra length itself, "2 ½ extra for each column over two to each letter." He reminded her that "what we pay you by agreement ($10 per letter) is just twice what we pay for any other European Correspondence," adding, "but we are very well aware that the quality justifies this." (Greeley's claim was not altogether true, for he was paying Dana in Paris the same amount.)[68] His object, he said, was that she be "entirely satisfied," whether she resumed writing for the paper or not.

Though he gave no indication of it in this letter, Greeley felt that Fuller had taken advantage of him and the *Tribune,* and in the fall of 1848 he finally told her how he felt about the cessation of her reporting. He had already vented his frustration about her abuse of him in her letters to family and friends. "It seems to me a clear case of infatuation," he wrote on 29 July, "that you, after requesting me to send you money to one especial place, should send for it and write about it to almost every body else, but not at all to the very place where you told me to send it, and where I accordingly *did* send it at the time I said I would, and whence I had assurance of its receipt months ago."[69] On 17 November, after the money issue had been cleared up, Greeley asked, "Can you wonder that I felt a little provoked about it?" He added,

> But then I was a little provoked with you on another ground, which I will state with entire frankness. The sum you asked me to advance was more than I had anticipated, and it came rather hard on me—but in truth I always am bothered about money. Well, just as I had forgotten that, along came your notification that you would write no more! —and that amazed me. Once a month would have served me very well, but to have you break off entirely, just as Italy and Europe were in the throes of a great Revolution, and when I tho't I had made an effort to oblige you, struck me as unkind. But let it all pass now, and, if useful, we can talk it over when we meet again.[70]

Unlike Fuller's friends in Boston and Cambridge, Greeley had not heard the rumors about her pregnancy, so to him her behavior seemed inexplicable.

Were it not for the fact that mail from America took at least a month to reach Rome, one would suspect that Greeley's letter of 17 November shamed Fuller into resuming her correspondence for the *Tribune.* She did so on 2 December

[68] See James Harrison Wilson, *The Life of Charles A. Dana* (New York: Harper & Bros., 1907), 62.

[69] Manuscript letter, Fuller Correspondence, Houghton Library, Harvard University.

[70] Manuscript letter, Fuller Correspondence, Houghton Library, Harvard University.

1848, after a six-month hiatus, writing two dispatches in one day. It is possible that she learned about Greeley's dismay through her family, who kept in touch with him, but more likely she began writing again because she needed money. On 23 November she told William Channing that though her heart was "full" and her mind "lively, engaged," she had "two terrible drawbacks, frequent failure of health and want of money. . . . Ah! my dear William, what a vast good would money be to me now, and I cannot get it."[71]

Another factor that influenced Fuller to resume her *Tribune* correspondence may have been the exciting events that had just transpired in Rome. Her two dispatches for 2 December, numbers 25 and 26, tell about the recall of troops from Lombardy by Ferdinand II and the pope, King Charles Albert's vacillation, defeat, and treachery, the assassination of the pope's minister, Count Pellegrino Rossi, the attack on the Quirinal Palace, and the pope's flight to Naples into the arms of "King Bomba." These two dispatches overflow with engaging material, and when Greeley received them, he dashed off a letter of thanks. "I trust you will hereafter let us hear from you at least monthly while you remain in Italy," he added. "Your friends here all feel personally obliged by a letter from you in the Tribune, and I should think that, if only to save yourself the trouble of writing private letters, you would keep up the thread of your correspondence. However, do as you think best."[72]

Fuller continued writing for the *Tribune*. Now, however, a new hard-hitting tone found its way into her correspondence. She was a different woman by the time she returned to Rome—more militant, more Italian, more certain than ever that her hopes were bound up with the fate of the revolutionary cause in Europe.[73] This partly explains why in dispatch 26 she could applaud the assassination of Rossi, saying, "certainly, the manner *was* grandiose," and why she could declare of Charles Albert that "had the people slain him in their rage, he well deserved it at their hands; and all his conduct since had confirmed that sudden verdict of passion." As she resumed her newspaper work, she began to assume the persona of Liberty in that figure's martial aspect—stoic, uncompromising, willing to shed blood if the cause demanded it.[74] Her dispatches gained in force and point as a result.

After the pope's flight from the city on 25 November 1848, there was a lull before the storm that occurred at the end of April 1849, when the French army

---

[71] Hudspeth 5:155.

[72] Manuscript letter, Fuller Correspondence, Houghton Library, Harvard University.

[73] See Reynolds 69.

[74] For a discussion of the contrasting and contested representations of Liberty during the revolutions of 1848–49, see Maurice Agulhon, *Marianne au combat: L'Imagerie et la symbolique républicaines de 1789 à 1880* (Paris: Flammarion, 1979), 110–33.

arrived to destroy the new Roman Republic. During this period, Fuller visited her son in Rieti at Christmas, then resumed work on her book about her European experiences, writing the *Tribune* whenever she had time and motive. Her book now was, in intent if not in fact, a full history and not merely a narrative of her impressions. In dispatch 25 she announced her plans for writing it and indicated that it would focus on the "realities" of contemporary Italian life—living men and women, as opposed to kings and princes and other "effigies of straw" who had been knocked down. Thus the project, like Carlyle's *Heroes and Hero Worship* and Melville's *Moby-Dick,* drew upon transcendental thought: it envisioned revolution and heroism as the struggle to penetrate to the essence of things by destroying mere semblances and forms. Whether the struggle would be successful or not, however, Fuller as yet did not know.

Fuller's conception of her "History" was very much a product of her times. She was obviously influenced by the genre as it had been practiced by European historians such as Carlyle and Michelet, whose passion and brilliance distinguished their work, and closer at home by America's more factual, less biased, but equally romantic historians Irving, Prescott, and Bancroft.[75] Fuller shared with her age assumptions about the writing of history—its documentary foundation, its multivolume format, its elevated status. Her work also has strong ties to the male-dominated professions (from which she was excluded)—the law, the ministry, politics, higher education. It was shaped by the unformulated premises that controlled contemporary history writing, especially the assumption that history is linear and progressive. Moreover, Sir Walter Scott's immensely popular historical romances had exerted a pervasive influence on the genre, causing practically all American historians of the age, Fuller included, to regard history as a creative form that combined attention to detail and the use of archival materials with sweeping narrative, heroic figures, and dramatic action.[76]

Fuller had been collecting the documentary ballast for her study for some time. Though handicapped by limited funds, Fuller saved newspaper clippings, pamphlets, books, and government documents, and she corresponded with friends and acquaintances in other parts of Europe asking them for accounts of revolutionary events they had witnessed. She included selected portions of this

[75] For an able discussion of Fuller's contemporary American historians, see David Levin, *History as Romantic Art: Bancroft, Prescott, Motley, and Parkman* (Stanford: Stanford University Press, 1959).

[76] For Scott's influence on historical writing, see George H. Callcott, *History in the United States, 1800–1860: Its Practice and Purpose* (Baltimore and London: Johns Hopkins University Press, 1970), 11–13.

research material in her *Tribune* dispatches, translating documents and newspaper articles into English for her readers and then contextualizing them with
her own commentary. She had an excellent knowledge of both Milanese and
Roman political figures and issues, and she read the newspapers daily to keep
herself up-to-date on recent developments throughout Europe. In February
1849 she informed her brother Richard, "I read little except the newspapers:
these take up an hour or two of the day. I am ardently interested in these present
struggles of the nations. I have my thoughts fixed daily on the bulletin of men
and things. I expect to write the history, because it is so much in my heart." [77]
The relationship she envisioned between the dispatches and her "History" was
that between sketches and an oil painting; the first done quickly and impres-
sionistically with the scene before her eyes; the second created in the studio
and showing the effects not only of contemplation and reflection, but also of
selection and arrangement. "Of all this great drama I have much to write,"
she informed her *Tribune* readers in December 1848, "but elsewhere in a more
full form, and where I can duly sketch the portraits of actors little known in
America. The materials are over-rich. I have bought my right in them by much
sympathetic suffering" (dispatch 25).

Fuller's use of the metaphors of drama and painting to describe her interest
in history writing is not unusual, for her contemporaries thought in the same
terms, but her proprietary attitude toward the events at hand, her tendency to
privilege the literary *use* of historical reality over that reality itself, stems from
an ideology tied to her profession as writer. As mentioned above, her devotion
to the literary often made her blur the distinction between life and art. Early
in her travels she regarded Europe as "a rich book" and resented taking time
"from studying it to write to my friends at home." [78] Her own life she regarded
in a similar fashion. In a letter to William Channing, she wrote that the places
she had seen in Europe "are only to me an illuminated margin on the text of
my inward life." [79] As her absorption in historical events grew, they too became
texts in her eyes, or rather the raw material for texts, valuable not necessarily
for their own sakes, but for the literary use she could make of them.

Though Fuller's immediate purposes were professional, her ultimate ones
were religious. For her, as for Emerson, history as reality, as opposed to history
as text, contained not merely specific events but evidence of an unseen force at
work in the world, a force spiritual and abstract in nature. Like the Puritans,
she often called this force "God," especially in letters to her mother, but she also
termed it "idea," "law," "principle," "Truth," "Spirit," "Destiny" and "Fate."

[77] Hudspeth 5:194.
[78] Hudspeth 5:273.
[79] Hudspeth 4:271.

The duty of the historian, in her view, was to discover and reveal this force at work. As early as her sixteenth dispatch, Fuller had declared that Americans "have no heart for *the idea,* for *the destiny* of our own great nation: how can they feel *the spirit* that is struggling now in this and others of Europe" (italics added). Similarly, in her eighteenth dispatch, written two months later, she predicted revolution by declaring that "still Europe toils and struggles with *her idea,* and, at this moment, all things bode and declare a new outbreak of the fire, to destroy old palaces of crime!" (italics added). Throughout her Italian dispatches, Fuller focused on the revolutionary idea or cause and insisted that because it was morally right, it would prevail.

She believed, like other romantic writers, that a poetic faculty of mind, called imagination or Reason, was necessary for the historian to perceive and express that which determined the course of historical events. In her 1846 essay "American Literature," she explained what was lacking in William Prescott's acclaimed histories of the Spanish conquests in the New World, praising his "industry and power of clear and elegant arrangement" but regretting that he lacked "the higher powers of the historian, great leading views, or discernment as to the motives of action and the spirit of an era." This failure of imagination, or "absence of thought," Fuller claimed, made Prescott unequal "to that great picture of Mexican life, with its heroism, its terrible but deeply significant superstition, its admirable civic refinement." Her friend George Bancroft, on the other hand, the second volume of whose ten-volume *History of the United States* had appeared, she praised in the same essay for "leading thoughts by whose aid he groups his facts." [80] And though Fuller claimed to possess limited knowledge of Bancroft's historical works, she surely took notice that his main "leading thoughts" centered upon democracy and the achievements of the American "people." In the writings and thought of Mazzini, whose motto was "God and the People" (*Dio e Popolo*), she encountered a similar democratic emphasis. Thus it is unsurprising that the *idea* Fuller saw impelling the European history she was living through and writing about was democracy: "The struggle is now fairly, thoroughly commenced between the principle of Democracy and the old powers, no longer legitimate," she wrote in dispatch 31. "That struggle may last fifty years, and the earth be watered with the blood and tears of more than one generation, but the result is sure. All Europe, including Great Britain, where the most bitter resistance of all will be made, is to be under Republican Government in the next century. 'God works in a mysterious way.'"

When the revolutions of 1848–49 failed, Fuller maintained the validity of her thesis by declaring that the struggle had not ended but had just begun,

[80] Reprinted in Joel Myerson, *Margaret Fuller: Essays on American Life and Letters* (New Haven: College and University Press, 1978), 385–86.

and that the future promised success. "The seeds for a vast harvest of hatreds and contempts are sown over every inch of Roman ground," she wrote in her last dispatch, "nor can that malignant growth be extirpated, till the wishes of Heaven shall waft a fire that will burn down all, root and branch, and prepare the earth for an entirely new culture. . . . A congress of great, pure, loving minds, and not a congress of selfish ambitions, shall preside" (dispatch 37). Knowing the improbability of such a future, Fuller at times shifted the ground of her narrative argument from the temporal to the spiritual, insisting that if not in this world, then in another, goodness and justice would prevail. As historian, her commitment to linearity and the concept of progress was so strong that though she witnessed reversals, ruptures, and outright cessation of the movement toward democracy in Europe, she would not forsake it. Her personal investment was too great.

In her dispatches, and one assumes in her lost "History" as well, Fuller searched for heroic protagonists, "great men" whom she could credit with embodying the leading principles of the age and guiding the movement toward brotherhood and equality. Though Pius IX seemed such a man to others, Fuller quickly saw that he could not and would not play such a role. Her turn to the "people" as the new heroes of the age did not entirely satisfy her either, for privately she disliked and found fault with them; in her journal, she calls the Italians "coarse," "selfish and ignorant."[81] Her public praise of the "people" was in part intended to counter the claim of the French general Oudinot that the Romans had instituted a "reign of terror" within the city. Fuller correctly pointed out that she could walk the streets of Rome in perfect safety during the siege. What she surely knew, but chose not to say, is that for members of the priesthood the city was dangerous. One of the Roman republicans, Callimaco Zambianchi, a former political exile, had his men kill a Dominican priest in cold blood during the battle of 30 April, and in the first week of May, according to the twentieth-century historian G.M. Trevelyan, he massacred "six persons in holy orders, whom he declared to have been preaching sedition and conspiring against the Republic."[82] The government and Mazzini knew about this terrorism, and tried to put a stop to it. Though Fuller surely found it abhorrent, she did not mention it.

Fuller eventually focused on Mazzini, Garibaldi, and their supporters and credited them with greatness. Her admiration for Mazzini was complete, but she had private doubts about Garibaldi and his followers. In a letter to Ossoli from Rieti in April 1849, Fuller related, "Garibaldi has no control over these desperadoes in his band. On Sunday they killed a priest, two citizens and per-

[81] See Rostenberg 218.
[82] Trevelyan 149–50.

haps nine, they say. Two bodies were found in the river. The presence of the regular troops could prevent these excesses. But certainly I don't now have courage to go out alone." [83] For her *Tribune* readers, on the other hand, she emphasized the courage and self-sacrifice of Garibaldi's men. In her dispatch of 21 June, she asserted that the defenders of Rome "are no mercenaries" but instead "the flower of the Italian youth, and the noblest souls of the age. . . . This is especially true of the Emigrant and Garibaldi legions" (dispatch 33).

One inspiration for Fuller's flattering public treatment was the denigration of the revolutionaries in the ultraconservative London *Times,* which disdained radicals of any kind. The paper's reporter, covering the siege of Rome by the French, traveled with the French army and had no first-hand knowledge of the state of affairs in Rome. Yet he insisted that the city was defended by "the degenerate remnant of the Roman people" and by "a nest of adventurers, from every part not only of Italy but of Europe." [84] In dispatches 32 and 37, Fuller directly attacked the falsehoods of the *Times,* and her knowledge of its version of current events informed her insistence that "the voice of this age shall yet proclaim the names of some of these Patriots whose inspiring soul was JOSEPH MAZZINI— men as nobly true to their convictions as any that have ever yet redeemed poor, stained Humanity" (dispatch 35).

By twentieth-century lights, the behavior of Pius IX and the French government certainly seems base, yet Mazzini's willful sacrifice of the lives of young men, after defeat became certain, for the purpose of dramatizing and magnifying Rome's martyrdom, can be interpreted as the self-aggrandizing behavior of a religious fanatic. Similarly, Garibaldi's failure of generalship on 3 June 1849, when he sent wave after wave of his men to their deaths as they attacked the entrenched French, suggests stupidity or ineptitude. At the least, we must say his intellectual and military abilities were less than considerable when guerrilla warfare was not the activity at hand. [85] Fuller's praise for the young soldiers who died or were wounded defending Rome seems better directed, yet here too one sees generic conventions shaping the history she tells. Her study of the classics made her naturally associate romantic heroism with the Roman character. "The genius of Rome," she wrote in 1840, "displayed itself in Character. . . . Everything turns your attention to what a man can become . . . by a single thought, an earnest purpose, and indomitable will, by hardihood, self-command, and force of expression." [86] These virtues of the ancient Roman she saw in the republicans defending contemporary Rome, especially those who lay wounded in

[83] Quoted in Chevigny 473.
[84] *The Times,* 11 May 1849, p. 4.
[85] See Trevelyan 180–93, 196–97.
[86] *Memoirs* 1:18.

the hospitals. "One kissed an arm which was cut off," she related in the *Tribune*; "another preserves pieces of bone which are being painfully extracted from his wound, as reliques of the best days of his life. . . . A spirit burns noble as ever animated the most precious facts we treasure from the heroic age" (dispatch 33).

Although one can naturally assume that her account is contrived, it seems that many of the young men defending Rome were well-educated students who had read the same works Fuller had as a child. Thus, her account of their attitudes and behavior may not be as fictional as it seems. Olivia Rosetti Agresti, the biographer of Nino Costa, one of the defenders of Rome, has described the education of her subject and his compatriots: "The men of that age were steeped in classic lore; the histories of Livy, of Tacitus, of Plutarch were to them the realities of life, the heroes of antiquity seemed to brood over them, moulding those moderns after their own image. . . . A noble idealism, an ardent love of country, that patriotism which the ancients considered the greatest of all virtues, and above all an invincible belief in the destinies and greatness of Rome, and a longing to see her return to her pristine glory, were sown in the hearts and brains of the youth, which was to yield so rich a harvest of heroism in 1848 and 1849." [87] If Agresti is reliable, then Fuller may be as well, as least as far as any historian can be.

As Hayden White has shown, all histories, and particularly those of the nineteenth century, depend on literary modes of emplotment (such as romance, tragedy, comedy, and satire) for their forms. No unmediated, or objective, history exists. The historian, by his or her selection of beginnings and endings, of events and emphasis, emplots historical reality. In Fuller's dispatches and private letters, one sees her continually searching for a plot which can explain the course of events. At first and at last, romance is the plot she perceives at work. As White has pointed out, romance is fundamentally "a drama of the triumph of good over evil, of virtue over vice, of light over darkness, and of the ultimate transcendence of man over the world in which he was imprisoned by the Fall." [88] For Fuller, Italy, like America, was destined to overthrow tyranny and enjoy the freedom and prosperity that had long been denied it. Sometime in the spring of 1849, though, she sensed that tragedy rather than romance might be the more accurate plot for the events she was witnessing.

In the fall of 1848 the Piedmontese had once again risen against the Austrian army, inspired by the Hungarian revolution in October 1848. On 23 March 1849, however, the Piedmontese suffered a devastating defeat at Novara, and

[87] Quoted in Trevelyan 170–71, n. 2.

[88] *Metahistory: The Historical Imagination in Nineteenth-Century Europe* (Baltimore and London: Johns Hopkins University Press, 1973), 9.

Charles Albert abdicated his throne in favor of his son Victor Emmanuel II. On 25 April 1849 the French landed at Cività Vecchia and soon began their march on Rome. These events combined to discourage republican hopes, and Fuller, who wrote a brief dispatch on 6 May, did not write again until 27 May. In the meantime she learned much about the routing of the French on 30 April, when they arrived outside the gates of Rome. Her reluctance to send a dispatch in response to this excitement can be attributed to the difficulty she faced as a self-proclaimed historian, for events had controverted the plot she had been using to narrate the history at hand. Her encounter with actual warfare, moreover, contributed to her uncertainty. "I have suspended writing in the expectation of some decisive event, but none such comes yet," she informed her readers at the beginning of dispatch 31. She went on to relate that "war near at hand seems to me even more dreadful than I had fancied it. . . . I have, for the first time, seen what wounded men suffer. The night of the 30th of April I passed in the hospital, and saw the terrible agonies of those dying or who needed amputation, felt their mental pains and longing for the loved ones. . . ." As she contemplated these experiences, Fuller started to speak of her own life as tragic, in letters to friends, and to replot the Roman revolution as a historical tragedy.

In such a plot, as White explains, "there are intimations of states of division among men more terrible than that which incited the tragic agon at the beginning of the drama. Still, the fall of the protagonist and the shaking of the world he inhabits which occur at the end of the Tragic play are not regarded as totally threatening to those who survive the agonic test. There has been a gain in consciousness for the spectators of the contest."[89] Such a gain and such an emphasis became Fuller's focus as the Roman Republic was destroyed before her eyes. By 10 June, when she mailed her thirty-second dispatch, the French general Oudinot had attacked Rome again (on 2 June) and begun the siege and bombardment that would last a month. When Mazzini saw that the plight of the republic was hopeless, yet decided to fight rather than capitulate, Fuller's dispatches helped him establish his version of history as truth. Indeed, later historians use and often quote from her dispatches in their accounts of the Roman revolution. For her, Mazzini became at the end a Christlike martyr. "Mazzini is immortally dear to me,—a thousand times dearer for all the trial I saw made of him in Rome," Fuller wrote a friend after Rome fell. "Many of his brave friends perished there. We who, less worthy, survive, would fain make up for the loss, by our increased devotion to him, the purest, the most disinterested of patriots, the most affectionate of brothers."[90] Though here Fuller's version of history is

---

[89] Ibid., 9.
[90] Hudspeth 5:250.

tragic, she returned to romantic emplotment in her final dispatches, after she had time to reflect and resolve "to seek the realization of all hopes and plans elsewhere,"[91] that is, in life after death.

With the fall of the Roman Republic, Fuller had closure for the historical tragedy she had been perceiving. Although she was to write three more dispatches for the *Tribune,* returning to a more optimistic romantic plot, she was nevertheless ready to prepare her other "History," the book manuscript, for publication. Accordingly, she wrote Carlyle asking his help in placing it with a London publisher. In August 1849 he informed Emerson that "waiting for me here, there was a letter from Miss Fuller in Rome, written about a month ago; a dignified and interesting letter; requesting help with Booksellers for some 'History of the late Italian revolution' she is about writing; and elegiacally recognizing the worth of Mazzini and other cognate persons and things. I instantly set about doing what little seemed in my power towards this object. . . . She has a beautiful enthusiasm; and is perhaps in the right stage of insight for doing that piece of business well."[92] Given Carlyle's antipathy toward the revolutionary movement, one wonders what he could have found to say in favor of Fuller's "piece of business." Whatever he said, on 5 September Fuller received a letter of rejection from the London publishers, "which indeed I had foreseen from previous advices or rather perhaps from a feeling of fate," she told her new friend Lewis Cass, Jr. "It has been my fate that when I worked for others I could always succeed; when I tried to keep the least thing for myself, it was not permitted."[93]

In the late summer and early fall of 1849, Fuller had to deal not only with the defeat of the Roman Republic and the rejection of what she hoped would be her magnum opus, but also with the sickness of her child. When she and Ossoli went to Rieti to join him, after the siege of Rome, they found him emaciated and near death; the young woman paid to care for him had fed him on wine rather than milk when the money stopped arriving from Rome. Fuller's anguish was great. Moreover, it was at this time that she learned about the death of young Pickie Greeley from his devastated father. "Ah Margaret," Greeley wrote, "the world grows dark with us! You grieve for Rome is fallen; I mourn, for Pickie is dead."[94] Fuller had loved Pickie dearly, and she wrote an affecting letter of condolence to Greeley, telling him about her own son and how sorry she felt about Pickie and the world:

[91] Hudspeth 5:260.

[92] Slater, *Correspondence of Emerson and Carlyle,* 456–57.

[93] Hudspeth 5:264.

[94] Manuscript letter, 23 July 1849, Fuller Correspondence, Houghton Library, Harvard University.

Ever sacred, my friend, be this bond between us—the love and knowledge of the child. I was his aunty; and no sister can so feel what you lose. My friend, I have never wept so for grief of my own, as now for yours. It seems to me *too* cruel. . . . My mother wrote me he said sometimes he would get a boat and carry yellow flowers to his Aunty Margaret. I suppose he had not yet quite forgotten that I used to get such for him. . . . Oh, it is all over; and indeed this life is over for me. The conditions of this planet are not propitious to the lovely, the just, the pure; it is these that go away; it is the unjust that triumph. Let us, as you say, purify ourselves; let us labor in the good spirit here, but leave all thought of results to Eternity.[95]

Given these sentiments, it is not surprising that Fuller's final three dispatches contain melancholy reflections on the state of the world as well as fierce, apocalyptic jeremiads directed at the unjust who have triumphed. These dispatches, which her brother Arthur did not include in his collection *At Home and Abroad,* contain some of Fuller's most powerful writing. They also show her moving closer to a revolutionary socialism than ever before. "The next revolution, here and elsewhere, will be radical . . . ," she warns. "Not only the Austrian, and every potentate of foreign blood, must be deposed, but every man who assumes an arbitrary lordship over fellow man, must be driven out. It will be an uncompromising revolution" (dispatch 37). Fuller's new friend in Florence, Elizabeth Barrett Browning, claimed that during her last months in Italy, before her ill-fated return to the United States, Fuller became "one of the out & out *Reds,*"[96] but this seems unlikely. Fuller's militancy had limits, as can be seen in her call for "the redress of the frightful social ills of Europe by a peaceful though radical revolution instead of bloody conflict." The figure of Christ permeates her final correspondence, and Christian socialism, on the order of that practiced by William Channing, seems to be the more accurate term to denote her late sociopolitical thought. Her last words to her *Tribune* readers speak of the "advent of EMMANUEL," and the giving of "glory to God in the highest" and "peace and love from man to man."

---

[95] Hudspeth 5:255–57.
[96] *The Letters of Elizabeth Barrett Browning to Mary Russell Mitford, 1836–1854,* ed. Meredith B. Raymond and Mary Rose Sullivan, 3 vols. (Winfield, Kan.: Wedgestone Press, 1983), 3:285.

THE DISPATCHES

FIRST IMPRESSIONS OF ENGLAND

AMBLESIDE, Westmoreland, 23d August, 1846 [1]

I take the first interval of rest and stillness to be filled up by some lines for The Tribune. Only three weeks have passed since leaving New-York, but I have already had nine days of wonder in England, and, having learned a good deal, suppose I may have something to tell.

Long before receiving this, you know that we were fortunate in the shortest voyage ever made across the Atlantic—only ten days and sixteen hours from Boston to Liverpool. The weather and all circumstances were propitious; and, if some of us were weak of head enough to suffer from the smell and jar of the machinery, or other ills by which the Sea is wont to avenge itself on the arrogance of its vanquishers, we found no pity. The stewardess observed that she thought "any one tempted God Almighty who complained on a voyage where they did not even have to put guards to the dishes!"

As many contradictory counsels were given us with regard to going in one of the steamers in preference to a sailing vessel, I will mention here, for the benefit of those who have not yet tried one, that he must be fastidious indeed who could complain of the Cambria.[2] The advantage of a quick passage and certainty as to the time of arrival, would, with us, have outweighed many ills; but, apart from this, we found more space than we expected and as much as we needed for a very tolerable degree of convenience in our sleeping-rooms, better ventilation than Americans in general can be persuaded to accept, general cleanliness and good attendance. In the evening, when the wind was favorable, and the sails set so that the vessel looked like a great winged creature darting across the apparently measureless expanse, the effect was very grand, but ah! for such a spectacle one pays too dear; I far prefer looking out upon "the blue and foaming sea" from a firm green shore.

Our ship's company numbered several pleasant members, and that desire prevailed in each to contribute to the satisfaction of all, which, if carried out through the voyage of life, would make this earth as happy as it is a lovely abode. At Halifax we took in the Governor of Nova-Scotia, returning from his very unpopular administration. His lady was with him, a daughter of

---

[1] First published as "Letters from England," *New-York Daily Tribune*, 24 September 1846, p. 2:1–3.

[2] The *Cambria* was a British steamer of the Cunard line. The captain was Charles H. E. Judkins (1811–76), the first commodore of the line (John W. Blassingame, ed., *The Frederick Douglass Papers* [New Haven: Yale University Press, 1979], 1:63–64).

William IV. and the celebrated Mrs. Jordan.[3] The English on board, and the Americans, following their lead, as usual, seemed to attach much importance to her left-handed alliance with one of the dullest families that ever sat upon a throne (and that is a bold word, too;) none to her descent from one whom Nature had endowed with her most splendid regalia, genius that fascinated the attention of all kinds and classes of men, grace and winning qualities that no heart could resist. Was the cestus buried with her, that no sense of Its preeminent value lingered, as far as I could perceive, in the thoughts of any except myself?

We had a foretaste of the delights of living under an aristocratical Government at the Custom-House, where our baggage was detained, and we waiting for it weary hours, because of the preference given to the mass of household stuff carried back by this same Lord and Lady Falkland.

Capt. Judkins of the Cambria, an able and prompt Commander, was the one who insisted upon Douglass being admitted to equal rights upon his deck with the insolent slaveholders, and assumed a tone toward their assumptions, which, if the Northern States had had the firmness, good sense and honor to use would have had the same effect, and put our country in a very different position from that she occupies at present. He mentioned with pride that he understood the New-York Herald called him 'the Nigger Captain,' and seemed as willing to accept the distinction as Colonel McKenney is to wear as his last title that of 'the Indian's friend.'[4]

---

[3] Lucius Bentinck Cary, tenth viscount of Falkland (1803–84), was the governor of Nova Scotia from 1840 to 1846. His job was to resist the demand for the full introduction of responsible government led by Joseph Howe (1804–73). Howe, a journalist, succeeded in ridiculing Lord Falkland so effectively that Falkland was forced to leave in 1846. Lord Falkland was accompanied home by his wife, Lady Falkland, the former Amelia Fitzclarence (?–1858) (Wallace W. Stewart, ed., *The Encyclopedia of Canada* [Toronto: University Associates of Canada, 1940], 2:317), who was the daughter of Dorothea Jordan (1762–1816), a famous actress and the mistress of the duke of Clarence (William IV). The "celebrated Mrs. Jordan" continued her theatrical career despite bearing ten children (*DNB*). Fuller suggests that Mrs. Jordan had earned, like the ancient Roman boxers, her own "cestus," or girdle of honor.

[4] Frederick Douglass (1817–95) published *The Narrative of the Life of Frederick Douglass, an American Slave* in 1845 and then visited Great Britain and France from 1845 to 1847. Douglass sailed for England on the *Cambria* on 16 August 1845. He was denied a cabin and forced to travel in steerage. The abolitionists on board objected, and Captain Judkins, who was sympathetic, provided an opportunity for Douglass to make a speech. A group of men, largely slave holders, objected, and the captain interfered in defense of Douglass (Booker T. Washington, *Frederick Douglass* [1907; rpt. New York: Greenwood, 1969], 100–101). Fuller had favorably reviewed Douglass's *Narrative* in the *New-York Daily Tribune*, 10 June 1845, p. 1:1–2.

Thomas Loraine McKenney (1785–1859) was the author of several books on Indians in

At the first sight of the famous Liverpool Docks, extending miles on each side of our landing, we felt ourselves in a slower, solider, and not on that account less truly active state of things than at home. That impression is confirmed. There is not as we travel that rushing, tearing and swearing, that snatching of baggage, that prodigality of shoe-leather and lungs that attend the course of the traveler in the United States; but we do not lose our "goods," we do not miss our car. The dinner if ordered in time, is cooked properly and served punctually, and at the end of the day, more that is permanent seems to have come of it than on the full-drive system. But more of that and with a better grace at a later day.

The day after our arrival we went to Manchester. There we went over the magnificent warehouse of ——— Phillips, in itself a Bazaar enough to furnish provision for all the wants and fancies of thousands. In the evening we went to the Mechanics' Institute and saw the boys and young men in their classes.[5] I have since visited the Mechanics' Institute at Liverpool, where more than seventeen hundred pupils are received, and with more thorough educational arrangements; but the excellent spirit, the desire for growth in wisdom and enlightened benevolence is the same in both. For a very small fee the mechanic, clerk, or apprentice, and the women of their families can receive various good and well-arranged instruction, not only in common branches of an English Education, but in mathematics, composition, the French and German languages, the practice and theory of the Fine Arts, and they are ardent in availing themselves of instruction in the higher branches. I found large classes, not only in architectural drawing, which may be supposed to be followed with a view to professional objects, but landscape also, and as large in German as in French. They can attend many good lectures and concerts without additional charge, for a due place is here assigned to Music as to its influence on the whole mind. The large and well-furnished libraries are in constant requisition, and the books in most constant demand are not those of amusement, but of a solid and permanent interest and value. Only for the last year in Manchester and for two in Liverpool, have these advantages been extended to girls; but now that part of the subject is looked upon as it ought to be, and begins to be treated more and more as it must and will be wherever true civilization is making its way.

North America (*DAB*); Fuller had used his *Sketches of a Tour to the Lakes* (1827) as a reference for her *Summer on the Lakes, in 1843* (Boston: Charles C. Little and James Brown, 1844).

[5] The Mechanics' Institutes were a major project of the Society for the Diffusion of Useful Knowledge, a Benthamite-oriented group established in 1826. These institutes were a part of the movement for promoting adult education (of a largely vocational character) and provided night school classes and modest libraries for artisans and skilled workers (Richard D. Altick, *Victorian People and Ideas* [New York: Norton, 1973], 257, and Mitchell, 488).

One of the handsomest houses in Liverpool has been purchased for the girls' school, and room and good arrangement been afforded for their work and their play. Among other things they are taught, as they ought to be in all American schools, to cut out and make dresses.

I had the pleasure of seeing quotations made from our Boston "Dial" in the address in which the Director of the Liverpool Institute, a very benevolent and intelligent man,[6] explained to his disciples and others its objects, and which concludes thus:

> But this subject of self-improvement is inexhaustible. If traced to its re-
> sults in action, it is, in fact, "The Whole Duty of Man." Here, however,
> we must stop. Much remains, of which there may be an opportunity to
> speak hereafter. Meantime, I have sought to impress one great principle,
> rather than to dwell on minor points, however useful;—a principle which,
> to us in our relations here, is unspeakably important, identifying, as it
> does, intellectual improvement with moral obligation and moral progress.
> What farther of detail it involves and implies, I know that you will, each
> and all, think out for yourselves. Beautifully has it been said—"Is not
> the difference between spiritual and material things just this; that in the
> one case we must watch details, in the other, keep alive the high resolve,
> and the details will take care of themselves? Keep the sacred central fire
> burning, and throughout the system, in each of its acts, will be warmth
> and glow enough.[7]

To sum up in a few words what I wish now to say. If you seek the power of speech and thought, (and they reciprocally aid each other) let the service of your fellows ever be in view; and in this service be not too curious to inquire whether, how, and when, your own happiness will be the result; be prepared even for unhappiness; in this world both are but means: if prosperity renders benevolence more beneficent, adversity renders it more sympathetic; if joy is the sunshine which makes your purposes of good bear the richest fruit, sorrow is a wind that will increase their strength, and strike their roots deeper into the heart. All outward fortune will thus contribute variously, but not unequally to your moral welfare.[8]

For myself, if I be asked what my purpose is in relation to you, I would briefly reply; it is that I may help, be it ever so feebly, to train up a race of young men, who shall escape vice by rising above it; who shall love truth because it is truth, not because it brings them wealth or honor; who

---

[6] William Ballantyne Hodgson (1815–80), an educator and reformer (*DNB*; Hudspeth 4:232n).

[7] *The Dial* 1 (1840): 188 [Fuller's note].

[8] The preceding paragraph is omitted from *AHA*.

shall regard life as a solemn thing, involving too weighty responsibilities to be wasted in idle or frivolous pursuits; who shall recognize in their daily labors not merely a tribute to the "hard necessity of daily bread," but a field for the development of their better nature by the discharge of duty; who shall judge in all things for themselves, bowing the knee to no sectarian or party watchwords of any kind; and who, while they think for themselves, shall feel for others, and regard their talents, their attainments, their opportunities, their possessions, as blessings held in trust for the good of their fellow-men. It may seem vain to aim at so high things with so humble means; but we must work with such means and such powers as we have; it is for us to seek what is right, it is for another to fix the measure of success which shall attend our search.

I found that The Dial had been read with earnest interest by some of the best minds in these especially practical regions, that it had been welcomed as a representative of some sincere and honorable life in America and thought the fittest to be quoted under this motto:

"What are noble deeds but noble thoughts realized?"

Among other signs of the times we bought Bradshaw's Railway Guide, and opening it found extracts from the writings of our countrymen Elihu Burritt and Charles Sumner,[9] on the subject of Peace, occupying a leading place in the "Collect" for the month, of this little hand-book, more likely, in an era like ours, to influence the conduct of the day than would an illuminated breviary. Now that peace is secured for the present between our two countries, the spirit is not forgotten that quelled the storm. Greeted on every side with expressions of feeling about the blessings of peace, the madness and wickedness of War, that would be deemed romantic in our darker land, I have answered to the speakers, "But you are mightily pleased, and illuminate for your victories in China and Ireland, do you not?" and they, unprovoked by the taunt, would mildly reply, "We do not, but it is too true that a large part of the nation fail to bring home the true nature and bearing of those events, and apply principle to conduct with as much justice as they do in the case of a nation nearer to them by kindred and

[9] George Bradshaw (1801–53), an engraver of maps, first produced *Bradshaw's Railway Time Tables* in 1839. *Bradshaw's Railway Companion* followed in 1840. Bradshaw, active in peace movements and educational reform for the poor, was a friend of Elihu Burritt (1810–79), a reformer and linguist, who edited *The Advocate of Peace and Universal Brotherhood* and exchanged "Friendly Addresses" (pleas for international peace) between American and British friends. Charles Sumner (1811–74), U.S. senator and ardent abolitionist, had shocked the largely military audience for the Boston Independence Day celebration in 1845 with a diatribe against war (*DAB* and *DNB*).

position. But we are sure that feeling is growing purer on the subject day by day, and that there will soon be a large majority against war on any occasion or for any object."

I heard a most interesting letter read from a tradesman in one of the country towns, whose daughters are self-elected instructors of the people in the way of cutting out from books and pamphlets fragments on the great subjects of the day, which they send about in packages, or paste on walls and doors. He said that one such passage pasted on a door, he had seen read with eager interest by hundreds to whom such thoughts were, probably, quite new, and with some of whom it could scarcely fail to be as a little seed of a large harvest. Another good omen I found in written tracts by Joseph Barker, a working-man of the town of Wortley, published through his own printing-press. I have one of these before me, "On the blessings of Free Trade," whose opening passage conveys in brief and simple fashion the kind of instruction most needed by America.[10]

> *Respected Chairman, my Friends.* —All I ask is that you will hear me with patience. I acknowledge that on various religious questions my opinions are different from those of most professors of religion; but I cannot consider myself as blamable on that account. My desire is in all things to know what is true and to reduce it to practice in my life. All I care for is to know what is right and do it. It is true I judge for myself what *is* right; but I leave others at liberty to do the same. I differ from others, but I allow others to differ from me; and there is not one of you but what differs as widely from me as I differ from you: why then should we not bear with one another? Why cannot we each enjoy our liberty with thankfulness, and leave the rest to God. I am accountable to God both for my opinions and practices, and that is enough. If I do wrong, God will punish me, and you have no need to wish to help him; and if I do right He will reward me, and you cannot hinder Him. And *you* also are accountable to God, and should rather be carefully preparing for your own reckoning, than judging whether others are prepared or not. If we can *mend* each other's religious opinions, let us do so at the proper time; but don't let us hate or persecute each other. Let us teach each other in gentleness and love, and then leave each other in the hands of God. To our own master we stand or fall.

[10] Joseph Barker (1806–75), a preacher, author, and workingman from Wortley, a suburb of Leeds, became a printer with help from the Unitarians in 1846. He wished to make publications available cheaply and began the Barker Library, a collection of 300 theological, philosophical, and ethical books. He turned to politics and advocated republicanism for England and repeal for Ireland. He published a weekly, *The People,* established in 1846, with a circulation of 20,000. Later in his life, he emigrated to America and became an active abolitionist (*DNB*). This sentence and the next eight paragraphs below were omitted in *AHA*.

I meet you at present as friends of liberty, as persons who rejoice in
the freedom and the welfare of mankind. We meet to express our joy and
thankfulness for that measure of freedom in trade which has been lately
granted to us. I stand forth to declare the joy and thankfulness of my own
soul, and to state my reasons for them. I stand forth to express my hopes
and wishes, and to show how they may be realized.

This is not mere talk, noise and bluster, it is the echo of a mighty voice from
the very heart of the nation. Like the simple close of Sir R. Peel's speech on
resigning the office of Premier, to retire to higher honors, it has that highest
eloquence of a plain and adequate sense of great facts.[11] We will not deny ourselves the pleasure of adding the working-man's tribute to the statesman who
has acted in the spirit of truth, of honor, of the genuine religion of manhood,
for a purpose which shall bear its harvest where no golden corn-field waves.

"I must add a few words about Sir Robert Peel. I know but little of his
former life, and I shall therefore say nothing about it. But his conduct of
late has been such as to incline me to believe that he has long been a lover
of liberty and peace, of knowledge and righteousness, a well-wisher to
the people of this empire, and to mankind at large. He has had his fears
no doubt, as all reformers have; he has been afraid of offending his party,
and of losing his friends; he has been afraid of losing his influence, and
lessening his power to do good; yet still, in my judgment, he has leaned to
the side of freedom and equity, and longed for the welfare of the people. I
do not at all agree with those who give him credit for nothing but a selfish
policy and superior tact and talent in what he has done; I believe him to
be a truly well-meaning man, and to have been influenced by an earnest
desire to promote the welfare of his countrymen and the welfare of the
world. His conduct for some time past has been truly noble and admirable. —The way in which he removed the pressure of taxation from the
poor to the rich; the manner in which he conducted himself in reference
to the Oregon dispute; the eagerness, the anxiety, the resolution, the

[11] Sir Robert Peel (1788–1850) became a member of Parliament in 1809 as a Tory (Conservative). He ruled Ireland from 1812 to 1818 and championed the Protestant cause. In
1823 he established a sound system of metallic currency and was home secretary from 1822
to 1827 and again in 1828. He was prime minister twice, 1834–35 and 1841–46. During
his second term, he reversed the traditional Tory position on protecting the interests of the
landowners and advocated free trade and repeal of the Corn Laws. These laws, enacted in
1815 and amended in 1828, restricted foreign imports of grain. The result was that the price
of bread was so high that workers could not afford it. After the narrow repeal of the Corn
Laws in 1846, Peel's government fell (*DNB*, Richard D. Altick, *Victorian People and Ideas*
[New York: Norton, 1973], 91).

straight-forwardness, the great patience and perseverance with which he
toiled and pleaded for Free Trade; the manly, the *Christian* fortitude with
which he braved reproach and persecution; the sacrifices which he made
for its sake; the firmness and calmness with which he endured the cruel
and disgraceful taunts and insults of his enemies, deserves the highest
praise. They have affected me very much. I never felt such a respect for a
Statesman before in all my life. It is impossible that he should be a hypo-
crite. I should as readily think of questioning the sincerity, the integrity
of the Apostle Paul as of Sir Robert Peel. If the conduct of Sir Robert Peel
for a length of time past does not prove him to be a good, an upright man;
a lover of truth and righteousness; a friend to peace and freedom; a real
well-wisher to the improvement and the welfare of his country and his
kind, then a tree can no longer be known by its fruits; then a fountain can
no longer be known by its streams. For myself I look on Sir Robert Peel
as one of the greatest and best-deserving men of our times. There is not
a Statesman on earth in whom I have greater confidence. I believe him to
be a sterling, Christian man, and I hope that the insults and persecutions
with which he has met, and with which he may continue to meet, will
only perfect his character, and prepare him for still greater usefulness in
days to come.

No doubt Sir Robert has his weakness, his failings; but so have the best
of men. He has allowed himself to be influenced at times by his fears; but
so have all reformers, from the days of Abraham to the present hour. He
has hoped to gain by policy what could only be gained by self-sacrifice;
but all good men have indulged such hopes. He has delayed good measures in hopes of winning over his party by time and the force of truth; but
the bravest reformers that ever lived have done the same. I do not believe
him to be perfect; much less do I believe him to have been always so; but
I still regard him as a great, good man, a *friend* as well as a benefactor to
his race.

There are many other things in the history of Sir R. Peel very much to
his credit, besides those to which I have alluded, but I cannot even refer to
them at present.

But what of his conduct toward O'Connell? [12] I answer; it is only fair

[12] Daniel O'Connell (1775–1847), an ardent Catholic and founder of the Young Ireland
movement, led an agitation against Peel in 1811. Peel responded by reviving the Insurrection Act of 1807 and establishing a peace preservation force in Ireland, the "Peelers." Unde-
terred, O'Connell was one of Peel's fiercest opponents and dedicated his life to promoting
nationalistic fervor in Ireland (*DNB*).

to suppose, that as he was one of a party who were not all as noble or as enlightened as himself, he might consent to certain measures which he did not quite approve. I cannot myself but construe his motives charitably. I like to illumine the darker portions of his life by the brighter, and not to obscure the brighter portions by the darker or the doubtful. In short, I have a right good, comfortable opinion of Sir R. Peel, and I am glad I have. I offer him my hearty thanks for his efforts in the cause of freedom and human happiness; I congratulate him on his great and glorious triumph; and I pray most heartily that God may spare his life, and favor him richly with the choicest of his blessings, and make him a still greater benefactor to his kind.

As for Cobden and his fellow-laborers, there is no need that I should dwell upon their merits.[13] Almost every one praises them. Sir Robert Peel has made the greatest sacrifices, and has been the greatest sufferer; I therefore sympathize the most with him." * * * * * * *

How great, how imperious the need of such men, of such deeds, we felt more than ever, while compelled to turn a deaf ear to the squalid and shameless beggars of Liverpool, or talking by night in the streets of Manchester to the girls from the Mills, who were strolling bare-headed, with coarse, rude and reckless air through the streets, seeing through the windows of its gin-palaces the women seated drinking, too dull to carouse. The homes of England! their sweetness is melting into fable; only the new Spirit in its holiest power can restore to those homes their boasted security of "each man's castle," for Woman, the warder, is driven into the street, and has let fall the keys in her sad plight. Yet, darkest hour of night is nearest dawn, and there seems reason to believe that

"There's a good time coming." [14]

Blest be those who aid—who doubt not that

"Smallest helps, if rightly given,
Make the impulse stronger;
'T will be strong enough one day."

Other things we saw in Liverpool—the Royal Institute, with the statue of

[13] Richard Cobden (1804–65) assisted other Manchester merchants in forming the Anti–Corn Law League in 1838. Until 1846, Cobden devoted his life to the repeal of the Corn Laws (*DNB*).

[14] Sir Walter Scott, *Rob Roy,* chap. 32 (London: Oxford University Press, 1829), 20:382.

Roscoe by Chantrey,[15] and in its collection from the works of the early Italian artists and otherwise, bearing traces of that liberality and culture by which the man, happy enough to possess them, and, at the same time engaged with his fellow-citizens in practical life, can do so much more to enlighten and form them than Prince or Noble possibly can with far larger pecuniary means. We saw the statue of Huskisson in the Cemetery.[16] It is fine as a Portrait Statue, but as a work of Art wants firmness and grandeur. I say it is fine as a portrait statue, though we were told it is not like the original; but it is a fine conception of an individuality which might exist, if it does not yet. It is by Gibson, who received his early education in Liverpool. I saw there, too, the body of an infant borne to the grave by women; for it is a beautiful custom here that those who have fulfilled all other tender offices to the little being, should hold to it the same relation to the very last.

From Liverpool we went to Chester, one of the oldest cities in England, a Roman station, Cestrea then, and abode of the "Twentieth Legion," "the Victorious." Tiles bearing this inscription, heads of Jupiter, other marks of their occupation have, not long ago, been detected beneath the sod. The town also bears the marks of Welsh invasion and domestic struggles. The shape of a cross in which it is laid out, its walls and towers, its four arched gateways, its ramparts and ruined towers, mantled with ivy, its old houses with biblical inscriptions, its cathedrals,—in one of which tall trees have grown up amid the arches, a fresh garden plot with flowers, bright green and red, has taken place of the altar and a crowd of reveling swallows supplanted the sallow choirs of a former priesthood—present a *tout-ensemble* highly romantic in itself and charming, indeed, to trans-Atlantic eyes. Yet not to all eyes would it have had charms, for one American traveler, our companion on the voyage, gravely assured us that we should find the "castles and that sort of thing all humbug," and that if we wished to enjoy them it would "be best to sit at home and read some *handsome* work on the subject."

At the hotel in Liverpool and that in Manchester I had found no bath, and asking for one at Chester, the chambermaid said with earnest good will, that

[15] William Roscoe (1753–1831) was one of the founders of the Liverpool society of the arts of painting and design, called the Royal Institute and established in 1817. The marble statue of Roscoe was publicly subscribed and placed in the Gallery of Art at the institute in 1841. In addition to the statue of Roscoe, Sir Francis Legatt Chantrey (1781–1841) sculpted many busts and statues of distinguished men, including Wordsworth, Sir Walter Scott, and George IV (*DNB* and *Great Britain* 348).

[16] William Huskisson(1790–1866) was a British statesman, financier, and leading advocate of free trade. John Gibson (1790–1866), an English sculptor, supervised (from 1844 to 1847) the erection of his statue of Huskisson in the mausoleum built by John Foster (1786–1846) in the St. James Cemetery (*DNB* and *OCA*).

"they had none, but she thought she could get me a note from her master to the Infirmary!! if I would go there." Luckily I did not generalize quite as rapidly as travelers in America usually do, and put in the note book—"*Mem:* None but the sick ever bathe in England;" [17] for in the next establishment we tried, I found the plentiful provision for a clean and healthy day, which I had read would be met *every where* in this country.

All else I must defer to my next, as the mail is soon to close.   ★

Dispatch 2

FROM CHESTER TO THE LAKE COUNTRY

AMBLESIDE, Westmoreland, 27th Aug. 1846 [1]

I forgot to mention, in writing of Chester, an object which gave me pleasure. I mentioned that the wall which enclosed the old town was two miles in circumference; far beyond this stretches the modern part of Chester, and the old gateways now overarch the middle of long streets. This wall is now a walk for the inhabitants, commanding a wide prospect, and three persons could walk abreast on its smooth flags. We passed one of its old picturesque towers, from whose top Charles I., poor, weak, unhappy king, looked down and saw his troops defeated by the Parliamentary army on the adjacent plain. [2] A little farther on, one of these picturesque towers is turned to the use of a Museum, whose stock, though scanty, I examined with singular pleasure, for it had been made up by truly filial contributions from all who had derived benefit from Chester, from the Marquis of Westminster, whose magnificent abode, Eton Hall, lies not far off, down to the merchant's clerk, who had furnished it in his leisure hours with a geological chart, the soldier and sailor who sent back shells, insects, and petrifactions from their distant wanderings, and a boy of thirteen, who had made, in wood, a model of its Cathedral and even furnished it with a bell to ring out the evening chimes. Many women had been busy in filling these magazines for the instruction and the pleasure of their fellow townsmen. Lady ———— , the wife of the Captain of the garrison, grateful for the gratuitous admission

[17] Fuller is taking a jibe at Frances Trollope (1780–1863), who made many such generalizations in her *Domestic Manners of the Americans* (1832).

[1] First published as "Things and Thoughts in Europe. No. II" in the *New-York Daily Tribune,* 29 September 1846, p. 1:1–3.

[2] The walls of Chester extend in a one-mile circuit; in the Middle Ages, several towers and gates were added. The King Charles Tower was the northeast corner of the Roman fortress. Charles I is said to have watched the defeat of his forces at Rowton Heath in 1645 from this point (*Treasures* 138).

of the soldiers once a month—a privilege of which the keeper of the Museum (a woman, also, who took an intelligent pleasure in her task) assured me that they were eager to avail themselves—had given a fine collection of butterflies, and a ship.—We had shown an untiring diligence in adding whatever might stimulate or gratify imperfectly educated minds. I like to see women perceive that there are other ways of doing good beside making clothes for the poor or teaching Sunday-school; these are well, if well directed, but there are many other ways, some as sure and surer, and which benefit the giver no less than the receiver.

I was waked from sleep at the Chester Inn by a loud dispute between the chambermaid and an unhappy elderly gentleman, who insisted that he had engaged the room in which I was, had returned to sleep in it, and consequently must do so. To her assurances that the lady was long since in possession, he was deaf; but the lock, fortunately for me, proved a stronger defence. With all a chambermaid's morality, the maiden boasted to me, "He said he had engaged 44, and would not believe me when I assured him it was 46; indeed, how could he? I did not believe myself." To my assurance that if I had known the room was his I should not have wished for it, but preferred taking a worse, I found her a polite but incredulous listener.

Passing from Liverpool to Lancaster by railroad, that convenient but most unprofitable and stupid way of traveling, we there took the canal-boat to Kendal, and passed pleasantly through a country of that soft, that refined and cultivated loveliness, which, however and forever we have heard of it, finds the American eye—accustomed to so much wildness, so much rudeness, such a corrosive action of man upon nature—wholly unprepared.[3] I feel all the time as if in a sweet dream, and dread to be presently awakened by some rude jar or glare, but none comes, and here in Westmoreland—but wait a moment, before we speak of that.

In the canal-boat we found two well-bred English gentlemen, apparently belonging to the "hupper airy-stokracy," and two well-informed German gentlemen, with whom we had some agreeable talk. With one of the former was a beautiful youth, about eighteen, whom I supposed, at the first glance, to be a type of that pure East-Indian race whose beauty I had never seen represented before except in pictures; and he made a picture, from which I could scarcely take my eyes a moment, and could as ill endure to part. He was dressed

[3] The "railway mania" of the mid-1840s had greatly increased the size of the railway system in England, and the Liverpool and Manchester railway was among the most successful and most heavily traveled (Mitchell 663–65).

in a broadcloth robe richly embroidered, leaving his throat and the upper part of his neck bare, except that he wore a heavy gold chain. A rich shawl was thrown gracefully round him, the sleeves of his robe were loose, with white sleeves below. He wore a black satin cap. The whole effect of this dress was very fine yet simple, setting off to the utmost advantage the distinguished beauty of his features, in which there was a mingling of national pride, voluptuous sweetness in that unconscious state of reverie when it affects us as it does in the flower, and intelligence in its newly awakened purity. As he turned his head, his profile was like one I used to have of Love asleep, while Psyche leans over him with the lamp, but his front face, with the full, summery look of the eye, was unlike that. He was a Bengalese, living in England for his education, as several others are at present. He spoke English well and conversed on several subjects, literary and political, with grace, fluency, and delicacy of thought. Passing from Kendal to Ambleside, we found a charming abode furnished us by the care of a friend[4] in one of the stone cottages of this region, almost the only one *not* ivy-wreathed, but commanding a beautiful view of the mountains, and truly an English home in its neatness, quiet, and delicate, noiseless attention to the wants of all within its walls. Here we have passed eight happy days, varied by many drives, boating excursions on Grasmere and Windermere, and the society of several agreeable persons. As the Lake district at this season draws together all kinds of people, and a great variety beside come from all quarters to inhabit the charming dwellings that adorn its hillsides and shores, I met and saw a good deal of the representations of various classes, at once. I found here two landed proprietors from other parts of England, both "traveled English," one owning a property in Greece, where he frequently resides, both warmly engaged in Reform measures, anti–Corn Law, anti–Capital Punishment—one of them an earnest student of Emerson's Essays. Both of them had wives, who kept pace with their projects and their thoughts, active and intelligent women, true ladies, skillful in drawing and music; all the better wives for the development of every power. One of them told me, with a glow of pride, that it was not long since her husband had been "cut" by all his neighbors among the gentry for the part he took against the Corn-Laws, but, she added, he was now a

---

[4] Harriet Martineau (1802–76) had built her home, The Knoll, in 1845–46 at Clappersgate, Westmoreland, following a protracted illness (*DNB* and *OCEL*). Fuller had met her in Boston in 1835 during Martineau's tour of the United States, the subject of her *Society in America* (1837), a book which Fuller disliked. Despite their differences of opinion about American society, Martineau received Fuller warmly and arranged for her and the Springs to occupy the little cottage at Ambleside.

favorite with them all. Verily, faith will remove mountains, if only you do join with it any fair portion of the dove and serpent attributes.

I found here, too, a wealthy Manufacturer, who has written many valuable pamphlets on popular subjects. He said: "Now that the progress of public opinion was beginning to make the Church and the Army narrower fields for the younger sons of 'noble' families, they sometimes wished to enter into trade, but, beside the aversion which had been instilled into them for many centuries, they had rarely patience and energy for the apprenticeship needed to give the needed knowledge of the world and habits of labor." Of Cobden he said: "He is inferior in acquirements to very many of his class, as he is self-educated and had every thing to learn after he was grown up, but in clear insight there is none like him."—A man of very little education, whom I met a day or two after in the stage-coach, observed to me: "Bright is far the more eloquent of the two, but Cobden is more felt, just *because* his speeches are so plain, so merely matter-of-fact and to the point."[5]

We became acquainted also with Dr. Gregory, Professor of Chemistry at Edinburgh, a very enlightened and benevolent man, who was in many ways of instruction and other benefit to us. He is the friend of Liebig, and one of his chief representatives here.[6] A pamphlet, lately translated by him from the German, was noticed in the "Evening Post" a short time before I left New-York, and the same extracts should have appeared in "The Tribune." I will here give the name of the pamphlet, as it is calculated to instruct so many in the United States, and will be sent for if known to exist. It is "Abstract of Researches on Magnetism, and on certain allied subjects, including a supposed new Imponderable, by Baron Von Reichenbach, translated and abridged from the German by William Gregory, M.D., F.R.S.E., M.R.I.A., Professor of Chemistry." (I give all these letters of the alphabet, because I have observed that with many persons they lend a charm to a work.)

We also met a fine specimen of the noble, intelligent Scotchwoman, such as Walter Scott and Burns knew how to prize. Seventy-six years have passed over her head, only to prove in her the truth of my theory that we need never

[5] John Bright (1811–89), a middle-class manufacturer who advocated free trade, was a champion of reform causes. A leader of the Anti–Corn Law League, he was elected member of Parliament for Manchester in 1847 (*DNB*).

[6] Dr. William Gregory (1803–58) had been elected to the chair of Chemistry at the University of Edinburgh in 1844. He was a student of the German chemist Justus von Liebig (1803–73), renowned for his work in organic chemistry and his abilities as a teacher. Gregory too gained prominence in the field of organic chemistry (*DNB*); Fuller was interested in his additional work in animal magnetism and telepathy, topics that had fascinated her for some years. The remainder of this paragraph is omitted in *AHA*.

grow old. She was "brought up" in the animated and intellectual circle of Edinburgh, in youth an apt disciple, in her prime a bright ornament of that society. She had been an only child, a cherished wife, an adored mother, unspoiled by love in any of these relations, because that love was founded on knowledge. In childhood she had warmly sympathized in the spirit that animated the American Revolution, and Washington had been her hero; later the interest of her husband in every struggle for freedom had cherished her own; she had known in the course of her long life many eminent men, knew minutely the history of efforts in that direction, and sympathized now in the triumph of the people over the Corn-Laws, as she had in the American victories with as much ardor as when a girl, though with a wiser mind. Her eye was full of light, her manner and gesture of dignity; her voice rich, sonorous, and finely modulated; her tide of talk marked by candor, justice,—showing in every sentence her ripe experience and her noble, genial nature. Dear to memory will be the sight of her in the beautiful seclusion of her home among the mountains, a picturesque, flower wreathed dwelling, where affection, tranquillity and wisdom were the gods of the hearth, to whom was offered no vain oblation. Grant us more such women, Time! Grant to men the power to reverence, to seek for such!

Our visit to Mr. Wordsworth was very pleasant.[7] He, also, is seventy-six, but his is a florid, fair old age. He walked with us to all his haunts about the house. Its situation is beautiful, and the "Rydalian Laurels" are magnificent. Still I saw abodes among the hills that I should have preferred for Wordsworth; more wild and still, more romantic—the fresh and lovely Rydal Mount seems merely the retirement of a gentleman, rather than the haunt of a Poet. He showed his benignity of disposition in several little things, especially in his attentions to a young boy we had with us. This boy had left the Circus, exhibiting its feats of horsemanship in Ambleside "for that day only," at his own desire to see Wordsworth, and I feared he would be disappointed, as I know I should have been at his age if, when called to see a Poet, I had found no Apollo, flaming with youthful glory, laurel-crowned and lyre in hand, but, instead, a reverend old man clothed in black, and walking with cautious step along the level garden path; however, he was not disappointed, but seemed in timid reverence to recognize the spirit that had dictated "Laodamia" and "Dion."—and Wordsworth, in his turn, seemed to feel and prize a congenial nature in this child.

Taking us into the house, he showed us the picture of his sister, repeating with much expression some lines of hers, and those so famous of his about

[7] William Wordsworth (1770–1850) was at this time near the end of his life. He had moved to Rydal Mount in 1813; when Fuller met him, he had been poet laureate for three years (*OCEL*).

her, beginning "Five Years" &c., also his own picture, by Inman, of whom he
spoke with esteem.[8] I had asked to see a picture in that room, which has been
described in one of the finest of his later poems.

There cannot be a better occasion to re-present, or, in many cases, present
for the first time, to the love of the reading world, a part of one of the finest
descriptive poems extant:

LINES
Suggested by a Portrait from the Pencil of F. Stone. [9]
BEGUILED into forgetfulness of care
Due to the day's unfinished task, of pen
Or book regardless, and of that fair scene
In Nature's prodigality displayed
Before my window, oftentimes and long
I gaze upon a portrait whose mild gleam
Of beauty never ceases to enrich
The common light; whose stillness charms the air
Or seems to charm it into like repose;
Whose silence for the pleasure of the ear
Surpasses sweetest music. There she sits
With emblematic purity attired
In a white vest, white as her marble neck
Is, and the pillar of the throat *would be*
But for the shadow by the drooping chin
Cast into that recess—the tender shade,
The shade and light, both there and every where.
And through the very atmosphere she breathes,
Broad, clear, and toned harmoniously, with skill
That might from Nature have been learnt in the hour
When the lone shepherd sees the morning spread
Upon the mountains. Look at her, whoe'er

[8] Henry Inman (1801–46), an American painter, traveled to England in 1844 to paint
portraits of Wordsworth and Macaulay (Bernard Myers, *Encyclopedia of Painting* [New York:
Crown, 1955]). The remainder of this paragraph, the next paragraph, and the entire poem
are omitted from *AHA*.

[9] The poem was first published in 1835. Frank Stone (1800–59), a painter, was a close
friend of Thackeray and Dickens. He had painted portraits of both Jemima and Rotha Quil-
linan in 1833. A copy of the portrait of Jemima was hung in the sitting room at Rydal Mount
(Alan G. Hill, ed., *The Letters of William and Mary Wordsworth,* 2d ed., vol. 6, "The Later
Years," Part III, 1835–1839, [Oxford: Oxford University Press, 1982], 234–35).

Thou be, that kindling with a Poet's soul
Hast loved the Painter's true Promethean craft
Intensely—from imagination take
The treasure, what mine eyes behold see thou,
Even though the Atlantic Ocean roll between.
A silver line, that from brow to crown,
And in the middle parts the braided hair,
Just serves to show how delicate a soil
The golden harvest grows in; and those eyes,
Soft and capacious as a cloudless sky
Whose azure depth their color emulates,
Must needs be conversant with *upward* looks,
Prayer's voiceless service; but now, seeking nought
And shunning nought, their own peculiar life
Of motion they renounce, and with the head
Partake its inclination toward earth
In humble grace, and quiet pensiveness
Caught at the point where it stops short of sadness.

Offspring of soul-bewitching art, make me
Thy confidant! say, whence derived that air
Of calm abstraction? Can the ruling thought
Be with some lover far away, or one
Crossed by misfortune, or of doubted faith?
Inapt conjecture! Childhood here, a moon
Crescent in simple loveliness serene,
Has but approached the gates of womanhood,
Not entered them; her heart is yet unpierced
By the blind archer-god, her fancy free;
The fount of feeling, if unsought elsewhere,
Will not be found.
        Her right hand, as it lies
Across the slender wrist of the left arm
Upon her lap reposing, holds—but mark
How slackly, for the absent mind permits
No firmer grasp—a little wild-flower, joined
As in a posy, with a few pale ears
Of yellowing corn, the same that overtopped
And in their common birthplace sheltered it
'Till they were plucked together; a blue flower

Called by the thrifty husbandman *a weed;*
But Ceres, in her garland, might have worn
That ornament, unblamed. The floweret, held
In scarcely conscious fingers, was, she knows,
(Her father told her so) in youth's gay dawn
Her mother's favorite; and the orphan girl,
In her own dawn—a dawn less gay and bright,
Loves it while there in solitary peace
She sits, for that departed mother's sake.
—Not from a source less sacred is derived
(Surely I do not err) that pensive air
Of calm abstraction through the face diffused
And the whole person.

  Words have something told,
More than the pencil can, and verily
More than is needed, but the precious art
Forgives their interference—art divine,
That both creates and fixes, in despite
Of death and time, the marvels it hath wrought.

  Strange contrasts have we in this world of ours!
That posture and the look of filial love
Thinking of past and gone, with what is left
Dearly united, might be swept away
From this fair portrait's fleshy archetype,
Even by an innocent fancy's slightest freak
Banished, nor ever, haply, be restored
To their lost place, or meet in harmony
So exquisite; but *here* do they abide,
Enshrined for ages. Is not then the art
Godlike, a humble branch of the divine,
In visible quest of immortality,
Stretched forth with trembling hope? In every realm,
From high Gibraltar to Siberian plains,
Thousands, in each variety of tongue
That Europe knows, would echo this appeal.

A hundred times had I wished to see this picture, yet when seen was not
disappointed by it. The light was unfavorable, but it had a light of its own,

"whose mild gleam
Of beauty never ceases to enrich
The common light."

Mr. Wordsworth is fond of the Hollyhock, a partiality scarcely deserved by the flower, but which marks the simplicity of his tastes. He had made a long avenue of them of all colors, from the crimson brown to rose, straw color and white, and pleased himself with having made proselytes to a liking for them among his neighbors.

I never have seen such magnificent Fuchsias as at Ambleside, and there was one to be seen in every cottage-yard. They are no longer here under the shelter of the green-house, as with us, and as they used to be in England. The plant, from its grace and finished elegance, being a great favorite of mine, I should like to see it as frequently and of as luxuriant a growth at home, and asked their mode of culture, which I here mark down, for the benefit of all who may be interested. Make a bed of bog-earth and sand, put down slips of the Fuchsia and give them a great deal of water—this is all they need. People have them out here in winter, but perhaps they would not bear the cold of our Januaries.

Mr. Wordsworth spoke with more liberality than we expected of the recent measures about the Corn Laws, saying that "the principle was certainly right, though as to whether existing interests had been as carefully attended to as was right, he was not prepared to say," &c. His neighbors were pleased to hear of his speaking thus mildly, and hailed it as a sign that he was opening his mind to more light on these subjects. They lament that his habits of seclusion keep him much ignorant of the real wants of England and the world, living in this region, which is cultivated by small proprietors, where there is little poverty, vice or misery, he hears not the voice which cries so loudly from other parts of England, and will not be stilled by sweet poetic suasion or philosophy, for it is the cry of men in the jaws of destruction. It was pleasant to find the reverence inspired by this great and pure mind warmest nearest home. Our landlady, in heaping praises upon him, added, constantly, "And Mrs. Wordsworth, too." "Do the people here," said I, "value Mr. Wordsworth most because he is a celebrated writer?" "Truly, Madam," said she, "I think it is because he is so kind a neighbor."

"True to the kindred points of Heaven and Home." [10]

---

[10] Wordsworth, "To a Skylark" (composed 1827). Stanza 2 reads:
Leave to the nightingale her shady wood;
A privacy of glorious light is thine;
Whence thou dost pour upon the world a flood
Of harmony, with instinct more divine;

Dr. Arnold, too, who lived, as his family still live, here—diffused the same ennobling and animating spirit among those who knew him in private, as through the sphere of his public labors.[11]

Miss Martineau has here a charming residence; it has been finished only a few months, but all about it is in unexpectedly fair order and promises much beauty after a year or two of growth. Here we found her restored to full health and activity, looking, indeed, far better than she did when in the United States. It was pleasant to see her in this home, presented to her by the gratitude of England for her course of energetic and benevolent effort, and adorned by tributes of affection and esteem from many quarters. From the testimony of those who were with her in and since her illness, her recovery would seem to be of as magical quickness and sure progress as has been represented. At the house of Miss M. I saw Milman, the author, I must not say Poet—a specimen of the polished, scholarly man of the world.[12]

I am here reminded that I have not spoken of James Martineau, whom I heard at Liverpool.[13] I will do so after I have heard other preachers of this land.

We passed one most delightful day in a visit to Langdale—the scene of the Excursion—and to Dungeon Gill Force.[14] I am finishing my letter at Carlisle on my way to Scotland, and will give a slight sketch of that excursion and one which occupied another day from Keswick to Buttermere and Crummock Water in my next.   ★

Type of the wise who soar, but never roam;
True to the kindred points of Heaven and Home!
(John O. Hayden, ed., *William Wordsworth: The Poems* [New Haven: Yale University Press, 1981], 2:613)

[11] Thomas Arnold (1795–1842), headmaster of Rugby School from 1827 to 1842, was the first to include mathematics, modern history, and modern languages in the school curriculum (*DNB*).

[12] Henry Hart Milman (1791–1868) was a translator, historian, and amateur poet. His major work was *History of the Jews* (1830); in 1849, he became dean of St. Paul's Cathedral in London (*DNB*).

[13] James Martineau (1805–1900), the younger brother of Harriet Martineau, was a Unitarian minister and a prominent theologian, who lived in Liverpool (*DNB*).

[14] Fuller refers to *The Excursion,* Wordsworth's poem in nine books, published in 1814. This poem was intended to be the middle part of *The Recluse,* which was never completed (*OCEL*). Dungeon Gill Force, a waterfall, is close to Ambleside, and one of Wordsworth's favorite destinations (*Great Britain* 427).

Dispatch 3

TOURIST ATTRACTIONS

EDINBURGH, 20th Sept. 1846 [1]

I have too long delayed writing up my journal. —Many interesting observations slip from recollection if one waits so many days: yet, while traveling, it is almost impossible to find an hour when something of value to be seen will not be lost while writing.

I said, in closing my last, that I would write a little more about Westmoreland; but so much has happened since that I must now dismiss that region with all possible brevity.

The first day of which I wished to speak was passed in visiting Langdale, the scene of Wordsworth's "Excursion." Our party of eight went in two of the vehicles called cars or droskas—open carriages, each drawn by one horse. They are rather fatiguing to ride in, but good to see from. In steep and stony places all alight, and the driver leads the horse. So many of these there are that we were four or five hours in going ten miles, including the pauses when we wished to *look*.

The scenes through which we passed are, indeed, of the most wild and noble character. The wildness is not savage but very calm. Without recurring to details, I recognized the tone and atmosphere of that noble poem, which was to me, at a feverish period in my life, as pure waters, free breezes and cold blue sky, bringing a sense of eternity that gave an aspect of composure to the rudest volcanic wrecks of time. We dined at a farm-house of the vale with its stone floors, old carved cabinet, (the pride of a house of this sort,) and ready provision of oaten cakes. We then ascended a near hill to the waterfall called Dungeon Gill Force, also a subject touched by Wordsworth's Muse. [2] You wind along a path for a long time, hearing the sound of the falling water, but you do not see it till, descending by a ladder the side of the ravine, you come to its very foot.— You find yourself then in a deep chasm, bridged over by a narrow arch of rock; the water falls at the farther end in a narrow column. Looking up, you see the sky through a fissure so narrow as to make it look very pure and distant. One of our party, passing in, stood some time at the foot of the waterfall, and added much to its effect, as his hight gave a measure by which to appreciate that of

---

[1] First published as "Things and Thoughts in Europe. No. III" in *New-York Daily Tribune*, 24 October 1846, p. 1:2–3.

[2] "The Idle Shepherd-Boys; or, Dungeon-Ghyll Force. A Pastoral." *William Wordsworth: The Poems* 1:425–28.

surrounding objects, and his look, by that light so pale and statuesque, seemed to inform the place with the presence of its genius.

Our circuit homeward from this grand scene led us through some lovely places, and to an outlook upon the most beautiful part of Westmoreland.— Passing over to Keswick we saw Derwentwater, and near it the Fall of Lodore. It was from Keswick that we made the excursion of a day through Borrowdale to Buttermere and Crummock Water, which I meant to speak of but I find it impossible at this moment.[3] The mind does not now furnish congenial colors with which to represent the vision of that day: it must still wait in the mind and bide its time, again to emerge to outer air.

At Keswick we went to see a model of the Lake Country which gives an excellent idea of the relative positions of all objects. Its maker had given six years to the necessary surveys and drawings. He said that he had first become acquainted with the country from his taste for fishing, but had learned to love its beauty till the thought arose of making this model; that while engaged in it, he visited almost every spot amid the hills and commonly saw both sunrise and sunset upon them; that he was happy all the time, but almost too happy when he saw one section of his model coming out quite right, and felt sure at last that he should be quite successful in representing to others the home of his thoughts. I looked upon him as indeed an enviable man to have a profession so congenial with his feelings, in which he had been so naturally led to do what would be useful and pleasant for others.

Passing from Keswick through a pleasant and cultivated country, we paused at 'fair Carlisle,' not voluntarily, but because we could not get the means of proceeding farther that day. So, as it was one in which

"The sun shone fair on Carlisle wall,"

we visited its Cathedral and Castle, and trod, for the first time, in some of the footsteps of the unfortunate Queen of Scots.

Passing next day the Border, we found the mosses all drained, and the very existence of some-time moss-troopers would have seemed problematical, but for the remains of Gilnockie, the tower of Johnie Armstrong, so pathetically recalled in one of the finest of the Scottish ballads.[4] Its size, as well as that of other

---

[3] Fuller's excursion includes a number of popular destinations of nineteenth-century tourists to the Lake District. Among the places she visited was Keswick, where Robert Southey lived at Greta Hall from 1803 to 1843 (*DNB*).

[4] Johnie Armstrong, or Armstrang, of Gilnockie was a popular historical figure. Fuller visited the remains of his home, a roofless tower near Langholm. In the ballad "Armstrong's Good-night," Armstrong is presented as the rebel leader of a plucky band of Scots who confront James V and an army of ten thousand in 1529. Despite the courage of the Bordermen, Armstrong is defeated and slain (Francis James Child, *English and Scottish Ballads* [Boston: Little, Brown, 1858], 6:37–45.)

keeps, towers and castles where ruins are reverentially preserved in Scotland, give a lively sense of the time when population was so scanty, and individual manhood grew to such force. Ten men in Gilnockie were stronger then in proportion to the whole, and, probably had in them more of intelligence, resource, and genuine manly power than ten regiments now of red-coats drilled to act out maneuvers they do not understand and use artillery which needs of them no more than the match to go off and do its hideous message.

Farther on we saw Branksome, and the water, in crossing which the Goblin Page was obliged to resume his proper shape and fly, crying, "Lost, lost, lost!"[5] Verily, these things seem more like home than one's own nursery, whose toys and furniture could not in actual presence engage the thoughts like these pictures, made familiar as household words by the most generous, kindly genius that ever blessed this earth.

On the coach with us was a gentleman coming from London to make his yearly visit to the neighborhood of Burns, in which he was born.[6] "I can now," said he, "go but once a year; when a boy I never let a week pass, without visiting the house of Burns." He afterward observed, as every step woke us to fresh recollections of Walter Scott, that Scott, with all his vast range of talent, knowledge and activity, was a poet of the past only, and in his inmost heart wedded to the habits of a feudal aristocracy, while Burns is the poet of the present and the future, the man of the People, and throughout a genuine man. This is true enough; but for my part I cannot endure such comparison by a breath of coolness to depreciate either. Both were wanted; each acted the important part assigned him by destiny with a wonderful thoroughness and completeness. Scott breathed the breath just fleeting from the forms of ancient Scottish heroism and -poesy into new—he made for us the bridge by which we have gone into the old Ossianic hall and caught the meaning just as it was about to pass from us forever. Burns is full of the noble, genuine democracy which seeks not to destroy royalty, but to make all men kings, as he himself was, in nature and in action. They belong to the same world; they are pillars of the same church, though they uphold its starry roof from opposite sides. Burns was much the rarer man; precisely because he had most of common nature on a grand scale; his humor, his passion, his sweetness, are all his own; they need no picturesque or romantic accessories to give them due relief: looked at by all lights they are the same.

[5] Fuller refers to *The Lay of the Last Minstrel* (1805) by Sir Walter Scott. The poem, written in six cantos, is set at Branksome Hall, and is based on a Border legend of the sixteenth century. The Goblin Page is the elfin page who causes mischief and on whom the complex plot turns (*OCEL*). Scott purchased Abbotsford on the Tweed and built a home there in 1811.

[6] The poet Robert Burns was born in Ayrshire, a county in southwestern Scotland (*DNB*).

Since Adam, there has been none that approached nearer fitness to stand up before God and angels in the naked majesty of manhood than Robert Burns;—
but there was a serpent in his field also! [7] Yet, but for his fault we could never
have seen brought out the brave and patriotic modesty with which he owned it.
Shame on him who could bear to think of fault in his rich jewel, unless reminded
by such confession.

We passed Abbotsford without stopping, intending to go there on our return. Last year five hundred Americans inscribed their names in its porter's
book. A raw-boned Scotsman, who gathered his weary length into our coach
on return from a pilgrimage thither, did us the favor to inform us that "Sir
Walter was a vara intelligent mon," and the guide-book mentions "the American Washington" as "a worthy old patriot." Lord safe us, cummers, what news
be there!

This letter, meant to go by the Great Britain, many interruptions force me to
close, unflavored by one whiff from the smoke of Auld Reekie. More and better
matter shall my next contain, for here and in the Highlands I have passed three
not unproductive weeks, of which more anon.   ★

Dispatch 4

THE NOTABLES OF EDINBURGH

EDINBURGH, Sept. 22d, 1846 [1]

The beautiful and stately aspect of this city has been the theme of admiration so
general that I can only echo it. We have seen it to the greatest advantage both
from Calton Hill and Arthur's Seat, and our lodgings in Princes-street allow us
a fine view of the Castle, always impressive, but peculiarly so in the moonlight
evenings of our first week here, when a veil of mist added to its apparent size,
and, at the same time, gave it the air with which Martin, in his illustrations of
"Paradise Lost," has invested the palace which "rose like an exhalation." [2]

On this our second visit, after an absence of near a fortnight in the Highlands, we are at a hotel nearly facing the new monument to Scott, and the
tallest buildings of the Old Town. From my windows I see the famous Kirk,
the spot where the old Tolbooth was, and can almost distinguish that where
Porteous was done to death, and other objects described in the most dramatic

[7] Burns fathered a number of illegitimate children.
[1] First published as "Things and Thoughts in Europe. No. IV" in *New-York Daily Tribune*,
5 November 1846, p. 1:1–2.
[2] John Martin (1789–1854) provided the illustrations for a new edition of *Paradise Lost*
(London: C. Whittingham, 1846).

part of "The Heart of Mid Lothian."[3] In one of these tall houses Hume wrote part of his History of England, and on that spot still nearer was the home of Allan Ramsay.[4] A thousand other interesting and pregnant associations present themselves every time I look out of the window.

In the open square between us and the Old Town is to be the terminus of the Railroad, but, as the building will be masked with trees, it is thought it will not mar the beauty of the place, yet Scott could hardly have looked without regret upon an object that marks so distinctly the conquest of the New over the Old, and, appropriately enough, his statue has its back turned that way. The effect of the monument to Scott is pleasing, though without strict unity of thought, or original beauty of design. The statue is too much hid within the monument, and wants that majesty of repose in the attitude and drapery which a sitting figure should have, and which might well accompany the massive head of Scott. Still, the monument is an ornament and an honor to the city. This is now the fourth that has been erected within two years to commemorate the triumphs of genius. Monuments that have risen from the same idea and in such quick succession, to Schiller, to Goethe, to Beethoven and to Scott, signalize the character of the new era still more happily than does the Railroad coming up almost to the foot of Edinburgh Castle.

The statue of Burns has been removed from the monument erected in his honor, to one of the public libraries, as being there more accessible to the public. It is, however, entirely unworthy its subject, giving the idea of a smaller and younger person, while we think of Burns as of a man in the prime of manhood, one who not only promised but *was,* and with a sunny glow and breadth of character of which this stone effigy presents no sign.

A Scottish gentleman told me the following story, which would afford the finest subject for a painter capable of representing the glowing eye and natural kingliness of Burns, in contrast to the poor, mean puppets he reproved.

Burns, still only in the dawn of his celebrity, was invited to dine with one of the neighboring so-called gentry, (unhappily quite void of true gentle blood). On arriving, he found his plate set in the servants' room!! After dinner he was invited into a room where guests were assembled, and a chair being placed for him at the lower end of the board, a glass of wine was offered, and he was re-

[3] The monument to Scott, designed by George Kemp with a statue of the novelist by Sir John Steele, was erected in Princes Street and inaugurated on 17 August 1846 (*DNB*). Scott's *The Heart of Mid-Lothian* was published in 1818.

[4] David Hume moved to Edinburgh in 1751 and began his *History of England* in 1752. The poet Allan Ramsay (1686–1758) founded the first circulating library in Scotland in 1726. He established a home on the north side of the Castle Rock in 1755 (*DNB*).

quested to sing one of his songs for the entertainment of the company. He drank off the wine and thundered forth in reply his grand song, "For a' that and a' that," with which it will do no harm to refresh the memories of our readers, for we doubt there may be, even in Republican America, those who need the reproof as much, and with far less excuse, than had that Scottish company:

"Is there for honest poverty
    That hangs his head, and a' that?
The coward-slave we pass him by,
    We dare be poor for a' that!
    For a' that, and a' that;
    Our toils obscure, and a' that,
The rank is but the guinea stamp,
    The man's the gowd for a' that.

What tho' on hamely fare we dine,
    Wear hoddin gray, and a' that;
Gie fools their silks, and knaves their wine,
    A man's a man for a' that;
    For a' that, and a' that,
    Their tinsel show, and a' that,
The honest man, though e'er sae poor,
    Is king o' men for a' that.

Ye see yon birkie, ca'd a lord,
    Wha struts and stares, and a' that;
Tho' hundreds worship at his word,
    He's but a coof for a' that;
    For a' that, and a' that,
    His riband, star, and a' that,
The man of independent mind,
    He looks and laughs at a' that.

A prince can mak a belted knight,
    A marquis, duke, and a' that;
But an honest man's aboon his might.
    Guid faith, he mauna fa' that!
    For a' that, and a' that,
Their dignities, and a' that
The pith of sense, and pride o' worth,
    Are higher ranks than a' that.

Then let us pray that come it may,

As come it will for a' that,
That sense and worth, o'er a' the earth,
   May bear the gree, and a' that;
   For a' that, and a' that
   It's coming yet, for a' that,
That man to man, the wide warld o'er
   Shall brothers be for a' that."

And, having finished this prophesy and prayer, Nature's nobleman left his churlish entertainers to hide their diminished heads in the home they had disgraced.

We have seen all the stock lions. The Regalia people still crowd to see, though the old natural feelings from which they so long lay hidden seem almost extinct. Scotland grows English day by day. The libraries of the Advocate's, Writers to the Signet, &c. are fine establishments.[5] The University and Schools are now in vacation; we are compelled by unwise postponement of our journey to see both Edinburgh and London at the worst possible season. We should have been here in April, there in June. There is always enough to see, but now we find a majority of the most interesting persons absent, and a stagnation in the intellectual movements of the place.

We have, however, the good fortune to find Dr. Andrew Combe, who, though a great invalid, was able and disposed for conversation at this time.[6] I was impressed with great and affectionate respect by the benign and even temper of his mind, his extensive and accurate knowledge, accompanied, as such should naturally be, by a large and intelligent liberality. Of our country he spoke very wisely and hopefully, though among other stories with which we, as Americans, are put to the blush here, there is none worse than that of the conduct of some of our publishers toward him. One of these stories I had heard in New-York, but supposed it to be exaggerated till I had it from the best authority.—It is one of our leading houses who were publishing on their own account and had stereotyped one of his works from an early edition. When this work had passed through other editions, when he had for years been busy in reforming and amending it, he applied to this house to republish from the later and better edition. They refused. In vain he urged that it was not only for his

---

[5] The Scottish Regalia, a crown made of Scottish gold for James V in 1540, a scepter, and a sword of state given by Pope Julius II to James IV are on display in the Crown Room of the Edinburgh Castle. The Library of the Faculty of Advocates, founded in 1682, is now called the National Library of Scotland (*Treasures* 180–82).

[6] Dr. Andrew Combe (1797–1847), physiologist and phrenologist, edited the *Phrenological Journal* (1823–37). His writings on physiology, health, and education were popular in England and, as Fuller indicates, in America (*DNB*).

own reputation as an author that he was anxious, but for the good of the great
country through which writings on such important subjects were to be circulated, that they should have the benefit of his labors, and best knowledge.——
Such arguments on the stupid and mercenary tempers of those addressed fell
harmless as on a buffalo's hide might a gold-tipped arrow. The book, they
thought, answered THEIR purpose sufficiently, for IT SELLS. Other purpose for
a book they knew none. And as to the natural rights of an author over the fruits
of his mind, the distilled essence of a life consumed in the severities of mental
labor, they had never heard of such a thing. His work was in the market, and
he had no more to do with it, that they could see, than the silk-worm with the
lining of one of their coats.

Mr. Greeley, the more I look at this subject, the more I must maintain, in
opposition to your views, that the publisher cannot, if a mere tradesman, be a
man of honor. It is impossible in the nature of things. He *must* have some idea
of the nature and value of literary labor, or he is wholly unfit to deal with its
products. He cannot get along by occasional recourse to paid critics or readers;
he must have himself some idea what he is about. One partner, at least, in
the firm, must be a man of culture. All must understand enough to appreciate
their position, and know that he who, for his sordid aims, circulates poison-
ous trash amid a great and growing people, and makes it almost impossible for
those whom Heaven has appointed as its instructors to do their office, are the
worst of traitors, and to be condemned at the bar of nations under a sentence
no less severe than false statesmen and false priests. This matter need and must
be looked to more conscientiously.

Dr. Combe, repelled with all this indifference to conscience and natural
equity by the firm who had taken possession of his work, applied to others. But
here he found himself at once opposed by the invisible barrier that makes this
sort of tyranny so strong and so pernicious. "It was the understanding among
the trade that they were not to interfere with one another; indeed, they could
have no chance," &c. &c. When at last he did get the work republished in
another part of the country less favorable for his purposes, the bargain made as
to the pecuniary part of the transaction was in various ways so evaded that up
to this time, he has received no compensation from that widely circulated work
except a lock of Spurzheim's hair!!

I was pleased to hear the true view expressed by one of the Messrs. Chambers.[7] These brothers have worked their way up to wealth and influence by

---

[7] William Chambers (1800–83) and Robert Chambers (1802–71), authors and publishers, established W&R Chambers, a very successful publishing company. William managed the firm and wrote travel literature. Robert, author of *Vestiges of the Natural History of
Creation* (1844), edited *Chambers' Edinburgh Journal* (DNB).

daily labor and many steps. One of them is more the business man, the other the literary curator of their journal. Of this journal they issue regularly eighty thousand copies, and it is doing an excellent work, by awakening among the people a desire for knowledge, and, to a considerable extent, furnishing them with good materials. I went over their fine establishment, where I found more than a hundred and fifty persons, in good part women, employed, all in well aired, well lighted rooms, seemingly healthy and content. Connected with the establishment is a Savings Bank, and evening instruction in writing, singing and arithmetic. There was also a reading room, and the same valuable and liberal provision we had found attached to some of the Manchester warehouses. Such accessories dignify and gladden all kinds of labor, and show somewhat of the true spirit of human brotherhood in the employer. Mr. Chambers said he trusted they could never look on publishing *chiefly* as *business* or a lucrative and respectable employment, but as the means of mental and moral benefit to their countrymen. To one so wearied and disgusted as I have been by vulgar and base avowals on such subjects, it was very refreshing to hear this from the lips of a successful publisher.

Dr. Combe spoke with high praise of Mr. Hurlbut's book, "Human Rights and their Political Guaranties," which was published at The Tribune office.[8] He observed that it was the work of a real thinker, and extremely well written. It is to be republished here. Dr. C. observed that it must make its way slowly, as it could interest those only who were willing to read thoughtfully, but that its success was sure at last.

He spoke with great interest and respect of Mrs. Farnham, of whose character and the influence she has exerted on the Female Prison at Sing Sing he had heard some account.[9]

A person of an opposite character and celebrity indeed is De Quincey, the English Opium-Eater, and who lately has delighted us again with the papers in Blackwood, headed SUSPIRIA DE PROFUNDIS.[10] I had the satisfaction, not easily attainable now, of seeing him for some hours, and in the mood of conversation.

[8] Elisha P. Hurlbut, *Essays on Human Rights and their Political Guaranties* (New York: Greeley and McElrath, 1845).

[9] In 1844 Eliza Wood Farnham became head matron of the women's section of the New York penitentiary at Sing Sing. She abandoned harsh treatment in favor of rehabilitation for the women inmates and was forced to resign in 1848 (Alden Whitman, ed., *American Reformers* [New York: H. W. Wilson, 1985]). Fuller visited Sing Sing on 20 October 1844 and wrote to Elizabeth Hoar of her favorable impressions of Farnham's innovations (Hudspeth 3:237–38). Fuller returned to Sing Sing and gave an address to the inmates on 25 December 1844 (Chevigny 335–37).

[10] Thomas De Quincey lived mostly in Edinburgh after 1822. *Suspiria de profundis* (1845) is a psychological inquiry into the faculty of dreaming (*OCEL; DNB*). In an enthusiastic

As one belonging to the Wordsworth and Coleridge constellation, (he too is now 76 years of age,) the thoughts and knowledge of Mr. De Quincey lie in the past, and oftentimes he spoke of matters now become trite to one of a later culture. But to all that fell from his lips, his eloquence, subtle and forcible as the wind, full and gently falling as the evening dew, lent a peculiar charm. He is an admirable narrator, not rapid, but gliding along like a rivulet through a green meadow, giving and taking a thousand little beauties not absolutely required to give his story due relief, but each, in itself, a separate boon.

I admired, too, his urbanity, so opposite to the rapid, slang, Vivian-Greyish style current in the literary conversation of the day.[11] "Sixty years since" men had time to do things better and more gracefully than now.

With Dr. Chalmers we passed a couple of hours.[12] He is old now, but still full of vigor and fire.—We had an opportunity of hearing a fine burst of indignant eloquence from him. "I shall blush to my very bones," said he, "if the *Chaarrch* (sound these two *rr*s with as much burr as possible and you will get an idea of his mode of pronouncing that unweariable word) "if the Chaarrch yields to the storm." He alluded to the outcry now raised by the Abolitionists against the Free Church, whose motto is, "Send back the money," *i. e.* money taken from the American Slaveholders. Dr. C. felt that if they did not yield from conviction they must not to assault. His manner in speaking of this gave me an idea of the nature of his eloquence. He seldom preaches now.

A fine picture was presented by the opposition of figure and lineaments between a young Indian, son of the celebrated Dwarkanauth Tagore, who happened to be there that morning, and Dr. Chalmers, as they were conversing together.[13] The swarthy, half timid, yet elegant face and form of the Indian

letter to Emerson, Fuller describes her meeting with De Quincey as a "real Grand Conversatione, quite in the Landor style, which lasted in full harmony some hours" (Hudspeth 4: 245–46).

[11] *Vivian Grey* by Benjamin Disraeli was published in 1826–27. The hero, a brilliant but difficult boy, is expelled from school and discovers that with his clever charm and social skills, he can advance himself in politics (*OCEL*).

[12] Thomas Chalmers, D.D. (1780–1847), theologian and philanthropist, founded the Free Church of Scotland in 1843. He is credited with the revival of evangelical life in Scotland and was a good friend of Thomas Carlyle's (*DNB*).

[13] Dwarkanauth Tagore (1794–1846) was the head of the famous Tagore family in Calcutta. Tagore was a wealthy businessman who founded the Union Bank in Bengali; he died in London in 1846. His son, Devendranath Tagore (1817–1905), was a renowned religious leader and thinker. He founded the journal *Tattvabodhini Patrika* in 1843 to promote culture and serious thinking. He wanted Indians to accept the good in Western culture and combine it with the best in Indian culture (Sachchidananda Bhattacharya, *A Dictionary of Indian History* [New York: Braziller, 1967]).

made a fine contrast with the florid, portly, yet intellectually luminous appearance of the Doctor, half shepherd, half orator, he looked a Shepherd King opposed to some Arabian story-teller.

I saw others in Edinburgh of a later date who haply gave more valuable as
well as fresher revelations of the Spirit, and whose names may be by-and-by
more celebrated than I have cited, but for the present this must suffice. It would
take a week, if I wrote half I saw or thought in Edinburgh, and I must close for
to-day. ★

Dispatch 5

LOST ON BEN LOMOND

BIRMINGHAM, Sept. 30th, 1846 [1]

I was obliged to stop writing at Edinburgh before the better half of my tale
was told, and must now begin there again, to speak of an excursion into the
Highlands, which occupied about a fortnight.

We left Edinburgh by coach for Perth, and arrived there about three in the
afternoon. I have reason to be very glad that I visit this island before the reign of
the stage-coach is quite over. I have been every where on the top of the coach,
even one day of drenching rain, and enjoy it highly.—Nothing can be more
inspiring than this swift, steady progress over such smooth roads, and placed
so high as to overlook the country freely, with the lively flourish of the horn
preluding every pause. Traveling by railroad is in my opinion the most stupid
process on earth; it is sleep without the refreshment of sleep, for the noise of the
train makes it impossible either to read, talk or sleep to advantage. Here the
advantages are immense; you can fly through this dull trance from one beautiful place to another, and stay at each during the time that would otherwise be
spent on the road. Already the Artists, who are obliged to find their home in
London, rejoice that all England is thrown open to them for sketching ground,
since, whereas, formerly they were obliged to confine themselves to a few 'green
and bowery' spots in the neighborhood of the metropolis, they can now avail
themselves of a day's leisure at a great distance and with choice of position. But
while you are in the car, it is to me that worst of purgatories, the purgatory of
dullness.

Well, on the coach we went to Perth, and passed through Kinross, and saw
Loch Leven, and the island where Queen Mary passed those sorrowful months,

[1] First published as "Things and Thoughts in Europe. No. V" in *New-York Daily Tribune,*
13 November 1846, p. 1:3–5.

before her romantic escape under care of the Douglas.[2] As this unhappy, lovely woman stands for a type in history, death, time, and distance do not destroy her attractive power; like Cleopatra, she has still her adorers; nay, some are born to her in each new generation of men. Lately she has for her chevalier the Russian Prince Labanoff, who has spent fourteen years in studying upon all that related to her, and thinks now that he can make out a story and a picture about the mysteries of her short reign, which shall satisfy the desire of her lovers to find her as pure and just as she was charming.[3] I have only seen of his array of evidence so much as may be found in the pages of Chambers's Journal, but that much does not disturb the original view I have taken of the case, which is that from a Princess educated under that Medici and Guise influence, engaged in the meshes of secret intrigue to favor the Roman Catholic faith, her tacit acquiescence, at least, in the murder of Darnley, after all his injurious conduct toward her, was just what was to be expected. From a poor, beautiful young woman, longing to enjoy life, exposed both by her position and her natural fas-

---

[2] Fuller refers to the ruin of a fourteenth-century castle on an island in the lake where Queen Mary of Scots was imprisoned in 1567 and escaped with the help of William Douglas (1533–91) in 1568. Scott's novel *The Abbot* (1820) is based on this episode and the battle that followed (*DNB*; Eagle 164; *Treasures* 281).

[3] Prince Alexandre Labanoff de Rostoff (1788–1866) was the author of the *Letters of Mary Stuart, Queen of Scotland, selected from the 'Recueil des lettres de Marie Stuart,' together with the Chronological Summary of Events during the Reign of the Queen of Scotland*, translated with notes and an introduction by William Turnbull, and published in 1845.

The publication of this book, the excerpts that appeared in *Chambers' Edinburgh Journal* 4 (1845), and Fuller's travels through Scotland heightened Fuller's interest in the dramatic events of Queen Mary's life. The imprisonment of Mary at Loch Leven followed a series of unwise personal and political actions that began with the death of her first husband, Francis II (1544–60), the son of Catherine de Medici. A widow, Mary returned to Scotland in 1561 with the hope of controlling the unruly Scottish nobility and protecting Scottish Catholicism. Her marriage to Henry Stewart, Lord Darnley (1545–67), proved disastrous. Darnley angered the Scottish nobles with his arrogance and a nervous Elizabeth I with his Tudor ancestry. Mary soon had her own difficulties with Darnley; he murdered her Italian secretary, David Rizzio, and openly attended Protestant services. The birth of their son, James, in 1567 did nothing to improve their relationship. Darnley died under suspicious circumstances following an explosion; many thought Mary planned his death in order to free herself for marriage to her third husband, James Hepburn, the earl of Bothwell (1536?–78). The marriage to Bothwell was equally unsuccessful; amid mounting political problems in Scotland, Bothwell was exiled and Mary was imprisoned at Loch Leven. There she was formally deposed in favor of her son, James. Following a brief year of freedom, Mary spent the remaining eighteen years of her life as a prisoner. After the exposure of a plot to assassinate Queen Elizabeth and bring about a Catholic uprising, Mary was tried by an English court and condemned to death. She was executed in 1587 at Fotheringay Castle (*DNB; New Cambridge Modern History* 3:109–33).

cinations to the utmost bewilderment of flattery whether prompted by interest
or passion, her other acts of folly are most natural, and let all who feel inclined
harshly to condemn her remember the verse,

> Then gently scan your brother man,
> Still gentler sister woman ————[4]

Surely in all the stern pages of life's account-book there is none on which a
more terrible price was exacted for every precious endowment. Her rank and
reign only made her powerless to do good, and exposed her to danger; her talents only served to irritate her foes and disappoint her friends; this most charming of women was the destruction of her lovers: married three times, she had
never any happiness as a wife, but in both the connections of her choice found
that either she had never possessed or could not retain, even for a few weeks,
the love of the men she had chosen, so that Darnley was willing to risk her life
and that of his unborn child to wreak his wrath upon Rizzio, and that after a
few weeks with Bothwell she was heard "calling aloud for a knife to kill herself with." A mother twice, and of a son and daughter; both the children were
brought forth in loneliness and sorrow, and separated from her early, her son
educated to hate her, her daughter at once immured in a convent. Add the eighteen years of her imprisonment, and the fact that this foolish, prodigal world,
when there was in it one woman fitted by her grace and loveliness to charm all
eyes and enliven all fancies, let her be shut up to water with her tears her dull
embroidery during all the full rose-blossom of her life, and you will hardly get
beyond this story for a tragedy not noble but pallid and forlorn.

Such were the bootless, best thoughts I had while looking at the dull blood-
stain and blocked-up secret stair of Holyrood, at the ruins of Loch Leven castle,
and afterward at Abbotsford where the picture of Queen Mary's head, as it lay
on the pillow when severed from the block, hung opposite to a fine caricature
of "Queen Elizabeth dancing high and disposedly." In this last the face is like
a mask—so frightful is the expression of cold craft, irritated vanity and the
malice of a lonely breast in contrast with the attitude and elaborate frippery of
the dress. The ambassador looks on dismayed; the little page can scarcely control the laughter which swells his boyish cheeks. Such can win the world which
better hearts (and such Mary's was, even if it had a large black speck in it) are
most like to lose.

It was a most lovely day in which we entered Perth, and saw in full sunshine
its beautiful meadows, among them the North Inch, the famous battle ground

---

[4] Robert Burns, "Address to the Unco Guid, or the Rigidly Righteous," *The Poems and
Songs of Robert Burns,* ed. James Kinsley (Oxford: Oxford University Press, 1968), 1:52–54.

commemorated in "The Fair Maid of Perth," adorned with graceful trees like those of the New England country towns.[5] In the afternoon we visited the modern Kinfauns, the stately home of Lord Grey. The drive to it is most beautiful, on the one side the Park, with noble hights that skirt it, on the other through a belt of trees was seen the river and the sweep of that fair and cultivated country. The house is a fine one, and furnished with taste, the library large, and some good works in marble. —Among the family pictures one arrested my attention, the face of a girl full of the most pathetic sensibility, and with no restraint of convention upon its ardent, gentle expression. She died young.

Returning, we were saddened, as almost always on leaving any such place, by seeing such swarms of dirty women and dirtier children at the doors of the cottages almost close by the gate of the avenue. To the horrors and sorrows of the streets in such places as Liverpool, Glasgow, and, above all, London, one has to grow insensible or die daily; but here in the sweet, fresh, green country, where there seems to be room for every body, it is impossible to forget the frightful inequalities between the lot of man and man, or believe that God can smile upon a state of things such as we find existent here. Can any man who has seen these things dare to blame the Associationists for their attempt to find prevention against such misery and wickedness in our land? Rather will not every man of tolerable intelligence and good feeling commend, say rather revere, every earnest attempt in that direction; nor dare interfere with any, unless he has a better to offer in its place?

Next morning we passed on to Crieff, in whose neighborhood we visited Drummond Castle, the abode, or rather one of the abodes, of Lord Willoughby D'Eresby. It has a noble park, through which you pass by an avenue of two miles long. The old keep still is ascended to get the fine view of the surrounding country; and during Queen Victoria's visit her Guards were quartered there. But what took my fancy most was the old-fashioned garden, full of old shrubs and new flowers, with its formal parterres in the shape of the family arms, and its clipped yew and box trees. It was fresh from a shower, and now glittering and fragrant in bright sunshine.

This afternoon we pursued our way, passing through the plantations of Ochtertyre, a far more charming place to my taste than Drummond Castle, freer and more various in its features. Five or six of these fine places lie in the neighborhood of Crieff, and the traveler may give two or three days to visiting them with a rich reward of delight. But we were pressing on to be with the lakes and mountains rather, and that night brought us to St. Fillan's, where we saw the moon shining on Loch Earn.

All this region and that of Loch Katrine and the Trosachs which we reached

[5] Scott's *The Fair Maid of Perth* was published in 1828.

next day, Scott has described exactly in "The Lady of the Lake;" nor is it possible to appreciate that poem without going thither, neither to describe the scene better than he has done after you have seen it.[6] I was somewhat disappointed in the pass of the Trosachs itself; it is very grand, but the grand part lasts so little while. The opening view of Loch Katrine, however, surpassed expectation. It was late in the afternoon when we launched our little boat there for Ellen's isle.

The boatmen recite, though not *con molto espressione,* the parts of the poem which describe these localities. Observing that they spoke of the personages, too, with the same air of confidence, we asked if they were sure that all this really happened. They replied, "Certainly; it had been told from father to son through so many generations." Such is the power of genius to interpolate what it will into the regular log-book of Time's voyage.

Leaving Loch Katrine the following day we entered Rob Roy's country, and saw on the way the house where Helen MacGregor was born and Rob Roy's sword, which is shown in a house by the wayside.[7]

We came in a row-boat up Loch Katrine, though both on that and Loch Lomond you *may* go in a hateful little steamer with a squeaking fiddle to play Rob Roy MacGregor O. I walked almost all the way through the pass from Loch Katrine to Loch Lomond; it was a distance of six miles; but you feel as if you could walk sixty in that pure, exhilarating air. At Inversnaid we took boat again to go down Loch Lomond to the little inn of Rowardennan, from which the ascent is made of Ben Lomond, the greatest elevation in these parts. The boatmen are fine, athletic men: one of these we had with us to-night, a handsome young man of two or three-and-twenty, sang to us some Gaelic songs. The first, a very wild and plaintive air, was the expostulation of a girl whose lover has deserted her and married another.[8] It seems he is ashamed and will not even look at her when they meet upon the road. She implores him, if he has not forgotten all that scene of by-gone love, at least to lift up his eyes and give her one friendly glance. The sad *crooning* burden of the stanzas in which she repeats this request was very touching. When the boatman had finished, he hung his head and seemed ashamed of feeling the song too much; then when we asked for another he said he would sing another about a girl that was happy. This one was in three parts. First, a tuneful address from a maiden to her absent lover. Second, his reply, assuring her of his fidelity and tenderness. Third, a

---

[6] Scott's *The Lady of the Lake,* a poem in six cantos, was published in 1810.

[7] Scott's *Rob Roy,* published in 1817, takes place just before the Jacobite uprising of 1715. Helen MacGregor was the bloodthirsty wife of Rob Roy (*OCEL*).

[8] Fuller herself had just learned by letter that the man she loved and hoped to be reunited with in England, James Nathan, had become engaged to another woman. Fuller never saw him again.

strain which expresses their joy when reunited. I thought this boatman had
sympathies which would prevent his tormenting any poor women, and perhaps
make some one happy, and this was a pleasant thought since probably in the
Highlands as elsewhere—

"Maidens lend an ear too oft
    To the careless wooer;
Maidens' hearts are *always soft*!
    Would that men's were truer."

I don't know that I quote the words correctly, but that is the sum and substance of a masculine report on these matters.

The first day at Rowardennan not being propitious to ascending the mountain, we went down the lake to sup, and got very tired in various ways, so that
we rose very late next morning. Then we found a day of ten thousand for our
purpose, but unhappily a large party had come with the sun and engaged all the
horses so that, if we went, it must be on foot. This was something of an enterprise for me, as the ascent is four miles and toward the summit quite fatiguing;
however, in the pride of newly gained health and strength, I was ready, and set
forth with Mr. S. alone.[9] We took no guide—and the people of the house did
not advise it as they ought. They told us afterward they thought the day was so
clear that there was no probability of danger, and they were afraid of seeming
mercenary about it. It was, however, wrong, as they knew what we did not,
that even the shepherds can be lost in these hills, if a mist comes on; that a
party of gentlemen were so a few weeks before, and only by accident found their
way to a house on the other side, and that a child which had been lost was not
found for five days, long after its death. We, however, nothing doubting, set
forth, ascending slowly, and often stopping to enjoy the points of view, which
are many, for Ben Lomond consists of a congeries of hills, above which towers
the true Ben or highest peak, as the head of a many-limbed body.

On reaching the peak, the night was one of beauty and grandeur such as
imagination never painted. You see around you no plain ground, but on every
side constellations or groups of hills exquisitely dressed in the soft purple of the
heather, amid which gleam the lakes like eyes that tell the secrets of the earth
and drink in those of the heavens. Peak beyond peak caught from the shifting
light all the colors of the prism, and on the farthest angel companies seemed
hovering in their glorious white robes.

---

[9] Marcus Spring (1810–74), a wealthy businessman, was married to Rebecca Buffum
Spring (1811–1911), the daughter of an abolitionist. Fuller accompanied them to Europe
and tutored their son Edward Adolphus Spring (1837–1907) (Hudspeth 4:49, nn. 1, 2).

Words are idle on such subjects; what can I say but that it was a noble vision that satisfied the eye and stirred the imagination in all her secret pulses? Had that been, as afterward seemed likely, the last act of my life, there could not have been a finer decoration painted on the curtain which was to drop upon it.

About four o'clock we began our descent. Near the summit the traces of the path are not distinct, and I said to Mr. S. after a while, that we had lost it. He said he thought that was of no consequence, we could find our way down. I said I thought it was, as the ground was full of springs that were bridged over in the pathway. He accordingly went to look for it, and I stood still because I was so tired I did not like to waste any labor.

Soon he called to me that he had found it, and I followed in the direction where he seemed to be.—But I mistook, overshot it and saw him no more.

In about ten minutes I became alarmed and called him many times. It seems he on his side did the same, but the brow of some hill was between us, and we neither saw nor heard one another.

I then thought I would make the best of my way down and I should find him when I arrived. But in doing so I found the justice of my apprehension about the springs, as so soon as I got to the foot of the hills I would sink up to my knees in bog, and have to go up the hills again, seeking better crossing places. Thus I lost much time; nevertheless in the twilight I saw at last the Lake and the Inn of Rowardennan on its shore.

Between me and it lay direct a high heathery hill, which I afterward found is called "The Tongue," because hemmed in on three sides by a water-course. It looked as if, could I only get to the bottom of that, I should be on comparatively level ground. I then attempted to descend in the water-course, but finding that impracticable, climbed on the hill again and let myself down by the heather, for it was very steep and full of deep holes. With great fatigue I got to the bottom, but when I was about to cross the water-course there it looked very deep, and I felt afraid; it looked so deep in the dim twilight. I got down as far as I could by the root of a tree and threw down a stone; it sounded very hollow, and I was afraid to jump. The shepherds told me afterward, if I had I should probably have killed myself, it was so deep and the bed of the torrent full of sharp stones.

I then tried to ascend the hill again, for there was no other way to get off it, but soon sank down utterly exhausted. When able to get up again and look about me, it was completely dark. I saw far below me a light that looked about as big as a pin's head, that I knew to be from the inn at Rowardennan, but heard no sound except the rush of the waterfall, and the sighing of the night-wind.

For the first few minutes that I perceived I had got to my night's lodging, such as it was, the prospect seemed appalling. I was very lightly clad—my feet and dress were very wet—I had only a little shawl to throw round me, and a cold autumn wind had already come, and the night-mist was to fall on me, all fevered and exhausted as I was. I thought I should not live through the night, or if I did, live always a miserable invalid. I had no chance to keep myself warm by walking, for, now it was dark, it would be too dangerous to stir.

My only chance, however, lay in motion, and my only help in myself, and so convinced was I of this, that I did keep in motion the whole of that long night, imprisoned as I was on such a little perch of that great mountain. *How* long it seemed under such circumstances only those can guess who may have been similarly circumstanced. The mental experience of the time, most precious and profound—for it was indeed a season lonely, dangerous and helpless enough for the birth of thoughts beyond what the common sunlight will ever call to being, may be told in another place and time.

For about two hours I saw the stars, and very cheery and companionable they looked; but then the mist fell and I saw nothing more, except such apparitions as visited Ossian on the hill-side when he went out by night and struck the bosky shield and called to him the spirits of the heroes and the white-armed maids with their blue eyes of grief.[10]—To me, too, came those visionary shapes; floating slowly and gracefully, their white robes would unfurl from the great body of mist in which they had been engaged, and come upon me with a kiss pervasively cold as that of Death. What they might have told me, who knows, if I had but resigned myself more passively to that cold, spirit-like breathing!

At last the moon rose. I could not see her, but her silver light filled the mist. Then I knew it was two o'clock, and that, having weathered out so much of the night, I might the rest; and the hours hardly seemed long to me more.

It may give an idea of the extent of the mountain, that though I called every now and then with all my force, in case by chance some aid might be near, and though no less than twenty men with their dogs were looking for me, I never heard a sound except the rush of the waterfall and the sighing of the night-wind, and once or twice the startling of the grouse in the heather. It was sublime indeed—a never-to-be-forgotten presentation of stern, serene realities.

At last came the signs of day, the gradual clearing and breaking up; some faint sounds, from I know not what; the little flies, too, arose from their bed amid the purple heather and bit me; truly they were very welcome to do so. But what was my disappointment to find the mist so thick that I could see neither

[10] James Macpherson (1736–96), a poet and translator, published *Fingal: An Ancient Poem* (1762) and *Temora: An Ancient Epic Poem* (1763), which he falsely represented as the works of Ossian, a Gaelic poet. Although the authenticity of the works was immediately challenged by Samuel Johnson and others, Ossian's romantic, visionary poems gained immense popularity in England, America, and Europe (*OCEL*).

lake nor inn, nor any thing to guide me. I had to go by guess, and, as it happened, my Yankee method served me well. I ascended the hill, crossed the torrent in the waterfall, first drinking some of the water which was as good at that
time as ambrosia. I crossed in that place because the waterfall made steps, as it
were, to the next hill; to be sure they were covered with water, but I was already
entirely wet with the mist, so that it did not matter. I then kept on scrambling,
as it happened, in the right direction, till about seven some of the shepherds
found me.—The moment they came all my feverish strength departed, though
if unaided I dare say it would have kept me up during the day, and they carried
me home, where my arrival relieved my friends of distress far greater than I had
undergone, for I had had my grand solitude, my Ossianic visions and the pleasure of sustaining myself, while they had had only doubt amounting to anguish
and a fruitless search through the night.[11]

Entirely contrary to my expectations I only suffered for this a few days, and
was able to take a parting look at my prison as I went down the lake with feelings of complacency. It was a majestic-looking hill, that Tongue, with the deep
ravines on either side, and the richest robe of heather I have seen any where.

Mr. S. gave all the men who were looking for me a dinner in the barn, and he
and Mrs. S. ministered to them, and they talked of Burns, really the national
writer, and known by them, apparently, as none other is, and of hair-breadth
'scapes by flood and fell. Afterwards they were all brought up to see me, and it
was pleasing indeed to see the good breeding and good feeling with which they
deported themselves on the occasion. Indeed, this adventure created quite an
intimate feeling between us and the people there. I had been much pleased with
them before, in attending one of their dances, at the genuine independence and
politeness of their conduct. They were willing and pleased to dance their Highland flings and strathspeys for our amusement, and did it as naturally and as
freely as they would have offered the stranger the best chair.

All the rest must wait awhile. I cannot economize time to keep up my record
in any proportion with what happens, nor can I get out of Scotland on this page,
as I had intended, without utterly slighting many gifts and graces.   ★

---

[11] In a letter to Emerson, Fuller refers to her night on Ben Lomond as her "hair-breadth
escape with life" (Hudspeth 4:246).

Dispatch 6

SCENES OF BEAUTY AND SORROW

PARIS, Nov. 1846[1]

I am very sorry to leave such a wide gap between my letters, but I was inevitably
prevented from finishing one that was begun for the steamer of 4th November.
I then hoped to prepare one after my arrival here in time for the Hibernia, but
a severe cold, caught on the way, unfitted me for writing. It is now necessary to
retrace my steps a long way, or lose sight of several things it has seemed desirable to mention to friends in America, though I shall make out my narrative
more briefly than if nearer the time of action.

If I mistake not, my last closed just as I was looking back on the hill where I
had passed the night in all the miserable chill and amid the ghostly apparitions
of a Scotch mist, but which looked in the morning truly beautiful, and (had I
not known it too well to be deceived) alluring, in its mantle of rich pink heath,
the tallest and most full of blossoms we anywhere saw, and with the waterfall
making music by its side, and sparkling in the morning sun.

Passing from Tarbet, we entered the grand and beautiful pass of Glencoe—
sublime with purple shadows with bright lights between, and in one place an
exquisitely silent and lonely little lake. The wildness of the scene was hight-
ened by the black Highland cattle feeding here and there. They looked much
at home, too, in the park at Inverary, where I saw them next day. In Inverary
I was disappointed. I found, indeed, the position of every object the same as
indicated in the "Legend of Montrose," but the expression of the whole seemed
unlike what I had fancied. The present abode of the Argyle family is a modern
structure, and it boasts very few vestiges of the old romantic history attached to
the name. The park and look out upon the lake are beautiful, but except from
a hasty pleasure in these, the old cross from Iona—that stands in the market-
place—and the drone of the bagpipe which lulled me to sleep at night playing
some melancholy air, there was nothing to make me feel that it was "a far cry
to Lochaw,"[2] but, on the contrary, I seemed in the very midst of the prose—
the civilized world.[3]

Leaving Inverary, we left that day the Highlands too, passing through

---

[1] First published as "Things and Thoughts in Europe. No. VI" in *New-York Daily Tribune*,
23 December 1846, p. 1:1–2.

[2] Scott, *Rob Roy*, chap. 29, 3.

[3] Inverary Castle was the seat of the Campbells, earls and dukes of Argyll. It is described
by James Boswell in *A Journal of a Tour of the Hebrides* (1785) and was greatly admired by
Scott, who used it as the setting for his *A Legend of Montrose* (1819), a novel about Montrose
and his rival, the Covenanter Archibald Campbell, the eighth earl (Eagle 140).

HELL'S GLEN, a very wild and grand defile. Taking boat then on Loch Long, we passed down the Clyde, stopping an hour or two on our way at Dumbarton.[4] Nature herself foresaw the era of picture when she made and placed this rock: there is every preparation for the artist's stealing a little piece from her treasures to hang on the walls of a room. Here I saw the sword of "Wallace wight," shown by a son of the 19th century, who said that this hero lived about fifty years ago, and who did not know the hight of this rock, in a cranny of which he lived, or at least ate and slept and "donned his clothes." From the top of the rock I saw sunset on the beautiful Clyde, animated that day by an endless procession of steamers, little skiffs, and boats. In one of the former, the Cardiff Castle, we embarked as the last light of day was fading, and that evening found ourselves in Glasgow.

I understand there is an intellectual society of high merit in Glasgow, but we were there only a few hours, and did not see any one. Certainly the place, as it may be judged of merely from the general aspect of the population and such objects as may be seen in the streets, more resembles an *Inferno* than any other we have yet visited. The people are more crowded together and the stamp of squalid, stolid misery and degradation more obvious and appalling. The English and Scotch do not take kindly to poverty like those of sunnier climes; it makes them fierce or stupid, and, life presenting no other cheap pleasure, they take refuge in drinking.

I saw here in Glasgow persons, especially women, dressed in dirty, wretched tatters, worse than none, and with an expression of listless, unexpecting woe upon their faces, far more tragic than the inscription over the gate of Dante's *Inferno*. To one species of misery suffered here to the last extent, I shall advert in speaking of London.

But from all these sorrowful tokens I by no means inferred the falsehood of the information that here was to be found a circle rich in intellect and in aspiration. The manufacturing and commercial towns, burning focuses of grief and vice, are also the centers of intellectual life, as in forcing beds the rarest flowers and fruits are developed by use of impure and repulsive materials. Where evil comes to an extreme, Heaven seems busy in providing means for the remedy. Need indeed is glaring throughout Scotland and England for the devoutest application of intellect and love to the cure of ills that cry aloud, and, without such application, *must* ere very long seek help by other means than words. Yet there is every reason to hope that those who ought to help are seriously, though slowly, becoming alive to the imperative nature of this duty, so we must not

[4] Dumbarton, an old town on the Clyde downriver from Glasgow, is commanded by a castle set on a rocky hill. This castle plays an important role in Scottish history (*Great Britain* 543, 545–46).

cease to hope, even in the streets of Glasgow and the gin palaces of Manchester, and the dreariest recesses of London.[5]

From Glasgow we passed to Stirling, like Dumbarton endeared to the mind, which cherishes the memory of its childhood still more by Miss Porter's Scottish Chiefs than by association with "Snowdon's Knight and Scotland's King."[6] We reached the town too late to see the Castle before the next morning, and I took up at the inn "The Scottish Chiefs," in which I had not read a word since ten or twelve years old. We are in the habit now of laughing when this book is named, as if it were a representative of what is most absurdly stilted or bombastic, but now, in reading, my maturer mind was differently impressed from what I expected, and the infatuation with which childhood and early youth regard this book and its companion, "Thaddeus of Warsaw," was justified. The characters and dialogue are, indeed, out of nature, but the sentiment that animates them is pure, true, and no less healthy than noble. Here is bad drawing, bad drama, but good music, to which the unspoiled heart will always echo, even when the intellect has learned to demand a better organ for its communication.

The Castle of Stirling is as rich as any place in romantic associations. We were shown its dungeons and its Court of Lions, where, says tradition, wild animals, kept in the grated cells adjacent, were brought out on festival occasions to furnish entertainment for the Court. So, while lords and ladies gay danced and sang above, prisoners pined and wild beasts starved below. This, at first blush looks like a very barbarous state of things, but, on reflection, one does not find that we have outgrown it in our present so-called state of refined civilization, only the present way of expressing the same facts is a little different. Still lords and ladies dance and sing above, unknowing or uncaring that the laborers who minister to their luxuries starve or are turned into wild beasts—below. Man need not boast his condition till he can weave his costly tapestry without the side that is kept under looking like that, methinks.

The Tournament Ground is still kept green and in beautiful order near Stirling Castle as a memento of the olden time, and as we passed away down the beautiful Firth, a turn of the river gave us a very advantageous view of it. So gay it looked, so festive in the bright sunshine, one almost seemed to see the graceful forms of knight and noble pricking their good steeds to the encounter,

---

[5] The above paragraph was omitted from *AHA*.

[6] Stirling is an ancient town north of Edinburgh, a favored residence of the Scottish sovereigns (*Great Britain* 547). Jane Porter (1776–1850) published her first romance, *Thaddeus of Warsaw*, in 1803. *The Scottish Chiefs* (1810) is her very popular novel about William Wallace, the Scottish patriot. "Snowdon's Knight and Scotland's King" refers to canto 6 of Scott's *The Lady of the Lake* (*DNB* and *OCEL*).

or the stalwart Douglas, vindicating his claim to be indeed a chief by conquest in the rougher sports of the yeomanry.

Passing along the Firth to Edinburgh we again passed two or three days in that beautiful city, which I could not be content to leave so imperfectly seen if I had not some hope of revisiting it when the bright lights that adorn it are concentered there. In Summer almost every one is absent. I was very fortunate to see as many interesting persons as I did. On this second visit I saw James Simpson, a well known philanthropist, and leader in the cause of popular education.[7] Infant schools have been an especial care of his, and America as well as Scotland has received the benefit of his thoughts on this subject. His last good work has been to induce the erection of public baths in Edinburgh, and the working people of that place, already deeply in his debt for the lectures he has been unwearied in delivering for their benefit, have signified their gratitude by presenting him with a beautiful model of a fountain in silver as an ornament to his study. Never was there a place where such a measure would be more important; if cleanliness be akin to godliness, Edinburgh stands at great disadvantage in her devotions. The impure air, the terrific dirt which surround the working people must make all progress in higher culture impossible, and I saw nothing which seemed to me so likely to have results of incalculable good, as this practical measure of the Simpsons, in support of the precept:

"Wash and be clean every whit."

We returned into England by the way of Melrose, not content to leave Scotland without making our pilgrimage to Abbotsford. The universal feeling, however, has made this pilgrimage so common that there is nothing left for me to say, yet though I had read a hundred descriptions, everything seemed new as I went over this epitome of the mind and life of Scott, as what constitutes the great man is more commonly some extraordinary combination and balance of qualities, than the highest development of any one. So you cannot but here be struck anew by the singular combination in his mind of love for the picturesque and romantic with the commonest common sense, a delight in heroic excess, with the prudential habit of order. Here the most pleasing order pervades emblems of what men commonly esteem disorder and excess.

Amid the exquisite beauty of the ruins of Dryburgh, I saw with regret that his body rests in almost the only spot that is not green and cannot well be made

---

[7] James Simpson (1718–1853), an author and friend of Scott's, was deeply interested in better elementary education and one of the founders of the Edinburgh modern infant school (*DNB*).

so, for the light does not reach it.—That is not a fit couch for him who dressed so many dim and time-worn relics with living green.

Always cheerful and beneficent, Scott seemed to the common eye, in like measure, prosperous and happy up to the last years, and the chair in which, under the pressure of the sorrows which led to his death, he was propped up to write when brain and eye and hand refused their aid, and the product remains only as a guide to the speculator as to the workings of the mind in case of insanity or approaching imbecility would by most persons be viewed as the only saddening relic of his career. Yet when I recall some passages in the Lady of the Lake, and the Address to his Harp, I cannot doubt that Scott had the full share of bitter in his cup, and feel the tender hope that we do about other gentle and generous guardians and benefactors of our youth, that in a nobler career they are now fulfilling still higher duties with serener mind, and trusting in us that we will try to fill their places with kindly deeds, ardent thoughts; nor leave the world in their absence,

"A dim, vast vale of tears,
   Vacant and desolate."[8]   ★

Dispatch 7

T H E   C A U S E   O F   P R O G R E S S

PARIS, 1846[1]

We crossed the moorlands in a heavy rain and reached Newcastle late at night. Next day we descended into a coal-mine; it was quite an odd sensation to be taken off one's feet and dropped down into darkness by the bucket. The stables under ground had a pleasant Gil-Blas air, though the poor horses cannot like it much;[2] generally they see the light of day no more after they have once been let down into these gloomy recesses, but pass their days in dragging cars along the rails of the narrow passages, and their nights in eating hay and dreaming of grass!! When we went down we meant to go along the gallery to the place where the miners were then at work, but found this was a walk of a mile and a

---

[8] See "Hymn to Intellectual Beauty," *The Poems of Shelley*, ed. Geoffrey Matthews and Kelvin Everest (London: Longman, 1989), 1:528.

[1] First published as "Things and Thoughts in Europe. No. VII" in *New-York Daily Tribune*, 5 January 1847, p. 1:1–2.

[2] *Gil Blas de Santillane* (1715, 1724, 1735), a picaresque romance by Alain-René Lesage (1668–1747), satirizes the ups and downs of the life of Gil Blas, who learns benevolence during a lengthy imprisonment.

half, and, beside the weariness of picking your steps slowly along by the light of a tallow candle, too wet and dirty an enterprise to be undertaken by way of amusement; so after proceeding half a mile or so, we begged to be restored to our accustomed level and reached it with minds slightly edified and face and hands much blackened.

Passing thence we saw York with its Minster, that dream of beauty realized. From its roof I saw two rainbows, overarching that lovely country. Through its aisles I heard grand music pealing. But how sorrowfully bare is the interior of such a cathedral, despoiled of the statues, the paintings, and the garlands that belong to the Catholic religion! The eye aches for them. Such a church is ruined by Protestantism; its admirable exterior seems that of a sepulchre; there is no correspondent life within.

Within the citadel, a tower half ruined and ivy-clad, is life that has been growing up while the exterior bulwarks of the old feudal time crumbled to ruin. George Fox, while a prisoner at York, for obedience to the dictates of his conscience, planted here a walnut and the tall tree that grew from it still "bears testimony" to his living presence on that spot.[3] The tree is old, but still bears nuts; one of them was taken away by my companions, and may perhaps be the parent of a tree somewhere in America that shall shade those who inherit the spirit, if they do not attach importance to the etiquettes of Quakerism.

In Sheffield I saw the sooty servitors tending their furnaces. I saw them also on Saturday night, after their work was done, going to receive its poor wages, looking pallid and dull, as if they had spent on tempering the steel that vital force that should have tempered themselves to manhood.

We saw, also, Chatsworth, with its park and mock wilderness, and immense conservatory, and really splendid fountains and wealth of marbles. It is a fine expression of modern luxury and splendor, but did not interest me; I found little there of true beauty or grandeur.

Warwick Castle, which we saw a day or two after, is a place entirely to my mind, a real representative of the English aristocracy in the day of its nobler life. The grandeur of the pile itself and its beauty of position introduce you fitly to the noble company with which the genius of Vandyke has peopled its walls. But a short time was allowed to look upon these nobles, warriors, statesmen and ladies, who look upon us in turn with such a majesty of historic association, yet was I very well satisfied; it is not difficult to see men through the eyes of Vandyke—his way of viewing character seems superficial though commanding;[4] he

[3] George Fox (1624–91), founder of the Society of Friends, had a religious experience in the early 1640s, became a great preacher, and was imprisoned many times for his beliefs (*DNB*).

[4] Sir Anthony Van Dyck (1599–1641), a Flemish painter, lived part of his life in England

sees the man in his action on the crowd, not in his hidden life; he does not, like some painters, amaze and engross us by his revelations as to the secret springs of conduct. I know not by what hallucination I forebore to look at the picture I most desired to see—that of Lucy, Countess of Carlisle. I was looking at something else, and when the fat, pompous butler announced her, I did not recognize her name from his mouth. Afterward it flashed across me, that I had really been standing before her and forgotten to look—but repentance was too late. I had passed the castle gate to return no more. I saw the picture of Gendimar, the Spanish Ambassador; that of Joanna, Queen of Naples, and that of Sir Philip Sidney, all three so admirably described by the German Prince.[5] I wonder his book upon England is not more read in our country; there are no better (subjective) descriptions than his, and subtle wit, high and general culture, and *abandon* of character combine in rare proportion to give charm to his page.

Pretty Leamington and Stratford are hackneyed ground. Of the latter I only observed what, if I knew, I had forgotten, that the room where Shakspeare was born has been an object of devotion only for forty years. England has learned much of her appreciation of Shakspeare from the Germans. In the days of innocence I fondly supposed that every one who could understand English and was not a cannibal, adored Shakspeare and read him on Sundays always for an hour or more, and on week days a considerable portion of the time. But I have lived to know some hundreds of persons in my native land, without finding ten who had any direct acquaintance with their greatest benefactor, and I dare say in England as large an experience would not end more honorably to its subjects. So vast a treasure is left untouched, while men are complaining of being poor, because they have not toothpicks exactly to their mind.

At Stratford I handled, too, the poker used to such good purpose by Geoffrey Crayon.[6] The muse had fled, the fire was out, and the poker rusty, yet a pleasant

---

and served as a painter to Charles I. He devoted much of the latter part of his life to portraits of the aristocracy and is famous for his representations of noblemen and women with proud faces and slender figures (*OCA*).

[5] Hermann Puckler-Muskau (1785–1871), a wealthy German writer and landscape gardener, traveled extensively in Europe and in England (Stanley J. Kunitz and Vineta Colby, eds., *European Authors, 1000–1900* [New York: Wilson, 1967]). His *Briefe eins Verstorbenen* (1832) is a witty account of his travels in England in 1826–28, which was reviewed in the *North American Review* as being similar in tone with respect to England as Frances Trollope's negative views about America ("Prince Puckler-Muscau [sic] and Mrs. Trollope," 36 [1833]: 1–48). Fuller greatly admired her "favorite prince" and recommended his *Tutti-Frutti: Aus den Papieren des Verstorbenen* (1834) to Caroline Sturgis (Hudspeth 2:61).

[6] Geoffrey Crayon, the pseudonym of Washington Irving (1783–1859), is the narrator for much of *The Sketch Book* (1819–20). In "Stratford-on-Avon," Geoffrey Crayon poses as the weary tourist, resting in a comfortable chair in the parlor of the Red Horse Inn in Stratford, which Irving had first visited in 1815. Commenting on the enjoyment of this moment

influence lingered even in that cold little room, and seemed to lend a transient glow to the poker under the influence of sympathy.

In Birmingham I heard two discourses from one of the rising lights of England, George Dawson, a young man of whom I had earlier heard much in praise.[7] He is a friend of the people, in the sense of brotherhood, not of social convenience or patronage; in literature catholic; in matters of religion anti-sectarian, seeking truth in aspiration and love.—He is eloquent, with good method in his discourse, fire and dignity when wanted, with a frequent homeliness in enforcement and illustration which offends the etiquettes of England, but fits him the better for the class he has to address. His powers are uncommon and unfettered in their play; his aim is worthy; he is fulfilling and will fulfil an important task as an educator of the people, if all be not marred by a taint of self-love and arrogance now obvious in his discourse. This taint is not surprising in one so young, who has done so much, and in order to do it has been compelled to great self-confidence and light heed of the authority of other minds, and who is surrounded almost exclusively by admirers; neither is it, at present, a large speck; it may be quite purged from him by the influence of nobler motives and the rise of his ideal standard; but, on the other hand, should it spread, all must be vitiated. Let us hope the best, for he is one that would ill be spared from the band who have taken up the cause of Progress in England.

In this connection I may as well speak of James Martineau, whom I heard in Liverpool, and W. J. Fox, whom I heard in London.[8]

Mr. Martineau looks like the over-intellectual, the partially developed man, and his speech confirms this impression. He is sometimes conservative, sometimes reformer, not in the sense of eclecticism, but because his powers and views

---

of leisure, Crayon remarks: "Let the world without go as it may; let kingdoms rise or fall, so along as he has the wherewithal to pay his bill, he is, for the time being, the very monarch of all he surveys. The arm-chair is his throne, the poker his sceptre, and the little parlour, some twelve feet square, his undisputed empire" (Washington Irving, *The Sketch Book of Geoffrey Crayon, Gent.* [New York: Dutton, 1963], 251; *OCAL*; Eagle 314).

[7] George Dawson (1821–76), preacher, lecturer, and politician, was appointed minister to a Baptist chapel in 1843 and became increasingly well known in Birmingham and Manchester for his lectures on historical and literary subjects. In 1847 he managed the Church of the Savior in Birmingham; he did much to popularize the ideas of Emerson and Carlyle. Dawson was a friend of Joseph Mazzini (1805–72), Louis Kossuth (1802–94), and other exiles (*DNB*).

[8] William Johnson Fox (1786–1864), preacher, politician, and man of letters, became a Unitarian minister in 1812. While he was coeditor of the *Monthly Depository,* the leading organ of the Unitarians, he purchased the copyright and in 1831 made it a journal of political and social reform as well as literary criticism. He was quick to recognize new talent, such as Robert Browning. A political activist, he was involved with Cobden in the Anti–Corn Law League (*DNB*).

do not find a true harmony. On the conservative side he is scholarly, acute,—
on the other, pathetic, pictorial, generous. He is no prophet and no sage, yet
a man full of fine affections and thoughts, always suggestive, sometimes satisfactory, he is well adapted to the wants of that class, a large one in the present
day, who love the new wine, but do not feel that they can afford to throw away
all their old bottles.

Mr. Fox is the reverse of all this: he is homogeneous in his materials and
harmonious in the results he produces. He has great persuasive power; it is
the persuasive power of a mind warmly engaged in seeking truth for itself. He
sometimes carries home convictions with great energy, driving in the thought
as with golden nails. A glow of kindly human sympathy enlivens his argument,
and the whole presents thought in a well-proportioned, animated body. But I
am told he is far superior in speech on political or social problems, than on such
as I heard him discuss.

I was reminded, in hearing all three, of men similarly engaged in our own
country, W. H. Channing and Theodore Parker.[9] None of them compare in
the symmetrical arrangement of extempore discourse or in pure eloquence and
communication of spiritual beauty with Channing, nor in fullness and sustained
flow with Parker, but, in power of practical and homely adaptation of their
thought to common wants, they are superior to the former, and all have more
variety, finer perceptions and are more powerful in single passages than Parker.

And now my pen has run to 1st October, and still I have such notabilities as
fell to my lot to observe while in London and these that are thronging upon me
here in Paris to record for you. I am sadly in arrears, but 'tis comfort to think
that such meats as I have to serve up are as good cold as hot. At any rate, it is
just impossible to do any better and I shall comfort myself, as often before, with
the triplet which I heard in childhood from a sage, (if only sages wear wigs!)

> As said the great prince Fernando,
> What *can* a man do,
> More than he can do?   ★

---

[9] The Unitarian clergymen William H. Channing (1810–85) was one of Fuller's closest
friends. Earnest and restless, he served as minister to congregations in New York, Boston,
and Cincinnati. He was a frequent contributor to the *Dial* and edited the *Western Messenger*.
After Fuller's death, he joined with Emerson and James Freeman Clarke in editing the *Memoirs*. Theodore Parker (1810–60), also a Unitarian minister and friend of Fuller's, was the
most renowned preacher of the Transcendentalists, known for his reasoned arguments and
encyclopedic knowledge. He contributed to the *Dial,* and Fuller admired and respected his
work (Chevigny 9–10, 68; *DAB*).

Dispatch 8

THE WORLD OF LONDON

PARIS, Dec. 1846[1]

I sit down here in Paris to narrate some recollections of London. The distance in space and time is not great, yet I seem in wholly a different world. Here in the region of wax lights, mirrors, bright wood fires, shrugs, vivacious ejaculations, wreathed smiles and adroit courtesies, it is hard to remember John Bull with his coal-smoke, hands in pockets, except when extended for ungracious demand of the perpetual half-crown or to pay for the all but perpetual mug of beer. John, seen on that side, is certainly the most churlish of clowns, and the most clownish of churls. But then there are so many other sides! When a gentleman he is so truly the gentleman, when a man so truly the man of honor! His graces, when he has any, grow up from his inmost heart.

Not that he is free from humbug, on the contrary, he is prone to the most solemn humbug, generally of the philanthropic or otherway moral kind. But he is always awkward beneath the mask, and can never impose upon anybody—but himself. Nature meant him to be noble, generous, sincere, and has furnished him with no faculties to make himself agreeable in any other way or mode of being. 'Tis not so with your Frenchman who can cheat you pleasantly, and move with grace in the devious and slippery path. You would be almost sorry to see him quite disinterested and straight-forward: so much of agreeable talent and naughty wit would thus lie hid for want of use. But John, oh John, we must admire, esteem or be disgusted with thee.

As to climate, there is not much to choose at this time of year. In London, for six weeks, we never saw the sun for coal-smoke and fog. In Paris we have not been blessed with its cheering rays above three or four days in the same length of time, and are, beside, tormented with an oily and tenacious mud beneath the feet, which makes it almost impossible to walk. This year, indeed, is an uncommonly severe one at Paris, and then if they have their share of dark, cold days, it must be admitted that they do all they can to enliven them.

But to dwell first on London—London, in itself a world. We arrived at a time which the well-bred Englishman considers as no time at all—quite out of "*the* season," when Parliament is in session, and London thronged with the equipages of her aristocracy, her titled, wealthy nobles.—I was listened to with a smile of polite contempt when I declared that the stock shows of London would

---

[1] First published as "Things and Thoughts in Europe. No. VIII" in *New-York Daily Tribune,* 2 February 1847, p. 1:1–3.

yield me amusement and employment more than sufficient for the time I had to stay. But I found that, with my way of viewing things, it would be to me an inexhaustible studio, and that if life were only long enough, I would live there for years obscure in some corner, from which I could issue forth day by day to watch unobserved the vast stream of life, or to decipher the hieroglyphics which ages have been inscribing on the walls of this vast palace (I may not call it a temple) which human effort has reared for means, not yet used efficaciously, of human culture.

And though I wish to return to London in "the season" when that city is an adequate representative of the state of things in England, I am glad I did not at first see all that pomp and parade of wealth and luxury in contrast with the misery, squalid, agonizing, ruffianly, which stares one in the face in every street of London and hoots at the gates of her palaces more ominous a note than ever was that of owl or raven in the portentous times when empires and races have crumbled and fallen from inward decay.

It is impossible, however, to take a near view of the treasures created by English genius, accumulated by English industry, without a prayer, daily more fervent, that the needful changes in the condition of this people may be effected by peaceful revolution which shall destroy nothing except the shocking inhumanity of exclusiveness, which now prevents their being used for the benefit of all.—May their present possessors look to it in time! A few already are earnest in a good spirit. For myself, much as I pitied the poor, abandoned, hopeless wretches that swarm in the roads and streets of England, I pity far more the English noble with this difficult problem before him, and such need of a speedy solution. Sad is his life if a conscientious man; sadder still, if not. Poverty in England has terrors of which I never dreamed at home. I felt that it would be terrible to be poor there, but far more so to be the possessor of that for which so many thousands are perishing. And the middle class, too, cannot here enjoy that serenity which the sages have described as naturally their peculiar blessing. Too close, too dark throng the evils they cannot obviate, the sorrows they cannot relieve. To a man of good heart, each day must bring purgatory, which he knows not how to bear—yet to which he fears to become insensible.

From these clouds of the Present it is pleasant to turn the thoughts to some objects which have cast a light upon the Past, and which, by the virtue of their very nature, prescribe hope for the Future. I have mentioned with satisfaction seeing some persons who illustrated the past dynasty in the progress of thought here: Wordsworth, Dr. Chalmers, De Quincey, Andrew Combe. With a still higher pleasure, because to one of my own sex whom I have honored almost above any, I went to pay my court, to Joanna Baillie.[2] I found on her brow not

[2] Joanna Baillie (1762–1851), a Scottish dramatist and poet, published her first volume

indeed a coronal of gold, but a serenity and strength undimmed and unbroken by the weight of more than fourscore years, or by the scanty appreciation which her thoughts have received.

I prize Joanna Baillie and Madame Roland[3] as the best specimens which have been hitherto offered of women of a Spartan, Roman strength and single-ness of mind, adorned by the various culture and capable of the various action opened to them by the progress of the Christian Idea. They are not sentimental; they do not sigh and write of withered flowers of fond affection, and woman's heart born to be misunderstood by the object or objects of her fond, inevitable choice. Love, (the passion,) when spoken of at all by them, seems a thing noble, religious, worthy to be felt. They do not write of it always; they did not think of it always; they saw other things in this great, rich, suffering world. In su-perior delicacy of touch they show the woman, but the hand is firm; nor was all their speech one continued utterance of mere personal experience. It contained things which are good, intellectually, universally.

I regret that the writings of Joanna Baillie are not more known in the United States. The Plays on the Passions are faulty in their plan—all attempts at comic, even at truly dramatic effect, fail—but there are masterly sketches of char-acter, vigorous expressions of wise thoughts, deep, fervent ejaculations of an aspiring soul!

We found her in her little calm retreat at Hampstead, surrounded by marks of love and reverence from distinguished and excellent friends. Near her was the sister, older than herself, yet still sprightly and full of active kindness, whose character and their mutual relation she has, in one of her last poems, indicated with such a happy mixture of sagacity, humor and tender pathos, and with so absolute a truth of outline. Although no autograph collector, I asked for theirs, and when the elder gave hers as "sister to Joanna Baillie," it drew a tear from my eye, a good tear, a genuine pearl, fit homage to that fairest product of the soul of man, humble, disinterested tenderness.

Hampstead has still a good deal of romantic beauty. I was told it was the favorite sketching ground of London artists, till the railroads gave them easy means of spending a few hours to advantage farther off. But, indeed, there is a wonderful deal of natural beauty lying in untouched sweetness near London.

---

of poems, *Fugitive Verses,* in 1790. Her career as a dramatist began with the publication of her first volume of the *Plays on the Passions* (1798), which included *Basil, The Trial,* and *De Montfort.* Because the volume was published anonymously, Scott was thought to be the author, and the two eventually became friends. The second volume was published in 1802 and included *Hatred* and *Ambition.* In 1806 she moved to Hampstead Heath with her sister and was visited by many eminent figures of the day (*DNB*).

[3] Pauline-Marie-Désirée Roland (1805–52) was a socialist and feminist. Fuller wrote to her mother that Madame Roland was an "interesting woman" (Hudspeth 4:253).

Near one of our cities it would all have been grubbed up the first thing. —But
we, too, are beginning to grow wiser.

At Richmond I went to see another lady of more than three score years' celebrity, more than fourscore in age, Miss Berry, the friend of Horace Walpole, and
for her charms of manner and conversation long and still a reigning power.[4] She
has still the vivacity, the careless nature or refined art that made her please so
much in earlier days—still is girlish and gracefully so. Verily, with her was no
sign of labor or sorrow.

From the older turning to the young, I must speak with pleasure of several
girls I knew in London who are devoting themselves to painting as a profession.
They had really wise and worthy views of the artist's avocation—if they remain
true to them, they will enjoy a free, serene existence, unprofaned by undue
care or sentimental sorrow. Among these, Margaret Gillies has attained some
celebrity; she may be known to some in America by engravings in the "People's
Journal" from her pictures, but, if I remember right, these are coarse things,
and give no just notion of her pictures, which are distinguished for elegance
and refinement; a little mannerized, but she is improving in that respect.[5]

Talking of coarse engravings, I must observe how shockingly that of Tennyson, which we see in Horne's "Spirit of the Age" metamorphosizes his picture
which I saw at Mr. Moxon's, as also a beautiful miniature of Keats from which
an engraving is being made for his "Life" by Milnes, soon to appear.[6] Tennyson's
eyes are very fine; a heavy lid, but looking as if the eye could glow into efful-

---

[4] Mary Berry (1763–1852) met Horace Walpole (1717–97) in 1788, when he was
seventy. Walpole wrote stories, such as his *Reminiscences of the Courts of George I and II* (1789),
for the amusement of Mary and her sister, Agnes. He bought a house for them in 1791, and
when he died he left them money, the house, and many gifts. Mary Berry edited most of
Walpole's works after his death. Her play *Fashionable Friends* was performed in 1802 (*DNB*).

[5] Margaret Gillies (1803–87), a watercolorist, painted miniatures of William Wordsworth and Charles Dickens (*DNB*). Fuller wrote Caroline Sturgis that Gillies "has given up
many things highly valued by English women to devote herself to Art, and attained quite
a high place in the profession; her pictures are full of grace, rather sentimental, but that
she is trying to shake off" (Hudspeth 4:240–41). Gillies's work also appeared in the *People's
Journal* (1846–48), founded by John Saunders (1810–95). Designed primarily as an organ
to promote societal reform, the *Journal* published the work of Mazzini as well as Harriet
Martineau and William and Mary Howitt (*DNB*).

[6] Richard Henry, or Hengist Horne (1803–84), was an author and friend of Elizabeth
Barrett Browning. Her "Cry of the Children" was inspired by his 1841 report on the employment of children and young people in mines and manufacturing companies. Horne's *A
New Spirit of the Age* (1844) was a collection of essays on contemporary figures. Two stories
for children were published in 1846: "The Good-natured Bear" and "Memoirs of a London
Doll." Edward Moxon (1801–58) established his publishing house at 44 Dover Street in
1833. He published volumes written by Charles Lamb and Wordsworth; with the publica-

gence. Talking of Mr. Horne, I saw him; he is a great favorite with his friends, and one can easily see why. I understand he is author of some very good children's books, a rare gift to his generation. One, "The History of a London Doll," I read with sincere edification. The Statesman's attempt to answer Dolly's letter is very good.[7]

The "People's Journal" comes nearer being a fair sign of the times than any other publication of England, apparently, if we except Punch. As for the Times, on which you all use your scissors so industriously, that is the Times' times, managed with vast ability, no doubt, but the blood would tingle many a time to the fingers' ends of the body politic before that solemn organ which claims to represent the heart, would dare to beat in unison.[8] Still it would require all the wise management of the Times or wisdom enough to do without it, and a wide range and diversity of talent, indeed, almost sweeping the circle, to make a People's Journal for England. The present is only a bud of the future flower.

Mary and William Howitt are its main support.[9] I saw them several times at their cheerful and elegant home. In Mary Howitt I found the same engaging traits of character we are led to expect from her books for children. Her husband is full of the same agreeable information communicated in the same lively yet precise manner we find in his books; it was like talking with old friends, except that now the eloquence of the eye was added. At their house I became acquainted with Dr. Southwood Smith, the well-known philanthropist. He is at present engaged on the construction of good tenements calculated to improve the condition of the working people. His plans look promising, and should they succeed, you shall have a detailed account of them. On visiting him, we saw an object which I had often heard celebrated and had thought would be revolting, but found on the contrary an agreeable sight; this is the skeleton of Jeremy

---

tion of *Poems* in 1833, he became Tennyson's publisher. Moxon was always looking for new talent; he published Browning's *Sordello* in 1840. Richard Monckton Milnes (1809–85), an author and politican, was instrumental in securing passage of the Copyright Act and assisted in establishing a Civil List pension for Tennyson. In 1848 he published *The Life and Letters of Keats* and later went to Paris, where he wrote "Letter to Lord Lansdown," supporting the Italian revolution (*DNB*).

[7] This paragraph is omitted in *AHA*.

[8] Fuller would come to detest the London *Times* because of its reactionary response to the revolutions of 1848. Emerson, however, had the highest regard for the paper and devoted a chapter of *English Traits* (1856) to it, crediting it with preventing revolution in England in 1848 (Reynolds 28–31).

[9] Mary Botham Howitt (1799–1888) married William Howitt (1792–1879) in 1821. They pursued a joint career as writers and editors. Mary wrote a number of children's stories and translated Hans Christian Andersen. William wrote travel literature and light essays (*DNB*).

Bentham.[10] It was at Bentham's request that the skeleton, dressed in the same dress he habitually wore, stuffed out to an exact resemblance of life, and with a portrait mask in wax, the best I ever saw, sits there as assistant to Dr. Smith in the entertainment of his guests and companion of his studies. The figure leans a little forward, resting the hands on a stout stick which Bentham always carried, and had named "Dapple;" the attitude is quite easy, the expression of the whole mild, winning, yet highly individual. It is a pleasing mark of that unity of aim and tendency to be expected throughout the life of such a mind, that Bentham, while quite a young man, had made a will, in which, to oppose in the most convincing manner the prejudice against dissection of the human subject, he had given his body after death to be used in service of the cause of science. "I have not yet been able," said the will, "to do much service to my fellow men by my life, but, perhaps, I may in this manner by my death." Many years after, reading a pamphlet by Dr. Smith on the same subject, he was much pleased with it, became his friend, and bequeathed his body to his care and use, with directions that the skeleton should finally be disposed of in the way I have described.

The countenance of Dr. Smith has an expression of expansive, sweet, almost child-like goodness. Miss Gillies has made a charming picture of him, with a favorite little grand-daughter nestling in his arms.

Another marked figure that I encountered on this great show-board was Cooper, the author of "The Purgatory of Suicides," a very remarkable poem, of which, had there been leisure before my departure, I should have made a review and given copious extracts in The Tribune. Cooper is as strong as and probably a milder man than when in the prison where that poem was written.[11] The earnestness in seeking freedom and happiness for all men which drew upon him that penalty, seems unabated; he is a very significant type of the new era, also an agent in bringing it near. One of the Poets of the People, also, I saw— the sweetest singer of them all,—Thom. "A Chieftain unknown to the Queen" is again exacting a cruel tribute from him.[12] I wish much that some of those of

[10] Thomas Southwood Smith (1788–1861) was a minister, doctor, and philanthropist in Edinburgh. He owned the skeleton of Jeremy Bentham (*DNB*). Bentham (1748–1832), an English philosopher and social theorist, advocated utilitarianism, the position that the aim of the individual and of the legislator in society should be to produce the greatest good for the greatest number. His *An Introduction to the Principles of Morals and Legislation* (1789) is a detailed articulation of this principle of conduct (*DNB*).

[11] Thomas Cooper (1805–92) served two years in jail for sedition, a direct result of his leadership role in the Chartist movement. He wrote *The Purgatory of Suicides,* a poem in Spencerian stanzas, while in prison in 1845 (*Chambers's Biographical Dictionary*).

[12] William Thom (1798–1848), a Scottish poet, was lame because he had been run over by a nobleman's carriage. His *Rhymes and Recollections of a Handloom Weaver* was published in 1844. Fuller reviewed the book in the *Tribune* (22 August 1845, p. 1:1–3). While in Europe, she headed an American subscription list to aid him (*DNB*).

New-York who have taken an interest in him would provide there a nook in which he might find refuge and solace for the evening of his days, to sing or to work as likes him best, and where he could bring up two fine boys to happier prospects than the parent land will afford them. Could and would America but take from other lands more of the talent, as well as the bone and sinew, she would be rich.

But the stroke of the clock warns me to stop now and begin to-morrow with fresher eye and hand on some interesting topics. My sketches are slight; still they cannot be made without time, and I find none to be had in this Europe except late at night. I believe it is what all the inhabitants use, but I am too sleepy a genius to carry the practice far.   ★

Dispatch 9

SIGHTS AND CELEBRITIES

[Undated] [1]

Again I must begin to write late in the evening. I am told it is the custom of the literati in these large cities to work in the night. It is easy to see that it must be almost impossible to do otherwise; but not only is the practice very bad for the health and one that brings on premature old age, but I cannot think this night-work will prove as firm in texture and as fair of hue as what is done by sunlight. Give me a lonely chamber, a window from which through the foliage you can catch glimpses of a beautiful prospect, and the mind finds itself tuned to action.

But London, London! I have yet some brief notes to make on London. We had scarcely any sunlight by which to see pictures, and I postponed all visits to private collections, except one, in the hope of being in England next time in the long Summer days. In the National Gallery I saw little except the Murillos; [2] they were so beautiful that with me, who had no true conception of his kind of genius before, they took away the desire to look into anything else at the same time. They did not affect me much either, except with a sense of content in this genius, so rich and full and strong. It was a cup of sunny wine that refreshed but brought no intoxicating visions. There is something very great in the genius of Spain, there is such an intensity and singleness; it seems to me it has not half shown itself, and must have an important part to play yet in the drama of this

[1] First published as "Things and Thoughts in Europe. No. IX" in *New-York Daily Tribune,* 19 February 1847, p. 1:1–3.

[2] Fuller refers to Bartolomé Esteban Murillo (1617–82), the Spanish painter. Among his important later works is *Two Trinities,* located in the National Gallery. Both *The Flower Girl* and *Peasant Boys* are located at the Dulwich Picture Gallery (*OCA*).

planet. At the Dulwich Gallery I saw the Flower Girl of Murillo, an enchanting picture, the memory of which must always

"Cast a light upon the day,
A light that will not pass away,
A sweet forewarning."

Who can despair when he thinks of a form like that, so full of life and bliss! Nature, that made human forms like that, to match the butterfly and the bee on June mornings when the lime-trees are in blossom, has surely enough of happiness in store to satisfy us all, somewhere, sometime.

It was pleasant, indeed, to see the treasures of those Galleries, of the British Museum, and of so charming a place as Hampton Court, open to everybody. In the National Gallery one finds a throng of nursery maids, and men just come from their work: true, they make a great deal of noise thronging to and fro on the uncarpeted floors in their thick boots, and noise from which, when penetrated by the atmosphere of Art, men, in the thickest boots, would know how to refrain, still I felt that the sight of such objects must be gradually doing them a great deal of good. The British Museum would, in itself, be an education for a man who should go there once a week, and think and read at his leisure moments about what he saw.

Hampton Court I saw in gloom and rain, and my chief recollections are of the magnificent yew-trees beneath whose shelter—the work of ages—I took refuge from the pelting shower. The expectations cherished from childhood about the Cartoons, were all baffled; there was no light by which they could be seen, but I must hope to visit Hampton Court again in the time of roses.[3]

The Zoological Gardens are another pleasure of the million, since, although something is paid there, it is so little that almost all can afford it.[4] To me, it is a vast pleasure to see animals where they can show out their habits or instincts, and to see them assembled from all climates and countries, amid verdure and with room enough as they are here, is a true poem. They have a fine Lion, the first I ever saw that realized the idea we have of the king of the animal world

[3] Fuller refers to Raphael's designs for tapestries depicting the lives of saints Peter and Paul. His "cartoons" had been located in the South Gallery at Hampton Court until their removal to the Victoria and Albert Museum when it opened in 1852. Raphael executed the cartoons for Pope Leo X in 1515–16; the tapestries were woven in Brussels for the Sistine Chapel of the Vatican (Karl Baedeker, *Handbook for London and Its Environs,* 6th ed. [London: Dulau, 1887]; F.R. Banks, *The Penguin Guide to London,* 7th ed. [New York: Penguin, 1977], 452).

[4] The Zoological Society of London established the gardens in an area of Regent's Park in 1828 (*London Encylopedia*).

—but the groan and roar of this one were equally royal. The Eagles were fine, but rather disgraced themselves. It is a trait of English piety, which would, no doubt, find its defenders among ourselves, not to feed the animals on Sunday, that their keepers may have rest—at least this was the explanation given us by one of these men of the state of ravenous hunger in which we found them on the Monday.—I half hope he was jesting with us. Certain it is that the Eagles were wild with famine, and even the grandest of them, who had eyed us at first as if we were not fit to live in the same zone with him, when the meat came round, after a short struggle to maintain his dignity, joined in wild shriek and scramble with the rest.

Sir John Soane's Museum I saw containing the sarcophagus described by Du Waagen, Hogarth's pictures, a fine Canaletto and a manuscript of Tasso.[5] It fills the house once the residence of his body, still of his mind. It is not a mind with which I have sympathy; I found there no law of harmony, and it annoyed me to see things all jumbled together as if in an old curiosity shop. Nevertheless it was a generous bequest, and much may perhaps be found there of value to him who takes time to seek. This house stands on one side of Lincoln's Inn Fields and on the other is the College of Surgeons. I visited their Anatomical Museum, and there the contents were so arranged by the light which has dawned on modern science, that even one as ignorant on the subject as I can read them as in a book.

The Museum of Economic Geology in like manner I saw with a great deal of pleasure, for its clear arrangement, which enables any one to get directly at what he wants. I believe there is none such in New-York; if not, it is well worthy imitation there. The Gardens at Kew I saw with delight; thereabouts all was so green and still one could indulge at leisure in the humorous and fantastic associations that cluster around the name of Kew, like the curls of a 'big wig' round the serene and sleepy face of its wearer. Here are fourteen green-houses: in one you find all the palms; in another the productions of the regions of snow; in one, of those squibs and humorsome utterances of Nature, the cactuses—ay! there I saw the great-grandfather of all the cactuses, a hoary, solemn plant—declared to be a thousand years old—disdaining to say if it is not really much older. In another the most exquisitely minute plants, delicate as the tracery of

---

[5] Sir John Soane (1753–1837) was an architect and founder of the Bank of England, who began a collection of antiquities, books, and works of art. In 1824 he purchased a celebrated alabaster sarcophagus brought from Egypt and placed it in his museum (*DNB* and *London Encyclopedia*). Fuller probably saw *A Rake's Progress* by William Hogarth (1697–1764), the English painter and engraver, and refers to Giovanni Antonio Canaletto (1697–1768), the Venetian painter, and Torquato Tasso (1544–95) (*OCA* and Lillian H. Hornstein, ed., *The Reader's Companion to World Literature* [New York: New American Library, 1956]).

frost-work, too delicate for the bowers of fairies, such at least as visit the grass brains of earthly poets.

The Reform Club was the only one of those splendid establishments that I visited.[6] Certainly the force of comfort can no farther go, nor can anything be better contrived to make dressing, eating, news-getting, and even sleeping, (for there are bedrooms as well as dressing rooms for those who will) be got through with as glibly as possible. Yet to me this palace of so many "single gentlemen rolled into one," seemed stupidly comfortable in the absence of that elegant arrangement and vivacious atmosphere which only Women can inspire. In the kitchen, indeed, I met them and, on that account, it seemed the pleasantest part of the building—though, even there, they are but the servants of servants. There reigned supreme a genius in his way, who has published a work on Cookery, and around him his pupils—young men who pay a handsome yearly fee for novitiate under his instruction. I am not sorry, however, to see men predominant in the cooking department, as I hope to see that and washing transferred to their care in the progress of things, since they are "the stronger sex."

The arrangements of this kitchen were very fine, combining great convenience with neatness, and even elegance. Fourier himself might have taken pleasure in them.[7] Thence we passed into the private apartments of the artist, and found them full of pictures by his wife, an artist in another walk. One or two of them had been engraved. *She* was an Englishwoman.

A whimsical little excursion we made on occasion of the anniversary of the wedding-day of two of my friends. They who had often enjoyed reading the account of John Gilpin's in America thought that now they were in England and near enough, they would celebrate their's also at "The Bell at Edmonton."[8]

---

[6] The Reform Club, 104–05 Pall Mall, was founded for Radicals in 1832 (*London Encyclopedia*).

[7] Francis-Marie-Charles Fourier (1772–1837) was a French utopian socialist who believed that society should be organized into a variety of cooperative groups, designed to meet the social and economic needs of the members (Newman). Fourier exerted a strong influence upon the Transcendentalists as a group, who were readers of his works. Brook Farm eventually became Fourieristic in 1845 and the *Tribune,* under Greeley's editorship, ardently supported Fourierist projects and ideas. Though skeptical of Fourierism while in America, Fuller came to regard it in Europe as offering the hope of the future.

[8] William Cowper (1731–1800) published *The Diverting History of John Gilpin* with his long poem *The Task* in 1785. John Gilpin, a Cheapside linen-draper, and his wife celebrate their twentieth anniversary with a trip to the Bell at Edmonton. Gilpin rides a horse while his wife, her sister, and their children ride in a chaise. Gilpin loses control of the horse, and the poem describes his wild ride to Edmonton, ten miles beyond to Ware, and back again (*OCEL*).

I accompanied them, with "a little foot page" to eke out the train, pretty and graceful and playful enough for the train of a princess. But our excursion turned out somewhat of a failure in an opposite way to Gilpin's. Whereas he went too fast, we went too slow. First we took coach and went through Cheapside to take omnibus at (strange misnomer!) the Flower-Pot. But Gilpin could never have had his race through Cheapside as it is in its present crowded state; we were obliged to proceed at a funeral pace. We missed the omnibus, and when we took the next one it went with the slowness of a "family horse" in the old chaise of a New-England Deacon, and after all, only took us half way. At the half-way house a carriage was to be sought. The lady who let it and all her grooms were to be allowed time to recover from their consternation at so unusual a move as strangers taking a carriage to dine at the little inn at Edmonton, now a mere ale-house, before we could be allowed to proceed. (The English stand lost in amaze at "Yankee notions" with their quick come and go, and it is impossible to make them "go ahead" in the zig-zag-chain-lightning path, unless you push them.) A rather odd part of the plan had been a pilgrimage to the grave of Lamb,[9] with a collateral view to the rural beauties of Edmonton, but night had fallen on all such hopes two hours at least before we reached the Bell. *There,* indeed, we found them somewhat more alert to comprehend our wishes; they laughed when we spoke of Gilpin, showed us a print of the race and the window where Mrs. Gilpin must have stood; balcony, alas! there was none; allowed us to make our own fire, and provided us a wedding dinner of tough meat and stale bread. Nevertheless we danced, dined, paid, (I believe) and celebrated the wedding quite to our satisfaction, though in the space of half an hour, as we knew friends were even at that moment expecting us to *tea* at some miles distance. But it is always pleasant in this world of routine to act out a freak, "such an one," said an English gentleman, "one of *us* would rarely never have dreamed of, much less acted." "Why, was it not pleasant?" "Oh, *very!* but *so* out of the way!"

Returning, we passed the house where Freiligrath [10] finds a temporary home, earning the bread of himself and his family in a commercial house. England

[9] Charles Lamb (1775–1834) is buried in Edmonton, where he died. Lamb, a close friend to Coleridge, was a poet and essayist. He collaborated with his emotionally unstable sister, Mary, to write *Tales from Shakespear* (1807) for children (*OCEL*).

[10] Ferdinand Freiligrath (1810–76), a German poet and political activist for German democracy, was living in exile when Fuller visited England. He returned to Germany in 1848 and was expelled again after the publication of his poem *Die Toten an die Lebenden* (1848) (*Chambers's Biographical Dictionary*). A translation of this poem entitled "The Dead to the Living" was published by J. B. Taylor in the *Tribune* (27 October 1848, p. 1:3–4); Taylor calls the poem the "boldest and fierest lyric the revolutions of '48 have produced."

houses the exile, but not without house-tax, window-tax, and head-tax. Where is the Arcadia that dares invite all genius to her arms, and change her golden wheat for their green laurels and immortal flowers? Arcadia!—would the name were America!

And here returns naturally to my mind one of the most interesting things I have seen here or elsewhere—the school for poor Italian boys, sustained and taught by a few of their exiled compatriots, and especially by the mind and efforts of Mazzini.[11] The name of Joseph Mazzini is well known to those among us who take an interest in the cause of human freedom, who, not content with the peace and ease bought for themselves by the devotion and sacrifices of their fathers, look with anxious interest on the suffering nations who are preparing for a similar struggle. Those who are not, like the brutes that perish, content with the enjoyment of mere national advantages, indifferent to the idea they represent, cannot forget that the human family is one,

"And beats with one great heart."

They know that there can be no genuine happiness, no salvation for any, unless the same can be secured for all.

To this universal interest in all nations and places where Man, understanding his inheritance, strives to throw off an arbitrary rule and establish a state of things where he shall be governed as becomes a man by his own conscience and intelligence, where he may speak the truth as it rises in his mind, and indulge his natural emotions in purity, is added an especial interest in Italy, the mother of our language and our laws, our greatest benefactress in the gifts of genius, the garden of the world, in which our best thoughts have delighted to expatiate, but over whose bowers now hangs a perpetual veil of sadness, and whose noblest plants are doomed to removal—for, if they cannot bear their ripe and perfect fruit in another climate, they are not permitted to lift their heads to heaven in their own.

Some of these generous refugees our country has received kindly, if not with a fervent kindness; and the word CORAGGIO is still in my ears as I heard it spoken in New-York by one whose heart long oppression could not paralyze. SPERANZA some of the Italian youth now inscribe on their banners, encouraged by some traits of apparent promise in the new Pope. However, their only true hope is in themselves, in their own courage, and in that wisdom which may

[11] Mazzini, the Italian revolutionary, was first exiled to France and, at the time Fuller was visiting, to England. In a letter to Caroline Sturgis, she commented enthusiastically on their first meeting, calling him "by far the most beauteous person I have seen" and "one in whom holiness has purified, but nowhere dwarfed the man" (Hudspeth 2:240).

only be learned through many disappointments as to how to employ it so that it may destroy tyranny, not themselves.

Mazzini, one of these noble refugees, is not only one of the heroic, the courageous, and the faithful—Italy boasts many such—but he is also one of the wise. One of those who, disappointed in the outward results of their undertakings, can yet "bate no jot of heart and hope," but *must* "steer right onward," for it was no superficial enthusiasm, no impatient energies, that impelled him, but an understanding of what *must* be the designs of Heaven with regard to Man, since God is Love, is Justice. He is one who can live fervently but steadily, gently, every day, every hour, as well as on great occasions, by the light of a hope, for, with Schiller, he is sure that "Those who live for their faith shall behold it living." [12] He is one of those same beings who, measuring all things by the ideal standard, have yet no time to mourn over failure or imperfection; there is too much to be done to obviate it.

Thus Mazzini, excluded from publication in his native language, has acquired the mastery both of French and English, and through his expressions in either shine the thoughts which animated his earlier effort, with mild and steady radiance. The misfortunes of his country have only widened the sphere of his instructions, and made him an exponent of the better era to Europe at large. Those who wish to form an idea of his mind could not do better than to read his sketches of the Italian Martyrs in the "People's Journal." They will find there, on one of the most difficult occasions, an ardent friend speaking of his martyred friends, the purity of impulse, warmth of sympathy, largeness and steadiness of view and fineness of discrimination which must belong to a legislator for a CHRISTIAN commonwealth.

But though I have read these expressions with great delight, this school was one, to me, still more forcible of the same ideas. Here these poor boys, picked up from the streets, are redeemed from bondage and gross ignorance by the most patient and constant devotion of time and effort. What love and sincerity this demands from minds capable of great thoughts, large plans and rapid progress, only their peers can comprehend, yet exceeding great shall be the reward; and as among the fishermen and poor people of Judea were picked up those who have become to modern Europe the leaven that leavens the whole mass, so may these poor Italian boys yet become more efficacious as missionaries to their people than would an Orphic poet at this period. These youths have very commonly good faces, and eyes from which that Italian fire that has

[12] Johann Christoph Friedrich Schiller (1759–1805), the romantic dramatist, was one of Fuller's favorite German authors (*OCGL*). She and James Freeman Clarke studied and translated many of Schiller's works in the 1830s.

done so much to warm the world glows out. We saw the distribution of prizes to the school, heard addresses from Mazzini, Pistrucci, Mariotti [13] (once a resident in our country) and an English gentleman who takes a great interest in the work, and then adjourned to an adjacent room where a supper was provided for the boys and other guests, among whom we saw some of the exiled Poles. The whole evening gave a true and deep pleasure, though tinged with sadness. We saw a planting of the Kingdom of Heaven, though now no larger than a grain of mustard-seed, and though, perhaps, none of those who watch the spot may live to see the birds singing in its branches.

I have not yet spoken of one of *our* benefactors, Mr. Carlyle, whom I saw several times. [14] I approached him with more reverence after a little experience of England and Scotland had taught me to appreciate the strength and hight of that wall of shams and conventions which he, more than any man, or thousand men, —indeed, he almost alone—has begun to throw down. Wherever there was fresh thought, generous hope, the thought of Carlyle has begun the work. He has torn off the veils from hideous facts; he has burnt away foolish illusions; he has awakened thousands to know what it is to be a man; that we must live, and not merely pretend to others that we live. He has touched the rocks and they have given forth musical answer; little more was wanting to begin to construct the city.

—But that little was wanting, and the work of construction is left to those that come after him: nay, all attempts of the kind he is the readiest to deride,

[13] The Italian Gratuitous School was founded in 1841 by Mazzini to benefit poor Italian boys brought to England to work as little more than slaves. In his autobiography, Mazzini explained that he and his friends "gave both moral and intellectual instruction to several hundred youths and children who were in a state of semi-barbarism" (*Joseph Mazzini, His Life, Writings, and Political Principles* [New York: Hurd and Houghton, 1872], 222). Filippo Pistrucci, a friend of Gabrielle Rosetti, was the director of the school; many prominent people provided financial support or, like Joseph Toynbee (1815–66), a well-known surgeon and philanthropist, taught classes without compensation (Stringfellow Bace, *Mazzini: Portrait of an Exile* [New York: Holt, 1935], 161–66). Antonio Carlo Napoleone Gallenga was a professor and fugitive who took the name Luigi Mariotti. He took refuge in the United States, where he became friends with Lowell and Longfellow, and in England, where he became a naturalized citizen in 1846. At the outbreak of the revolution, he returned to Italy with Mazzini and joined the Piedmontese army. (Margaret C. W. Wicks, *The Italian Exiles in London, 1816–1848* [Freeport, N.Y.: Books for Libraries Press, 1937], 178–80).

[14] Thomas Carlyle (1795–1881) and his wife, Jane Welsh Carlyle (1801–66), were very hospitable to Fuller and invited her to their home, where she met George Henry Lewes (1817–78) and W. J. Fox. The Carlyles also visited Fuller and the Springs on an evening when Mazzini was visiting. As Hudspeth has pointed out, Fuller caught Carlyle at a bad time, for he was restless at not working on a book and he had just quarreled with his wife (Hudspeth 4:249n).

fearing new shams worse than the old, unable to trust the general action of a thought, and finding no heroic man, no natural king to represent it and challenge his confidence. Accustomed to the infinite wit and exuberant richness of his writings, his talk is still an amazement and a splendor scarcely to be faced with steady eyes. He does not converse—only harangues. It is the usual misfortune of such marked men (happily not one invariable or inevitable) that they cannot allow other minds room to breathe and show themselves in their atmosphere, and thus miss the refreshment and instruction which the greatest never cease to need from the experience of the humblest. Carlyle allows no one a chance, but bears down all opposition, not only by his wit and onset of words resistless in their sharpness as so many bayonets, but by actual physical superiority, raising his voice and rushing on his opponent with a torrent of sound. This is not the least from unwillingness to allow freedom to others; on the contrary, no man would more enjoy a manly resistance to his thought, but it is the impulse of a mind accustomed to follow out its own impulse as the hawk its prey, and which knows not how to stop in the chase. Carlyle, indeed, is arrogant and overbearing, but in his arrogance there is no littleness, no self-love: it is the heroic arrogance of some old Scandinavian conqueror—it is his nature and the untamable impulse that has given him power to crush the dragons. You do not love him, perhaps, nor revere, and perhaps, also, he would only laugh at you if you did, but you like him heartily, and like to see him the powerful smith, the Siegfried, melting all the old iron in his furnace till it glows to a sunset red, and burns you if you senselessly go too near. He seemed to me quite isolated, lonely as the desert, yet never was man more fitted to prize a man, could he find one to match his mood. He finds them, but only in the past. He sings rather than talks. He pours upon you a kind of satirical, heroical, critical poem, with regular cadences, and generally catching up near the beginning some singular epithet, which serves as a *refrain* when his song is full, or with which as with a knitting needle he catches up the stitches if he has chanced now and then to let fall a row. For the higher kinds of poetry he has no sense, and his talk on that subject is delightfully and gorgeously absurd; he sometimes stops a minute to laugh at it himself, then begins anew with fresh vigor—for all the spirits he is driving before him seem to him as Fata Morganas, ugly masks, in fact, if he can but make them turn about, but he laughs that they seem to others such dainty Ariels. He puts out his chin sometimes till it looks like the beak of a bird, and his eyes flash bright instinctive meanings like Jove's bird; yet he is not calm and grand enough for the eagle; he is more like the falcon, and yet not of gentle blood enough for that either. He is not exactly like anything but himself, and therefore you cannot see him without the most hearty refreshment and good will, for he is original, rich and strong enough to afford a thousand faults; one expects some wild land in a rich kingdom. His talk, like his books, is full of pictures, his critical strokes masterly; allow for his point of view, and his survey is admirable. He is a large subject; I cannot speak more or wiselier of him now, nor needs it; his works are true, to blame and praise him, the Siegfried of England, great and powerful, if not quite invulnerable, and of a might rather to destroy evil than legislate for good. At all events, he seems to be what Destiny intended, and represents fully a certain side; so we make no remonstrance as to his being and proceeding for himself, though we sometimes must for us.

I had meant some remarks on Sarnee's pictures, and the little I saw of the Theatre in England; but these topics must wait till my next, when they will connect themselves naturally enough with what I have to say of Paris.   ★

Dispatch 10

FROM   LONDON   TO   PARIS

PARIS [Undated] [1]

When I wrote last I could not finish with London, and there remain yet two or three things I wish to speak of before passing to my impressions of this wonderfull Paris.

I visited the model-prison at Pentonville; but though in some respects an improvement upon others I have seen—though there was the appearance of great neatness and order in the arrangements of life—kindness and good judgment in the discipline of the prisoners—yet there was also an air of bleak forlornness about the place, and it fell short of what my mind demands of such abodes considered as Redemption schools. [2] But as the subject of prisons is now engaging the attention of many of the wisest and best, and the tendency is in what seems to me the true direction, I need not trouble myself to make crude and hasty suggestions; it is a subject to which persons who would be of use should give the earnest devotion of calm and leisurely thought.

The same day I went to see an establishment which gave me unmixed pleasure; it is a bathing establishment put at a very low rate to enable the poor

---

[1] First published as "Things and Thoughts in Europe. No. X" in *New-York Daily Tribune*, 3 March 1847, p. 1:1–4.

[2] The 520-cell Pentonville prison, opened in 1842, became the model for fifty-four new prisons built in England (Mitchell 639–41). Fuller may have restrained herself from making "crude and hasty suggestions" about the prisons because she recalled Charles Dickens's generalizations about prisons from his visit to the Eastern Penitentiary in Pennsylvania, recorded in his *American Notes* (1842), about which she commented in *Summer on the Lakes* (1844).

to avoid one of the worst miseries of their lot, and which yet promises *to pay.* Joined with this is an establishment for washing clothes, where the poor can go and hire, for almost nothing, good tubs, water ready heated, the use of an apparatus for rinsing, drying and ironing, all so admirably arranged that a poor woman can in three hours get through an amount of washing and ironing that would, under ordinary circumstances, occupy three or four days. Especially the drying closets I contemplated with great satisfaction, and hope to see in our own country the same arrangements throughout the cities and even in the towns and villages.—Hanging out the clothes is a great exposure for women, even when they have a good place for it, but when, as is so common in cities, they must dry them in the house, how much they suffer! In New-York I know those poor women who take in washing endure a great deal of trouble and toil from this cause; I have suffered myself from being obliged to send back what had cost them so much toil, because it had been, perhaps inevitably, soiled in the drying or ironing, or filled with the smell of their miscellaneous cooking. In London it is much worse. An eminent physician told me he knew of two children whom he considered to have died because their mother, having but one room to live in, was obliged to wash and dry clothes close to their bed when they were ill. The poor people in London naturally do without washing all they can, and beneath that perpetual fall of soot the result may be guessed. All but the very poor in England put out their washing, and this custom ought to be universal in civilized countries, as it can be done much better and quicker by a few regular laundresses than by many families, and 'the washing day' is so malignant a foe to the peace and joy of households that it ought to be effaced from the calendar. But, as long as we are so miserable as to have any very poor people in this world, *they* cannot put out their washing, because they cannot earn enough money to pay for it, and, preliminary to something better, washing establishments like this of London are desirable.

One arrangement that they have here in Paris will be a good one, even when we cease to have any very poor people, and, please Heaven, also to have any very rich. These are the *Crèches*—houses where poor women leave their children to be nursed during the day while they are at work. I have not yet been to see one of these, and must postpone speaking of them more fully to another letter.

I must mention that the superintendent of the washing establishment observed, with a legitimate triumph, that it had been built without giving a single dinner or printing a single puff—an extraordinary thing, indeed, for England!

To turn to something a little gayer—the embroidery on this tattered coat of civilized life—I went into only two theatres, Old Drury—once the scene of great glories, now of execrable music and more execrable acting. If anything can

be invented more excruciating than an English Opera, such as was the fashion
at the time I was in London, I am sure no sin of mine deserves the punishment
of bearing it.[3]

At Sadler's Wells I saw a play which I had much admired in reading it, but
found still better in actual representation; indeed, it seems to me there can be
no better acting play: this is 'The Patrician's Daughter,' by J. W. Marston.[4] The
movement is rapid yet clear and free, the dialogue natural, dignified and flowing—the characters marked with few but distinct strokes. Where the tone of
discourse rises with manly sentiment or passion, the audience applauded with
bursts of generous feeling that gave me great pleasure, for this play is one that,
in its scope and meaning, marks the new era in England; it is full of an experience which is inevitable to a man of talent there, and is harbinger of the day
when the noblest commoner shall be the only noble possible in England.

But how different all this acting to what I find in France! Here the theatre
is living; you see something really good, and good throughout. Not one touch
of that stage strut and vulgar bombast of tone which the English actor fancies
indispensable to scenic illusion is tolerated here. For the first time in my life I
saw something represented in a style uniformly good, and should have found
sufficient proof, if I had needed any, that all men will prefer what is good to
what is bad, if only a fair opportunity for choice be allowed. When I came here,
my first thought was to go and see Mademoiselle Rachel.[5] I was sure that in
her I should find a true genius, absolutely the diamond, and so it proved.—I

[3] From 1838 to 1848 Sir Julius Benedict, composer of the operas *The Brides of Venice*
and *The Crusaders,* was the music director at the Drury Lane Theatre. Under his direction a
series of English romantic operas were performed, including *The Bohemian Girl* by Michael
William Balfe (1808–70) and *Mathilde of Hungary* by William Vincent Wallace (1812–65)
(*Grove, OCM*).

[4] The Theatre Royal, Drury Lane, the fourth theater erected on this site, was built
in 1809–12. Sadler's Wells, which began performances in 1685 on Rosebury Avenue in
Finsbury, is where Fuller saw *The Patrician's Daughter* (1842) by John Westland Marston
(1819–90); she had reviewed the play in the *Dial* 4 (1844):307–49. Marston joined a mystical group gathered around James Pierrepont Greaves (1777–1842) that loosely followed
the ideas of the New England Transcendentalists. *The Patrician's Daughter* was based on
Marston's courtship of his wife, Eleanor Jane Potts (*DNB*).

[5] Elisabeth Félix (1821–58) became Rachel, the most celebrated actress of her day
(Oscar G. Brockett, *History of the Theatre,* 4th ed. [Boston: Allyn and Bacon, 1982]). Fuller
especially admired her performance in *Phèdre* (1677) by Jean Racine (Bernard Sobel, *The
Theatre Handbook and Digest of Plays* [New York: Crown, 1940]). Fuller wrote to Caroline
Sturgis, "I am engrossed in Rachel; she surpasses my hopes." And later, "There is nothing
like her voice; she speaks the language of the Gods. To the noblest genius is joined the
severest culture. She has a really bad reputation as woman. A liberal Frenchman says to me
'Me *Sand* has committed what are called errors, but we doubt not the nobleness of her soul,

went to see her seven or eight times, always in parts that required great force of soul and purity of taste even to conceive them, and only once had reason to find fault with her. On one single occasion I saw her violate the harmony of the character to produce effect at a particular moment; but almost invariably I found her a true artist, worthy Greece, and worthy at many moments to have her conceptions immortalized in marble.

Her range even in high tragedy is limited. She can only express the darker passions, and grief in its most desolate aspects. Nature has not gifted her with those softer and more flowery attributes that lend to pathos its utmost tenderness. She does not melt to tears or calm or elevate the heart by the presence of that tragic beauty that needs all the assaults of Fate to make it show its immortal sweetness. Her noblest aspect is when sometimes she expresses truth in some severe shape, and rises, simple and austere, above the mixed elements around her. On the dark side, she is very great in hatred and revenge. I admired her more in PHEDRE than in any other part in which I saw her, the guilty love inspired by the hatred of a goddess was expressed in all its symptoms with a force and terrible naturalness that almost suffocated the beholder. After she had taken the poison, the exhaustion and paralysis of the system—the sad, cold, calm submission to Fate—were still more grand.

I had heard so much about the power of her eye in one fixed look, and the expression she could concentrate in a single word, that the utmost results could only satisfy my expectations. It is, indeed, something magnificent to see the dark cloud give out such sparks, each one fit to deal a separate death, but it was not that I admired most in her.—It was the grandeur, truth and depth of her conception of each part, and the sustained purity with which she represented it.

For the rest, I shall write somewhere a detailed *critique* upon the parts in which I saw her. It is she who has made me acquainted with the true way of viewing French tragedy. I had no idea of its powers and symmetry till now, and have received from the revelation high pleasure and a crowd of thoughts.

The French language from her lips is a divine dialect; it is stripped of its national and personal peculiarities and becomes what any language must— moulded by such a genius—the pure music of the heart and soul. I never could remember her tone in speaking any word; it was too perfect; you had received the thought quite direct. Yet, had I never heard her speak a word, my mind would be filled by her attitudes. Nothing more graceful can be conceived, nor could the genius of sculpture surpass her management of the antique drapery.

She has no beauty except in the intellectual severity of her outline, and bears marks of race that will grow stronger every year, and make her ugly before long.

but it is said that the private life of *Mlle Rachel* has nothing in common with the apparition of the Artist.' Do not speak of this in America" (Hudspeth 4:250–52).

Still it will be a *grandiose,* gypsy, or rather Sibyline ugliness, well adapted to the expression of some tragic parts. Only it seems as if she could not live long; she expends force enough upon a part to furnish out a dozen common lives.

Though the French tragedy is well acted throughout, yet unhappily there is no male actor now with a spark of fire, and these men seem the meanest pigmies by the side of Rachel—so on the scene, beside the tragedy intended by the author, you see also that common tragedy, a woman of genius who throws away her precious heart, lives and dies for one unworthy of her. In parts this effect is productive of too much pain. I saw Rachel one night with her brother and sister. The sister imitated her so closely that you could not help seeing she had a manner, and an imitable manner. Her brother was in the play her lover; a wretched automaton, and presenting the most unhappy family likeness to herself. Since then I have hardly cared to go and see her. We could wish with geniuses as with the Phenix[6]—to see only one of the family at a time.

In the pathetic or sentimental drama Paris boasts another young actress, nearly as distinguished in that walk as Rachel in hers. This is Rose Cheny, whom we saw in her 98th personation of *Clarissa Harlowe,* and afterward in Genevieve and the *Protegé sans le savoir*—a little piece written expressly for her by Scribe.[7] The 'Miss Clarisse' of the French drama is a feeble and partial reproduction of the heroine of Richardson; indeed the original in all its force of intellect and character would have been too much for the charming Rose Cheny, but, to the purity and lovely tenderness of Clarissa she does full justice. In the other characters she was the true French girl, full of grace and a mixture of naïveté and cunning, sentiment and frivolity, that is winning and *piquant,* if not satisfying. Only grief seems very strange to those bright eyes; we do not find that they can weep much and bear the light of day, and the inhaling of charcoal seems near at hand to their brightest pleasures.

At the other little theatres you see excellent acting and a sparkle of wit unknown to the world out of France. The little pieces in which all the leading topics of the day are reviewed are full of drolleries that make you laugh at each instant. *Paudre-coton* is the only one of these I have seen; in this, among other jokes, Dumas, in the character of Monte-Christo and in a costume half Ori-

---

[6] The Phoenix, a mythological bird symbolizing rebirth and immortality, supposedly lived alone in the Arabian desert for hundreds of years before being consumed in fire, only to rise again from its own ashes.

[7] Rose Cheney was an eighteenth-century actress who performed in London from 1763 to 1782. She would have been much too old for the performance described here. Either this is a less well known actress with the same name or Fuller (or the *Tribune*) got the name wrong. Eugène Scribe (1791–1861) wrote comedies, opera libretti, and serious drama (*OCFL*).

ental, half juggler, is made to pass the other theatres in review while seeking candidates for his new one.[8]

Dumas appeared in court yesterday and defended his own cause against the editors who sue him for evading some of his engagements. I was very desirous to hear him speak and went there in what I was assured would be very good season, but a French audience, who knew the ground better, had slipped in before me, and I returned, as has been too often the case with me in Paris, having seen nothing but endless staircases, dreary vestibules, and *gens d'armes.* The hospitality of *le grande nation* to the stranger is, in many respects, admirable. Galleries, libraries, cabinets of coins, museums, are opened in the most liberal manner to the stranger, warmed, lighted, ay, and guarded, for him almost all days in the week; treasures of the past are at his service; but when anything is happening in the present, the French run quicker, glide in more adroitly, and get possession of the ground. I find it not the most easy matter to get to places even when there is nothing going on—there is so much tiresome fuss of getting *billets* from one and another to be gone through; but when something is happening it is still worse. I missed hearing M. Guizot in his speech on the Montpensier marriage, which would have given a very good idea of his manner, and which, like this defence of M. Dumas, was a skillful piece of work as regards evasion of the truth.[9] The good feeling toward England which had been fostered with so much care and toil seems to have been entirely dissipated by the mutual recriminations about this marriage, and the old dislike flames up more fiercely for having been hid awhile beneath the ashes. I saw the little Duchess, the innocent or ignorant topic of all this disturbance, when presented at Court. She went round the circle on the arm of the Queen. Though only fourteen she

[8] Alexandre Dumas *père* (1802–70) was a prolific writer of plays and novels. *The Count of Monte Cristo,* one of his most famous works, was published in 1844–45. Dumas was constantly in debt because of his extravagant lifestyle and took on many more projects than he could possibly complete (Anthony Thorlby, *The Penguin Companion to World Literature* [New York: McGraw-Hill, 1967]).

[9] François-Guillaume Guizot (1787–1874), historian and statesman, had served Louis Philippe from 1830. From 1840 to 1848 he was the minister of foreign affairs and the de facto head of the ministry. His arrangement of the Montpensier marriage was an attempt to strengthen the alliance between the House of Bourbon and the House of Orléans. The marriage of the infanta Maria Luisa Fernanda to the duc de Montpensier (the son of Louis Philippe) took place on 11 October 1846 at the same time as Isabella II was married to the infante Francisco de Asis. "The Affair of the Spanish Marriages," as it was called, outraged the British government, which lodged an official protest. During the French revolution of February 1848, Guizot was dismissed by Louis Philippe in a futile attempt to preserve the monarchy (Newman).

looks twenty, but has something fresh, engaging, and girlish about her. I fancy it will soon be rubbed out under the drill of the royal household.

I attended not only at the presentation but at the ball given at the Tuileries directly after; these are fine shows, as the suite of apartments is very handsome, brilliantly lighted, the French ladies surpassing all others in the art of dress; indeed, it gave me much pleasure to see them; certainly there are many ugly ones, but they are so well dressed and have such an air of graceful vivacity, that the general effect was of a flower-garden. As often happens, several American women were among the most distinguished for positive beauty; one from Philadelphia, who is by many persons considered the prettiest ornament of the dress circle at the Italian Opera, was especially marked by the attention of the King. However, these ladies, even if here a long time, do not attain the air and manner of French-women: the magnetic fluid that envelops them is less brilliant and exhilarating in its attractions.

It was pleasant to my eye, which has always been so wearied in our country by the sombre masses of men that overcloud our public assemblies, to see them now in so great variety of costume, color and decoration.

Among the crowd wandered Leverrier in the costume of Academician, looking as if he had lost, not found, his planet.[10] French *savants* are more generally men of the world and even men of fashion than those of other climates; but, in his case, he seemed not to find it easy to exchange the music of the spheres for the music of fiddles.

Speaking of Leverrier leads to another of my disappointments. I went to the Sorbonne to hear him lecture, nothing dreaming that the old pedantic and theological character of those halls was strictly kept up in these days of light. An old guardian of the inner temple seeing me approach had his speech all ready, and, manning the entrance, said with a disdainful air, before we had time to utter a word, "Monsieur may enter if he pleases, but Madame must remain here," (*i.e.* in the court-yard.) After some exclamations of surprise I found an alternative in the Hotel de Cluny,[11] where I passed an hour very delightfully while waiting for my companion. The rich remains of other centuries are there so arranged that they can be seen to the best advantage; many of the works in ivory, china and carved wood are truly splendid or exquisite. I saw a dagger with

---

[10] Urbain Jean LeVerrier (1811–77), an astronomer, predicted the existence of the planet Neptune in 1846 (Patricia Moore, ed., *The International Encyclopedia of Astronomy* [New York: Orion, 1987]).

[11] The Hôtel de Cluny, established as a residential palace by Jean de Bourbon, abbot of Cluny, in 1480, had been opened as a national museum of antiquities in 1843 (*Gallignani's New Paris Guide for 1869* [Paris: A. and W. Gallignani, 1869]).

jeweled hilt which talked whole poems to my mind. In the various 'Adorations of the Magi' I found constantly one of the wise men black, and with the marked African lineaments. Before I had half finished, my companion came and wished me at least to visit the lecture-rooms of the Sorbonne now that the talk, too good for female ears, was over. But the guardian again interfered to deny me entrance. "You can go, Madame," said he "to the College of France; you can go to this and t'other place, but you cannot enter here." [12] "What, sir," said I, "is it your institution alone that remains in a state of barbarism?" "Que voulez vous, Madame," he replied, and, as he spoke, his little dog began to bark at me "Que voulez vous, Madame, c'est la regle,"—"What would you have, Madame, IT IS THE RULE,"—a reply which makes me laugh even now, as I think how the satirical wits of former days might have used it against the bulwarks of learned dullness.

I was more fortunate in hearing Arago, and he justified all my expectations. Clear, rapid, full and equal, his discourse is worthy its celebrity, and I felt repaid for the four hours one is obliged to spend in going, in waiting and in hearing, for the lecture begins at half past one and you must be there before twelve to get a seat, so constant and animated is his popularity. [13]

Generally the most celebrated lecturers are silent at this moment. Michelet is ill. Mickiewicz, highly vaunted by discriminating hearers for a various and inspired eloquence, is absent. [14] Sated with lectures in our own country, I have not felt willing to give my hours to the less distinguished, even although for me, as stranger and Columbian ignoramus, I know they would have many a kernel worth disengaging from the husks, if strength and time were more abundant.

I have attended with some interest two discussions at the Athenée—one on Suicide, the other on The Crusades. They are amateur affairs where, as always at such times, one hears much nonsense and vanity, much making of phrases and sentimental mental grimace; but there was one excellent speaker, adroit and rapid as only a Frenchman could be. With admirable readiness, skill and rhe-

[12] The prestigious Collège de France was independent of the universities. The lectures were open to the public; no degrees or diplomas were granted (Newman).

[13] The astronomer François Arago (1786–1853) was the director of the Paris Observatory (Moore). Following the 1848 French revolution he served as a minister of the Provisional Government and then a member of the Constituent Assembly in the new French Republic.

[14] Jules Michelet (1798–1874) was a prominent historican whose six-volume *Histoire de France* appeared from 1833 to 1844. Michelet was a lecturer at the Collège de France from 1838 to 1851 and was enormously popular for his speeches advocating a republican France. Adam Mickiewicz (1798–1855), a Polish poet and revolutionary who also lectured at the college, was living in Paris and met Fuller during her stay (Newman). This paragraph is omitted in *AHA*.

torical polish, he examined the arguments of all the others and built upon their failures a triumph for himself. His management of the language, too, was masterly, and French is the best of languages for such a purpose—clear, flexible, full of sparkling points and quick, picturesque turns, with a subtle blandness that makes the dart tickle while it wounds. Truly he pleased the fancy, filled the ear and carried us pleasantly along over the smooth, swift waters; but then came from the crowd a gentleman, not one of the appointed orators of the evening, but who had really something in his heart to say—a grave, dark man, with Spanish eyes, and the simple dignity of honor and earnestness in all his gesture and manner. He said in few and unadorned words his say, and the sense of a real presence filled the room and those charms of rhetoric faded, as vanish the beauties of soap-bubbles from the eyes of astonished childhood.

I was present on one good occasion at the Academy the day that M. Remusat was received there in the place of Royer Collard.[15] I looked down from one of the tribunes upon the flower of the celebrities of France, that is to say, of the celebrities which are authentic, *comme il faut*. Among them were many marked faces, many fine heads; but, in reading the works of poets we always fancy them about the age of Apollo himself, and I found with pain some of my favorites quite old, and very unlike the company on Parnassus as represented by Raphael. Some however, were venerable, even noble, to behold. Indeed the literary dynasty of France is growing old, and here, as in England and Germany, there seems likely to occur a serious gap before the inauguration of another, if indeed another is coming.

However, it was an imposing sight; there are men of real distinction now in the Academy, and Molière would have a fair chance if he were proposed to-day. Among the audience I saw many ladies of fine expression and manner as well as one or two *Precieuses Ridicules,* a race which is never quite extinct.

M. Rémusat, as is the custom on these occasions, painted the portrait of his predecessor; the discourse was brilliant and discriminating in the details, but the orator seemed to me to neglect drawing some obvious inferences which would have given a better point of view for his subject.

A *sceance* to me much more impressive and interesting was one which borrowed nothing from dress, decorations, or the presence of titled pomp. I went to call on La Mennais, to whom I had a letter.[16] I found him in a little study; his

[15] François-Marie-Charles, comte de Rémusat (1797–1875), was a politican and author who published *Essais de philosophie* in 1842 and *Abelard* in 1845; he played a small role in the revolutions of 1848. Pierre-Paul Royer-Collard (1763–1845) was a philosopher, doctrinaire royalist, and a professor at the Sorbonne. His students included Rémusat and Guizot (Newman).

[16] Félicité-Robert de Lamennais (1797–1854) was a liberal Catholic priest, philosopher, and political writer. He rose to prominence with his *Essais sur l'indifférence en matière de religion*

secretary was writing in a larger room through which I passed. With him was a somewhat citizen-looking, but vivacious, elderly man, whom I was at first sorry to see, having wished for half an hour's undisturbed visit to the apostle of Democracy. But how quickly were those feelings displaced by joy when he named to me the great national lyrist of France, the unequaled Beranger.[17] I had not expected to see him at all, for he is not one to be seen in any show place; he lives in the hearts of the people, and needs no homage from their eyes. I was very happy in that little study in presence of these two men, whose influence has been so great, so real. To me Beranger has been much; his wit, his pathos, his exquisite lyric grace, have made the most delicate strings vibrate, and I can feel, as well as see, what he is in his nation and his place. I have not personally received anything from La Mennais, as, born under other circumstances, mental facts to which he, once the pupil of Rome, has passed through such ordeals, are at the basis of all my thoughts. But I see well what he has been and is to Europe, and of what great force of nature and spirit. He seems suffering and pale, but in his eyes is the light of the future.

These are men who need no flourish of trumpets to announce their coming— no band of martial music upon their steps—no obsequious nobles in their train. They are the true kings, the theocratic kings, the judges in Israel. The hearts of men make music at their approach; the mind of the age is the historian of their passage; and only men of destiny like themselves shall be permitted to write their eulogies, or fill their vacant seat.

Wherever there is a genius like his own, a germ of the finest fruit still hidden beneath the soil, the *"Chante pauvre petit"* of Beranger shall strike, like a sunbeam, and give it force to emerge, and wherever there is the true Crusade— for the spirit, not the tomb of Christ—shall be felt an echo of the *"Que tes armes soient benis jeune soldat"* of La Mennais.   ★

(1817–23). He denounced the passivity of religion and advocated a church that was active in social justice (Sandra W. Dolbow, *Dictionary of Modern French Literature: From the Age of Reason through Reaslism* [New York: Greenwood, 1986]). Fuller's new friend, George Sand, had been a disciple of Lamennais's but had broken with him in 1841 (Hudspeth 4:258).

[17] Fuller was delighted to meet Pierre-Jean de Béranger (1780–1857), the French poet, playwright, and songwriter (*OCFL*). When she wrote Lamennais to thank him for receiving her, she said of Béranger that he is "the genuine poet, the genuine man of France. I have felt all the enchantment of the lyre of Béranger; have paid my warmest homage to the truth and wisdom adorned with such charms, such wit and pathos. It was a great pleasure to see himself" (Hudspeth 4:254).

Dispatch 11

ART, MUSIC, AND ETHER

[Undated][1]

It needs not to speak in this cursory manner of the treasures of art, pictures, sculptures, engravings, and the other riches which France lays open so freely to the stranger in her Musées. Any examination worth writing of such objects, or account of the thoughts they inspire, demands a place by itself and an ample field in which to expatiate. The American, first introduced to some good pictures by the truly great geniuses of the religious period in Art, must, if capable at all of mental approximation to the life therein embodied, be too deeply affected, too full of thoughts, to be in haste to say anything, and, for me, I bide my time.

No such great crisis, however, is to be apprehended from acquaintance with the productions of the modern French school. They are, indeed, full of talent and of vigor, but also melo-dramatic and exaggerated to a degree that seems to give the nightmare passage through the fresh and cheerful day. They sound no depth of soul, and are marked with the signet of a degenerate age.

Thus speak I generally; to the pictures of Horace Vernet one cannot but turn a gracious eye—they are so faithful a transcript of the life which circulates around us in the present state of things, and we are willing to see his nobles and generals mounted on such excellent horses.[2] De la Roche gives me pleasure; there is in his pictures a simple and natural poesy; he is a man who has in his own heart a well of good water where he draws for himself when the streams are mixed with strange soil and bear offensive marks of the bloody battles of life.[3]

The pictures of Leopold Robert I find charming.[4] They are full of vigor and nobleness; they express a nature where all is rich, young and on a large scale. Those that I have seen are so happily expressive of the thoughts and perceptions of early manhood, I can hardly regret he did not live to enter on another stage of life—the impression now received is so single.

---

[1] First published as "Things and Thoughts in Europe. No. XI" in *New-York Daily Tribune*, 31 March 1847, p. 1:1–3.

[2] Antoine-Charles Horace Vernet (1758–1835) painted large battle pieces. His *Battle of Marengo* and *Morning of Austerlitz* are at Versailles (*OCA*).

[3] Hippolyte Delaroche (1797–1856) depicted subjects from English and French history; his best works are small paintings of incidents from the Passion (*OCFL*).

[4] Louis Leopold Robert (1794–1835) was born in Switzerland but studied in France. Many of his paintings are at the Louvre, such as *L'Improvisateur napolitain* (S. Spooner, *A Biographical Dictionary of the Fine Arts* [New York: J.W. Bouton, 1865]).

The effort of the French school in Art, as also its main tendency in Literature, seems to be to turn the mind inside out, in the coarsest acceptation of such
a phrase. Always art is art, only by presenting an adequate outward symbol of
some fact in the interior life. But then it *is* a symbol that Art seeks to present
and not the fact itself. These French painters seem to have no idea of this; they
have not studied the method of Nature. With the true Artist, as with Nature
herself, the more full the representation the more profound and enchanting is
the sense of mystery. We look and look as on a flower of which we cannot scruti-
nize the secret life, yet by looking seem constantly drawn nearer to the soul that
causes and governs that life. But in the French pictures suffering is represented
by streams of blood—wickedness by the most ghastly contortions.

I saw a movement in the opposite direction in England; it was in Turner's
pictures of the later period. It is well known that Turner, so long an idol of the
English public, paints now in a manner which has caused the liveliest dissensions in the world of connoisseurs. There are two parties, one of which main-
tains, not only that the pictures of the late period are not good, but that they
are not pictures at all—that it is impossible to make out the design or find
what Turner is aiming at by those strange blotches of color. The other party
declares that these pictures are not only good but divine—that whoever looks
upon them in the true manner will not fail to find there somewhat ineffably and
transcendently admirable—the soul of Art. Books have been written to defend
this side of the question.[5]

I had become much interested about this matter as the fervor of feeling on
either side seemed to denote that there was something real and vital going on,
and, while time would not permit my visiting other precious collections in London and its neighborhood, I insisted on taking it for one of Turner's pictures. It
was at the house of one of his devoutest disciples, who has arranged everything
in the rooms to harmonize with them.[6] There were a great many of the earlier
period; these seemed to me charming but superficial views of Nature. They
were of a character that he who runs may read—obvious, simple, graceful. The
later pictures were quite a different matter; mysterious looking things—hieroglyphics of picture, rather than picture itself. Sometimes you saw a range of
red dots, which, after long looking, dawned on you as the roofs of houses—
shining streaks turned out to be most alluring rivulets, if traced with patience

[5] John Ruskin's *Modern Painters* was the most famous defense of Joseph Mallord William
Turner (1775–1851). Volumes 1 and 2 of this five-volume work had appeared in 1843
and 1846.

[6] In a letter to an unknown recipient, Fuller refers to visits to private collections of both
Turner's and Clarkson Stanfield's paintings. Stanfield (1793–1867) was known, like Turner,
for his landscape paintings (Hudspeth 4:244–45).

and a devout eye. Above all, they charmed the eye and the thought. Still, these pictures, it seems to me, cannot be considered fine works of Art, more than the mystical writing common to a certain class of minds in the United States can be called good writing. A great work of Art demands a great thought or a thought of beauty adequately expressed.—Neither in Art nor Literature more than in Life can an ordinary thought be made interesting because well-dressed. But in a transition state, whether of Art or Literature, deeper thoughts are imperfectly expressed, because they cannot yet be held and treated masterly. This seems to be the case with Turner. He has got beyond the English gentleman's conventional view of Nature, which implies a *little* sentiment and a *very* cultivated taste; he has become awake to what is elemental, normal, in Nature— such, for instance, as one sees in the working of water on the sea-shore. He tries to represent these primitive forms. In the drawings of Piranesi, in the pictures of Rembrandt, one sees this grand language exhibited more truly.[7] It is not picture, but certain primitive and leading effects of light and shadow, or lines and contours, that captivate the attention. I see a picture of Rembrandt's at the Louvre, whose subject I do not know and have never cared to inquire. I cannot analyze the group, but I understand and feel the thought it embodies. At somewhat similar Turner seems aiming; an aim so opposed to the practical and outward tendency of the English mind, that, as a matter of course, the majority find themselves mystified and thereby angered, but for the same reason answering to so deep and seldom satisfied a want in the minds of the minority as to secure the most ardent sympathy where any at all can be elicited.

Upon this topic of the primitive forms and operations of Nature, I am reminded of something interesting I was looking at yesterday. These are botanical models in wax with microscopic dissections by an artist from Florence, a pupil of Calamajo, the Director of the Wax-Model Museum there. I saw collections of ten different *genera,* or fifty to sixty species of Fungi, mosses and lichens detected and displayed in all the beautiful secrets of their lives; many of them as observed by Dr. Leveille of Paris. The artist told me that a fisherman, introduced to such acquaintance with the marvels of love and beauty which we trample under foot or burn in the chimney each careless day, exclaimed, " 'T is the good God who protects us on the sea that made all that," and a similar recognition, a correspondent feeling, will not be easily evaded by the most callous observer. This artist has supplied many of these models to the magnificent collection of the *Jardin des Plantes,* to Edinburgh and to Bologna, and would fur-

---

[7] Giovanni Battista Piranesi (1720–78) was an etcher, archeologist, and architect whose etchings of ancient and modern Rome shaped the Romantic notions of Rome, especially his *Vedute di Roma* (OCA).

nish them to our Museums at a much cheaper rate than they can elsewhere be obtained. I wish the Universities of Cambridge, New-York, and other leading institutions of our country might avail themselves of the opportunity. Address

"M. Rossi, *Chez* Mr. Dolay, Protestant Library, Rue Tronchet, Paris."

I have not been very fortunate here in meeting the best music. The *Conservatoire,* said to give as fine concerts as there are in the world, has given two or three; but I have not been able to obtain admission; it is very difficult. At the different Opera Houses, the orchestra is always good, but the vocalization, though far superior to what I have heard at home, falls so far short of my ideas and hopes that—except to the Italian Opera—I have not been often. The *Opera Comique* I visited only once; it was tolerably well and no more, and, for myself, I find the tolerable intolerable in music. At the Grand Opera I heard *'Robert le Diable'* and *'Guillaume Tell'* almost with ennui; the decorations and dresses are magnificent, the instrumentation good, but not one fine singer to fill these fine parts. Duprez has had a great reputation, and probably has sung better in former days; still, he has a vulgar mind and can never have had any merit as an artist.[8] At present I find him detestable—he forces his voice, sings in the most coarse, showy style, and aims at producing effects without regard to the harmony of his part; fat and vulgar, he still takes the part of the lover and young chevalier; to my sorrow I saw him in Ravenswood and he has well nigh disenchanted for me "The Bride of Lammermoor."

The Italian Opera is as well sustained, I believe, as any where in the world at present, and there, indeed, all is quite good, but alas! nothing excellent, nothing admirable. Yet no! I must not say nothing: Lablache is excellent—voice, intonation, manner of song, action. Ronconi I found good in the Doctor of *'L'Elisir d'Amore.'* But for the higher parts Grisi, though now much too large for some of her parts, and without a particle of poetic grace or dignity, has certainly beauty of feature, and from Nature a fine voice.[9] But I find her conception of her parts equally coarse and shallow. Her love is the love of a peasant; her anger the rage of a fishwife—though truly, with the Italian picturesque richness and vigor, it is the anger of an Italian fishwife, entirely unlike anything in the same rank elsewhere; her despair is that of a person in the toothache, or who has drawn a blank in the lottery. The first time I saw her was in *'Norma;'* then

[8] Gilbert-Louis Duprez (1806–96) was a premier tenor at the Paris Opéra (Jean Gourret, *Dictionnaire des chanteurs de l'Opéra de Paris* [Paris: Editions Albatross, 1982]). He appeared in both Meyerbeer's *Robert le diable* and Rossini's *Guillaume Tell* (Quaintance Eaton, *Opera Production II: A Handbook* [Minneapolis: University of Minnesota Press, 1977]).

[9] Fuller heard a number of famous opera singers in Paris, including the bass Luigi Lablache, the baritone Giorgio Ronconi, and the soprano Giulia Grisi (Kobbé and *Grove*).

the beauty of her outline, which becomes really enchanting as she recalls the first emotions of love, the force and gush of her song, filled my ear and charmed the senses so that I was pleased, and did not perceive her great defects; but with each time of seeing her I liked her less, and now I do not like her at all.

Persiani is more generally a favorite here; she is indeed skillful both as an actress and in the management of her voice, but I find her expression meretricious, her singing mechanical. Neither of these women is equal to Pico in natural force, if she had but the same advantages of culture and environment. In hearing 'Semiramide' here I first learned to appreciate the degree of talent with which it was cast in New-York.[10] Grisi indeed is a far better Semiramis than Borghese, but the best parts of the Opera lost all their charm from the inferiority of Me. Brambilla, who took Pico's place. Mario has a charming voice, grace and tenderness; he fills very well the part of the young, chivalric lover, but he has no range of power. Coletti is a very good singer; he has not from Nature a fine voice or personal beauty; but he has talent, good taste and often surpasses the expectation he has inspired. Gardoni, the new singer, I have only heard once; that was in a love-sick shepherd part; he showed delicacy, tenderness and tact. In fine, among all these male singers there is much to please, but little to charm; and for the women they never fail absolutely to fill their parts, but no ray of the Muse has fallen on them.[11]

When we first came, there was great talk about a new Opera which Rossini was to give, 'Robert Bruce,' but everybody foreboded it would prove a new Opera made up from his old music, and I understand it is even so.[12] We were anxious to go to the first representation, as all the celebrities of Paris were to be there, and we had not then enjoyed an opportunity of gazing upon them, but the tickets had been taken long beforehand, and one was not to be obtained for less than forty-eight francs, which we declined to pay. After, the accounts I heard of the Opera did not incline me to give an evening to it.

I heard 'The Two Foscari,' Verdi's favorite Opera, and found it is a whole fable, without sufficient *motif*, and wanting in melody. It boasts, however, striking and impressive passages. But I did not find this Composer one of my geniuses.

[10] Fuller had been to a performance of Rossini's *Semiramide* in January or February 1845 and had written about Rosina Pico for the *New-York Daily Tribune* on 14 May 1846, p. 2:2 (Hudspeth 4:50, n.4).

[11] The Brambilla family included three renowned sisters: Marietta (1807–75), a contralto; Teresa (1813–95), a soprano; and Giuseppina (1819–1903), a contralto; [Mario] Giuseppe Comte de Candia (1810–83), a tenor, was a rival of Duprez. Filippo Coletti (1811–94) was an Italian baritone; and Gardoni (known to have performed in the early 1840s) was a tenor (*Grove*; Jean Gourret, *Dictionnaire des chanteurs de l'Opéra de Paris* [Paris: Editions Albatros, 1982]).

[12] At this point in his life, Rossini was in poor health and was doing little new or original work (*Grove*).

Very different is the sincere pleasure given by hearing the *'Barber of Seville'* and *'Don Giovanni.'* After hearing all one's life all this charming music piecemeal, it was so refreshing to get at it at last in its natural order! [13]

'Don Giovanni' conferred on me a benefit, of which certainly its great author never dreamed.—I shall relate it—first begging pardon of Mozart and assuring him I had no thought of turning his music to the account of a "vulgar utility,"— it was quite by accident. After suffering several days very much with the tooth- ache, I resolved to get rid of the cause of sorrow by the aid of the Ether, not sorry, either, to try its efficacy, after all the marvelous stories I had heard. The first time I inhaled it, I did not for several seconds feel the effect, and was just thinking, "Alas! this has not power to soothe nerves so irritable as mine," when suddenly I wandered off, I don't know where, but it was a sensation like wan- dering in long garden walks, and through many alleys of trees, many impres- sions, but all pleasant and serene. The moment the tube was removed I started into consciousness and put my hand to my cheek, but, sad! the throbbing tooth was still there. The dentist said I had not seemed to him insensible. He then gave me the Ether in a stronger dose, and this time I quitted the body instantly, and cannot remember any detail of what I saw and did, but the impression was as in the Oriental tale, where the man has his head in the water an instant only, but in his vision a thousand years seem to have passed. I experienced that same sense of an immense length of time and succession of impressions; even now the moment my mind was in that state seems to me a far longer period in time than my life on earth does as I look back upon it. Suddenly I seemed to see the old dentist as I had for the moment before I inhaled the gas, amid his plants, in his night-cap and dressing-gown; in the twilight the figure had somewhat of a Faust-like, magical air, and he seemed to say *"C'est inutile."* Again I started up, fancying that once more he had not dared to extract the tooth, but it was gone. What is worth noticing is the mental translation I made of his words, which my ear must have caught, for my companion tells me he said *"C'est le moment,"* a phrase of just as many syllables, but conveying just the opposite sense.

Ah! how I wished, then, that you had settled there in the United States who really brought this means of evading a portion of the misery of life into use. But as it was, I remained at a loss whom to apostrophize with my benedictions, whether Dr. Jackson, Morton or Wells, and somebody thus was robbed of his due—neither does Europe know whom to address her medals. [14]

[13] *I due Foscari,* by Verdi, was based on Byron's *The Two Foscari* (*Grove*). The above two paragraphs were omitted in *AHA*.

[14] The first use of ether as a surgical anesthetic was in the United States in 1846 (Roderick E. McGrew and Margaret P. McGrew, *Encyclopedia of Medical History* [New York: McGraw-Hill, 1985], 14–16). Fuller refers to the controversy over the exact order of dis-

However, there is no evading the heavier part of these miseries. You escape the effort of screwing up your courage to one of these moments, and escape the moment of suffering, but not the jar to the whole system. I found the effect of having taken the Ether bad for me. I seemed to taste it all the time, and neuralgic pain continued; this lasted three days yet. In the evening of the third I had taken a ticket to '*Don Giovanni*,' and could not bear to give up this Opera, which I had always been longing to hear; still I was in much suffering, and, as it was the sixth day I had been so, much weakened. However I went, expecting to be obliged to come out; but the music soothed the nerves at once. I hardly suffered at all during the Opera; however, I supposed the pain would return as soon as I came out; but no! it left me from that time. Ah! if physicians only understood the influence of the mind over the body, instead of treating, as they so often do, their patients like machines and according to precedent! But I must pause here for to-day.   ★

Dispatch 12

THE NEED FOR RADICAL REFORM

[Undated] [1]

I bade adieu to Paris the twenty-fifth of February, just as we had had one fine day. It was the only one of really delightful weather, from morning till night, that I had to enjoy all the while I was at Paris, from the thirteenth November till the twenty-fifth February. Let no one abuse our climate; even in Winter it is delightful, compared to the Parisian Winter of mud and mist.

This one fine day brought out the Parisian world in its gayest colors. I never saw anything more animated or prettier, of the kind, than the promenade that day in the *Champs Elysées*. Such crowds of gay equipages, with *cavaliers* and their *amazons* flying through their midst on handsome and swift horses! On the

---

covery and use of ether by Americans. Horace Wells (1815–48), a dentist and anesthesiologist, first tried nitrous oxide on himself in 1844. He botched a demonstration at Harvard, however, and eventually committed suicide. William Thomas Green Morton (1819–68) practiced with Wells in 1842–43 and later worked with Charles A. Jackson (1805–80), a chemist and geologist, who suggested to Morton that ether might be used in tooth extraction in 1846. Morton obtained a patent for sulphuric ether ("letheon") in 1846 and announced "his" discovery to the French Academy of Sciences in December 1846. For the rest of their lives, Jackson and Morton engaged in a controversy over who was the actual discoverer. Fuller was clearly one of the earliest patients on whom ether was used; the first recorded use in France was in Paris, 15 December 1846 (*DAB*).

[1] Published as "Things and Thoughts in Europe. No. XII" in *New-York Daily Tribune*, 15 May 1847, p. 1:1–3.

promenade what groups of passably pretty ladies, with excessively pretty bonnets, announcing in their hues of light green, peach blossom and primrose the approach of Spring, and charming children—for French children are charming. I cannot speak with equal approbation of the files of men sauntering arm in arm; one sees few fine-looking men in Paris: the air half-military, half dandy, of self-esteem and *savoir-faire,* is not particularly interesting; nor are the glassy stare and fumes of bad cigars exactly what one most desires to encounter, when the heart is opened by the breath of Spring zephyrs and the hope of buds and blossoms.

But a French crowd is always gay, full of quick turns and drolleries; most amusing when most petulent, it represents what is so agreeable in the character of the nation. We have now seen it on two good occasions, the festivities of the new year and just after we came was the *mardi gras,* and the procession of the *Fat Ox,* described, if I mistake not, by Eugene Sue.[2] An immense crowd thronged the streets this year to see it, but few figures and little invention followed the emblem of plenty; indeed few among the people could have had the heart for such a sham, knowing how the poorer classes have suffered from hunger this Winter. All signs of this are kept out of sight in Paris. A pamphlet, called "The Voice of Famine," stating facts, though in the tone of vulgar and exaggerated declamation, unhappily common to productions on the Radical side, was suppressed almost as soon as published, but the fact cannot be suppressed that the people in the Provinces have suffered most terribly amid the vaunted prosperity of France.

While Louis Philippe lives, the gases, compressed by his strong grasp, may not burst up to light; but the need of some radical measures of reform is not less strongly felt in France than elsewhere, and the time will come before long when such will be imperatively demanded.[3] The doctrines of Fourier are making considerable progress, and wherever they spread the necessity of some practical application of the precepts of Christ, in lieu of the mummeries of a worn-out ritual, cannot fail to be felt. The more I see of the terrible ills which infests the body politic of Europe, the more indignation I feel at the selfishness or stupidity of those in my own country who oppose an examination of these subjects— such as is animated by the hope of prevention. The mind of Fourier is, in many

---

[2] Eugène Sue was immensely popular as a chronicler of Parisian low life. Fuller probably refers to *Les Mystères de Paris,* which was serialized from 1842 to 1843 (*OCFL*).

[3] Fuller visited France during an uneasy time. Louis-Philippe (1773–1850), the "citizen king," who had come to power on 9 August 1830, was increasingly unpopular with a middle class anxious for societal and political reforms. With Guizot, whom he appointed as foreign minister in 1840, Louis-Philippe maintained a precarious control until he was forced to abdicate on 24 February 1848 (Newman).

respects, uncongenial to mine. Educated in an age of gross materialism, he is tainted by its faults; in attempts to reorganize society, he commits the error of making soul the result of health of body, instead of body the clothing of soul— but his heart was that of a genuine lover of his kind, of a philanthropist in the sense of Jesus—his views are large and noble,—his life was one of devout study on these subjects, and we should pity the person who, after the briefest sojourn in Manchester and Lyons—the most superficial acquaintance with the population of London and Paris,—could seek to hinder a study of his thoughts or be wanting in reverence for his purposes. But always, always, the unthinking mob has found stones on the highway to throw at the prophets.

Amid so many great causes for thought and anxiety, how childish has seemed the endless gossip of the Parisian press on the subject of the Spanish marriage— how melancholy the flimsy falsehoods of M. Guizot—more melancholy the avowal so naïvely made, amid those falsehoods that to his mind expediency is the best policy. This is the policy, said he, that has made France so prosperous.—Indeed, the success is correspondent with the means though in quite another sense than that he meant. I went to the *Hotel des Invalides,* supposing I should be admitted to the spot where repose the ashes of Napoleon, for though I love not pilgrimages to sepulchres, and prefer paying my homage to the living spirit, rather than to the dust it once animated, I should have liked to muse a moment beside his urn, but as yet the visiter is not admitted there. But in the library one sees the picture of Napoleon crossing the Alps, opposite to that of the present King of the French. Just as they are they should serve as frontispieces to two chapters of history.—In the first, the seed was sewn in a field of blood indeed, but the seed of all that is vital in the present period. By Napoleon the career was really laid open to talent, and all that is really great in France now consists in the possibility that talent finds of struggling to the light. Paris is a great intellectual center, and there is a Chamber of Deputies to represent the people very different from the poor, limited Assembly politically so called. Their tribune is that of literature, and one needs not to beg tickets to mingle with the audience. To the actually so-called Chamber of Deputies I was indebted for two pleasures. First and greatest, a sight of the manuscripts of Rousseau treasured in their Library.[4] I saw them and touched them—those manuscripts just as he has celebrated them, written on the fine white paper, tied with ribbon—yellow and faded age has made them, yet at their touch I seemed

---

[4] Rousseau was an important precursor to the romantic movement because of his focus on sentiment and his celebration of man in his natural, as opposed to civilized, state. The writers of the American renaissance were quite familiar with Rousseau's writings, especially his *Confessions* (1781–88).

to feel the fire of youth, immortally glowing, more and more expansive, with which his soul has pervaded this century. He was the precursor of all we most prize; true, his blood was mixed with madness, and the course of his actual life made some detours through villanous places, but his spirit was intimate with the fundamental truths of human nature, and fraught with prophecy: there is none who has given birth to more life for this age; his gifts are yet untold; they are too present with us; but he who thinks really must often think with Rousseau, and learn him even more and more: such is the method of genius to ripen fruit for the crowd by those rays of whose heat they complain.

The second pleasure was in the speech of M. Berryer, when the Chamber was discussing the address to the King. Those of Thiers and Guizot had been, so far, more interesting, as they stood for more that was important—but M. Berryer is the most eloquent speaker of the House.[5] His oratory is, indeed, very good, not logical, but plausible, full and rapid, with occasional bursts of flame and showers of sparks, though indeed no stone of size and weight enough to crush any man was thrown out by the crater. Although the oratory of our country is very inferior to what might be expected from the perfect freedom and powerful motive for development of genius in this province, it presents several examples of persons superior in both force and scope and equal in polish to M. Berryer.

Nothing can be more pitiful than the manner in which the infamous affair of Cracow is treated on all hands.[6] There is not even the affectation of noble feeling about it. La Mennais and his coadjutors published in *La Reforme* an honorable and manly Protest, which the public rushed to devour the moment it was out of the press—and no wonder! for it was the only crumb of comfort offered to those who have the nobleness to hope that the confederation of nations may yet be conducted on the basis of divine justice and human right. Most men who touched the subject, apparently weary of feigning, appeared in their genuine colors of the calmest, most complacent selfishness. As described by Körner in the prayer of such a man:

"O God, save me
Thy wife, child, and hearth,
Then my harvest also;

[5] Pierre-Antoine Berryer (1790–1868), lawyer and politician, entered the Chamber of Deputies in 1830. He earned a reputation as an outstanding orator. In 1848 he was elected to the Constituent Assembly of the Second Republic. Louis-Adolphe Thiers (1797–1877) occupied a central position in French political life from the early 1820s through the 1870s (Newman).

[6] The Republic of Cracow, the last vestige of free Poland, was absorbed by Austria in March 1846 (Robertson 201).

Then will I bless thee,
Though thy lightning scorch to
    blackness all the
rest of human kind."[7]

A sentiment which finds its paraphrase in the following vulgate of our land:

"O Lord, save me,
My wife, child, and brother Sammy,
Us four *and no more.*"

The latter clause, indeed, is not quite frankly avowed as yet by politicians.

It is very amusing to be in the Chamber of Deputies when some dull person is speaking. The French have a truly Greek vivacity; they cannot endure to be bored. Though their conduct is not very dignified, I should like a corps of the same kind of sharp-shooters in our legislative assemblies when honorable gentlemen are addressing their constituents and not the assembly, repeating in lengthy, windy, clumsy paragraphs what has been the truism of the newspaper press for months previous, wickedly wasting the time that was given us to learn something for ourselves, and help our fellow creatures. In the French Chamber, if a man who has nothing to say ascends the tribune, the audience swarm with the noise of a myriad bee-hives; the President rises on his feet, and passes the whole time of the speech in taking the most violent exercise, stretching himself to look imposing, ringing his bell every two minutes, shouting to the Representatives of the Nation to be decorous and attentive, in vain. The more he rings, the more they won't be still. I saw an orator in this situation, fighting against the desires of the audience, as only a Frenchman could—certainly a man of any other nation would have died of embarrassment rather—screaming out his sentences, stretching out both arms with an air of injured dignity, panting, growing red in the face, the hubbub of voices were stopped an instant. At last he pretended to be exhausted, stopped and took out his snuff-box. Instantly there was a calm. He seized the occasion, and shouted out a sentence; but it was the only one he was able to make heard. They were not to be trapped so a second time. When any one is speaking that commands interest, as Berryer did, the effect of this vivacity is very pleasing; the murmur of feeling that rushes over the

---

[7] Karl Theodor Körner (1791–1813) was a poet and playwright, the son of Schiller's friend and biographer Christian Gottfried Körner (*OCGL*). Fuller's translations of some of Körner's poems were published as "Dissatisfaction. Translated from Theodore Körner" in *Life Without and Life Within,* ed. Arthur B. Fuller (Boston: Brown, Taggard and Chase, 1860), 377–78. She also published an essay on Körner in the *Western Messenger* 4 (1838):306–11 and 369–75.

assembly is so quick and electric—light, too, as the ripple on the lake. I heard Guizot speak one day for a short time. His manner is very deficient in dignity—has not even the dignity of station; you see the man of cultivated intellect, but without inward strength, nor is even his panoply of proof.

I saw in the Library of Deputies some books intended to be sent to our country through M. Vattemare. The French have shown great readiness and generosity with regard to his project, and I earnestly hope that our country, if it accept these tokens of good-will, will show both energy and judgment in making a return. I do not speak from myself alone, but from others whose opinion is entitled to the highest respect, when I say it is not by sending a great quantity of documents of merely local interest, that would be esteemed lumber in our garrets at home, that you pay respect to a nation able to look beyond the binding of a book. If anything is to be sent, let persons of ability be deputed to make a selection honorable to us and of value to the French. They would like documents from our Congress—what is important as to commerce and manufactures; they would also like much what can throw light on the history and character of our Aborigines. This project of international exchange could not be carried on to any permanent advantage without accredited agents on either side, but in its present shape it wears an aspect of good feeling that is valuable and may give a very desirable impulse to thought and knowledge. M. Vattemare has given himself to the plan with indefatigable perseverance, and I hope our country will not be backward to accord him that furtherance he has known how to conquer from his countrymen.

To his complaisance I was indebted for opportunity of a leisurely survey of the *Imprimeri Royale,* which gave me several suggestions I shall impart at a more favorable time, and of the operations of the Mint also. It was at his request that the Librarian of the Chamber showed me the manuscripts of Rousseau, which are not always seen by the stranger. He also introduced me to one of the Evening Schools of the *Frères Chrétiens,* where I saw, with pleasure, how much can be done for the working classes, only by evening lessons. In reading and writing, adults had made surprising progress, and still more so in drawing. I saw with the highest pleasure, excellent copies of good models made by hard-handed porters and errand-boys with their brass badges on their breasts. The benefits of such an accomplishment are, in my eyes, of the highest value, giving them, by insensible degrees, their part in the glories of art and science, in the tranquil refinements of home. Visions rose in my mind of all that might be done in our country by associations of men and women who have received the benefits of literary culture giving such evening lessons throughout our cities and villages. Should I ever return, I shall propose to some of the like-minded, an association for such a purpose, and try the experiment of one of these schools of Christian

brothers with the vow of disinterestedness, but without the robe and the subdued priestly manner, which even in these men, some of whom seemed to me
truly good, I could not away with.

I visited also a Protestant institution called that of the Deaconesses, which
pleased me in some respects. Beside the regular *Crèche,* they take the sick children of the poor, and nurse them till they are well. They have also a refuge like
that of the Home which the ladies of New-York have provided, through which
members of the most unjustly treated class of society may return to peace and
usefulness. There are institutions of the kind in Paris, but too formal—and the
treatment shows ignorance of human nature. I see nothing that shows so enlightened a spirit as The Home, a little germ of good which I hope flourishes
and finds active aid in the community. I remember that last year much regret
was felt that application had not been made previous to the general breaking-
up of the 1st of May for such gifts of household stuff as families are usually glad
to spare from their transit, and the humblest of which would be useful there.
I hope the appeal has been made this year. I am sure it would be effectual in
many instances. I have collected many facts with regard to this suffering class of
women, both in England and in France. I have seen them under the thin veil of
gayety, and in the horrible tatters of utter degradation. I have seen the hearts
of men with regard to their condition and a general heartlessness in women of
more favored and protected lives, which I can only ascribe to utter ignorance of
the facts. If a proclamation of some of them can remove it, I hope to make such
a one in the hour of riper judgment, and after a more extensive survey.

Sad as are many features of the time, we have at least the satisfaction of feeling that if something true can be revealed—if something wise and kind shall be
perseveringly tried, it stands a chance of nearer success than ever before—for
much light has been let in at the windows of the world, and many dark nooks
have been touched by a consoling ray. The influence of such a one I felt in visiting
the School for Idiots, near Paris. Idiots, so called long time by the impatience
of the crowd—for there are really none such, but only beings so below the aver-
age standard, so partially organized that it is difficult for them to learn or to
sustain themselves. I wept the whole time I was in this place a shower of sweet
and bitter tears, of joy at what had been done, grief for all that I and others
possess and cannot impart to these little ones. But patience, and the Father of
All will give them all yet. A good angel these of Paris have in their master; I
have seen no man that seemed to me more worthy of envy, if one could envy
happiness so pure and tender. He is a man of seven or eight-and-twenty, who
formerly came there only to give lessons in writing, but became so interested in
his charge that he came at last to live among them and to serve them. They sing
the hymns he writes for them, and as I saw his fine countenance looking in love

on those distorted and opaque vases of humanity, where he had succeeded in waking up a faint flame, I thought his heart could never fail to be well-warmed and buoyant. They sang well, both in parts and in chorus, went through gymnastic exercises with order and pleasure, then stood in a circle and kept time, while several danced extremely well. One little fellow, with whom the difficulty seemed to be that an excess of nervous sensibility paralyzed instead of exciting the powers, recited poems with a touching childish grace and perfect memory. They wrote well, drew well, make shoes and do carpenters' work. One of the cases most interesting to the metaphysician is that of a boy, brought there about two years and a half ago, at the age of thirteen, in a state of brutality—and of ferocious brutality. I read the Physician's report of him at that period: he discovered no ray of decency or reason; entirely beneath the animals in the exercise of the senses; he discovered a restless fury beyond that of beasts of prey, breaking and throwing down whatever came in his way, was a voracious glutton, and every way grossly sensual. Many trials and vast patience were necessary before an inlet could be obtained to his mind; then it was through the means of mathematics. He delights in the figures, can draw and name then all, detects them by the touch when blindfolded. Each mental gesture of the kind he still follows up with an imbecile chuckle; as indeed his face and whole manner are still that of an idiot, but he has been raised from his sensual state, and can now discriminate and name colors and perfumes which before were all alike to him. He is partially redeemed; earlier, no doubt, far more might have been done for him, but the degree of success is an earnest which must encourage to perseverance in the most seemingly hopeless cases. I thought sorrowfully of the persons of this class whom I have known in our country, who might have been so raised and solaced by similar care. I hope ample provision may ere long be made for these Pariahs of the human race; every case of the kind brings its blessings with it, and observation of these subjects would be as rich in suggestion for the thought as such acts of love are balmy for the heart.[8]   ★

---

[8] Here Fuller reflects the late eighteenth- and early nineteenth-century fascination with the "idiot" child. According to Alan Bewell, such a child was "a privileged object of observation and commentary in the heated arguments of philosophers and theologians concerning the origins and conditions of language and memory and their role in defining man" (*Wordsworth and the Enlightenment: Nature, Man, and Society in the Experimental Poetry* [New Haven: Yale University Press, 1989], 57).

Dispatch 13

FROM PARIS TO NAPLES

[Undated][1]

In the last days at Paris I was fortunate in hearing some delightful music. A friend of Chopin's took me to see him, and I had the pleasure, which the delicacy of his health makes a rare one for the public, of hearing him play.[2] All the impressions I had received from hearing his music imperfectly performed were justified, for it has marked traits which can be veiled but not travestied: but to feel it as it merits, one must hear himself; only a person as exquisitely organized as he can adequately express these subtle secrets of the creative spirit.

It was with a very different sort of pleasure that I listened to the Chevalier Neukomm, the celebrated composer of "David," which has been so popular in our country.[3] I heard him improvise on the *Orgue Expressif,* and afterward on a great organ which has just been built here by Cavaillé[4] for the Cathedral of Ajaccio. Full, sustained, ardent, yet exact, the stream of his thought bears with it the attention of hearers of all characters, as his character, full of *bonhommie,* open, friendly, animated and sagacious, would seem to have something to present for the affection and esteem of all kinds of men. One was the minstrel, the other the orator of music: we want them both—the mysterious whispers and the resolute pleadings from the better world which calls us not to slumber here, but press daily onward to claim all our heritage.

Paris! I was sad to leave thee, thou wonderful focus, where ignorance ceases to be a pain, because there we find such means daily to lessen it.[5] It is the only school where I ever found abundance of teachers who could bear being examined by the pupil in their special branches. I must go to this school more before I again cross the Atlantic, where often for years I have carried about some

---

[1] First published as "Things and Thoughts in Europe. No. XIII" in *New-York Daily Tribune,* 29 May 1847, p. 1:1–2.

[2] Johanna [Jane] Wilhelmina Stirling, a student of Chopin, took Fuller to hear the pianist play on 14 February 1847. Chopin was a lover of George Sand, with whom Fuller became friendly (*OCM;* Hudspeth 4:261–62 and 5:53–54).

[3] Sigsimund von Neukomm (1778–1858) was an Austrian pianist and composer who wrote the oratorio *David,* first performed in England in 1834 (*OCM*). Fuller heard him play in the company of Jane Stirling, referring to him in a letter as the "dear kind Chevalier" (Hudspeth 4:261–62 and 5:54).

[4] Aristide Cavaillé-Col (1811–99) built nearly 500 organs for cathedrals in France, Spain, and South America (Stanley Sadie, ed., *The New Grove Dictionary of Musical Instruments,* 3 vols. [London: Macmillan, 1984]).

[5] Fuller and the Springs left Paris for Italy on 25 February 1847.

trifling question without finding the person who could answer it. Really deep questions we must all answer for ourselves—the more the pity not to get more quickly through with a crowd of details, where the experience of others might accelerate our progress.

Parting by *diligence,* we pursued our way from twelve o'clock on Thursday till twelve at night on Friday, thus having a large share of magnificent moonlight upon the unknown fields we were traversing. At Chalons we took boat and reached Lyons betimes that afternoon. So soon as refreshed, we sallied out to visit some of the garrets of the weavers. As we were making inquiries about these, a sweet little girl who heard us offered to be our guide. She led us by a weary, winding way, whose pavement was much easier for her feet in their wooden *sabots* than for ours in Paris shoes, to the top of a hill from which we saw for the first time "the blue and arrowy Rhone."[6] Entering the high buildings on this high hill, I found each chamber tenanted by a family of weavers, all weavers, wife, husband, sons, daughters—from nine years old upward—each was helping. On one side were the looms, nearer the door the cooking apparatus, the beds were shelves near the ceiling: they climbed up to them on ladders. My sweet little girl turned out to be a wife of six or seven years' standing, with two rather sickly looking children; she seemed to have the greatest comfort that is possible amid the perplexities of a hard and anxious lot, to judge by the proud and affectionate manner in which she always said "mon maré," and by the courteous gentleness of his manner toward her.—She seemed, indeed, to be one of those persons on whom "the Graces have smiled in their cradle" and to whom a natural loveliness of character makes the world as easy as it can be made while the evil spirit is still so busy choking the wheat with tares. I admired her graceful manner of introducing us into those dark little rooms, and she was affectionately received by all her acquaintance. But alas! that voice, by nature of such bird-like vivacity, repeated again and again, "Ah! we are all very unhappy now." "Do you sing together or go to evening schools?" "We have not the heart.—When we have a piece of work we do not stir till it is finished, and then we run to try and get another; but often we have to wait idle for weeks.— It grows worse and worse, and they say it is not likely to be any better. We can think of nothing but whether we shall be able to pay our rent. Ah! the workpeople are very unhappy now." This poor, lovely little girl, at an age when the merchants' daughters of Boston and New-York are just making their first experiences of "society," knew the price of every article of food and clothing that is

[6] Fuller and the Springs followed a similar route through the countryside of France as that of Charles Dickens, whose *Pictures from Italy* was published in 1846. Fuller may be echoing Dickens's description of the "Arrowy Rhone" in *American Notes and Pictures from Italy* (New York: Oxford University Press, 1957), 271.

wanted by such a household to a farthing, her thought by day and her dream by night was, whether she should long be able to procure a scanty supply of these, and Nature had gifted her with precisely those qualities, which, unembarrassed by care, would have made her and all she loved really happy, and she was fortunate now, compared with many of her sex in Lyons—of whom a gentleman who knows the class well said to me, "When their work fails they have no resource except in the sale of their persons. There are but these two ways open to them, of weaving or prostitution to gain their bread." And there are those who dare to say that such a state of things is *well enough,* and what Providence intended for man—who call those who have hearts to suffer at the sight, energy and zeal to seek its remedy, visionaries and fanatics! To themselves be woe, who have eyes and see not, ears and hear not, the convulsions and sobs of injured Humanity!

My little friend told me she had nursed both her children—though almost all of her class are obliged to put their children out to nurse; "but," said she, "they are brought back so little, so miserable, that I resolved, if possible, to keep mine with me."—Next day in the steamboat I read a pamphlet by a physician of Lyons in which he recommends the establishment of *Crèches* not merely, like those of Paris, to keep the children by day, but to provide wet nurses for them. Thus by the infants receiving nourishment from more healthy persons, and who, under the supervision of directors, would treat them well, he hopes to counteract the tendency to degenerate in this race of sedentary workers, and to save the mothers from too heavy a burden of care and labor, without breaking the bond between them and their children, whom, under such circumstances, they could visit often and see them taken care of—as they, brought up to know nothing except how to weave, cannot take care of them.—Here, again, how is one reminded of Fourier's observations and plans, still more enforced by the recent developments at Manchester as to the habit of feeding children on opium, which has grown out of the position of things there.

Descending next day to Avignon, I had the mortification of finding the banks of the Rhone still sheeted with white, and there waded through melting snow to Laura's tomb.[7] We did not see Mr. Dickens's Tower and Goblin; it was too late in the day—but we saw a snow-ball fight between two bands of the military in the Castle-yard that was gay enough to make a goblin laugh.[8] And next

[7] Laura de Noves of Avignon is thought to be the woman to whom Petrarch addressed his poems (Hudspeth 4:262; Bondanella).

[8] Fuller refers to Dickens's humorous account of his tour of the ruins of the Palace of the Popes, where the Inquisition conducted its inquiries and persecutions. The "Goblin" was the name Dickens gave to his guide, "A little old, swarthy woman, with a pair of flashing black eyes—proof that the world hadn't conjured down the devil within her," who took a fiendish delight in showing Dickens through the dank dungeons and the tower that housed the executioner of the Inquisition (*American Notes and Pictures from Italy,* 270–78).

day, on to Arles, still snow, snow and cutting blasts in the South of France, where everybody had promised us bird-songs and blossoms to console us for the dreary winter of Paris. At Arles, indeed, I saw the little saxifrage blossoming on the steps of the Amphitheatre, and fruit-trees in flower amid the tombs. Here was the first time I saw the great hand-writing of the Romans in its proper medium of stone, and I was content. It looked as grand and solid as I expected, as if life in those days was thought worth the having, the enjoying and the using. The sunlight was warm this day; it lay deliciously still and calm upon the ruins. One old woman sat knitting where twenty-five thousand persons once gazed down in fierce excitement on the fights of men and lions. Coming back, we were refreshed all through the streets by the sight of the women of Arles. They answered to their reputation for beauty; tall, erect and noble, with high and dignified features, and a full, earnest gaze of the eye, they looked as if the Eagle still waved its wings over their city. Even the very old women still have a degree of beauty, because when the colors are all faded and the skin wrinkled, the face retains this dignity of outline. The men do not share in these charac-teristics; some Priestess, well beloved of the powers of old religion, must have called down an especial blessing on her sex in this town.

Hence to Marseilles—where is little for the traveler to see, except the mix-ture of Oriental blood in the crowd of the streets. Thence by steamer to Genoa. Of this transit, he who has been on the Mediterranean in a stiff breeze well understands I can have nothing to say, except "I suffered." It was all one dull, tormented dream to me and, I believe, to most of the ship's company—a dream too of thirty hours' duration, instead of the promised sixteen.

The excessive beauty of Genoa is well known, and the impression upon the eye alone was correspondent with what I expected, but, alas! the weather was still so cold I could not realize that I had actually touched those shores to which I had looked forward all my life, where it seemed that the heart would expand, and the whole nature be turned to delight. Seen by a cutting wind, the marble palaces, the gardens, the magnificent water-view of Genoa failed to charm, "I *saw, not felt,* how beautiful they were." Only at Naples have I found *my* Italy, and here not till after a week's waiting—not till I began to believe that all I had heard in praise of the climate of Italy was fable, and that there is really no Spring anywhere except in the imagination of poets. For the first week was an exact copy of the miseries of a New-England Spring; a bright sun came for an hour or two in the morning just to flatter you forth without your cloak, and then—and then—came up a villanous, horrible wind, exactly like the worst East wind of Boston, breaking the heart, racking the brain and turning hope and fancy to an irrevocable green and yellow hue in lieu of their native rose.

However, here at Naples I *have* at last found *my* Italy; I have passed through the Grotto of Pausilippo, visited Cuma, Baia, and Capri—ascended Vesuvius, and found all familiar, except the sense of enchantment, of sweet exhilaration this scene conveys.

"Behold how brightly breaks the morning!"

and yet all new, as if never described, for Nature here, most prolific and exuberant in her gifts, has touched them all with a charm unhackneyed, unhackneyable, which the boots of English dandies cannot trample out, nor the raptures of sentimental tourists daub or fade. Baia had still a hid divinity for me, Vesuvius a fresh baptism of fire, and Sorrento—oh Sorrento was beyond picture, beyond poesy, for the greatest Artist had been at work there in a temper beyond the reach of human art.

Beyond this, reader, my old friend and valued acquaintance on other themes, I shall tell you nothing of Naples, for it is a thing apart in the journey of life, and, if represented at all, should be so in a fairer form than offers itself at present. Now the actual life here is over, I am going to Rome, and expect to see that fane of thought the last day of this week.

At Genoa and Leghorn, I saw for the first time Italians in their homes. Very attractive I found them, charming women, refined men, eloquent and courteous.[9] If the cold wind hid Italy, it could not the Italians. A little group of faces, each so full of character, dignity, and what is so rare in an American face, the capacity for pure, exalting passion, will live ever in my memory—the fulfillment of a hope!

We came from Leghorn in an English boat, highly recommended, and as little deserving of such praise as many another bepuffed article. In the middle of a fine, clear night, she was run into by the mail steamer, which all on deck perfectly saw coming upon her, for no reason that could be ascertained except that the man at the wheel said *he* had turned the right way, and it never seemed to occur to him that he could change when he found the other steamer had taken the same direction. To be sure the other steamer was equally careless, but as a change on our part would have prevented an accident that narrowly missed sending us all to the bottom, it hardly seemed worth while to persist for the sake of convicting them of error.

Neither the Captain nor any of his people spoke French, and we had been much amused before by the chambermaid acting out the old story of "Will you lend me the loan of a gridiron?" A Polish lady was on board with a French

---

[9] One of these women was Mazzini's mother, Maria, whom Fuller and the Springs visited in Genoa. Maria Mazzini was so taken with Fuller that she wrote her son hinting that he should consider marriage to her (Chevigny 422).

waiting-maid, who understood no word of English. The daughter of John Bull would speak to the lady in English, and, when she found it of no use, would say imperiously to the *suivante*—"Go and ask your mistress what she will have for breakfast." And now when I went on deck there was a parley between the two steamers, which the Captain was obliged to manage by such interpreters as he could find; it was a long and confused business. It ended at last in the Neapolitan steamer taking us in tow for an inglorious return to Leghorn. When she had decided upon this she swept round, her lights glancing like sagacious eyes, to take us. The sea was calm as a lake; the sky full of stars; she made a long detour with her black hull, her smoke and lights, which look so pretty at night, then came round to us like the bend of an arm embracing. It was a pretty picture, worth the stop and the fright—perhaps the loss of twenty-four hours, though I did not think so at the time. At Leghorn we changed the boat, and, retracing our steps, came now at last to Naples,—to this priest-ridden, misgoverned, full of dirty, degraded men and women, yet still most lovely Naples,—of which the most I can say is that the divine aspect of Nature *can* make you forget the situation of Man in this region, which was surely intended for him as a princely child, angelic in virtue, genius and beauty, and not as a begging, vermin-haunted, image-kissing Lazzarone.[10]   ★

Dispatch 14

ART, POLITICS, AND THE HOPE OF ROME

ROME, May 1847[1]

There is very little that I can like to write about Italy. Italy is beautiful, worthy to be loved and embraced, not talked about. Yet I remember well that when afar I liked to read what was written about her; now all thought of it is very tedious.[2]

The traveler passing along the beaten track, vetturinoed from inn to inn, ciceroned from gallery to gallery, thrown, through indolence, want of tact, or ignorance of the language, too much into the society of his compatriots, sees

---

[10] A loafer or vagabond.

[1] First published as "Things and Thoughts in Europe. No. XIV" in *New-York Daily Tribune*, 31 July 1847, p. 1:1–3.

[2] Fuller had been fascinated with Italy for years and was quite familiar with travel literature about the country; in a letter to Caroline Sturgis, she mentions reading Beckford's *Italy: with Sketches of Spain and Portugal* (1834) (Hudspeth 1:298).

the least possible of the country; fortunately, it is impossible to avoid seeing a great deal. The great features of the past pursue and fill the eye.

Yet I find that it is quite out of the question to know Italy; to say anything of her that is full and sweet, so as to convey any idea of her spirit, without long residence, and residence in the districts untouched by the scorch and dust of foreign invasion, (the invasion of the dilettanti I mean,) and without an intimacy of feeling, an abandonment to the spirit of the place, impossible to most Americans; they retain too much of their English blood; and the traveling English, as a tribe, seem to me the most unseeing of all possible animals. There are exceptions; for instance, the perceptions and pictures of Browning seem as delicate and just here on the spot as they did at a distance; but, take them as a tribe, they have the vulgar familiarity of Mrs. Trollope without her vivacity, the cockneyism of Dickens without his graphic power and love of the odd corners of human nature.[3] I admired the English at home in their island; I admired their honor, truth, practical intelligence, persistent power. But they do not look well in Italy; they are not the figures for this landscape. I am indignant at the contempt they have presumed to express for the faults of our semi-barbarous state. What is the vulgarity expressed in our tobacco-chewing, and way of eating eggs, compared to that which elbows the Greek marbles, guide-book in hand—chatters and sneers through the Miserere of the Sistine Chapel, beneath the very glance of Michel Angelo's Sibyls,—praises St. Peter's as *"nice,"* talks of *"managing"* the Colosseum by moonlight,—and snatches *"bits"* for a *"sketch"* from the sublime silence of the Campagna.

Yet I was again reconciled with them, the other day, in visiting the studio of Macdonald.[4] There I found a complete gallery of the aristocracy of England, for each lord and lady who visited Rome has considered it a part of the ceremony to sit to him for a bust. And what a fine race! how worthy the marble! what heads of orators, statesmen, gentlemen; of women chaste, grave, resolute and tender! Unfortunately they do not look as well in flesh and blood; then they show the habitual coldness of their temperament, the habitual subservience to frivolous conventions; they need some great occasion, some crisis, to excite them, to make them look as free and dignified as these busts; yet is the beauty

[3] In a letter to Evert A. Duyckinck, Fuller comments, "Admirable as Browning's sketches of Italian scenery and character seemed before, they seem far finer now that I am close to the objects. The best representation of the spirit of Italy which our day affords. It is difficult to speak with any truth of Italy: it requires *genius, talent,* which is made to serve most purposes now, entirely fails here" (Hudspeth 4:272).

[4] Lawrence Macdonald (1799–1878), a sculptor, who with others established the British Academy of Arts in Rome in 1823. He executed a bust of Scott (1831) and many other public figures (*DNB*).

there, though imprisoned and clouded—and such a crisis would show us more than one Boadicea, more than one Alfred. Tenerani has just completed a statue which is highly spoken of; it is called the Angel of the Resurrection.[5] I was not so fortunate as to find it in his studio. In that of Wolff I saw a Diana, ordered by the Emperor of Russia. It is modern and sentimental; as different from the antique Diana as the trance of a novel-read young lady of our day from the thrill with which the ancient shepherds deprecated the magic pervasions of Hecate, but very beautiful and exquisitely wrought. He has also lately finished the Four Seasons, represented as children. Of these, Winter is graceful and charming.

Among the sculptors I delayed longest in the work-rooms of Gott.[6] I found his groups of young figures connected with animals very refreshing after the grander attempts of the present time. They seem real growths of his habitual mind—fruits of Nature, full of joy and freedom. His spaniels and other frisky poppets would please Apollo far better than most of the marble nymphs and muses of the present day.

Our Crawford has just finished a bust of Mrs. Crawford, which is extremely beautiful, full of grace and innocent sweetness.[7] All its accessories are charming—the wreaths, the arrangement of drapery, the stuff of which the robe is made. I hope it will be much seen on its arrival in New York. He has also a Herodias in the clay, which is individual in expression, and the figure of distinguished elegance. I liked the designs of Crawford better than those of Gibson, who is estimated as highest in the profession now.[8]

Among the studios of the European painters I have visited only that of Overbeck.[9] It is well known in the United States what his pictures are. I have much to say at a more favorable time of what they represented to me. He himself looks as if he had just stepped out of one of them,—a lay monk, with a pious eye and habitual morality of thought which limits every gesture.

Painting is not largely represented here by American artists at present. Terry has two pleasing pictures on the easel; one is a costume picture of Italian life,

[5] The sculptor Pietro Tenerani (1789–1869) lived in Rome (Giuliano Dogo, *Treasures of Italy* [New York: Norton, 1976]).

[6] Joseph Gott (1785–1860), a sculptor, was a student at the Royal Academy and was sent to Rome with the help of patrons (*DNB*).

[7] Thomas Crawford (1813–57) was an American sculptor of Irish descent. His works include the equestrian *George Washington* (1857) in Richmond, Virginia, and *The Armed Liberty* (1860) on top of the Capitol dome in Washington, D.C. (*OCA*).

[8] John Gibson (1790–1866) was an English sculptor from Liverpool who spent most of his life in Rome (*OCA*).

[9] Friedrich Overbeck (1789–1869) was a German painter who converted to Catholicism in 1813 and made extensive use of religious symbolism in his work (*OCA*).

such as I saw it myself, enchanted beyond my hopes, as coming from Naples I approached Santa Agatha a day of *gran festa*.[10] Cranch sends soon to America a picture of the Campagna, such as I saw it on my first entrance into Rome, all light and calmness.[11] Hicks, a charming half-length of an Italian girl, holding a mandolin: it will be sure to please; his pictures are full of life, and give the promise of some real achievement in Art.[12]

Of the fragments of the great time, I have now seen nearly all that are treasured up here; I have, however, as yet nothing of consequence to say of them. I find that others have often given good hints as to how they *look*; and as to what they *are,* it can only be known by approximating to the state of soul out of which they grew. They should not be described, but reproduced. They are many and precious, yet is there not so much of high excellence as I had expected: they will not float the heart on a boundless sea of feeling, like the starry night on our Western Prairie. Yet I love much to see the galleries of marbles, even when there are not many separately admirable, amid the cypresses and ilexes of Roman villas; and a picture that is good at all looks very good in one of these old palaces.

The Italian painters whom I have learned most to appreciate, since I came abroad, are Dominichino and Titian. Of others one may learn something by copies and engravings: but not of these. The portraits of Titian look upon me from the walls things new and strange. They are portraits of men such as I have not known. In his picture, absurdly called *Sacred and Profane Love,* in the Bor-

[10] Luther Terry (1813–69) was a portrait and figure painter who settled permanently in Rome in 1838 (Groce).

[11] Christopher Pearse Cranch (1813–92), a poet and painter, left the Unitarian ministry in 1840 and went to live in Italy from 1846 to 1849 (Groce). Fuller had known Cranch since her years in Boston; a former Brook Farmer, Cranch admired Fuller and saw her often during her time in Rome. She reviewed his *Poems* in the *Tribune* (12 December 1844, p. 1:1), and after her death he wrote a poem celebrating her heroism (see *Collected Poems of Christopher Pearse Cranch,* ed. Joseph M. DeFalco [Gainesville, Fla.: Scholars' Facsimiles and Reprints, 1971], 167–68).

[12] Thomas Hicks (1823–90), a portrait and landscape painter, went abroad in 1845 to study in London, Florence, and Rome; he returned to New York in 1849 (Groce). Soon after meeting the twenty-three-year-old Hicks, Fuller apparently fell in love with him and sent him a letter declaring her feelings and asking for an answer. Claiming to be too old at heart for her, he replied, "It is you who are young for every pulse of your being is full and warm with Love. Why would you be endeared to me? I am the child of autumn. . . . Do you not see that I cannot make you happy? May I hope not to offend you in writing so?" The two remained friends; during the siege of Rome Hicks painted Fuller's portrait and later refused to part with it or with her letters (Chevigny 423–25).

ghese Palace, one of the figures has developed my powers of gazing to an extent unknown before.[13]

Dominichino seems very unequal in his pictures; but when he is grand and free, the energy of his genius perfectly satisfies. The frescoes of Carracci and his scholars in the Farnese Palace have been to me a source of the purest pleasure, and I do not remember to have heard of them.[14] I loved Guercino much before I came here, but I have looked too much at his pictures and begin to grow sick of them; he is a very limited genius.[15] Leonardo I cannot yet like at all, but I suppose the pictures are good for some people to look at; they show a wonderful deal of study and thought.[16] That is not what I can best appreciate in a work of art. I hate to see the marks of them. I want a simple and direct expression of soul. For the rest the ordinary cant of connoisseurship on these matters seems in Italy even more detestable than elsewhere.

I cannot yet recover from my pain at finding the frescoes of Raphael in such a state enough to look at them happily. I had heard of it, but could not realize it. However, I have gained nothing by seeing his pictures in oil, which are well preserved. I find I had before the full impression of his genius. Michel Angelo's frescoes in like manner I seem to have seen as far as I can. But it is not the same with the sculptures: my thought had not risen to the height of the Moses. It is the only thing in Europe, so far, which has entirely outgone my hopes.[17] Michel Angelo was my demigod before; but I find no offering worthy to cast at the feet of the Moses. I like much his Christ too, (in the Church of Maria sopra Minerva,)—it is a refreshing contrast with all the other representations of the same subject. I like it even as contrasted with Raphael's Christ of the Transfiguration or that of the cartoon of *Feed my Lambs*.

I have heard owls hoot in the Colosseum by moonlight, and they spoke more to the purpose than I ever heard any other voice upon that subject. I have seen all the pomps and shows of Holy Week in the Church of St. Peter, and found

[13] Titian's *Sacred and Profane Love* (c. 1516), an enigmatic allegory, inaugurated a new phase in the artist's career during which he produced several religious, mythological, and portrait paintings (*OCA*).

[14] Annibale Carracci completed the frescoed ceiling of the Farnese palace in 1600 (Ann Hill, ed., *A Visual Dictionary of Art* [Greenwich, Ct.: New York Graphic Society]).

[15] Gian-Francesco Barbieri (1591–1666) was called Guercino because of his squint (*OCA*).

[16] In *Pictures from Italy,* Dickens commented on the poor condition of *The Last Supper* in the refectory of Santa Maria delle Grazie, Milan.

[17] Michelangelo designed *Moses* as one of forty large figures for the tomb of Pope Julius II. It and two slaves were the only part of the work that he completed (*OCA*).

them less imposing than an habitual acquaintance with the place with processions of monks and nuns stealing in now and then, or the swell of vespers from some side chapel. I have ascended the dome and seen thence Rome and its Campagna, its villas with their cypresses and pines serenely sad as is nothing else in the world, and the fountains of the Vatican Garden gushing hard by. I have been in the Subterranean to see a poor little boy introduced, much to his surprise, to the bosom of the Church; and then I have seen by torch-light the stone Popes where they lie on their tombs, and the old mosaics, and Virgins with gilt caps. It is all rich and full,—very impressive in its way. St. Peter's must be to each one a separate poem.

The ceremonies of the Church have been numerous and splendid during our stay here; and they borrow unusual interest from the love and expectation inspired by the present Pontiff. He is a man of noble and good aspect, who, it is easy to see, has set his heart upon doing something solid for the benefit of Man. But pensively, too, must one feel how hampered and inadequate are the means at his command to accomplish these ends. The Italians do not feel it, but deliver themselves, with all the vivacity of their temperament, to perpetual hurra, vivas, rockets, and torch-light processions. I often think how grave and sad must the Pope feel, as he sits alone and hears all this noise of expectation.[18]

A week or two ago the Cardinal Secretary published a circular inviting the departments to measures which would give the people a sort of representative council. Nothing could seem more limited than this improvement but it was a great measure for Rome. At night the Corso, in which we live, was illuminated, and many thousands passed through it in a torch-bearing procession. I saw them first assembled in the Piazza del Popolo, forming around its fountain a great circle of fire. —Then, as a river of fire, they streamed slowly through the Corso, on their way to the Quirinal to thank the Pope, upbearing a banner on which the edict was printed. The stream of fire advanced slowly with a perpetual surge-like sound of voices; the torches flashed on the animated Italian

---

[18] In 1846 Giovanni Maria Mastai-Ferretti (1792–1878) suceeded Pope Gregory XVI (1765–1846) to become Pope Pius IX. Pope Gregory had been strongly opposed to democractic progress and had not been inclined to increase political freedom in the Papal States. Pius IX granted a general amnesty to political exiles and prisoners on 16 July 1846 and began a series of popular reform movements. On 19 April 1847 he established an advisory council of laymen from various provinces; on 5 July 1847 he established the Civic Guard, and on 29 December 1847 he established a Cabinet Council. The enactment of these reforms was not, however, indicative of the new pope's willingness to extend his liberal views to include the commencement of a war with Austria, and his allocution of 29 April 1848 shocked and surprised those who had hoped he would take a stronger stand. By 24 November 1848, the revolution was such that the pope fled Rome in disguise to Gaeta. He did not return until 12 April 1850 (*NCE*).

faces. I have never seen anything finer. Ascending the Quirinal they made it a mount of light. Bengal fires were thrown up, which cast their red and white light on the noble Greek figures of men and horses that reign over it. The Pope appeared on his balcony: the crowd shouted three vivas; he extended his arms: the crowd fell on their knees and received his benediction; he retired, and the torches were extinguished, and the multitude dispersed in an instant.

The same week came the natal day of Rome. A great dinner was given at the Baths of Titus, in the open air. The company was on the grass in the area; the music at one end; boxes filled with the handsome Roman women occupied the other sides. It was a new thing here, this popular dinner, and the Romans greeted it in an intoxication of hope and pleasure. Sterbini, author of "The Vestal," presided: many others, like him long time exiled and restored to their country by the present Pope, were at the tables.[19] The Colosseum and Triumphal Arches were in sight; an effigy of the Roman wolf with her royal nursling was erected on high; the guests, with shouts and music, congratulated themselves on the possession in Pius IX. of a new and nobler founder for another State. Among the speeches that of the Marquis d'Azelgio, a man of literary note in Italy, and son-in-law of Manzoni,[20] contained this passage, (he was sketching the past history of Italy): "The crown passed to the head of a German monarch; but he wore it not to the benefit but the injury of Christianity—of the world. The Emperor Henry was a tyrant who wearied out the patience of God. God said to Rome, 'I give you the Emperor Henry;' and from these hills that surround us, Hildebrand, Pope Gregory VII. raised his austere and potent voice to say to the Emperor, *'God did not give you Italy that you might destroy her,'* and Italy, Germany, Europe, saw her butcher prostrated at the feet of Gregory in penitence. Italy, Germany, Europe, had then kindled in the heart the first spark of Liberty."

The narrative of the dinner passed the censure and was published: the Ambassador of Austria read it, and found, with a modesty and candor truly admirable, that this passage was meant to allude to his Emperor. He must take his passports if such home-thrusts are to be made. And so the paper was seized, and the account of the dinner only told from mouth to mouth, from those who had already read it. Also the idea of a dinner for the Pope's fete day is abandoned, lest something too frank should again be said; and they tell me here,

[19] Pietro Sterbini (1795–1863) was a part of Mazzini's Young Italy movement in 1846. He was appointed by Pius IX as a member of the ministry in November 1848 (*NCE;* Hudspeth 5:151, 153).

[20] The poet and novelist Alessandro Manzoni became active in the 1848 uprising in Milan. Fuller met him on 10 August 1847 and was impressed by his tenderness, frankness, elevation, and simplicity of manner (see Hudspeth 4:287).

with a laugh, "I fancy you have assisted at the first and last popular dinner."
Thus we may see that the liberty of Rome does not yet advance with seven-
leagued boots; and the new Romulus will need to be prepared for deeds at least
as bold as his predecessor, if he is to open a new order of things.

I cannot well wind up my gossip on this subject better than by translating
the programme of the CONTEMPORANEO, which represents the hope of Rome
at this moment, and which is offered you in exchange for *The Tribune*. It is conducted by men of well known talent.

"The *Contemporaneo* (Contemporary) is a journal of progress,[21] but tempered,
as the good and wise think best, in conformity with the will of our best of
Princes, and the wants and expectations of the public.[22]

"There are men rooted in old habits, absolutely hostile to every innovation.
These see disorder and anarchy in the most innocent attempts at progress, suggested by the zeal for humanity, the most noble and generous Christian love.
The Crèches, asylums for children, houses to provide for children when they
leave those asylums, associations to aid laborers who cannot find work, savings'
banks, societies of mutual aid for artists and artisans, penitentiaries for prisoners, houses of refuge for young offenders, Sunday and evening schools for the
people, and the like good works which are the glory of our age, have always
been opposed by them. What wonder if they are likewise hostile to steam-
engines, railways, banks, Scientific Congresses, and other means taken by modern civilization in aid of commerce, industry and knowledge?

"These are not usually bad persons; they enjoy rather (and not always without ground) the reputation of being good; but they are cowardly in soul and
thoughts—servile to the excuse 'it has always been done thus,' and fear a deadly
ambush in every novelty. So the ancient superstitions have succeeded in the
present day the fear of the Demon of Revolution, which, at the annunciation of
anything new, trembles lest new Robespierres come to mow off human heads.
With this class of timid retrogradists, since the civilization of the day cares not
for them, and, thank God, need not fear them, we wage no war, considering
all that as good as buried in the brains of childish and decrepit minds, and forgotten by the great living public.

"There are deceitful men who feign moderation, and are really retrogradists,
as to whom silence is the best. There are abject souls over whom any and every
successful opinion has sway. The *Contemporaneo* will pay no attention to these,
who are the dregs and disgrace of society. There are men eager and impatient for

[21] *Il contemporaneo*, established first as a weekly and then as a daily newspaper in 1846,
was progressive but moderate. Although the paper at first supported Pius IX, it became
increasingly critical of his policies (Berkeley 2:103–04).
[22] The following three paragraphs were omitted from *AHA*.

novelty agitated by lively passions, mostly moved by generous intentions, but so fervent and exaggerated that they can never see an obstacle, but must effect in a single day all desired reforms. These are men by nature formed for good, who ought not to be opposed and repressed, but rather enrolled in the ranks of Social Progress, taught to temper that heat by prudence, and work by reason rather than impulse. To those who constitute the greater part of our youth the *Contemporaneo* especially addresses its affection and its thoughts; as, being the journal of Progress, it must hope to be the journal of the young. It invites all minds to a sacred league in aid of this Social Progress. It will receive into its columns all Italian writers who may desire to study measures for the aid of society, and will accept all those who wish to proclaim principles of progress in the temper of moderation.

"Through discussion it desires to prepare minds to receive reforms so soon and far as they are favored by the law of *opportunity*.

"Every attempt which is made contrary to this social law must fail. It is vain to hope fruits from a tree out of season, and equally in vain to introduce the best measures into a country not prepared to receive them."

And so on. I intended to have translated in full the programme, but time fails, and the law of opportunity does not favor, as my "opportunity" leaves for London this afternoon. I have given enough to mark the purport of the whole. It will easily be seen that it was not from the platform assumed by the *Contemporaneo* that Lycurgus legislated, and Socrates taught; that the Christian religion was propagated, neither its reform by Luther. The opportunity that the Martyrs found here in the Colosseum, from whose blood grew up this great tree of Papacy, was not of the kind waited for by these moderate Progressists. Nevertheless, they may be good schoolmasters for Italy, and are not to be disdained in these piping times of peace.

More anon, of old and new, from Tuscany.   ★

Dispatch 15

SUMMER IN NORTHERN ITALY

MILAN, August 9, 1847 [1]

Since leaving Rome, I have not been able to steal a moment from the rich and varied objects before me to write about them. I will, therefore, take a brief retrospect of the ground.

I passed from Florence to Rome by the Perugia route, and saw, for the first

[1] First published as "Things and Thoughts in Europe. No. XV" in *New-York Daily Tribune*, 11 September 1847, p. 1:1–3.

time, the Italian vineyards. The grapes hung in little clusters. When I return they will be full of light and life, but the fields will not be so enchantingly fresh, nor so enamelled with flowers.

The profusion of red poppies, which dance on every wall and glitter throughout the grass, is a great ornament to the landscape. In full sunlight their vermillion is most beautiful. Well might Ceres gather *such* poppies to mingle with her wheat.

We climbed the hill to Assisi, and my ears thrilled as with many old remembered melodies when an old peasant, in sonorous phrase, bade me look out and see the plain of Umbria. I looked back and saw the carriage toiling up the steep path, drawn by a pair of those light-colored oxen Shelley so much admired.[2] I stood near the spot where Goethe met with a little adventure which he has described with even more than his usual delicate humor.[3]—Who can ever be alone for a moment in Italy? Every stone has a voice, every grain of dust seems instinct with spirit from the Past, every step recalls some line, some legend of long-neglected lore. Assisi was exceedingly charming to me. So still!—all temporal noise and bustle seem hushed down yet by the presence of the saint. So clean!— the rains of Heaven wash down all impurities into the valley. I must confess that, elsewhere, I have shared the feelings of Dickens toward St. Francis and St. Sebastian, as the "Mounseer Tonsons" of Catholic art.[4] St. Sebastian I have not been so tired of, for the beauty and youth of the figure make the monotony with which the subject of his martyrdom is treated somewhat less wearisome. But St. Francis is so sad, and so ecstatic, and so brown, so entirely the monk—and St. Clara so entirely the nun! I have been very sorry for her that he was able to draw her from the human to the heavenly life, she seems so sad and so worn out by the effort. But here at Assisi, one cannot help being penetrated by the spirit that flowed from that life. Here is the room where his father shut up the boy to punish his early severity of devotion. Here is the picture which represents him despoiled of all outward things, even his garments—devoting himself, body and soul, to the service of God in the way he believed most acceptable. Here is the underground chapel, where rest those weary bones, saluted by the tears of so many weary pilgrims who have come hither to seek strength from his ex-

---

[2] Shelley's "milk-white oxen slow" appear in his "Lines Written Among the Euganean Hills," line 220 (Roger Ingpen and Walter E. Peck, eds., *The Complete Works of Percy Bysshe Shelley* [New York: Grove Press, 1965], 2:55).

[3] Fuller had studied the works of Goethe from an early age (*OCGL*). Her first book was a translation of *Eckermann's Conversations with Goethe* (1839), and she had accumulated materials for a never-completed biography of Goethe. She refers here to Goethe's *Italienische Reise* (1816–29), which she reviewed for the *New-York Tribune* on 18 December 1845.

[4] Fuller refers again to *Pictures from Italy*.

ample. Here are the churches above, full of the works of earlier art, animated by the contagion of a great example. It is impossible not to bow the head and feel how mighty an influence flows from a single soul, sincere in its service of Truth, in whatever form that truth comes to it. A troop of neat, pretty school-girls attended us about, going with us into the little chapels adorned with pictures which open at every corner of the streets, smiling on us at a respectful distance.—Some of them were fourteen or fifteen years old. I found reading, writing and sewing were all they learned at their school; the first, indeed, they knew well enough, if they could ever get books to use it on. Tranquil as Assisi was, on every wall was read *Viva* Pio IX. and we found the guides and workmen in the shop full of a vague hope from him. The old love which has made so rich this aerial cradle of St. Francis glows warm as ever in the breasts of men; still, as ever, they long for hero-worship, and shout aloud at the least appearance of an object.

The church at the foot of the hill, *Santa Maria degli Angeli,* seems tawdry after Assisi. It also is full of records of St. Francis, his pains and his triumphs. Here, too, on a little chapel is the famous picture by Overbeck;[5] too exact a copy, but how different in effect from the early art we had just seen above! Harmonious but frigid, grave but dull, childhood is beautiful, but not when continued or rather transplanted into the period where we look for passion, varied means and manly force.

Before reaching Perugia, I visited the Etrurian tomb, which is a little way off the road; it is said to be one of the finest in Etruria. The hill-side is full of them, but excavations are expensive and not frequent. The effect of this one was beyond my expectations; in it were several female figures, very dignified and calm as the dim lamp-light fell on them by turns. The expression of these figures shows that the position of woman in these states was noble. Their Eagles' nests cherished well the female Eagle who kept watch in the eyrie.

PERUGIA too is on a noble hill: what a daily excitement such a view taken at every step; life is worth ten times as much in a city so situated.—Perugia is full, overflowing, with the treasures of early art. I saw them so rapidly it seems now as if in a trance—yet certainly with a profit, a manifold gain, such as Mahomet thought he gained from his five minutes' visits to other spheres. Here are two portraits of Raphael as a youth; it is touching to see what effect this angel had upon all that surrounded him from the very first.

FLORENCE!—I was there a month, and in a sense saw Florence: that is to say, I took an inventory of what is to be seen there, and not without great intel-

---

[5] Fuller probably saw a copy of his most famous painting, *The Rose Miracle of St. Francis* (1829) (*OCA* and *ODA*).

lectual profit, too. There is too much that is really admirable in art—the nature of its growth lies before you too clear to be evaded.—Of such things more elsewhere.

Florence I do not like as I do cities more purely Italian. The natural character is ironed out here, and done up in a French pattern; yet there is no French vivacity, nor Italian either. The Grand Duke—more and more agitated by the position in which he finds himself between the influence of the Pope and that of Austria—keeps imploring and commanding his people to keep still, and they *are* still and glum as death.[6] This is all on the outside; within, Tuscany burns and flutters. Private culture has not been in vain, and there is, in a large circle, mental preparation for a very different state of things from the present, with an ardent desire to diffuse the same amid the people at large. The Sovereign has been obliged for the present to give more liberty to the press, and there was an immediate rush of thought to the new vent; if it is kept open a few months, the effect on the body of the people cannot fail to be great. I intended to have translated some passages from the programme of the *Patria,* one of the papers newly started at Florence, but time fails. One of the articles in the same number by Lambruschini, on the Duties of the Clergy at this juncture, contains views as liberal as can be found in print anywhere in the world.[7] More of these things when I return to Rome in the Autumn, when I hope to find a little leisure to think over what I have seen, and, if found worthy, to put the result in writing.

I visited the studios of our sculptors: Greenough has in clay a David which promises high beauty and nobleness, a bas-relief, full of grace and tender expression; he is also modeling a head of Napoleon, and justly enthusiastic in the study.[8] His great group I did not see in such a state as to be secure of my impression—the face of the Pioneer is very fine, the form of the woman graceful and expressive; but I was not satisfied with the Indian. I shall see it more as a whole on my return to Florence.

As to the Eve and the Greek Slave I could only join with the rest of the world in admiration of their beauty and the fine feeling of nature which they exhibit. The statue of Calhoun is full of power, simple and majestic in attitude and ex-

---

[6] Leopold II, grand duke of Tuscany, was known for his repressive rule. With Pius IX and Charles Albert, he was among the most powerful leaders in Italy (Berkeley 3:23).

[7] Cardinal Luigi Lambruschini (1776–1854) had been a favorite of Pope Gregory XVI. When Pius IX was elected Pope in 1846, Lambruschini opposed his constitutionalism (*NCE*; Berkeley 3:461).

[8] Horatio Greenough (1805–52) was an American neoclassical sculptor, who lived mostly in Italy. Emerson thought Greenough a mediocre sculptor but a promising intellectual. Greenough created the large figure of George Washington in a Roman toga that stands outside the Capitol in Washington, D.C. (*OCA*).

pression. In busts Powers seems to me unrivaled; still, he ought not to spend his best years on an employment which cannot satisfy his ambition nor develop his powers.[9] If our country loves herself, she will order from him some great work before the prime of his genius has been frittered away and his best years spent on lesser things.

I saw at Florence the festivals of St. John, but they are poor affairs to one who has seen the Neapolitan and Roman people on such occasions.

Passing from Florence, I came to BOLOGNA—learned Bologna, indeed an Italian city, full of expression, of physiognomy—so to speak. A woman should love Bologna, for there has the spark of intellect in Woman been cherished with reverent care. Not in former ages only, but in this, Bologna raised a woman who was worthy to the dignities of its University, and in their Certosa they proudly show the monument to Clotilda Tambroni, late Greek Professor there. Her letters, preserved by her friends, are said to form a very valuable collection. In their Anatomical Hall is the bust of a woman, Professor of Anatomy. In Art they have Properzia di Rossi, Elizabetta Sirani, Lavinia Fontana, and delight to give their works a conspicuous place.[10]

In other cities the men alone have their *Casino dei Nobili,* where they give *balls converzazioni* and similar entertainments. Here women have one, and are the soul of society.

In Milan, also, I see in the Ambrosian Library the bust of a female Mathematician. These things make me feel that if the state of Woman in Italy is so depressed, yet a good will toward a better is not wholly wanting. These things, and still more the reverence to the Madonna and innumerable female Saints, who if, like St. Teresa, they had intellect as well as piety, became counselors no less than comforters to the spirits of men.

Ravenna, too, I saw and its old Christian art, the Pineta where Byron loved to ride, and the paltry apartments where, cheered by a new affection,[11] in which

---

[9] The sculptor Hiram Powers (1805–73) enjoyed depicting Americans as Romans. His full-length portrayal of John C. Calhoun was destroyed around 1850. He completed *Eve Tempted* in 1842, and his celebrated *The Greek Slave* in 1843. (*ODA*; William L. Vance, *America's Rome* [New Haven: Yale University Press, 1989], 1:233–37). Though much admired, the latter struck many as sexually provocative.

[10] The Certosa was a former Carthusian monastery, which housed paintings by Elizabetta Sirani (1638–65) and the monument to Clotilda Tambroni (1794–1817), a professor of Greek. Mme. Mazzoni was a professor of anatomy at the university. Among the women artists Fuller mentions, Properzia di Rossi (1490–1530) was a sculptor and Livinia Fontana (1552–1614) achieved fame as a portrait painter (Baedeker 1:344, 360; *OCA*).

[11] Byron's "new affection" was Countess Teresa Gambia Guiccioli, the wife of Count Alessandro Guiccioli. She met Bryon in Venice in April 1819, and he became her para-

was more of tender friendship than of passion, he found himself less wretched than at beautiful Venice or stately Genoa.

All the details of this visit to Ravenna are pretty. I shall write them out some time. Of Padua, too, the little to be said should be said in detail.

Of Venice and its enchanted life I could not speak; it should only be echoed back in music. There only I began to feel in its fullness Venetian Art. It can only be seen in its own atmosphere. Never had I the least idea of what is to be seen at Venice. It seems to me as if no one ever yet had seen it—so entirely wanting is any expression of what I felt myself. Venice! on this subject I shall not write a word till time, place and mode agree to make it fit.

Venice, where all is past, is a fit asylum for the dynasties of the Past. The Duchess de Berri owns one of the finest palaces on the Grand Canal; the Duke de Bordeaux rents another;[12] Mlle. Taglioni[13] has bought the famous Casa d'Oro, and it is under repair. Thanks to the fashion which has made Venice a refuge of this kind; the palaces, rarely inhabited by the representatives of their ancient names, are valuable property, and the Palladian structures will not be suffered to lapse into the sea, above which they rose so proudly. The restorations, too, are made with excellent taste and judgment—nothing is spoiled. Three of these fine palaces are now hotels, so that the transient visiter can enjoy from their balconies all the wondrous shows of the Venetian night and day as much as any of their former possessors did. I was at the Europa, formerly the Giustiniani Palace, with better air than those on the Grand Canal, and a more unobstructed view than Danieli's.

We are fortunate in our consul at Venice. Mr. Sparks speaks well the foreign languages and is, by education and fine tact, fitted to understand and act in foreign society, as few Americans are. His wife—a fair, pale flower from the South—may well give an attractive idea of the charms of our gardens. The Venetian women have much beauty and more charm, but in a style as differ-

---

mour. Her husband resented the liaison but liked and respected Byron. (*DNB* and Leslie A. Marchand, *Bryron: A Biography,* 3 vols. [New York: Knopf, 1957], 2:773–75).

12 Caroline Ferdinande Louise de Bourbon (1798–1870) married Charles Ferdinand, duc de Berri (1778–1820) in 1816. In 1820 the duc de Berri was assassinated, and after the July revolution in 1830, Mme. de Berri fled France to Italy with her son, Henri Charles Dieudonné, comte de Chambord (1820–83), who, as a grandson of Charles X, was a claimant to the French throne (*Chambers's Biographical Dictionary*).

13 Maria Taglioni (1804–84) was a member of a famous family of dancers and choreographers. A talented dancer, she performed in theaters all over Europe and in Russia. After her last appearance in Paris in 1847, she retired and lived in Italy until 1860 (*Grande dizionario enciclopedico Utet,* 19 vols. [Turin: Unione Tipografico-Editrice Torinese, 1972]).

ent from that of Mrs. C. as from the bold, noble contours and coloring of the Roman women.[14]

Madame de Berri gave an entertainment on the birthnight of her son, and the old Duchess d'Angoulême came from Vienna to attend it.[15] 'T was a scene of fairy land; the palace full of light, so that from the canal could be seen even the pictures on the walls. Landing from the gondolas, the elegantly dressed ladies and gentlemen seemed to rise from the water; we also saw them glide up the great stair, rustling their plumes, and, in the reception rooms, make and receive the customary grimaces. A fine band stationed on the opposite side of the canal played the while, and a flotilla of gondolas lingered there to listen. I, too, amid the mob, a pleasant position in Venice alone, thought of the Stuarts, Bourbons, Bonapartes, here in Italy, and offered up a prayer that other names when the possessors have power without the heart to use it for the emancipation of mankind, might be added to the list, and other princes, more rich in blood than brain, might come to enjoy a perpetual *villeggiatura* [16] in Italy. It did not seem to me a cruel wish. The show of greatness will satisfy every legitimate desire of such minds. A gentle punishment for the distributors of *lettres de cachet* and Spielberg dungeons to their fellow men.

Having passed more than a fortnight at Venice, I have come here, stopping at Vicenza, Verona, Mantua, Lago di Garda, Brescia. Certainly I have learned more than ever in any previous ten days of my existence, and have formed an idea what is needed for the study of Art and its history in these regions. To be sure, I shall never have time to follow it up, but it is a delight to look up those glorious vistas, even when there is no hope of entering them.

A violent shower obliged me to stop on the way. It was late at night and I was nearly asleep, when, roused by the sound of bubbling waters, I started up and asked, "Is that the Adda?" and it was. So deep is the impression made by a simple natural recital, like that of Renzo's wanderings in the *Promessi Sposi,* that the memory of his hearing the Adda in this way occurred to me at once, and the Adda seemed familiar as if I had been a native of this region.[17]

As the Scottish lakes seem the domain of Walter Scott, so does Milan and its neighborhood in the mind of a foreigner belong to Manzoni. I have seen him

[14] This paragraph was omitted from *AHA*.

[15] The formidable Marie Thérèse of Austria, the duchess d'Angoulême (1778–1851), was the aunt of Mme. de Berri's son, Henri Charles Dieudonné (*Chambers's Biographical Dictionary*).

[16] A country holiday or summer vacation.

[17] The poet and novelist Alessandro Manzoni (1785–1873) published *I promessi sposi* (The betrothed) in 1827.

since, the gentle lord of this wide domain; his hair is white, but his eyes still beam as when he first saw the apparitions of truth, simple tenderness and piety has so admirably recorded for our benefit. Those around lament that the fastidiousness of his taste prevents his completing and publishing more, and that thus a treasury of rare knowledge and refined thought will pass from us without our reaping the benefit. We, indeed, have no title to complain, what we do possess from his hand is so excellent.

At this moment there is great excitement in Italy. A supposed spy of Austria has been assassinated at Ferrara, and Austrian troops are marched there.[18] It is pretended that a conspiracy has been discovered in Rome; the consequent disturbances have been put down. The National Guard is forming. All things seem to announce that some important change is inevitable here, but what? Neither Radicals nor Moderates dare predict with confidence, and I am yet too much a stranger to speak with assurance of impressions I have received.—But it is impossible not to hope. Time fails, as usual. The clock strikes, the postbag opens and leaves only time to make the sign of ★

Dispatch 16

THE ITALIAN LAKES
AND THE COMING STORM

ROME, October 1847 [1]

I think my last letter was from Milan, and written after I had seen Manzoni. This was to me a great pleasure.[2] I have now seen the most important representatives who survive of the last epoch in thought. Our age has still its demonstrations to make, its heroes and poets to crown.

Although the modern Italian literature is not poor, as many persons at a distance suppose—but, on the contrary, surprisingly rich in tokens of talent—if we consider the circumstances under which it struggles to exist, yet very few writers have or deserve an European, an American reputation. Where a whole country is so kept down, her best minds cannot take the lead in the progress of the age; they have too much to suffer, too much to explain. But among the few

[18] Field Marshal Count Joseph Radetzky (1766–1858) led his Austrian troops in a well-planned and quickly executed seizure of the city of Ferrara (Robertson 331–32; *New Cambridge Modern History* 10:562–64).

[1] First published as "Things and Thoughts in Europe. No. XVI" in *New-York Daily Tribune,* 25 December 1847, p. 3:1–2.

[2] Fuller met Manzoni in Milan on 10 August 1847 and was quite taken with him and his young, second wife, Lucia (Hudspeth 4:287).

who, through depth of spiritual experience and the beauty of form in which it is expressed, belong not only to Italy, but to the world, Manzoni takes a high rank. The passive virtues he teaches are no longer what is wanted; the manners he paints with so delicate a fidelity are beginning to change—but the spirit of his works—the tender piety, the sensibility to the meaning of every humblest form of life, the delicate humor and satire so free from disdain—these are immortal.

Young Italy rejects Manzoni, though not irreverently; Young Italy prizes his works, but feels that the doctrine of "Pray and wait" is not for her at this moment, that she needs a more fervent hope, a more active faith.[3] She is right.

It is well known that the traveler, if he knows the Italian as written in books, the standard Tuscan, still finds himself a stranger in many parts of Italy, unable to comprehend the dialects, with their lively abbreviations and witty slang. That of Venice I had understood somewhat, and could enter into the drollery and *naïveté* of the gondoliers, who, as a class, have an unusual share of character. But the Milanese I could not at first understand at all. Their language seemed to me detestably harsh and their gestures unmeaning. But after a friend,[4] who possesses that large and ready sympathy—easier found in Italy than anywhere else—had translated for me verbatim into French some of the poems written in the Milanese, and then read them aloud in the original, I comprehended the peculiar inflection of voice and idiom in the people, and was charmed with it, as one is with the instinctive wit and wisdom of children.

There is very little to see at Milan compared with any other Italian city, and this was very fortunate for me, allowing an interval of repose in the house, which I cannot take when there is so much without tempting me to incessant observation and study. I went through the North of Italy with a constantly increasing fervor of interest.[5] When I had thought of Italy, it was always of the South—of the Roman States—of Tuscany. But now I became deeply interested in the history, the institutions, the art of the North. The fragments of the Past mark the progress of its waves so clearly, I learned to understand, to prize them every day more, to know how to make use of the books about them. I shall have much to say on these subjects some day.

Leaving Milan, I went on the Lago Maggiore, and afterward into Switzerland. Of this tour I shall not speak here; it was a beautiful little romance by

[3] Giovine Italia (Young Italy), founded in 1831 by Joseph Mazzini in exile at Marseilles, was a subversive organization that worked for Italian unification under a republican form of government, with Rome as the capital (Bondanella).

[4] Probably Costanza Arconati-Visconti (1800–71), who became one of Fuller's closest friends in Italy (Hudspeth 4:14, 279n; Deiss 73–74).

[5] Fuller was now traveling on her own. She had parted with the Springs in Venice.

itself, and infinitely refreshing to be so near Nature in these grand and simple forms, after so much exciting thought of Art and Man. The day passed in the St. Bernardin, with its lofty peaks and changing lights upon the distant snows; its holy, exquisite valleys, and waterfalls, its stories of eagles and chamois, was the greatest refreshment I ever experienced: it was bracing as a cold bath after the heat of a crowd amid which one has listened to some most eloquent oration.

Returning from Switzerland I passed a fortnight on the Lake of Como, and afterward visited Lugano. There is no exaggeration in the enthusiastic feeling with which artists and poets have viewed these Italian lakes. Their beauties are peculiar, enchanting, innumerable. The *"Titan"* of Richter, the *"Wanderjahre"* of Goethe, the Elena of Taylor, the pictures of Turner, had not prepared me for the visions of beauty that daily entranced the eyes and heart in those regions.[6] To our country, Nature has been most bounteous, but we have nothing in the same class that can compare with these lakes, as seen under the Italian heaven. As to those persons who have pretended to discover that the effects of light and atmosphere were no finer than they found in our own lake scenery, I can only say that they must be exceedingly obtuse in organization—a defect not uncommon among Americans.

Nature seems to have labored to express her full heart in as many ways as possible, when she made these Lakes molded and planted their shores. Lago Maggiore is grandiose, resplendent in its beauty; the view of the Alps gives a sort of lyric exaltation to the scene. Lago di Garda is so soft and fair—so glittering sweet on one side—the ruins of ancient palaces rise so softly with the beauties of that shore; but at the other end, amid the Tyrol, it is so sublime, so calm, so concentrated in its meaning! Como cannot be better described in generals than in the words of Taylor:

"Softly sublime, profusely fair."

Lugano is more savage, more free in its beauty. I was on it in a high gale; there was a little danger, just enough to exhilarate; its waters wild and clouds blowing across its peaks. I like very much the boatmen on these lakes; they have strong and prompt character; of simple features, they are more honest and manly than

---

6 *Titan*, a novel by Johann Paul Friedrich Richter (1763–1825), was published in 1800–1803 (*OCGL*). Known for his beautiful and evocative descriptions of landscape, Richter inspired Fuller to write a poem as well as several reviews of his work. *Wilhelm Meisters Wanderjahre oder Die Enstagenden* was published by Goethe in 1821 as a sequel to *Wilhelm Meisters Lehrjahre* (1795–96) (*OCGL*). Henry Taylor (1800–1886) wrote *Philip Van Artevelde*, a dramatic romance in two parts, which was set in this region. "The Lay of Elena" is a poem-prologue that begins part 2 (*DNB*). Fuller reviewed Taylor's romance in the *Western Messenger*, 1 (December 1835):398–408; rpt. in *Life Without and Life Within*, 371–73.

Italian men are found in the thoroughfares; their talk is not so witty as that of the Venetian gondoliers, but picturesque and what the French call *incisive*. Very touching were some of their histories, as they told them to me while pausing sometimes on the lake.[7] Grossi gives a true picture of such a man in his family relations; the story may be found in "Marco Viscount." The idea of the situation is borrowed from Walter Scott, but many touches are his own.[8] At Riva di Trento (Lago di Garda) De Henry, called on me. He is an Irish gentlemen, author of a Temperance tract which has been widely circulated in the United States. He gave me a little piece of playful doggerel which may be inserted here as a good description of the journey from Trent to Riva. Unhappily in the refrain *Adige* must be mispronounced to make it rhyme with *carriage*.

FROM TRENT TO RIVA ON THE LAGO DI GARDA.
June 7, 1847.

At five leave Trent
   In coach and pair,
For Riva bent
   And cooler air,

My wife and I
   And daughter tall
And Maestro Monti,
   Four in all.

Good company,
   In sooth, are we,
And for six hours
   May well agree.

If quarrels come,
   As poets teach,
From too free use
   Of the parts of speech,

For we no word have
   Of Italian,

No English he
   Nor cramp Germanian,

Nor hath as yet
   Th' acquaintance made
Even of Miss French,
   That common jade,

That walks at ease
   Wide Europe's streets
And chats and laughs
   With all she meets.

Pleasant the view is
   As our carriage
Rolls smoothly down
   The vale of Adige;

Toward southern suns
   And genial skies
Gently sloped
   That valley lies;

---

[7] The remainder of this paragraph and all of the poem were omitted in *AHA*.

[8] Tommaso Grossi (1790–1853) was a poet, novelist, and close friend of Manzoni. His chief historical novel, *Marco Visconti, a Romance of the Fourteenth Century* (1843), was written in the tradition of Sir Walter Scott and Manzoni. In the novel is a prisoner's song, "Rondi-nella pellgina" (The little swallow), which was popular among Italian prisoners in Austria during the Risorgimento (Bondanella).

From wintry blasts
   North, east and west,
Alpine steeps
   Defend its breast;

And with a thousand
   Ice-fed rills
Water its fields
   And turn its mills,

And cool the sultry
   Summer air,
And play sweet music
   To the ear.

Here the cliffs
   Are bleak and bare;
With pine forests
   Covered there;

Or with various
   Carpet spread
Of fern and heath,
   The black cock's bed.

Here mica schist,
   Red porphyry
And granite peaks
   Invade the sky;

There slumbering marble
   Waits the hand
That bids it into
   Life to stand;

Lower down
   The sandstone rock,
At our feet
   The boulder block.

Pleasant the view is
   As our carriage
Rolls smoothly down
   The vale of Adige;

Trellised vines
   Stretch far and near,
Through fields of lentil,
   Maize and xere;

Chesnut and walnut
   Stately stand
Flanking the road
   On either hand;

And gentler willow
   Lends its shade
And droops and arches
   Overhead;

And sunburnt peasants'
   Hands rapacious
Call the mulberry's
   Foliage precious;

The sacks stand full,
   The carts are loaded,
The patient oxen
   Yoked and goaded;

The master hears
   With ears of pleasure
The axle groan
   Beneath the treasure;

Let six weeks pass,
   The work is done,
The worms are fed,
   The cocoons spun,

The crysalis killed,
   Its intricate clue
Unraveled nice
   And spun anew

Into a firm,
   Tenacious line,
Yellow as gold,
   As gossamer fine;

Parent of
   The bombazine,
Rustling sarsnet
   Satin sheen

Of the sofa's
   Gay brocade;
Of the lutestring—
   Quilted bed;

Of the flag
   That floats on high
Defiance to
   The enemy;

Of the garter,
   Of the pall,
Wond'rous thread
   That mak'st them all!

Pleasant the view is
   As our carriage
Rolls smoothly down
   The vale of Adige

On our right hand
   The broad river,
Gay and clear
   And sparkling ever,

In its stony
   Channel dashing,
Raving, fretting,
   Foaming, splashing;

What though still
   Its course is forward,
What though still
   It rushes onward;

Downward still,
   Although its motion
Toward the vast,
   Absorbing ocean;

See! each wavelet
   Backward curls;[9]
See! reversed
   Each eddy swirls;

See! it casts
   Its lingering look
Toward the scenes
   It hath forsook,

Toward its native
   Orteler mountain,
Toward its parent
   Glacier fountain;

Life's traveler so
   Casts back his view
On the dear scenes
   His childhood knew;

With face reverted
   So 't is borne
Down the rough road
   Whence no return,

And plunged at last
   Into the sea
By finites called
   Eternity.

Pleasant the view is
   As our carriage
Rolls smoothly down
   The vale of Adige;

[9] When the bed of a river is smooth and its water deep, its waves break and fall in the direction of the course of the river. When on the contrary, the water is shallow, the bed rocky, and the descent considerable, the waves receiving a contrary impulse from the impeding rocks turn over and fall backward (*i.e.* in the opposite direction to that in which the

We thread the gorge
  Where Lagerthal
In battle saw
  Sanseverin fall;

Leave on our right
  Old Castel Barco,
And hear thy tower,
  Holy San Marco,

Chime night's first watch
  In Rovereith,
As we arrive
  At half past eight.

After supper,
  Fresh and merry,
We turn us west
  Toward Adige ferry;

And where 'twixt banks
  Of flowery rushes
Deep, silent, smooth,
  The river gushes;

Carriages and all
  Across it float
In broad, flat-bottomed,
  Lugger boat;

Dark though it be
  Small fear have we,
And Maestro's still
  Good company;

And part by signs,
  And part by looks,
And part by words
  Picked out of books,

Contrives to let us
  Understand

He guides us through
  No unknown land;

Guides us through Meri's
  Village rude:
'T were picturesque
  By daylight viewed;

Past Loppio's lake
  With islands dotted,
Past Loppio's rocks
  With lichen spotted;

Then where our passing
  Lamp-light falls
On yonder gray,
  Time-eaten walls;

Awful from
  the rocky steep
Frowned, Nago, once
  The castled keep.

Our downward course
  Is fair and free
From those drear hights
  To Torbole,

Where snugly moored
  In Morpheus' arms
Lake Garda's boatmen
  Dream of storms;

Hung on lines
  Their nets are drying,
High on the strand
  Their boats are lying.

Cross we thus
  Hoarse Saresas's bridge
And turn Mont Brion's
  Jutting ridge;

---

river is flowing). A similar phenomenon is produced in all large collections of water, and very remarkable in the sea, by a wind adverse to the course of the water. [Fuller's note]

Where scantly may
  The strait road sweep
'Twixt the deep lake
  And mountain steep,

Overboard
  Swings, drearily,
The glimmering lamp
  Of a Calvary;

With widows' oil
  That lamp is fed,
A widow's tears
  On that slab are read:

"Fellow sinner
  Bend thy knee,
Fellow sinner
  Pray with me

"For him that in
  The tempest's shock,
Foundering sank
  By yonder rock.

"Mother of God!
  The sailor save
On Lake Garda's
  Dangerous wave."

Two short miles more
  Run quickly past
And Riva safe
  We reach at last,

And just as cocks
  And clocks tell one,
At "Il Jardino"
  Are set down.

Here Maestro Monti
  Bids 'Good night;'
And all to bed
  In weary plight.

On this lake, also, I met Lady Franklin, wife of the celebrated navigator. She has been in the United States, and showed equal penetration and candor in remarks on what she had seen there. She gave me interesting particulars as to the state of things in Van Diemen's Land, where she passed seven years when her husband was in authority there.[10]

I returned to Milan for the great feast of the Madonna, 8th September, and those made for the Archbishop's entry, which took place the same week. These excited as much feeling as the Milanese can have a chance to display, this Archbishop being much nearer the public heart than his predecessor, who was a poor servant of Austria.

The Austrian rule is always equally hated, and time, instead of melting away differences, only makes them more glaring. The Austrian race have no faculties that can ever enable them to understand the Italian character; their policy, so well contrived to palsy and repress for a time, cannot kill, and there is always a force at work underneath which shall yet, and I think now before long, shake off

[10] Lady Jane Franklin (1792–1875) was the wife of the Arctic explorer Sir John Franklin (1786–1847). Lady Franklin accompanied her husband on a series of trips to Syria, Asia Minor, Van Dieman's Land (Tasmania), Australia, and New Zealand (*DNB*).

the incubus. The Italian nobility have always kept the invader at a distance; they have not been at all seduced or corrupted by the lures of pleasure or power, but have shown a passive patriotism highly honorable to them. In the middle class ferments much thought—a capacity for effort; in the present system it cannot show itself, but it is there; it ferments, and will yet produce a wine that shall set the Lombard veins on fire when the time for action shall arrive. The lower part of the population is in a dull state indeed; the censure of the press prevents all easy, natural ways of instructing them; there are no public meetings, no free access to them by more instructed and aspiring minds:—the Austrian policy is to allow them a degree of material well-being, and though so much wealth is drained from the country for the service of the foreigner, yet enough must remain on these rich plains comfortably to feed and clothe the inhabitants. Yet the great moral influence of the Pope's action, though obstructed in their case, does reach and rouse them, and they, too, felt the thrill of indignation at the occupation of Ferrara. The base conduct of the police toward the people when, at Milan, some youths were resolute to sing the Hymn in honor of Pius IX. when the feasts for the Archbishop afforded so legitimate an occasion—roused all the people to unwonted feeling; the nobles protested, and Austria had not courage to resist as usual. She could not sustain her police, who rushed upon a defenceless crowd that had no share in what excited their displeasure, except by sympathy, and, driving them like sheep, wounded them *in the backs*. Austria feels that there is now no sympathy for her in these matters; that it is not the interest of the world to sustain her. Her policy is, indeed, too thoroughly organized to change except by revolution; its scope is to serve, first, a reigning family instead of the people; second, with the people to seek a physical in preference to an intellectual good; and third, to prefer a seeming outward peace to an inward life. This policy may change its opposition from the tyrannical to the insidious; it can know no other change, yet do I meet persons who call themselves Americans—miserable, thoughtless Esaus, unworthy their high birthright— who think that a mess of pottage can satisfy the wants of Man, and that the Viennese listening to Strauss's waltzes, the Lombard peasant supping full of his polenta, is *happy enough*. Alas! I have the more reason to be ashamed of my countrymen, that it is not among the poor, who have so much toil that there is little time to think, but those who are rich, who travel—in body, that is, they do not travel in mind—absorbed at home by the lust of gain, the love of show, abroad they see only the equipages, the fine clothes, the food—they have no heart for the idea, for the destiny of our own great nation: how can they feel the spirit that is struggling now in this and others of Europe?

But of the hopes of Italy I will write more fully in another letter, and shall state what I have seen, what felt, what thought. I went from Milan to Pavia, and saw its magnificent Cortesa. I passed several hours in examining its riches, especially the sculptures of its façade, full of force and spirit. I then went to Florence by Parma and Bologna. In Parma, though ill, I went to see all the works of the Masters; a wonderful beauty it is that informs them, not mine— not, I mean, what is the chosen food of my soul, yet wonderful and which did its message to me also. Those works are failing; it will not be useless to describe them in a book. Beside these pictures, I saw nothing in Parma and Modena; these States are obliged to hold their breath while their poor, ignorant sovereigns skulk in corners, hoping to hide from the coming storm. Of all this more in my next.   ★

Dispatch 17

ITALIAN PATRIOTISM

ROME, October 18, 1847 [1]

In the Spring, when I came to Rome, the people were in the intoxication of joy at the first serious measures of reform taken by the Pope. I saw with pleasure their childlike joy and trust: I saw with pleasure the Pope, who has not in his expression the signs of intellectual greatness so much as of nobleness and tenderness of heart, of large and liberal sympathies. Heart had spoken to heart between the Prince and the People; it was beautiful to see the immediate good influence of human feeling, generous designs, on the part of a ruler: he had wished to be a father, and the Italians, with that readiness of genius that characterizes them, entered at once into the relation; they, the Roman people, stigmatized by prejudice as so crafty and ferocious, showed themselves children, eager to learn, quick to obey, happy to confide.

Still, doubts were always present whether all this joy was not premature. The task undertaken by the Pope seemed to present insuperable difficulties. It is never easy to put new wine into old bottles, and our age is one where all things tend to a great crisis, not merely to revolution but to radical reform. [2]

---

[1] First published as "Things and Thoughts in Europe. No. XVII" in *New-York Daily Tribune*, 27 November 1847, p. 1:1–3.

[2] Mazzini had written a letter to the pope on 8 September 1847, in which he asserted it was possible that Pius IX could unite Italy under a democracy based on spiritual sanctions. The letter was privately printed and thrown into the pope's carriage by a friend. Mazzini shared the letter with Fuller and wrote to her in December, telling her that the pope might be the instrument for reform in Italy: "As king he has neither genius nor energy. He fears the Jesuits and fears us. As a Pope he has been sent *to give the last blow to the papacy;* and it will be seen when he dies, 'Old bottles will not contain new wine'" (Rostenberg 76). To

From the people themselves the help must come, and not from princes: in the new state of things there will be none but natural princes, great men. From the aspirations of the general heart, from the teachings of conscience in individuals, and not from an old ivy-covered church, long since undermined, corroded by Time and gnawed by vermin, the help must come. Rome, to resume her glory, must cease to be an ecclesiastical Capital; must renounce all this gorgeous mummery, whose poetry, whose picture charms no one more than myself, but whose meaning is all of the Past and finds no echo in the Future. Although I sympathized warmly with the warm love of the people, the adulation of leading writers, who were so willing to take all from the hand of the prince, of the Church, as a gift and a bounty instead of implying steadily that it was the right of the people, was very repulsive to me. The Moderate party, like all who, in a transition state, manage affairs with a constant eye to prudence, lacks dignity always in its expositions; it is disagreeable and depressing to read them.[3]

Passing into Tuscany, I found the Liberty of the Press just established, and a superior preparation to make use of it. The *'Alba,'* the *'Patria,'* were begun, and have been continued with equal judgment and spirit. Their aim is to educate the youth, to educate the lower people; they see that this is to be done by promoting Thought fearlessly, yet urge temperance in action, while the time is yet so difficult, and many of its signs dubious. They aim at breaking down those barriers between the different States of Italy, relics of a barbarous state of polity, artificially kept up by the craft of her foes. While anxious not to break

---

Emerson, Fuller wrote, "I don't know whether you take an interest in the present state of things in Italy, but you would if you were here. It is a fine time to see the people. As to the Pope, it is as difficult here as elsewhere to put new wine into old bottles, and there is something false as well as ludicrous in the spectacle of the people first driving their princes to do a little justice, and then *viva*-ing them at such a rate. This does not apply to the Pope; he is a real great heart, a generous man. The love for him is geniune, and I like to be within its influence. It was his heart that gave the impulse, and this people has shown, to the shame of English and other prejudice, how unspoiled they were at the core, how open, nay, how wondrous swift to answer a generous appeal!" (Hudspeth 4:315).

[3] The "Moderate party" was composed principally of liberal nobles and members of the bourgeoisie, located primarily in Sardinia with supporters in Lombardy and Venetia. The Moderates wanted the establishment of a constitutional monarchy and believed that economic unification of Italy had to precede political unification. The two other factions working for the unification of Italy were Mazzini and his followers, who believed in the principle of popular sovereignty and a strong nation; and the Neo-Guelph movement, led by Vincenzo Gioberti (1801–52), who advocated a federation of Italian states under the leadership of the pope, with executive authority placed in the hands of a college of princes (Charles Breunig, *The Age of Revolution and Reaction: 1789–1850* [New York: Norton, 1970], 227–29). During her years in Italy, Fuller witnessed the clash of these three different perspectives on Italian unification.

down what is really native to the Italian character, defences and differences that give individual genius a chance to grow and the fruits of each region to ripen in their natural way, they aim at a harmony of spirit as to measures of education and for the affairs of business, without which Italy can never, as one nation, present a front strong enough to resist foreign robbery, and for want of which so much time and talent are wasted here, and internal development almost wholly checked.

There is in Tuscany a large corps of enlightened minds, well prepared to be the instructors, the elder brothers and guardians of the lower people, and whose hearts burn to fulfil that noble office. Hitherto it had been almost impossible to them, for the reasons I have named in speaking of Lombardy; but, during these last four months that the way has been opened by the Freedom of the Press and establishment of the National Guard—so valuable, first of all, as giving occasion for public meetings and free interchange of thought between the different classes, it is surprising how much light they have been able to diffuse already.

A Bolognese, to whom I observed, "How can you be so full of trust when all your hopes depend, not on the recognition of principles and wants throughout the people, but on the life of one mortal man?" replied, "Ah! but you don't consider that his life gives us a chance to effect that recognition. If Pius IX. be spared to us five years, it will be impossible for his successors ever to take a backward course. Our people is of a genius so vivacious; we are unhappy but not stupid, we Italians; we can learn as much in two months as other nations in twenty years." This seemed to me no brag when I returned to Tuscany and saw the great development and diffusion of thought that had taken place during my brief absence. The Grand Duke, a well-intentioned, though dull man, had dared to declare himself "*an* ITALIAN *Prince*," and the heart of Tuscany had bounded with hope. It is now deeply as justly felt that *the* curse of Italy is foreign intrusion, that if she could dispense with foreign aid and be free from foreign aggression, she would find the elements of salvation within herself. All her efforts tend that way, to reestablish the natural position of things: may Heaven grant them success! For myself I believe they will attain it. I see more reason for hope, as I know more of the people. Their rash and baffled struggles have taught them prudence; they are wanted in the civilized world as a peculiar influence; their leaders are thinking men, their cause is righteous. I believe that Italy will revive to new life, and probably a greater, a more truly rich and glorious, than at either epoch of her former greatness.

During the period of my absence, the Austrians had entered Ferrara.[4] It is

---

[4] The Austrian goverment, under the guise of maintaining order, had occupied Ferrara on 17 July 1847. Their intent was to provoke hostilities which could justify military suppres-

well that they hazarded this step, for it showed them the difficulties in acting against a Prince of the Church who is at the same time a friend to the People. The position was new, and they were probably surprised at the result, surprised at the firmness of the Pope, surprised at the indignation, tempered by calm resolve, on the part of the Italians. Louis Philippe's mean apostacy has this time turned to the advantage of Freedom. He renounced the good understanding with England which it had been one of the leading features of his policy to maintain, in the hope of aggrandizing and enriching his family (not France; he did not care for France) he did not know that he was paving the way for Italian Freedom. England now is led to play a part a little nearer her pretensions as the Guardian of Progress than she often comes, and the ghost of Lafayette looks down, not unappeased, to see the "Constitutional King" decried by the subjects he has cheated and lulled so craftily. The King of Sardinia is a worthless man, in whom nobody puts any trust so far as regards his heart or honor, but the stress of things seems likely to keep him on the right side. The little sovereigns blustered at first, then ran away affrighted when they found there was really a spirit risen at last within the charmed circle, a spirit likely to defy, to transcend, the spells of haggard premiers and imbecile monarchs.

I arrived in Florence, unhappily, too late for the great fete of the 12th September, in honor of the grant of the National Guard. But I wept at the mere recital of the events of that day, which, if it should lead to no important results, must still be hallowed for ever in the memory of Italy for the great and beautiful emotions that flooded the hearts of her children. The National Guard is hailed with no undue joy by Italians, as the earnest of Progress, the first step toward truly national institutions and a representation of the people. Gratitude had done its natural work in their hearts; it had made them better. Some days before were passed by reconciling all strifes, composing all differences between cities, districts, and individuals. They wished to drop all petty, all local differences, to wash away all stains, to bathe and prepare for a new great covenant of brotherly love, where each should act for the good of all. On that day they all embraced in sign of this—strangers, foes, all, exchanged the kiss of faith and love; they exchanged banners as a token that they would fight for, would animate, one another. All was done in that beautiful poetic manner peculiar to this artist people, but it was the spirit, so great and tender, that melts my heart to think of. It was the spirit of true religion—such, my Country; as welling freshly from some great hearts in thy early hours, won for thee all of value

---

sion of the reform movement in central Italy (*Cambridge Modern History* 11:77). Shortly thereafter, the Austrian government made a pact with the duke of Modena, and in December they moved into Parma (Fejtö 117).

that thou canst call thy own, whose ground-work is the assertion, still sublime though thou hast not been true to it, that all men have equal rights, and that these are *birth*-rights, derived from God alone.[5]

I rejoice to say that the Americans took their share in this occasion, and that Greenough—one of the few Americans who, living in Italy, takes the pains to know whether it is alive or dead; who penetrates beyond the cheats of trades-men and the cunning of a mob corrupted by centuries of slavery, to know the real mind, the vital blood, of Italy—took a leading part. I am sorry to say that a large portion of my countrymen here take the same slothful and prejudiced view as the English, and, after many years' sojourn, betray entire ignorance of Italian literature and Italian life beyond what is attainable in a month's passage through the thoroughfares. However, they did show, this time, a becoming spirit, and erected the American Eagle where its cry ought to be heard from afar, where a Nation is striving for independent existence and a Government to represent the People. Crawford here in Rome has had the just feeling to join the Guard, and it is a real sacrifice for an artist to spend time on the exercises; but it well becomes the sculptor of Orpheus, of him who had such faith, such music of divine thought, that he made the stones move, turned the beasts from their accustomed haunts and shamed Hell itself into sympathy with the grief of love. I do not deny that such a spirit is wanted here in Italy; it is everywhere if anything great, anything permanent, is to be done. In reference to what I have said of many Americans in Italy, I will only add that they talk about the corrupt and degenerate state of Italy as they do about that of our slaves at home. They come ready trained to that mode of reasoning which affirms that, because men are degraded by bad institutions, they are not fit for better.

For the English, some of them, are full of generous, intelligent sympathy, as indeed what is more solidly, more wisely good than the right sort of English-men, but others are like a gentleman I traveled with the other day, a man of intelligence and refinement too as to the details of life and outside culture, who observed, "he did not see what the Italians wanted of a National Guard unless to wear these little caps." He was a man who had passed five years in Italy, but always covered with that non-conductor called by a witty French writer "the Britannic fluid."[6]

Very sweet to my ear was the continual hymn in the streets of Florence, in honor of Pius IX. It is the Roman hymn, and none of the new ones written in

---

[5] Here Fuller makes her first comment on her increasing opposition to slavery in the United States. In later dispatches she develops this theme more fully.

[6] In *Summer on the Lakes* Fuller had referred to a young British woman visiting northern Illinois as a "young lady who showed herself to have been bathed in the Britannic fluid" (41).

Tuscany have been able to take its place.—The people thank the Grand Duke when he does them good, but they know well from whose mind that good originates, and all their love is for the Pope. Time presses, or I would fain describe in detail the troupe of laborers of the lowest class, marching home at night; keeping step as if they were in the National Guard, filling the air and cheering the melancholy moon, by the patriotic hymns sung, with the mellow tone and in the perfect time which belong to Italians. I would describe the extempore concerts in the streets, the rejoicings at the theatres, where the addresses of liberal souls to the people, through that best vehicle, the drama, may now be heard. But I am tired; what I have to write would fill volumes, and my letter must go. I will only add some words upon the happy augury I draw from the wise docility of the people. With what readiness they listened to wise counsel and the hopes of the Pope that they would give no advantage to his enemies at a time when they were so fevered by the knowledge that conspiracy was at work in their midst. That was a time of trial. On all these occasions of popular excitement their conduct is like music, in such order and with such union of the melody of feeling with discretion where to stop; but what is wonderful is that they acted in the same manner on that difficult occasion. The influence of the Pope here is without bounds; he can always calm the crowd at once. But in Tuscany where they have no such one idol, they listened in the same way on a very trying occasion. The first announcement of the regulation for the Tuscan National Guard terribly dissappointed the people; they felt that the Grand Duke, after suffering them to demonstrate such trust and joy on this feast of the 12th, did not really trust, on his side; that he meant to limit them all he could; they felt baffled, cheated; hence young men in anger tore down at once the symbols of satisfaction and respect; but the leading men went among the people, begged them to be calm, and wait till a deputation had seen the Grand Duke. The people listened at once to men who, they were sure, had at heart their best good— waited; the Grand Duke became convinced, and all ended without disturbance. If the people continue to act thus, their hopes cannot be baffled. Certainly I, for one, do not think that the present road will suffice to lead Italy to her goal. But it *is* an onward, upward road, and the people learn as it advances. Where they can now seek and think fearless of prisons and bayonets, a healthy circulation of blood begins, and the heart frees itself from disease.

I earnestly hope some expression of sympathy from my country toward Italy. Take a good chance and do something; you have shown much good feeling toward the Old World in its physical difficulties—you ought to do so still more in its spiritual endeavor. This cause is OURS, above all others; we ought to show that we feel it to be so. At present there is no likelihood of war, but in case of it I trust the United States would not fail in some noble token of sympathy toward this country. The Soul of our Nation need not wait for its Government; these things are better done by the effort of individuals. I believe some in the United States will pay attention to these words of mine, will feel that I am not a person to be kindled by a childish, sentimental enthusiasm, but that I must be sure that I have seen something of Italy to speak as I do. I have been here only seven months, but my means of observation have been uncommon. I have been ardently desirous to judge fairly, and I had no prejudices to prevent; beside, I was not ignorant of the history and literature of Italy and had some common ground on which to stand with its inhabitants, and hear what they have to say. In many ways she is of kin to us; she is the country of Columbus, of Amerigo, of Cabot. It would please me much to see a cannon here bought by the contributions of Americans, at whose head should stand the name of Cabot, to be used by the Guard for salutes on festive occasions, if they should be so happy as to have no more serious need. In Tuscany they are casting one to be called the "Gioberti," from a writer who has given a great impulse to the present movement. I should like the gift of America to be called the AMERICA, the COLUMBO, or the WASH-INGTON. Please think of this, some of my friends, who still care for the Eagle, the 4th July, and the old cries of Hope and Honor. See, if there are any objections that I do not think of, and do something if it is well and brotherly. Ah! America, with all thy rich boons, thou hast a heavy account to render for the talent given; see in every way that thou be not found wanting.[7]   ★

Dispatch 18

N E W   A N D   O L D   W O R L D   D E M O C R A C Y

[Undated][1]

This letter will reach the United States about the 1st of January; and it may not be impertinent to offer a few New-Year's reflections. Every new year, indeed, confirms the old thoughts, but also presents them under some new aspects.

The American in Europe, if a thinking mind, can only become more American. In some respects it is a great pleasure to be here. Although we have an independent political existence, our position toward Europe, as to Literature

[7] Fuller had written to Francis G. Shaw, a successful, reform-minded businessman, asking him to consider expressing his sympathies for Italy in the United States. In early November a general meeting of citizens gathered in New York to publicly express their sympathy with the aims and hopes of the Italian people for a unified Italy. Among the organizers were Theodore Sedgwick and Horace Greeley (Hudspeth 4:15, 308; Marraro 5).

[1] First published as" Things and Thoughts in Europe. No. XVIII" in *New-York Daily Tribune,* 1 January 1848, p. 1:1–3.

and the Arts, is still that of a colony, and one feels the same joy here that is experienced by the colonist in returning to the parent home. What was but picture to us becomes reality; remote allusions and derivations trouble no more: we see the pattern of the stuff, and understand the whole tapestry. There is a gradual clearing up on many points, and many baseless notions and crude fancies are dropped. Even the post-haste passage of the business American through the great cities, escorted by cheating couriers, and ignorant *valets de place,* unable to hold intercourse with the natives of the country, and passing all his leisure hours with his countrymen, who know no more than himself, clears his mind of some mistakes—lifts some mists from his horizon.

There are three species: first, the servile American—a being utterly shallow, thoughtless, worthless. He comes abroad to spend his money and indulge his tastes. His object in Europe is to have fashionable clothes, good foreign cookery, to know some titled persons, and furnish himself with coffee-house gossip, which he wins importance at home by retailing among those less traveled, and as uninformed as himself.

I look with unspeakable contempt on this class—a class which has all the thoughtlessness and partiality of the exclusive classes in Europe, without any of their refinement, or the chivalric feeling which still sparkles among them here and there. However, though these willing serfs in a free age do some little hurt, and cause some annoyance at present, it cannot last: our country is fated to a grand, independent existence, and as its laws develop, these parasites of a bygone period must wither and drop away.

Then there is the conceited American, instinctively bristling and proud of— he knows not what—He does not see, not he, that the history of Humanity for many centuries is likely to have produced results it requires some training, some devotion, to appreciate and profit by. With his great clumsy hands only fitted to work on a steam-engine, he seizes the old Cremona violin, makes it shriek with anguish in his grasp, and then declares he thought it was all humbug before he came, and now he knows it; that there is not really any music in these old things; that the frogs in one of our swamps make much finer, for *they* are young and alive. To him the etiquettes of courts and camps, the ritual of the Church, seem simply silly—and no wonder, profoundly ignorant as he is of their origin and meaning. Just so the legends which are the subjects of pictures, the profound myths which are represented in the antique marbles, amaze and revolt him; as, indeed, such things need to be judged of by another standard from that of the Connecticut Blue-Laws. He criticises severely pictures, feeling quite sure that his natural senses are better means of judgment than the rules of connoisseurs—not feeling that to see such objects mental vision as well as fleshly eyes are needed, and that something is aimed at in Art beyond the imitation of the commonest forms of Nature.

This is Jonathan in the sprawling state, the booby truant, not yet aspiring enough to be a good school-boy. Yet in his folly there is meaning; add thought and culture to his independence, and he will be a man of might: he is not a creature without hope, like the thick-skinned dandy of the class first specified.

The Artistes form a class by themselves. Yet among them, though seeking special aims by special means may also be found the lineaments of these two classes, as well as of the third, of which I am to speak.

3d. The thinking American—a man who, recognizing the immense advantage of being born to a new world and on a virgin soil, yet does not wish one seed from the Past to be lost. He is anxious to gather and carry back with him all that will bear a new climate and new culture. Some will dwindle; others will attain a bloom and stature unknown before. He wishes to gather them clean, free from noxious insects. He wishes to give them a fair trial in his new world. And that he may know the conditions under which he may best place them in that new world, he does not neglect to study their history in this.

The history of our planet in some moments seems so painfully mean and little, such terrible bafflings and failures to compensate some brilliant successes—such a crashing of the mass of men beneath the feet of a few, and these, too, of the least worthy—such a small drop of honey to each cup of gall, and, in many cases, so mingled, that it is never one moment in life purely tasted,— above all, so little achieved for Humanity as a whole, such tides of war and pestilence intervening to blot out the traces of each triumph, that no wonder if the strongest soul sometimes pauses aghast! No wonder if the many indolently console themselves with gross joys and frivolous prizes. Yes! those men *are* worthy of admiration who can carry this cross faithfully through fifty years; it is a great while for all the agonies that beset a lover of good, a lover of men; it makes a soul worthy of a speedier ascent, a more productive ministry in the next sphere. Blessed are they who ever keep that portion of pure, generous love with which they began life! How blessed those who have deepened the fountains, and have enough to spare for the thirst of others! Some such there are; and, feeling that, with all the excuses for failure, still only the sight of those who triumph gives a meaning to life or makes its pangs endurable, we must arise and follow.

Eighteen hundred years of this Christian culture in these European Kingdoms, a great theme never lost sight of, a mighty idea, an adorable history to which the hearts of men invariably cling, yet are genuine results rare as grains of gold in the river's sandy bed! Where is the genuine Democracy to which the rights of all men are holy? where the child-like wisdom learning all through life more and more of the will of God? where the aversion to falsehood in all its myriad disguises of cant, vanity, covetousness, so clear to be read in all the history of Jesus of Nazareth? Modern Europe is the sequel to that history, and see this hollow England, with its monstrous wealth and cruel poverty, its conventional life and low, practical aims; see this poor France, so full of talent, so adroit, yet so shallow and glossy still, which could not escape from a false position with all its baptism of blood; see that lost Poland and this Italy bound down by treacherous hands in all the force of genius; see Russia with its brutal Czar and innumerable slaves; see Austria and its royalty that represents nothing, and its people who, as people, are and have nothing! If we consider the amount of truth that has really been spoken out in the world, and the love that has beat in private hearts—how Genius has decked each spring-time with such splendid flowers, conveying each one enough of instruction in its life of harmonious energy, and how continually, unquenchably the spark of faith has striven to burst into flame and light up the Universe—the public failure seems amazing, seems monstrous.

Still Europe toils and struggles with her idea, and, at this moment, all things bode and declare a new outbreak of the fire, to destroy old palaces of crime! May it fertilize also many vineyards!—Here at this moment a successor of St. Peter, after the lapse of near two thousand years, is called "Utopian" by a part of this Europe, because he strives to get some food to the mouths of the *leaner* of his flock. A wonderful state of things, and which leaves as the best argument against despair that men do not, *cannot* despair amid such dark experiences— and thou, my country! will thou not be more true? does no greater success await thee? All things have so conspired to teach, to aid! A new world, a new chance, with oceans to wall in the new thought against interference from the old!— Treasures of all kinds, gold, silver, corn, marble, to provide for every physical need! A noble, constant, starlike soul, an Italian, led the way to its shores, and, in the first days, the strong, the pure, those too brave, too sincere for the life of the Old World hastened to people them. A generous struggle then shook off what was foreign and gave the nation a glorious start for a worthy goal. Men rocked the cradle of its hopes, great, firm, disinterested men who saw, who wrote, as the basis of all that was to be done, a statement of the rights, the inborn rights of men, which, if fully interpreted and acted upon, leaves nothing to be desired.

Yet, oh Eagle, whose early flight showed this clear sight of the Sun, how often dost thou near the ground, how show the vulture in these later days! Thou wert to be the advance-guard of Humanity, the herald of all Progress; how often hast thou betrayed this high commission! Fain would the tongue in clear triumphant accents draw example from thy story, to encourage the hearts of those who almost faint and die beneath the old oppressions. But we must stammer and blush when we speak of many things. I take pride here that I may really say the Liberty of the Press works well, and that checks and balances naturally evolve from it which suffice to its government. I may say the minds of our people are alert, and that Talent has a free chance to rise. It is much. But dare I say that political ambition is not as darkly sullied as in other countries? Dare I say that men of most influence in political life are those who represent most virtue or even intellectual power? Is it easy to find names in that career of which I can speak with enthusiasm? Must I not confess in my country to a boundless lust of gain? Must I not confess to the weakest vanity, which bristles and blusters at each foolish taunt of the foreign press; and must I not admit that the men who make these undignified rejoinders seek and find popularity so? Must I not confess that there is as yet no antidote cordially adopted that will defend even that great, rich country against the evils that have grown out of the commercial system in the old world? Can I say our social laws are generally better, or show a nobler insight into the wants of man and woman? I do, indeed, say what I believe, that voluntary association for improvement in these particulars will be the grand means for my nation to grow and give a nobler harmony to the coming age. But it is only of a small minority that I can say they as yet seriously take to heart these things; that they earnestly meditate on what is wanted for their country,—for mankind,—for our cause is, indeed, the cause of all mankind at present. Could we succeed, really succeed, combine a deep religious love with practical development, the achievements of Genius with the happiness of the multitude, we might believe Man had now reached a commanding point in his ascent, and would stumble and faint no more. Then there is this horrible cancer of Slavery, and this wicked War, that has grown out of it.[2] How dare I speak of these things here? I listen to the same arguments against the emancipation of Italy, that are used against the emancipation of our blacks; the same arguments in favor of the spoliation of Poland as for the conquest of Mexico. I find the cause of tyranny and wrong everywhere the same—and lo! my Country the darkest offender, because with the least excuse, foresworn to the high calling with which she was called,—no champion of the rights of men, but a robber and a jailer; the scourge hid behind her banner; her eyes fixed, not on the stars, but on the possessions of other men.

[2] Fuller alludes to the Mexican War (1846–48), viewed by many in America as a means to extend slavery territory. It was precipitated by the annexation of Texas by the United States in December 1845. Hostilities began in April 1846 when Mexicans resisted the crossing of the disputed boundary of southern Texas by American troops. The treaty of Guadalupe-Hildalgo, signed on 2 February 1848, gave the United States two-fifths of Mexico's territory, including California *(OCAL)*

How it pleases me here to think of the Abolitionists! I could never endure to be with them at home, they were so tedious, often so narrow, always so rabid and exaggerated in their tone.[3]

But, after all, they had a high motive, something eternal in their desire and life; and, if it was not the only thing worth thinking of it was really something worth living and dying for to free a great nation from such a terrible blot, such a threatening plague. God strengthen them and make them wise to achieve their purpose!

I please myself, too, with remembering some ardent souls among the American youth who, I trust, will yet expand and help to give soul to the huge, over fed, too hastily grown-up body. May they be constant. "Were Man but constant he were perfect!" it has been said; and it is true that he who could be constant to those moments in which he has been truly human—not brutal, not mechanical—is on the sure path to his perfection and to effectual service of the Universe.

It is to the youth that Hope addresses itself, to those who yet burn with aspiration, who are not hardened in their sins. But I dare not expect too much of them. I am not very old, yet of those who, in life's morning, I saw touched by the light of a high hope, many have seceded. Some have become voluptuaries; some mere family men, who think it is quite life enough to win bread for half a dozen people and treat them decently; others are lost through indolence and vacillation. Yet some remain constant. "I have witnessed many a shipwreck, yet still beat noble hearts."

I have found many among the youth of England, of France—of Italy also— full of high desire, but will they have courage and purity to fight the battle through in the sacred, the immortal band? Of some of them I believe it and await the proof. If a few succeed amid the trial, we have not lived and loved in vain.

To these, the heart of my country, a Happy New Year! I do not know what I have written. I have merely yielded to my feelings in thinking of America; but something of true love must be in these lines—receive them kindly, my friends; it is, by itself, some merit for printed words to be sincere.   ★

[3] In the early 1840s Fuller expressed indifference toward the antislavery movement and refused to devote one of her "conversations" to abolition when Maria Weston Chapman asked her to do so. In 1845, however, she published seven pieces in the *Tribune* against slavery, and she twice reviewed Chapman's annual abolition anthology (Chevigny 238–39, 286, 288, 340–42).

Dispatch 19

ROMAN SIGHTS AND CEREMONIES

ROME, Dec. 17, 1847 [1]

This seventeenth day of December I rise to see the floods of sunlight blessing us as they have almost every day since I returned to Rome—two months and more; with scarce three or four days of rainy weather. I see the fresh roses and grapes still each morning on my table, though both these I expect to give up at Christmas.

This autumn is *"something like,"* as my country men say at home. Like *what,* they do not say, so I always supposed they meant like the ideal standard. Certainly this weather corresponds with mine, and I begin to believe the climate of Italy is really what it has been represented.[2] Shivering here last Spring in an air no better than the cruel east wind of Puritan Boston, I thought all the praises lavished on

"Italia, O Italia!" [3]

would turn out to be figments of the brain, and that even Byron, usually accurate beyond the conception of plodding pedants, had deceived us when he says you have the happiness in Italy to

"See the sun set sure he'll rise to-morrow,"

and not according to a view which exercises a withering influence on the enthusiasm of youth in my native land be forced to regard each pleasant day as a *"weather-breeder."*

How delightful, too, is the contrast between this time and the Spring in another respect! Then I was here, like travelers in general, expecting to be driven away in a short time. Like others, I went through the painful process of

[1] First published as "Things and Thoughts in Europe. No. XIX" in *New-York Daily Tribune,* 29 January 1848, p. 1:1–4.

[2] Fuller's autumn in Italy had been an idyllic time in her life. She was in love with Giovanni Angelo Ossoli (1821–50), the younger son of a noble family, whom she had met in April 1847 (Deiss 53–57 and Hudspeth 5:6). Her reunion with him in the fall had clearly been a happy one. Although she did not confide in her family and friends, she wrote glowing letters of her happy life. To her mother she wrote: "My life at Rome is thus far all I hoped. I have not been so well since I was a child, nor so happy ever as during the last six weeks. . . . The air of Rome agrees with me as it did before and Rome is so dear I do not know how I can ever be willing to live anywhere else" (Hudspeth 4:312).

[3] "Childe Harold's Pilgrimage," canto 4, 42, 6 (Ernest Hartley Coleridge, ed., *The Works of Lord Byron* [New York: Scribners, 1899], 2:361).

sight-seeing, so unnatural everywhere, so counter to the healthful methods and true life of the mind. You rise in the morning knowing there are around you a great number of objects worth knowing, which you may never have a chance to see again. You go every day, in all moods, under all circumstances; you feel, probably, in seeing them, the inadequacy of your preparation for understanding or duly receiving them; this consciousness would be most valuable if you had time to think and study, being the natural way in which the mind is lured to cure its defects—but you have no time, you are always wearied, body and mind, confused, dissipated, sad. The objects are of commanding beauty or full of suggestion, but you have no quiet to let that beauty breathe its life into your soul—no time to follow up these suggestions and plant for your proper harvest. Many persons run about Rome for nine days and then go away; they might as well expect to see it so, as to appreciate the Venus by throwing a stone at it. I stayed in Rome nine weeks and came away unhappy as he who, having been taken in the visions of night through some wondrous realm, wakes unable to recall anything but the hues and outlines of the pageant, the real knowledge, the recreative power induced by familiar love, the assimilation of its soul and substance—all the true value of such a revelation—is wanting, and he remains a poor Tantalus, hungrier even when he most needed to be fed.

No; Rome is not a nine-days' wonder, and those who try to make it such lose the ideal Rome (if they ever had it) without gaining any notion of the real. For those who travel, as they do everything else—only because others do—I do not speak to them; they are nothing. Nobody counts in the estimate of the human race who has no character.

For one, I now really live in Rome, and I begin to see and feel the real Rome. She reveals herself now; she tells me some of her life. Now I never go out to see a sight, but I walk every day, and here I cannot miss of some object of consummate interest to end a walk. In the evenings, which are long now, I am at leisure to follow up the inquiries suggested by the day.

As one becomes familiar, ancient and modern Rome—at first so painfully and discordantly jumbled together, are drawn apart to the mental vision. You see where objects and limits anciently were; the superstructures vanish, and you recognize the local habitation of so many thoughts. When this begins to happen it is that one feels first truly at ease in Rome. Then the old Kings, the Consuls, and Tribunes, the Emperors, drunk with blood and gold, the warriors of eagle sight and remorseless beak, return for us, and the toga'd procession finds room to sweep across the scene; the seven hills tower, the innumerable temples glitter, and the Via Sacra swarms with triumphal life once more.

Ah! how joyful to see once more *this* Rome, instead of the pitiful, peddling, Anglicised Rome first viewed in unutterable dismay from the coupe of the vettura: a Rome all full of taverns, lodging houses, cheating chambermaids, vilest vile *valets de place* and fleas!! A Niobe of Nations, indeed! ah, why! secretly the heart blasphemed, did the Sun omit to kill her, too, when all the glorious race which wore her crown, fell beneath his ray!

Thank heaven, it is possible to wash away all this dirt and come at the marble yet.

Then the later Papal Rome: it requires much acquaintance, much thought, much reference to books, for the child of Protestant, Republican America to see where belong the legends illustrated by rite and picture, the sense of all the rich tapestry where it has a united and poetic meaning, where it is broken by some accident of history. For all these things, a senseless mass of juggleries to the uninformed eye, are really growths of the human spirit struggling to develop its life, and full of instruction for those who learn to understand them.

Then Modern Rome—still ecclesiastical, still darkened and damp in the shadow of the Vatican, but where bright hopes gleam now amid the ashes. Never was a people who have had more to corrupt them—bloody tyranny, and incubus of priestcraft, the invasions, first of Goths, then of trampling emperors and kings, then of sight-seeing foreigners, everything to turn them from a sincere, hopeful, fruitful life, and they are much corrupted, but still a fine race. I cannot look merely with a pictorial eye on the lounge of the Roman Dandy, the bold, Juno gait of the Roman Contadina. I love them, (Dandies and all?) I believe the natural expression of these fine forms will animate them yet. Certainly there never was a people that showed a better heart than they do in this day of love, of purely moral influence. It makes me very happy to be for once in a place ruled by a father's love, and where the pervasive glow of one good, generous heart is felt in every pulse of every day.

I have seen the Pope several times since my return, and it is a real pleasure to see him in the thoroughfares, where his passage is always greeted as that of *the* living soul.

The first week of November there is much praying for the dead here in the Chapels of the Cemeteries.[4] I went to Santo Spirito. This Cemetery stands high, and all the way up the slope was lined with beggars petitioning for alms, in every attitude and tone, (I mean tone that belongs to the professional beggar's gamut, for that is peculiar,) and under every pretext imaginable, from the quite legless elderly gentleman to the ragged ruffian with the roguish twinkle in his

---

[4] The series of buildings along the Via Giulia, a thoroughfare designed in the sixteenth century as an approach to St. Peter's (it was never finished). At the end of the street is a good view of Rome. Santo Spirito, one of many churches near St. Peter's, is built on the site of an eighth-century settlement of Saxons (Masson 145–48; Baedeker 2:305).

eye, who has merely a slight stiffness in one arm and one leg. I could not help laughing; it was such a show; greatly to the alarm of my attendant, who declared they would kill me, if ever they caught me alone, but I was not afraid. I am sure the endless falsehood in which such creatures live must make them very cowardly. We entered the Cemetery; it was a sweet, tranquil place, lined with cypresses, and soft sunshine lying on the stone coverings where repose the houses of clay in which once dwelt joyous Roman hearts—for the hearts here do take pleasure in life. There were several Chapels; in one boys were chanting, in others people on their knees silently praying for the dead. In another was one of the groups in wax exhibited in such Chapels through the first week of November. It represented St. Carlo Borromeo as a beautiful young man in a long scarlet robe, pure and brilliant, as was the blood of the martyrs, relieving the poor who were grouped around him—old people and children, the halt, the maimed, the blind; he had called them all in to the feast of love; the Chapel was lighted and draped so as to give very good effect to this group; the spectators were mainly children and young girls, listening with ardent eyes, while their parents or the Nuns explained to them the group, or told some story of the Saint. It was a pretty scene, only marred by the presence of a villanous looking man, who ever and anon shook the poor's box. I cannot understand the bad taste of choosing him, when there were *frati*[5] and priests enough of expression less unprepossessing.

I next entered a court-yard, where the stations, or different periods in the Passion of Jesus, are painted on the wall. Kneeling around at these were many persons: here a Franciscan, in his brown robe and cord; there a pregnant woman, uttering, doubtless, some tender aspiration for the welfare of the yet unborn dear one; there some boys, with gay yet reverent air; while all the while these fresh young voices were heard chanting. It was a beautiful moment, and despite the wax saint, the ill-favored friar, the professional mendicants, and my own removal, wide as pole from pole, from the position of mind indicated by these forms, their spirit touched me and I prayed too—prayed for the distant, every way distant—for those who seem to have forgotten me, and with me all we had in common—prayed for the dead in spirit, if not in body—prayed for myself, that I might never walk the earth

   "The tomb of my dead self,"

and prayed in general for all unspoiled and loving hearts, no less for all who suffer and find yet no helper.

Going out, I took my road by the Cross, which marks the brow of the hill.

---

[5] Monks

Up the ascent still wound the crowd of devotees, and still the beggars beset them. Amid that crowd how many lovely, warm hearted women! The women of Italy are intellectually in a low place, *but*—they are unaffected; you can see what Heaven meant them to be, and I believe they will be yet the mothers of a great and generous race. Before me lay Rome—how exquisitely tranquil in the sunset! Never was an aspect that for serene grandeur could vie with that of Rome at sunset.

Next day was the feast of the Milanese saint, whose life has been made known to some Americans by Manzoni, when speaking in his popular novel of the cousin of St. Carlo, Federigo Borromeo. The Pope came in state to the Church of St. Carlo, in the Corso.[6] The show was magnificent; the church is not very large, and was almost filled with the Papal court and guards, in all their splendid harmonies of color. An Italian child was next me, a little girl of four or five years, whom her mother had brought to see the Pope. As in the intervals of gazing the child smiled and made signs to me, I nodded in return and asked her name: "Virginia," said she; "and how is the Signora named?" "Margherita." "My name," she rejoined, "is Virginia Gentili." I laughed, but did not follow up the cunning, graceful lead—still I chatted and played with her now and then. At last, she said to her mother, "La Signora e molto cara," (the Signora is very dear,) or, to use the English equivalent, *a darling;* "show her my two sisters." So the mother, herself a fine-looking woman, introduced two handsome young ladies, and with the family I was in a moment pleasantly intimate for the hour.

Before me sat three young English ladies the pretty daughters of a noble Earl; their manners were a strange contrast to this Italian graciousness, best expressed by their constant use of the offish pronoun that—*"See that man,"* (i.e. some high dignitary of the church,) "Look at that dress," dropped constantly from their lips. Ah! without being a Catholic one may well wish Rome was not dependent on English sight-seers who violate her ceremonies with acts that bespeak their thoughts full of wooden shoes and warming-pans. Can any thing be more sadly expressive of times out of joint than the fact that Mrs. Trollope is a resident in Italy? Yes! she is fixed permanently in Florence, as I am told, pensioned at the rate of two thousand pounds a year to trail her slime over the fruit of Italy. She is here in Rome this winter, and after having violated the virgin beauty of America, will have for many a year her chance to sully the imperial

[6] The church of St. Carlo in the Corso is dedicated to St. Carlo Borromeo (1538–84), the archbishop of Milan. His strong interest in social problems and his heroic dedication in the plague year of 1576 made him greatly revered by the people. The Feast of St. Carlo is celebrated on 4 November (*NCE*). Fuller is thinking of Manzoni's *I promessi sposi* (The betrothed, 1827).

matron of the civilized world. What must the English public be, if it wishes to pay two thousand pounds a year to get Italy Trollopified?[7]

But, to turn to a pleasanter subject. When the Pope entered, borne in his chair of state amid the pomp of his tiara and his white and gold robes, he looked to me thin, or as the Italians murmur anxiously at times *consumato,* or wasted. But during the ceremony he seemed absorbed in his devotions, and at the end I think he had become exhilarated by thinking of St. Carlo, who was such another lover of the human race as himself, and his face wore a bright glow of faith. As he blessed the people he raised his eyes to Heaven, with a gesture quite natural: it was the spontaneous act of a soul which felt that moment more than usual its relation with things above it, and sure of support from a higher Power. I saw him to still greater advantage a little while after when riding on the Campagna with a young gentleman who had been ill; we met the Pope on foot, taking exercise. He often quits his carriage at the gates and walks in this way. He walked rapidly, robed in a simple white drapery, two young priests in a spotless purple walked on either side; they gave silver to the poor who knelt beside the way, while the beloved Father gave his benediction. My companion knelt; he is not a Catholic but he felt that "this blessing would do him no harm." The Pope saw at once he was ill and gave him a mark of interest with that expression of melting love, the true, the only charity, which assures all who look on him that were his power equal to his will, no living thing would ever suffer more. This expression the artists try in vain to catch; all busts and engravings of him are caricatures; it is a magnetic sweetness, a lambent light that plays over his features, and of which only great genius or a soul tender as his own would form an adequate image.

The Italians have one term of praise peculiarly characteristic of their highly endowed nature. — They say of such and such, *"Ha una phisonomia simpatica,"* — "He has a sympathetic expression;" and this is praise enough. This may be pre-eminently said of that of Pius IX. *He* looks, indeed, as if nothing human could be foreign to him. Such alone are the genuine kings of men.

He has shown undoubted wisdom, clear-sightedness, bravery and firmness, but it is above all, his generous human heart that gives him his power over this people. His is a face to shame the selfish, redeem the skeptic, alarm the wicked and cheer to new effort the weary and heavy-laden. — What form the issues of his life may take is yet uncertain: in my belief they are such as he does not think of; but they cannot fail to be for good. — For my part, I shall always rejoice to have been here in this time. The working of his influence confirms all my

[7] Fuller's negative opinion of Frances Trollope and her *Domestic Manners of the Americans* had not changed since the publication of *Summer on the Lakes.*

theories, and it is a positive treasure to me to have seen him. I have never been presented, not wishing to approach so real a presence in the path of mere etiquette; I am quite content to see him standing amid the crowd, while the band plays the music he has inspired.

"Sons of Rome, awake!"[8]

Yes, awake, and let no police officer put you again to sleep in prison, as has happened to those who were called by the Marseillaise.

Affairs look well here. The King of Sardinia has at last, though with evident distrust and heartlessness, entered the upward path in a way that makes it difficult to return. The Duke of Modena, the most senseless of all these ancient gentlemen, after publishing a declaration which made him more ridiculous than would the bitterest pasquinade penned by another, that he would fight to the death against Reform, finds himself obliged to lend an ear as to the league for the Customs; and if he joins that, other measures follow of course. Austria trembles; and, in fine, cannot sustain the point of Ferrara. The King of Naples, after having shed much blood, for which he has a terrible account to render, (ah! how many sad, fair romances are to tell already about the Calabrian difficulties!)[9] still finds the spirit fomenting in his people; he cannot put it down; the dragon's teeth are sown, and the lazzaroni may be men yet! The Swiss affairs have taken the right direction, and good will ensue, if other powers act with decent honesty, and think of healing the wounds of Switzerland, rather than merely of tying her down, so that she cannot annoy them.[10]

[8] "The Awakening of Italy" was a spirited song of the Italian liberation movement; the lyrics were by Secchidi Casali and the music by Herrman S. Saroni. According to the *Tribune*, William Cullen Bryant translated the Italian words into English for the Hall & Son publication of the piece. "It is," the *Tribune* declared, "one of the best of the modern Revolutionary lyrics which we have seen, and we have no doubt will be very popular" (30 June 1848, p. 3). The song obviously echoes the French "Marseillaise," which begins (in translation), "Ye Sons of France awake to Glory."

[9] Calabria, located in southern Italy and at this time a part of the Kingdom of Naples, was the scene, in 1844, of an insurrection organized by Emilio and Attilio Bandiera. Forced to serve in the Austrian army, they nonetheless wished to be a part of Young Italy and join Mazzini in the Italian cause. Their correspondence with Mazzini was intercepted by the British postmaster-general, who communicated the details of their plans to the Austrians. As a result, the Austrians eventually were able to thwart the insurrection, and the Bandiera brothers were captured and shot to death (Maurice 118–20).

[10] On 4 November 1847 the liberal Diet of the Swiss Confederation declared war on the Sonderbund, the seven Catholic and conservative cantons who refused to dissolve their outlawed coalition; civil war resulted but lasted only twenty-three days. The victorious government showed considerable clemency toward the dissident cantons, merely imposing fines upon them (Fejtö 62–63).

In Rome, here, the new Council is inaugurated, and elections have given tolerable satisfaction. Already struggles, by-passed in other places, begin to be renewed here as to gas-lights, introduction of machinery, &c. We shall see at the end of the Winter how they have gone on. At any rate, the wants of the people are in some measure represented; and already the conduct of those who have taken to themselves so large a portion of the loaves and fishes on the very platform supposed to be selected by Jesus for a general feeding of his sheep, begins to be the subject of spoken as well as whispered animadversion. Torlonia is assailed in his bank, Campana amid his urns or his Monte di Pieti—but these assaults have yet to be verified.[11]

On the day when the Council was to be inaugurated, great preparations were made by representatives of other parts of Italy, and also foreign nations friendly to the cause of Progress. It was considered to represent the same thought as the feast of 12th Sept. in Tuscany, the dawn of an epoch when the people should find their wants and aspirations represented and guarded. The Americans showed a warm interest; the gentlemen subscribing to buy a flag (the United States having none before in Rome) and the ladies meeting to make it. The same distinguished individual, indeed, who at Florence, made a speech to prevent "the American Eagle being taken out on so trifling an occasion," with similar perspicuity and superiority of view, on the present occasion was anxious to prevent "rash demonstrations, which might embroil the United States with Austria;" but the rash youth here present rushed on, ignorant how to value his Nestorian prudence—fancying, hot-headed simpletons, that the cause of Freedom was the cause of America and her Eagle at home, wherever the Sun shed a warmer ray, and, there was reason to hope, a happier life for Man. So they hurried to buy their silk—red, white and blue, and inquired of recent arrivals how many States there are this Winter in the Union, in order to making the proper number of stars. A magnificent spread Eagle was procured, not without difficulty, as this, once the eyrie of the king of birds, is now a rookery rather, full of black ominous fowl, ready to eat the harvest sown by industrious hands.[12] This eagle having previously spread its wings over a piece of furniture where its back was sustained by the wall was somewhat deficient in a part of its anatomy. But we flattered

[11] Giovanni Torlonia (1754–1829) founded a bank in Rome in 1814; in 1848 his son, Prince Alessandro Torlonia (1800–86) was "assailed" for his conduct of bank affairs (Hudspeth 5:73–74). Giovanni Pietro Campana, an antiquarian, was the director of the Monte di Pietà, since 1604 a pawn office. His management resulted in financial difficulties for which he was sentenced to a year in prison, later changed to a sentence of exile (Zorzi 58; Baedeker 2:221).

[12] Fuller's allusion is to the Jesuit priests, hated because of their reactionary politics and secret intrigue against reform (*Cambridge Modern History* 11:76).

ourselves he should be held so high that no Roman eye, if disposed, could carp and criticise. When lo! just as the banner was ready to unfold its young glories in the home of Horace, Virgil and Tacitus, an ordinance appeared, prohibiting the display of any but the Roman ensign.

This ordinance was, it is said, caused by representations made to the Pope that the Obscurantists,[13] ever on the watch to do mischief, meant to make this the occasion of disturbance; as it is their policy to seek to create irritation here; that the Neapolitan and Lombardo-Venetian flags would appear draped with black, and thus the signal be given for tumult. I cannot help thinking these fears were groundless, that the people, on their guard, would have indignantly crushed at once any of these malignant efforts. However that may be, no one can ever be really displeased with any measure of the Pope, knowing his excellent intentions. But the limitation of the festival deprived it of the noble character of the brotherhood of nations and an ideal aim, worn by that of Tuscany. The Romans, chilled and disappointed, greeted their Councilors with but little enthusiasm. The procession, too, was but a poor affair for Rome. Twenty-four carriages had been lent by the princes and nobles, at the request of the city, to convey the Councilors. I found something symbolical in this. Thus will they be obliged to furnish from their old grandeur the vehicles of the new ideas. Each deputy was followed by his target and banner. When the deputy for Ferrara passed, many garlands were thrown upon his carriage. There has been deep respect and sympathy felt for the citizens of Ferrara; they have conducted so well under their late trying circumstances. They contained themselves, knowing that the least indiscretion would give a handle for aggression to the enemies of the good cause. But the daily occasions of irritation must have been innumerable, and they have shown much power of wise and dignified self-government.

After the procession passed, I attempted to go on foot from the Café Novo in the Corso to St. Peter's, to see the decorations of the streets, but it was impossible. In that dense but most vivacious, various and good-humored crowd, with all best will on their part to aid the foreigner, it was impossible to advance. So I saw only themselves; but that was a great pleasure. There is so much individuality of character here that it is a great entertainment to be in the crowd.

In the evening there was a ball given at the Argentina.[14] Lord Minto was there; Prince Corsini, now Senator; the Torlonias, in uniform of the Civic Guard; Princess Torlonia, in a sash of their colors, given her by the Civic Guard, which she waved often in answer to their greetings. But the beautiful show of

---

[13] Fuller's derogatory name for the Jesuits.

[14] The Teatro Argentina, a theater described by William Wetmore Story (1819–95) as dedicated to comedy, farce, and second-rate opera (Story 1:210).

the evening was the Trasteverini dancing the Saltarello in their most brilliant costume. I saw them thus to much greater advantage than ever before; several were nobly handsome, and danced admirably; it was really like Pinelli.[15]

The Saltarello enchants me; in this is really the Italian wine, the Italian sun. The first time I saw it danced one night very unexpectedly near the Colosseum; it carried me quite beyond myself, so that I most unamiably insisted on staying while the friends in my company, not heated by enthusiasm like me, were shivering and catching cold from the damp night-air. I dare say they remember it against me, nevertheless I cherish the memory of the moments wickedly stolen at their expense; for it is only the first time seeing such a thing that you enjoy that peculiar delight. But since, I love to see and study it much.

The Pope, in receiving the Councilors, made a speech; such as the King of Prussia entrenched himself in on a similar occasion, only much better and shorter; implying that he meant only to improve, not to *reform,* and should keep things *in statu quo,* safe locked with the keys of St. Peter. This little speech was made, no doubt, more to reassure Czars, Emperors and Kings than from the promptings of the spirit. But the fact of its necessity, as well as the inferior freedom and spirit of the Roman journals to those of Tuscany, seems to say that the Pontifical government, though from the accident of this one man's accession, it has taken the initiative to better times, yet may not, after a while, from its very nature, be able to keep in the vanguard.

A sad contrast to the feast of this day was presented by the same persons, a fortnight after, following the body of Silvani, one of the Councilors, who died suddenly. The Councilors, the different Societies of Rome, a corps *frati* bearing tapers, the Civic Guard with drums slowly beating, the same state carriages with their liveried attendants all slowly, sadly moving, with torches and banners, drooped along the Corso in the dark night. A single horseman, with his long white plume and torch reversed, governed the procession: it was the Prince Aldobrandini. The whole had that grand effect, so easily given by this artist-people, who seize instantly the natural poetry of an occasion and with unanimous tact hasten to represent it. More and much anon.   ★

---

[15] Elliot Gilbert, second earl of Minto (1782–1859), was a British statesman in Italy on a diplomatic mission to report to the British government on Italian affairs, to assist Pius IX in his reform measures, and to improve relationships with Sardinia and Tuscany. Tommaso Corsini (1767–1856) was an ambassador at the court of Napoleon in Paris from 1796 to 1805. He was a senator in Rome in 1818 and then in 1847, a leader who, after the flight of Pius IX, helped adopt a moderate government for the city. He later fled to Florence and did not take part in creating the short-lived Roman Republic (*DNB;* Zorzi 58). The Trasteverini were the poor of Rome who lived by the Tiber on the west side of the city in the Trastevere quarter. Bartolomeo Pinelli (1781–1835), a painter, engraver, and sculptor, depicted everyday Roman life (Zorzi 58).

Dispatch 20

R A I N Y - D A Y S'   O B S E R V A T I O N S

ROME, Dec. 30, 1847 [1]

I could not, in my last, content myself with praising the glorious weather. I wrote in the last day of it. Since, we have had a fortnight of rain falling incessantly, and whole days and nights in torrents such as are peculiar to the "clearing-up" shower in our country.

Under these circumstances, I have found my lodging in the Corso not only has its dark side, but is all dark, and that one in the Piazza di Spagne would have been better for me in this respect that on those days, the only ones when I wish to stay at home and write and study, I should have had the light. Now, if I consulted the good of my eyes, I should have the lamp lit when I first rise in the morning.

"Every sweet must have its sour," and the exchange from the brilliance of the Italian heaven to weeks and months of rain and such black cloud, is unspeakably dejecting. For myself, at the end of this fortnight without exercise or light, and in such a damp atmosphere, I find myself without strength, without appetite, almost without spirits.[2] The life of the German scholar who studies fifteen hours out of the twenty-four, or that of the Spielberg prisoner who could live through ten, fifteen, twenty years of dark prison with only half an hour's exercise in the day, is to me a mystery.—How can the brain, the nerves ever support it?—We are made to keep in motion, to drink the air and light; to me these alone make life supportable; the physical state is so difficult and full of pains at any rate.

I am sorry for those who have arrived just at this time, hoping to enjoy the Christmas festivities.—Everything was spoiled by the weather. I went at half-past ten to San Luigi Francese, a church adorned with some of Domenichino's finest frescoes on the life and death of St. Cecilia.[3]

This name leads me to a little digression. In a letter to Mr. Phillips, the dear friend of our revered Dr. Channing, I asked him if he remembered what recumbent statue it was of which Dr. Channing was wont to speak as of a sight that

[1] First published as "Things and Thoughts in Europe. No. XX" in *New-York Daily Tribune,* 7 February 1848, p. 1:1–3.

[2] The glorious autumn that Fuller had spent with Ossoli had come to an end, and she undoubtedly realized that she was pregnant.

[3] The national church of France, S. Luigi dei Francesi, was begun in 1523 and completed in 1578. Although the Domenichino frescoes are very fine, the great treasures of the church are Caravaggio's paintings in the Chapel of St. Matthew: the *Calling,* the *Martyrdom of St. Matthew,* and *St. Matthew with the Angel* (Masson 164–65).

impressed him more than anything else in Rome.[4] He said indeed his mood, and the unexpectedness in seeing this gentle, saintly figure lying there as if Death had just struck her down, had, no doubt, much influence upon him, but still he believed the work had a peculiar holiness in its expression. I recognized at once the theme of his description (the name he himself had forgotten) as I entered the other evening the lonely Church of St. Cecilia in Trastevere. As in his case, it was twilight; one or two nuns were at their devotions, and there lay the figure in its grave-clothes with an air so gentle, so holy, as if she had only ceased to pray as the hand of the murderer struck her down. Her gentle limbs seemed instinct still with soft, sweet life; the expression was not of the heroine, the martyr, so much as of the tender angelic woman. I could well understand the deep impression made upon his mind. The expression of the frescoes of Domenichino is not inharmonious with the suggestions of this statue.[5]

Finding the mass was not to begin for some time, I set out for the Quirinal to see the Pope return from that noble church, Santa Maria Maggiore, where he officiated this night. I reached the mount just as he was returning; a few torches gleamed before his door; perhaps a hundred people were gathered together round the fountain; last year an immense multitude waited for him there to express their affection in one grand good night; the change was occasioned partly by the weather, partly by other causes of which I shall speak by and by. —Just as he returned, the moon looked palely out from amid the wet clouds, and shone upon the fountain and the noble figures above it, and the long white cloaks of the Guardia Nobile who followed his carriage on horseback; darker objects could scarcely be seen, except by the flickering light of the torches, much blown by the wind. I then returned to San Luigi; the effect of the night service there was very fine; those details which often have such a glaring, mean look by day are lost sight of in the night, and the unity of impression from the service much more undisturbed. The music, too, descriptive of that era which promised peace on earth, good will to men, was very sweet, and the *pastorale* particularly soothed the heart amid the crowd and pompous ceremonial. But here, too, the sour had its sweet in the vulgar vanity of the leader of the orchestra, too common to such, who, not content with marking the time for

---

[4] Dr. William Ellery Channing (1780–1842), the highly respected liberal Unitarian clergyman whose idealism paved the way for transcendentalism, was an important influence on Fuller in her early life (*DAB*). Jonathan Phillips, once one of Channing's atheistical college friends, became one of his deacons. Called by Channing "one of the intuitive men," Phillips was invited to attend an early Transcendental Club meeting (Ralph L. Rusk, *The Life of Ralph Waldo Emerson* [New York: Scribner's, 1949], 244).

[5] The sculptor Stefano Maderno (1576–1636) completed his statue of St. Cecilia in 1600 (*ODA*).

the musicians, made his stick heard in the remotest nook of the church, so that what would have been sweet music and flowed in upon the soul, was vulgarized to make you remember the performers and their machines.

On Monday the leaders of the Guardia Civica paid their respects to the Pope, who, in receiving them, expressed his constantly-increasing satisfaction in having given this institution to his people. The same evening there was a procession with torches to the Quirinal to pay the homage due to the day, (Feast of St. John and name-day of the Pope, *Giovanni Maria Mastai,*) but all the way the rain continually threatened to extinguish the torches, and the Pope could give but a hasty salute under an umbrella, when the heavens were again opened, and such a cataract of water descended as drove both man and beast to seek the nearest shelter.

On Sunday, I went to see a nun take the veil. She was a person of high family; a princess gave her away, and the Cardinal Ferreti, Secretary of State, officiated.[6] It was a much less effective ceremony than I expected from the descriptions of travelers and romance-writers. There was no moment of throwing on the black veil; no peal of music, nor salute of cannon. The nun, an elegantly dressed woman of five or six and twenty, pretty enough, but whose quite worldly air gave the idea that it was one of those arrangements made because no suitable establishment could otherwise be given her, came forward, knelt and prayed; her confessor, in that strained, unnatural whine, too common among preachers of all churches and all countries, praised himself for having induced her to enter on a path which would lead her fettered steps "from palm to palm, from triumph to triumph." Poor thing! she looked as if the domestic olives and poppies were all she wanted; and, lacking these, tares and wormwood must be her portion. She was then taken behind a grating, her hair cut, and her clothes exchanged for the nun's vestments; the black-robed sisters who worked upon her, looking like crows or ravens at their ominous feasts. All the while the music played, first sweet and thoughtful, then triumphant strains.—The effect on my mind was revolting and painful to the last degree. Were monastic seclusion always voluntary, and could it be ended whenever the mind required a change back from seclusion to common life, I should have nothing to say against it; there are positions of the mind which it suits exactly, and even characters that might choose it all through life; certainly to the broken-hearted it presents a shelter that Protestant communities do not provide; but where it is enforced or repented of no hell could be worse; nor can a more terrible responsibility be in-

---

[6] Gabriele Ferretti (1795–1860), cardinal and secretary of state in 1847, originally favored the Italian national cause but sided with Pius IX on the question of declaring war against Austria (*NCE*).

curred than by him who has persuaded a novice that the snares of the world are less dangerous than the demons of solitude.

Festivities in Italy have been of great importance, since for a century or two back, the thought, the feeling, the genius of the people have had more chance to expand, to express themselves, there than anywhere else. Now, if the march of Reform goes forward, this will not be so; there will be also speeches, made freely on public occasions, without having the life pressed out of them by the censure. Now we hover betwixt the old and the new; when the many uses and reasons of the new prevail, I hope what is poetical in the old will not be lost. The ceremonies of New-Year are before me, but as I may probably have to send this letter on New-Year's day; in that case I cannot describe them.

The Romans begin now to talk of the mad gayeties of Carnival, and the Opera is open. They have begun with 'Attila,' as, indeed, there is little hope of hearing in Italy other music than Verdi's. Great applause waited on the following air. (The music is in itself very pleasing, but that was not the reason.)

EZIO (THE ROMAN LEADER)
E gittata la mia sorte,
    Pronto sono ad agri guerra,
S'io cadrò, cadrò da forte,
    E il mio nome restorà.

Non vedrò l'amata terra
    Svener lenta e farri a brano
Sopra l'ultimo Romano
    Tutta Italia piangerà.[7]

And at these words:

'O brave man
Whose supreme power can raise thy country from such dire distress;
From the immortal hills, radiant with glory, let the shades of our ancestors
    arise, oh! only one day, one instant arise to look upon us!'

It was an Italian who sang this strain, though singularly enough here in the heart of Italy, so long reputed the home of music, three principal parts were filled by persons bearing the foreign names of Ivanoff, Mitrovich, and Nissren.[8]

Naples continues in a state of great excitement, which now pervades the

[7] My lot is fixed and I stand ready for every conflict. If I must fall, I shall fall as a brave man, and my fame will survive. I shall not see my beloved country fall to pieces and slowly perish, and over the last Roman all Italy will weep [Fuller's translation].

[8] *Attila* by Giuseppe Verdi (1813–1901) had premiered in Venice on 17 March 1846 (*OCM,* Kobbé). Nicola Ivanoff (1810–80) was a Russian-born tenor (*Grove*).

upper classes, as several young men of noble families have been arrested, among them one young man, much beloved, son of Prince Terella, who, it is said, was certainly not present on the occasion for which he was arrested, and that the measure was taken because he is known to sympathize strongly with the Liberal movement. The nobility very generally have not feared to go to the house of his father to express their displeasure at the arrest and interest in the young man. The Ministry, it is said, are now persuaded of the necessity of a change of measures. The King alone remains inflexible in his stupidity.

The stars of Bonaparte and Byron show again a conjunction by the almost simultaneous announcement of changes in the lot of women with whom they were so intimately connected, the Arch-duchess of Parma, Maria Louisa, is dead; the Countess Guiccioli is married.[9] The Countess I have seen several times; she still looks young, and retains the charms which she is reputed to have had by the contemporaries of Byron; they never were of a very high order; her best expression is that of a good heart. I always supposed that Byron, weary and sick of the world such as he had known it, became attached to her for her good disposition and sincere, warm tenderness for him; the sight of her and the testimony of a near relative confirmed this impression. This friend of hers added that she had tried very hard to remain devoted to the memory of Byron, but was quite unequal to the part, being one of those affectionate natures that must have some one near with whom to be occupied, and now, it seems, she has resigned herself publicly to abandon her romance. However, I fancy the manes of Byron remain undisturbed.

We all know the worthless character of Maria Louisa, the indifference she showed to a husband who, if he was not her own choice, yet would have been endeared to almost any woman as one fallen from an immense height into immense misfortune, and the father of her child. No voice from her penetrated to cheer his exile: the unhappiness of Josephine was well avenged; and that child, the poor Duke of Reichstadt, of a character so interesting and with obvious elements of greatness, withering beneath the mean, cold influence of his

[9] Marie-Louise von Habsburg (1791–1847) was Napoleon's second empress (1810–14), whom he married when he divorced Empress Josephine in 1809. The marriage was arranged with a view toward the advantages of an alliance between the French and the Austrians, and a son, Napoleon-Francis-Joseph-Charles (the duke of Reichstadt, 1811–33), was born on 20 March. After Napoleon's abdication, Marie-Louise had no further contact with her husband and returned to Austria, where she became the mistress of Count Adam Adalbert von Neipperg. She was given the duchy of Parma in 1830 (Owen Connelly, *Historical Dictionary of Napoleonic France* [Westport, Conn.: Greenwood Press, 1976]). Teresa Gambia Guiccioli took Bryon as her lover. Her husband, Count Guiccioli, died in 1840, and she married the marquis de Boissy in 1847 (*DNB*; Leslie A. Marchand, *Byron: A Biography,* 3 vols. [New York: Knopf, 1957], 2:773–75).

grandfather, what did she do for him? she, appointed by Nature to be his inspiring genius, his protecting angel? I felt for her a most sad and profound contempt last Summer, as I passed through her injured dominion, a little sphere,
in which, if she could not save it from the usual effects of the Austrian rule, she
might have done so much private, womanly good, might have been a genial
heart to warm it, and where she had let so much ill be done. A journal an-
nounces her death in these words: "The Arch-duchess is dead, a woman who
might have occupied one of the noblest positions in the history of the age," and
there makes expressive pause.

Parma, passing from bad to worse, falls into the hands of the Duke of
Modena, and the people and magistracy have made an address to their new
ruler which I translate as a specimen of the temperate and free manner which is
to be admired now in such acts here. The address has received many thousand
signatures, and seems quite sincere, except in the assumption of good will in
the Duke of Modena, and this is merely an insincerity of etiquette.[10]

> ROYAL HIGHNESS; The Government now terminated by the death of her
> highness Maria Louisa, which, in the beginning, cheered the subjects by
> good laws, reasonable civil liberty, mild and generous exercise of power,
> gradually became corrupted in the hands of persons incapable, or not
> sufficiently acquainted with the laws, their administration, the condi-
> tion and wants of the country, and at last fell into the power of one who
> knew no law other than despotism. Sustained by military power and the
> interference of the police, these things were endured, with an, as it were,
> inevitable patience by the citizens, through a not unreasonable fear of
> foreign invasion, and some hope that the natural good disposition of the
> Duchess would, at last, show her the cause of the ill and lead her to seek
> its remedy. But already remonstrances had been made to the magistracies
> of Piacentia and Parma; we were on the point of addressing the sovereign,
> herself, just complaints, just requests, when her illness prevented.
>
> What we were constrained to say to Maria Louisa, we can with more
> confidence address to your Royal Highness, who, not through perverse,
> stupid, credulous, prejudiced, or crafty, tyrannical or abject ministers,
> but YOURSELF, can see the State impoverished by money lying fruitless
> in the Treasury, Agriculture repressed by too heavy taxes, the citizens
> irritated and dejected by the presence of troops, which not only consume
> the public treasure, but imagine and then aver seditions, surpass the law,
> offend and calumniate the citizens, and are (though, perhaps, through

---

[10] The remainder of this dispatch was omitted in *AHA*.

fault of a few only) not the defence, but the terror and disgrace of the City.

Your Highness will see also instruction contaminated by barbarism, the censure of the press and even of thought governed, not by reason and intellect, but by arbitrary suspicion, by insolent caprice; will see the Police violate the security of the person, the liberty of innocent citizens; will see it corrupt the sacredness of home, degrade, disunite the citizens by espionage, put fear and doubt everywhere—in the street, the shop, the house, and thence even in the palace and the ear of the Prince.

In such a state of things your Royal Highness may divine with how much desire and hope these dukedoms expect you, secure that you must mean to reform Public Instruction, to impose laws on the Police, reasonable limits to the censure of the Press, to embrace the League of the Customs, make Railroads, raise degraded Commerce, confide to the citizens the election of municipal officers, reorder the communes on a freer and broader basis, and give that institution which proves the mutual confidence between Prince and subjects, assuring the public quiet and defence by means of those who most have desire and need to preserve them.

Such institutions being demanded by the wants of the time, were they quite untried, ought to be hoped from the descendants of Princes who knew how by great administrative intelligence to promote the civilization of their age; but they are not untried, nor unpleasing to your Highness, and therefore with confidence we expect them.

We might enumerate many other good things to be done, many other ills to remove, but there will be persons who will approach your Highness to represent them, and you will know how to examine and relieve with the sense of a Prince who has said he wished *to govern by love alone.*

Our words, Highness, moved yesterday in a method more mild, more cool, more composed, but if the violence used yesterday evening against the only Magistracy legal here at this moment render them not less sincere, not less just, although more excited and lively in tone, we hope they will not have the less effect on your wisdom," &c.

Meanwhile the Duke of Modena prepares to answer these appeals dignified in justice by crowding his dominions with Austrian troops. Still they are not made in vain; they find their echo, and will be duly heard in another generation if not in this.

They find their echo on other shores. Since beginning this letter, I have received the paper containing an account of the meeting in New-York upon Italian affairs. I read it and was proud of my country; the tone of the letters and speeches generally is so intelligent, so noble; the Address to the Pope is excellent.[11] I have sent it to the *Circolo Romano* to be read by the editors; I presume there will be a notice of it in the papers before the reception of the Address. Of this and many other things I must write in my next letter, which will go by the French steamer. Much more there was I had to say, but time fails, and it must wait for the next letter.   ★

Dispatch 21

THE POPE AND HIS PEOPLE

ROME, New-Year's Eve of 1848 [1]

This morning I sent off a letter which was obliged to be mailed to day in order to reach the steamer of the 16th. So far am I from home, that even steam does not come nigh to annihilate the distance.

This afternoon I went to the Quirinal Palace to see the Pope receive the new municipal officers.—He was to-day in his robes of white and gold, with his usual corps of attendants in pure red and white, violet and white. The new officers were in black velvet dresses with broad white collars. They took the oaths of office and then actually kissed his foot. I had supposed this was never really done, but only a very low obeisance made: the act seemed to me disgustingly abject. A Heavenly Father does not want his children at his feet, but in his arms, on a level with his heart.

After this was over the Pope went to the Gesù,[2] a very rich church belonging to the Jesuits, to officiate at Vespers, and we followed. The music was beautiful, and the effect of the church with its richly-painted dome and altar-piece

---

[11] Fuller refers to the speech that Horace Greeley, chair of the committee to prepare the address to the pope, gave on 29 November 1847 at the Broadway Tabernacle in New York. In the speech, which was adopted by acclamation, Greeley had compared the situation in Italy to that of the United States: "We unite in this tribute, not as Catholics, which some of us are while the greater number are not, but as Republicans and lovers of Constitutional Freedom. Recent as is our national origin, wide as is the ocean which separates our beloved land from your sunny clime, we know well what Italy was in the proud days of her unity, freedom and glory—what she has since been while degraded by foreign rule and internal dissension—and we have faith that a lofty and benignant destiny awaits her when her People shall again be united, independent and free. In the great work of her regeneration, we hail you as a Heaven-appointed instrument; and we ardently pray that your days may be prolonged until you shall witness the consummation of the wise and beneficent policy which is destined to render your name immortal" (Marraro 7, 315).

[1] First published as "Things and Thoughts in Europe. No. XXI" in *New-York Daily Tribune,* 19 February 1848, p. 1:1–5.

[2] The Gesù, the principal church of the Jesuits in Rome, was built in 1568–75 (Baedeker 2:215).

in a blaze of light, while the assembly were in a sort of brown darkness, was very fine.

A number of Americans there, new arrivals, kept requesting in the midst of the music to know when "*it* would begin:" "Why this is *it*," some one at last had the patience to answer: "You are hearing Vespers now." "What," they replied, "is there no oration, no speech!" So deeply rooted in the American mind is the idea that a sermon is the only real worship!

This church is indelibly stamped on my mind. Coming to Rome this time, I saw in the diligence a young man, whom his uncle, a priest of the convent that owns this church, had sent for, intending to provide him employment here. Some slight circumstancs tested the character of this young man, and showed it what I have ever found it, singularly honorable and conscientious. He was led to show me his papers, among which was a letter from a youth for whom, with that true benevolence only possible to the poor, because only they *can* make great sacrifices had so benefited as to make an entire change in his prospects for life. Himself a poor orphan, with nothing but a tolerable education at an Orphan Asylum, and a friend of his dead parents to find him employment on leaving it, he had felt for this young man, poorer and more uninstructed than himself, had taught him at his leisure to read and write, had then collected from friends and given himself till he had gathered together sixty francs, and procuring also for his protege a letter from monks, who were friends of his, to the convents on the road, so that wherever there was one, the poor youth had lodging and food gratis. Thus armed, he set forth on foot for Rome; Piacurza, their native place, affording little hope, even of gaining bread in the present distressed state of that dominion. The latter was to say that he had arrived, and been so fortunate as to find employment immediately in the studio of Benzoni, the sculptor. The poor patron's eyes sparkled as I read the letter. "How happy he is," said he, "and does he not spell and write well; I was his only master."

But the good do not inherit the earth, and, less fortunate than his protege, Germano on his arrival found his uncle ill of the Roman fever. He came to see me much agitated. "Can it be, Signorina," says he, "that God, who has taken my father and mother, will also take from me the only protector I had left, and just as I arrive in this strange place, too?"—After a few days he seemed more tranquil and told me that, though he had felt as if it would console him and divert his mind to go to some places of entertainment, he had forborne and applied the money to have masses said for his uncle. "I feel," he said, "as if God would help me." Alas! at that moment the uncle was dying. Poor Germano came next day with a receipt for masses said for the soul of the departed, (his simple faith in these being apparently indestructible,) and amid his tears he said, "The Fathers were so unkind they were hardly willing to hear me speak a word; they were so afraid I should be a burden to them, I shall never go there again. But the most cruel thing was I offered them a scudo (dollar) to say six masses for the soul of my poor uncle; they said they would only say five and must have seven baiocchi (cents) more for that."

A few days after I happened to go into their church and found it thronged, while a preacher, panting, sweating, leaning half out of the pulpit was exhorting his hearers to "imitate Christ." With unspeakable disgust I gazed on this false shepherd of those who had just so failed in their duty to a poor stray lamb. Their church is so rich in ornaments, the seven baiocchi were hardly needed to burnish it. Their altar-piece is a very imposing composition, by an artist of Rome, still in the prime of his powers, Capalti. It represents the Circumcision, with the cross and six waiting angels on the back-ground; Joseph who holds the child, the priest and all the figures in the foreground seem intent upon the barbarous rite, except Mary the mother; her mind seems to rush forward into the future, and understand the destiny of her child; she sees the cross—she sees the angels, too.

Now I have mentioned a picture, let me say a word or two about art and artists, by way of parenthesis in this otherwise political letter. We laugh a little here at some words that come from your City on this subject. Artists are told "they would do better to come home and *study*." They are at the same time informed that "The Life and Antique drawing school is shut up *because*—there is not money to pay for the gas!!" This is certainly a great and grave joke in a City like New-York. Here they have plenty of schools and plenty of models, if no gas!

We also hear their landscapes show a want of familiarity with Nature; they need to return to America and see her again. But, friends, Nature wears a different face in Italy from what she does in America. Do you not want to see her Italian face; it is very glorious! We thought it was the aim of art to reproduce all forms of Nature, and that you would not be sorry to have transcripts of what you have not always round you. American art is not necessarily a reorganization of American nature alone.

Hicks has made a charming picture of familiar life, which those who cannot believe in Italian daylight would not tolerate. I am not sure that all eyes are made in the same manner for I have known those who declare they see nothing remarkable in these skies, these hues; and always complain when they see them reproduced in picture. I have yet seen no picture by Cropsey on an Italian subject, but his sketches from Scotch scenes are most poetical and just presentations of those lakes, those mountains, with their mourning veils.[3] He is an

---

[3] Jasper Francis Cropsey (1823–1900), a landscape-painter and architect, lived in Europe from 1847 to 1850 (*Groce*).

artist of great promise. Cranch has made a picture for Mr. Ogden Haggerty of a fine mountain-hold of old Colonna story. I wish he would write a ballad about it too; there is plenty of material.

But to return to the Jesuits. One swallow does not make a Summer, nor am I who have seen so much hard-heartedness and barbarous greed of gain in all classes of men, so foolish as to attach undue importance to the demand in those who have dared to appropriate peculiarly to themselves the sacred name of Jesus from a poor orphan, and for the soul of one of their own order of "seven baiocchi more." But I have always been satisfied from the very nature of their institutions that the current prejudice against them must be correct. These Institutions are calculated to harden the heart and destroy entirely that truth which is the con-servative principle in character. Their influence is and must be always against the free progress of humanity. The more I see of its working, the more I feel how pernicious it is, and were I a European, to no object should I lend myself with more ardor than to the extirpation of this cancer. True, disband the Jesuits, there would still remain Jesuitical men, but singly they would have infinitely less power to work mischief.[4]

The influence of the Obscurantist foe has shown itself more and more plainly in Rome, during the last four or five weeks. A false miracle is devised: the Madonna del Popolo, (who has her handsome house very near me,) has cured a paralytic youth, (who, in fact, was never diseased,) and appearing to him in a vision, takes occasion to criticise severely the measures of the Pope. Rumors of tumult in one quarter are circulated to excite it in another. Inflammatory hand-bills are put up in the night. But the Roman thus far resists all intrigues of the foe to excite him to bad conduct.

On New-Year's Day, however, success was near. The people, as usual, asked permission of the Governor to go to the Quirinal and receive the benediction of the Pope. This was denied and not as it might truly have been because the Pope was unwell, but in the most ungracious, irritating manner possible by saying, "He is tired of these things: he is afraid of disturbance." Then the people being naturally excited and angry, the Governor sends word to the Pope that there is excitement, without letting him know why and has the guards doubled on the posts. The most absurd rumors are circulated among the people that the can-non of St. Angelo are to be pointed on them, &c. But they with that singular discretion that they show now, instead of rising, as their enemies had hoped,

---

[4] The Society of Jesus reappeared in France in 1814 (after their dissolution in 1764). Con-cerned with the nature of education, the Jesuits set about regaining control of many schools in France. Secularists opposed them, and the debate became heated. Fundamentally, the Jesuits believed that liberalism derived from the Protestants and as such was incompatible with true religion. Consequently, revolutionaries in both France and Italy were united in their opposition to the Jesuits (Newman; *New Cambridge Modern History* 10:565).

went to ask counsel of their lately appointed Senator, Corsini. He went to the
Pope, found him ill, entirely ignorant of what was going on and much distressed when he heard it. He assured the people they should be satisfied, that
since they had not been allowed to come to him, he would go to them. Accordingly the next day, though rainy and of a searching, miserable cold like that of
a Scotch mist, we had all our windows thrown open and the red and yellow tapestries hung out. He passed through the principal parts of the city, the people
throwing themselves on their knees and crying out "O Holy Father, don't desert
us; don't forget us; don't listen to our enemies." The Pope wept often and replied, "Fear nothing my people, my heart is yours." At last seeing how ill he
was, they begged him to go in, and he returned to the Quirinal, the present
Tribune of the People, as far as rule in the heart is concerned, Ciceraucchio,
following his carriage. I shall give some account of this man in another letter.[5]

For the moment the difficulties are healed, as they long will be whenever the
Pope directly shows himself to the people. Then his generous affectionate heart
will always act and act on them, dissipating the clouds which others have been
toiling to darken.

In speaking of the intrigues of these emissaries of the power of darkness, I
will mention that there is a report here that they are trying to get an Italian Consul for the United States, and one in the employment of the Jesuits. This rumor
seems ridiculous; yet it is true that Dr. Beecher's panic about the Catholic influence in the United States is not quite unfounded, and that there is considerable
hope of establishing a new dominion there.[6] I hope the United States will appoint no Italian, no Catholic, to a Consulship. The representative of the United
States should be American; our national character and interests are peculiar and
cannot be fitly represented by a foreigner, unless like Mr. Ombrosi of Florence,
he has passed part of his youth in the United States.[7] It would, indeed, be well
if Government paid attention to qualification for the office in the candidate,
and not to pretensions founded on partisan service. It would be well to appoint
men of probity who would not stain the national honor in the sight of Europe.

[5] Fuller refers to Angelo Brunetti, nicknamed Ciceruacchio, because of his size; he was
a wine and horse dealer who was devoted to the Pope at this time. Widely regarded as a
natural leader of the people, he was later a fervid supporter of the Roman Republic (Robertson 362–63; Deiss 84–85; Leona Rostenberg, "Mazzini to Margaret Fuller, 1847–1849,"
American Historical Review 47 (1941): 79n).

[6] Lyman Beecher (1775–1863), the father of Harriet Beecher Stowe, was a Presbyte-
rian clergyman who was strongly Calvinist and evangelical in orientation. In 1831, he had
preached a series of sermons against Catholicism (*DAB*).

[7] James Ombrosi (1777?–1852) was United States consul at Florence (Hudspeth 5:
269n).

It would be well not to appoint men entirely ignorant of foreign manners, customs, ways of thinking, even of any language in which to communicate with
foreign society, making the country ridiculous by all sorts of blunders. But,
't were pity if a sufficient number of Americans could not be found, honest,
with some knowledge of Europe and gentlemanly tact, and able at least to speak
French.

To return to the Pope, although the shadow that has fallen on his popularity
is in a great measure the work of his enemies, yet there is real cause for it too.
His conduct in deposing for a time one of the Censors, about the banners the
15th of December, his speech to the Council the same day, his extreme displeasure at the sympathy of a few persons with the triumph of the Swiss Diet,
because it was a Protestant triumph,[8] and in fine, his speech to the Consistory,
so deplorably weak in thought and obsolete in manner, show a man less strong
against domestic than foreign foes, instigated by a generous humane heart to
advance, but fettered by the prejudices of education, and terribly afraid to be
or seem to be less the Pope of Rome, in becoming a Reform Prince, and father
to the fatherless. I insert a passage of this document, which seems to say that
whenever there shall be collision between the Priest and the Reformer, the
Priest shall triumph:

"Another subject there is which profoundly afflicts and harasses our mind.
It is not certainly unknown to you, Venerable Brethren, that many enemies of Catholic truth have, in our times especially, directed their efforts
in the desire to place certain monstrous offsprings of opinion on a par with
the doctrine of Christ, or to blend them therewith, seeking to propagate
more and more that impious system of *indifference* toward all Religion
whatever.

"And lately some have been found, dreadful to narrate! who have
offered such an insult to our name and Apostolic dignity, as slanderously
to represent us participators in their folly, and favorers of that most iniquitous system above named. These have been pleased to infer from the
counsels (certainly not foreign to the sanctity of the Catholic Religion)
which in certain affairs pertaining to the civil exercise of the Pontific sway
we had benignly embraced for the increase of public prosperity and good,
and also from the pardon bestowed in clemency upon certain persons
subject to that sway, in the very beginning of our Pontificate, that we
had such benevolent sentiments toward every description of persons as to
believe that not only the sons of the Church, but others also, remaining

[8] The Swiss Civil War ended in victory for the Swiss Diet on 30 November 1847.

aliens from Catholic Unity, are alike in the way of salvation and may attain
eternal life. Words are wanting to us, from horror, to repel this new and
atrocious calumny against us. It is true that with intimate affection of
heart we love all mankind, but not otherwise than in the charity of God
and of our Lord Jesus Christ, who came to seek and to save that which
had perished, who wisheth that all men should be saved and come to a
knowledge of the truth;—and who sent His Disciples through the whole
world to preach the Gospel to every creature, declaring that those who
should believe and be baptized should be saved, but those who should
not believe, be condemned. Let those therefore who seek salvation come
to the pillar and support of the Truth, which is the Church,—let them
come, that is, to the true Church of Christ, which possesses in its Bishops
and the supreme head of all, the Roman Pontiff, a never interrupted succession of Apostolic authority, and which for nothing has ever been more
zealous than to preach and with all care preserve and defend the doctrine
announced as the mandate of Christ by His Apostles;—which Church
afterward increased, from the time of the Apostles, in the midst of every
species of difficulties, and flourished throughout the whole world, radiant
in the splendor of miracles, amplified by the blood of Martyrs, ennobled
by the virtues of Confessors and Virgins, corroborated by the testimony
and most sapient writings of the Fathers; as it still flourishes throughout all lands, refulgent in perfect unity of the Sacraments, of Faith, and
of holy discipline. We who, though unworthy, preside in this supreme
chair of the Apostle Peter, in which Christ our Lord placed the foundation
of that His Church, have at no time abstained from any cares or toils to
bring, through the grace of Christ Himself, those who are in ignorance
and error to this sole way of truth and salvation. Let those, whoever they
be, that are adverse, remember that heaven and earth shall pass away, but
nothing can ever perish of the words of Christ, nor be changed in the doctrine which the Catholic Church received, to guard, defend and publish,
from Him.

"Next to this we cannot but speak to you, Venerable Brethren, of the
bitterness of sorrow by which we were affected, on seeing that a few days
since, in this our fair city the fortress and center of the Catholic Religion,
it proved possible to find some—very few indeed and well-nigh frantic
men, who, laying aside the very sense of humanity, and to the extreme
disgust and indignation of other citizens of this town, were not withheld
by horror from triumphing openly and publicly over the most lamentable intestine war lately excited among the Helvetic people; which truly

fatal war we sorrow over from the depths of our heart, as well considering the blood shed by that nation, the slaughter of brothers, the atrocious, daily recurring and fatal discords, hatreds and dissensions (which usually redound among nations in consequence especially of civil wars;) as the detriment which we learn the Catholic Religion has suffered, and fear it may yet suffer, in consequence of this; and, finally, the deplorable acts of sacrilege committed in the first conflict, which our soul shrinks from the narration of."

It is probably on account of these fears of Pius IX. that he shall be called a Protestant Pope, that the Roman journals thus far in translating the American address to the Pope have not dared to add any comment. But if the heart, the instincts of this good MAN have been beyond his thinking powers, that only shows him the Providential agent to work out aims beyond his ken. A wave has been set in motion, which cannot stop till it casts up its freight upon the shore, and if Pius IX. does not suffer himself to be surrounded by dignitaries, to hear the signs of the times through the medium of others, if he does not suffer the knowledge he had of general society as a simple Prelate, to become incrusted by the ignorance habitual to Princes, he cannot fail long to be a most important agent in fashioning a new and better era for this beautiful, injured land.

I gave in my last letter the address of the magistracy of Parma to their new Sovereign. I now give another document as a specimen of the dignity and religious mildness given by a deep sense of justice in their claims to the Italian mind at this juncture. It is truly a remonstrance as in the hearing of God, and though probably made quite in vain for the most stupid Majesty to whom it is addressed, will not be without its effect elsewhere. It is now in Rome for the purpose of receiving signatures[9]:

KINGDOM OF THE TWO SICILIES.

"Il Risorgimento," the able Journal established at Turin by a Society of Men of Letters, among whom a principal part is taken by Cesare Balbo, has printed the following "proposal for a petition to the King of the Two Sicilies by the Italians of the Union"

SIRE: Though not subjects of your Majesty, but Italians of other Provinces, and as such deeply interested in the welfare of your people and crown, as in that of our common country; we approach your throne with the intention, Sire, of entreating you to accede to the policy of Pius IX, of Leopold and Charles Albert, to the policy of Italy, of Providence—that of pardon, Christian civilization and charity.

[9] This paragraph and the document below are omitted from *AHA*.

Sire, at this moment Italy is expecting you, Europe fixing her attention
upon you—Deity summoning you. We do not enter into the remem-
brances of the past; we know that a merciful God has regard in the case of
each individual to the difficulties, the incitements and good intentions,
with which he may have acted, or even erred; and we know that on earth,
as in Heaven, every man remains justified or not according to the last
determining facts of his life.

And now, Sire, you have arrived at the culminating point, the highest
act of your life, the course that must be decisive to that which remains of
it; now your conscience can no longer remain doubtful, since the will of
Providence is no longer doubtful. Look up, and extend your gaze over all
Italy; behold the joy of a nation risen to new life, the satisfaction of the
Sovereigns, authors of that resurrection! behold reciprocal union, peace
and innocence, and consider the high character of all these our actions,
blest by the Pontiff, blest by the consent of all Christianity; and then
judge whether we are accomplishing a foolish and impious revolution, or
a good, holy, and most happy mutation, seconding therein the will of the
Almighty.

Sire, your obedience to that Will, the accession of your authority to
that mutation, will render it more facile, more felicitous and moderate
than ever; and adding a second to the first third of the Italians now regenerate, will constitute a great plurality on the side of the regenerate
in our Nation; will render it impregnable to its enemies, independent
even of its friends among strangers, free and compact in itself, giving it
force, dignity, and time to accomplish in peace the whole of the admirable
work undertaken; will render the destinies of Italy, in fine, as far as human
things can be, secure.

Should you refuse, on the contrary, to follow the fortune and virtue
of Italy, then, Sire, her destinies would indeed be disturbed in the magnificent path where they are now advancing, but not averted therefrom.
Never, never can Italy remain below, adverse, or contrary to Christian
Civilization; that civilization which triumphs in omnipotence not only
over all these petty internal obstacles, but over all human powers, all the
nations with their civilization that are not Christian. Whoever may be,
now or any time, the enemies and the cold or false friends of Italy, she will
take her place in the triumph of Christian nations.—Possibly, as already
has been the case, obstacles may impede the progress; perhaps your refusal
(which God forbid) may cut short by violence the most important questions in the regeneration of Italy, or even have the effect of degrading the
cause, which might not continue, as hitherto, blameless, holy, without

example in the world and the course of ages! Therefore it is, Sire, that we
cry from the depths of our hearts and souls: May God forbid it! May God
forbid it! and we Italians, independent of you, come as suppliants to pray,
after God, to You that this may never be.

We are, with profound respect,

Your Majesty's most humble and devoted servants.[10]

I will now give another document, which may be considered as representing
the view taken by the Democratic party called "Young Italy" of what is now
passing. Should it in any other way have reached the United States yet, it will
not be amiss to have it translated for *The Tribune,* as many of your readers may
not othewise have a chance of seeing this noble document, one of the milestones
in the march of Thought.

Letter to the Most High Pontiff. Pius IX. from JOSEPH MAZZINI—(Printed at
Paris, 1847.)

PREFACE OF THE EDITOR. Convinced that I shall please those Italians,
who truly love their country, and at the same time aid the cause of truth
by so doing, I publish this letter, which, although we know it has been
delivered into the hands for which it was destined, yet by passing in
manuscript from person to person, and from country to country, might
suffer such alterations as no longer to appear the work of him who dictated
it. And I believe in publishing it that I have a right, not only to the approbation of the author, but to his thanks, because it cannot displease him
that the feelings expressed by him with such loyalty, should be known by
all, and especially by those who, deceived as to him, believe them quite
different from what they really are. I believe, also, that his letter will
aid one day the history of a new era, as that which, more than any other,
manifests the opinions and hopes of an entire people, and the true way to
attain the desired results.

Those powerful ones, on whom depends in part the hastening or
delaying this epoch, ought to consider the grandeur and the truth of
the courageous thought developed in this little work, and no less than
generous reason should keep them from embracing it. MARRIMO FABI.

Paris, 25th November, 1847.
The letter itself is dated London, 8th September, 1847:

---

[10] Here follow the names of Balbo, the other directors of the Journal, Robert D'Azelgio,
Silvio Pellico, and many others, among whom are a Provincial and Doctor of Theology of
the Franciscan Religions [Fuller's note].

LETTER.

MOST HOLY FATHER: Permit an Italian, who has studied your every step
for some months back with an immense hope, to address you, in the midst
of the applauses, often far too servile and unworthy of you, which resound
near you, some free and profoundly sincere words. Take to read them some
moments from your infinite cares. From a simple individual animated by
holy intentions may come, sometimes, a great counsel; and I write to you
with so much love, with so much emotion of my whole soul, with so much
faith in the destiny of my country, which may be revived by your means,
that my thoughts ought to speak truth.

And first, it is needful, Most Holy Father, that I should say to you
somewhat of myself. My name has probably reached your ears, but accompanied by all the calumnies, by all the errors, by all the foolish
conjectures which the police, by system, and many men of my party
through want of knowledge or poverty of intellect, have heaped around
it. I am not a subverter, nor a communist, nor a man of blood, nor a hater,
nor intolerant, nor exclusive adorer of a system, or of a form imagined
by my mind. I adore God, and an idea which seems to me of God, Italy
an angel of moral unity and of progressive civilization for the nations of
Europe. Here and everywhere I have written the best I knew how against
the vices of materialism, of egotism, of reaction, and against the destruc-
tive tendencies which contaminate many of our party. If the people should
rise in violent attack against the selfishness and bad government of their
rulers, I, while rendering homage to the right of the people, shall be,
probably, among the first to prevent the excesses and the vengeance which
long slavery has prepared. I believe profoundly in Religious Principle,
supreme above all social ordinances; in a Divine Order which we ought
to seek to realize here on earth; in a Law, in a Providential Design, which
we all ought, according to our powers to study and to promote. I believe
in the inspiration of my immortal Soul, in the Tradition of Humanity,
which shouts to me through the deeds and words of all its Saints, incessant
progress for all through the work of all my brothers toward a common
moral amelioration, toward the fulfilment of the Divine Law. And in the
great Tradition of Humanity I have studied the Tradition of Italy, and
have found there Rome twice directress of the world—first through the
Emperors, later through the Popes. I have found there that every manifestation of Italian life, has also been a manifestation of European life; and
that always when Italy fell, the moral Unity of Europe began to fall apart
in analysis, in doubt, in anarchy. I believe in yet another manifestation of
the Italian Idea; and I believe that another European world ought to be

revealed from the Eternal City, that had the Capitol and has the Vatican.
And this faith has not abandoned me ever through years, poverty, delu-
sions, and griefs which God alone knows. In these few words lies all my
being, all the secret of my life. I may err in the intellect, but the heart has
always remained pure. I have never lied through fear or hope, and I speak
to you as I should speak to God beyond the sepulchre.

I believe you good. There is no man this day, I will not say in Italy, but
in all Europe, more powerful than you; you then have, most Holy Father,
vast duties. God measures these according to the means which he has
granted to his creatures.

Europe is in a tremendous crisis of doubts and desires.—Through
the work of time, accelerated by your predecessors of the hierarchy of
the Church, Faith is dead, Catholicism is lost in Despotism; Protestantism is lost in Anarchy. Look around you; you will find superstitions and
hypocrites, but not believers. The intellect travels in a void. The bad
adore calculation, physical good; the good pray and hope; nobody *believes*.
Kings, governments, the ruling classes combat for a power usurped; illegitimate, since it does not represent the worship of truth, nor disposition
to sacrifice oneself for the good of all; the people combat because they
suffer, because they would fain take their turn to enjoy; nobody fights for
Duty; nobody, because the war against evil and falsehood is a holy war,
the crusade of God. We have no more a Heaven; hence we have no more a
Society.

Do not deceive yourself, most Holy Father; this is the present state of
Europe.

But Humanity cannot exist without a Heaven. The idea of Society is
only a consequence of the idea of Religion. We shall have then, sooner
or later, Religion and Heaven. We shall have these not in the kings and
the privileged classes—their very condition excludes Love, the soul of
all religions—but in the people. The spirit from God descends on many
gathered together in his name. The people has suffered for ages on the
cross and God will bless it with a faith.

You can, most Holy Father, hasten that moment. I will not tell you
my individual opinions on the religious development which is to come;
these are of little importance. But I will say to you that, whatever be the
destiny of the creeds now subsistent, you can put yourself at the head of
it. If God wills that they should revive, you can make them revive; if God
wills that they should be transformed, that leaving the foot of the Cross,
dogma and worship should be purified by rising a step nearer God, the
Father and Educator of the world, you can put yourself between the two

epochs, and guide the world to the conquest and the practice of Religious Truth, extirpating a hateful egotism, a barren negation.

God preserve me from tempting you with ambition; that would be profanation. I call you in the name of the power which God has granted you, and has not granted without a reason, to fulfil the good, the regenerating, European work. I call you after so many ages of doubt and corruption, to be apostle of Eternal Truth. I call you to make yourself the "Servant of All," to sacrifice yourself, as needful so that "the will of God may be done on the Earth as it is in Heaven;" to hold yourself ready to glorify God in Victory, or to repeat with resignation, if you must fail, the words of Gregory VII, "I die in exile, because I have loved Justice and hated Iniquity."

But for this, to fulfil the mission which God confides to you, two things are needful,—to be a believer, and to unify Italy. Without the first you will fall in the middle of the way, abandoned by God and by men: without the second, you will not have the lever with which only you can effect great, holy and durable things.

Be a believer; abhor to be King, Politician, Statesman. Make no compromise with error; do not contaminate yourself with diplomacy, make no compact with fear, with expediency, with the false doctrines of a *legality*, which is merely a falsehood invented when faith failed. Take no counsel except from God, from the inspirations of your own heart, and from the imperious necessity of rebuilding a temple to Truth, to Justice, to Faith. Ask of God, self-collected in enthusiasm of love for Humanity, and apart from every Human regard, that He will teach you the way; then enter upon it, with the faith of a conqueror on your brow, with the irrevocable decision of the martyr in your heart; look neither to the right hand or the left, but straight before you and up to Heaven. Of every object that meets you on the way, ask of yourself—"Is this just or unjust; true or false; law of men or law of God?" Proclaim aloud the result of your examination and act accordingly. Do not say to yourself—"if I speak and work in such a way, the Princes of the earth will disagree; the Ambassadors will present notes and protests!" What are the quarrels of selfishness from Princes or their notes before a syllable of the eternal Evangelist of God. They have had importance till now, because, though phantoms, they had nothing to oppose them but phantoms; oppose to them the Reality of a man who sees the Divine view, unknown to them of human affairs, of an immortal soul conscious of a high mission, and these will vanish before you as vapors accumulated in darkness before the sun which rises in the East.—Do not let yourself be affrighted by intrigues; the Creature who fulfills a duty belongs not to men, but to God. God will protect you; God will spread round you such a halo of love, that neither the perfidy of men irreparably lost, nor the suggestions of Hell can break through it. Give to the world a spectacle new, unique: you will have results new, not to be foreseen by human calculation. Announce an Era; declare that Humanity is sacred, and a daughter of God; that all who violate her rights to progress, to association, are on the way of error; that in God is the source of every Government; that those who are best by intellect and heart, by genius and virtue, must be the guides of the People; bless those who suffer and combat; blame, reprove those who cause suffering, without regard to the name they bear, the rank that invests them; the People will adore in you the best interpreter of the Divine design, and your conscience will give you rest, strength and ineffable comfort.

Unify Italy, your country. For this you have no need to work, but to bless Him who works through you and in your name. Gather round you those who best represent the national party. Do not beg alliances with Princes. Continue to conquer the alliance of our own people; say, "the Unity of Italy ought to be a fact of the Nineteenth Century" and it will suffice; we shall work for you. Leave our pens free; leave free the circulation of ideas in what regards this point, vital for us, of the National Unity; treat the Austrian Government, even when it no longer menaces your territory with the reserve of one who knows that it governs by usurpation in Italy and elsewhere; combat it with words of a just man wherever it contrives oppressions and violations of the rights of others out of Italy. — Invite, in the name of the God of Peace, the Jesuits allied with Austria in Switzerland to withdraw from that country, where their presence prepares an inevitable and speedy effusion of the blood of the citizens. Give a word of sympathy which shall become public to the first Pole of Gallicia who comes into your presence. Show us, in fine, by some fact, that you tend not only to improve the physical condition of your own few subjects, but that you embrace in your love the twenty four millions of Italians, your brothers; that you believe them called by God to unite in family unity under one and the same compact; that you would bless the National banner wherever it should be raised by pure and incontaminate hands; and leave the rest to us. We will cause to rise around you a nation over whose free and popular development you, living, shall preside. We will found a Government unique in Europe, which shall destroy the absurd divorce between spiritual and temporal power, and in which you shall be chosen to represent the principle of which the men chosen by the Nation will make the application. We shall know how to translate into a potent fact the instinct which palpitates through all Italy. We will excite for you active support among the nations of Europe; we will find you friends even in the ranks of Austria; we alone, because we alone have unity of design, believe in the truth of our principle, and have never betrayed it. Do not fear excesses from the people once thrown upon this way; the people only commits excesses when it is left to its own impulses without any guide whom it respects.—Do not pause before the idea of becoming a cause of war. War exists, everywhere, open or latent, but near breaking out, inevitable; nor can human power prevent it. Nor do I, it must be said frankly, most holy Father, address to you these words because I doubt in the least of our destiny, or because I believe you the sole, the indispensable means of the enterprise. The Unity of Italy is work of God. A part of the design of Providence and now of all, even of those who show themselves most satisfied with local improvements, and who, less sincere than I wish to make them means of attaining their own aims, it will be fulfilled with you or without you. But I address it to you because I believe you worthy to take the initiative in a work so vast; because your putting yourself at the head of it would much abridge the road and diminish the dangers, the injury, the blood; because with you the conflict would assume a religious aspect, and be freed from many dangers of reaction and civil errors; because might be attained at once under your banner a political result and a vast moral result; because the revival of Italy under the aegis of a religious idea, of a standard, not of rights, but of duties, would leave behind all the revolutions of other countries, and place her immediately at the head of European progress; because it is in your power to cause that God and the People, terms too often fatally disjoined, should meet at once in beautiful and holy harmony, to direct the fate of Nations.

If I could be near you, I would invoke from God power to convince you, by gesture, by accent, by tears; now I can only confide to the paper the cold corpse, as it were of my thought; nor can I ever have the certainty that you have read and meditated a moment what I write. But I feel an imperious necessity of fulfilling this duty toward Italy and you, and whatsoever you may think of it, I shall find myself more in peace with my conscience for having thus addressed you.

Believe, most holy Father, in the feelings of veneration and of high hope which professes for you your most devoted   JOSEPH MAZZINI.

Whatever may be the impression of the reader as to the ideas and propositions contained in this document, I think he cannot fail to be struck with its simple nobleness, its fervent truth.

JANUARY 10.

A thousand petty interruptions have prevented my completing this letter, till now the hour of closing the mail for the Steamer is so near I shall not have time to look over it, either to see what I have written or make slight corrections. However, I suppose it represents the feelings of the last few days, and shows that without having lost any of my confidence in the Italian movement, the office of the Pope in promoting it has shown narrower limits and sooner than I had expected.

This does not at all weaken my personal feelings toward this excellent man, whose heart I have seen in his face, and can never doubt. It was necessary to be a great thinker, a great genius, to compete with the difficulties of his position. I never supposed he was that; I am only disappointed that his good heart has not carried him on a little father. With regard to the reception of the American Address, it is only the Roman Press that is so timid; the private expressions of pleasure have been very warm; the Italians say: "The Americans are indeed our brothers."

For the rest, it remains to be seen, when Pius IX. receives the Address, whether the Man, the Reforming Prince or the Pope is uppermost at that moment.   ★

Dispatch 22

KINGCRAFT AND PRIESTCRAFT

ROME, January 1848 [1]

I think I closed my last letter without having had time to speak of the ceremonies that precede and follow Epiphany. This month, no day, scarcely no hour, has passed unmarked by some showy spectacle or some exciting piece of news.

On the last day of the year died Don Carlo Torlonia, brother of the banker, a man greatly beloved and regretted. The public felt this event the more that its proximate cause was an attack made upon his brother's house by Paradisi, now imprisoned in the Castle of St. Angelo, pending a law process for proof of his accusations.[2] Don Carlo had been ill before, and the painful agitation caused

---

[1] First published as "Things and Thoughts in Europe. No. XXII" in *New-York Daily Tribune,* 13 March 1848, p. 1:1–3.

[2] Don Carlo Torlonia was the brother of the banker Alessandro Torlonia, whose conduct of his business was the object of great resentment. Paradisi, a journalist, published an article in *The Contemporary* in November 1847, attacking the business practices of Alessandro Torlonia, accusing him of a series of financial irregularities in his administration of

by these circumstances decided his fate. The public had been by no means displeased at this inquiry into the conduct of Don Alessandro Torlonia, believing
that his assumed munificence is, in this case, literally a robbery of Peter to pay
Paul, and that all he gives to Rome is taken from Rome. But it sympathized no
less with the affectionate indignation of his brother, too good a man to be made
the confidant of wrong, or have eyes for it, if such exist.

Thus, in the poetical justice which does not fail to be, at least, done in the
prose narrative of life—while men hastened, the moment one chanced to raise
the cry against Don Alessandro, to echo it back by all kinds of imputations
both on himself and his employees, every man held his breath and many wept
while passed the mortal remains of Don Carlo; feeling that in him was lost a
benefactor, a brother, a simple, just man.

Don Carlo was a Knight of Malta, but with him the celebate life had not
hardened the heart—but only left it free on all sides to general love. Not less
than half a dozen pompous funerals were given in his honor, by his relatives,
the brotherhoods to which he belonged, and the battalion of the Civic Guard
to which he was commander-in-chief. But in his own house the body lay in no
other state than that of a simple Franciscan, the Order to which he first belonged, and whose vow he had kept through half a century, by giving all he had
for the good of others. He lay on the ground in the plain dark robe and cowl—
no unfit subject for a modern picture of little angels descending to shower lilies
on a good man's corpse. The long files of armed men, the rich coaches and
liveried retinues of the princes, were little observed in comparison with more
than a hundred orphan girls whom his liberality had sustained and who followed the bier in mourning-robes and long white veils, spirit-like in the dark
night. The trumpet's wail, and soft melancholy music from the bands, broke
at times the roll of the muffled drum; the hymns of the Church were chanted
and volleys of musketry discharged in honor of the departed—but much more
musical was the whisper in which the crowd, as passed his mortal spoil, told
anecdotes of his good deeds.

I do not know when I have passed more consolatory moments than in the
streets one night of all this pomp and picturesque show—for once not empty of
all meaning as to the present time, recognizing that somewhat healthy which
remains at bottom in the human being, ineradicable by all ill, and promises that
our poor injured natures shall rise and bloom again from present corruption to
immortal purity. If Don Carlo had been a thinker, a man of strong intellect, he
might have devised means of using his money to more radical advantage than

---

salt and tobacco for the public. Paradisi demanded a trial, but Torlonia denounced him for
libel, and Paradisi was put in jail to await trial as Fuller says (Zorzi 122).

simply to give it in alms; he had only a kind human heart, but from that heart distilled a balm which made all men bless it, happy in finding cause to bless.

As in the moral little books with which our nurseries are entertained, followed another death in violent contrast. One of those whom the new arrangements deprived of power and the means of unjust gain was the Cardinal Prince Massimo, a man a little younger than Don Carlo, but who had passed his forty years in a very different manner—He remonstrated; the Pope was firm, and at last is said to have answered with sharp reproof for the past. The Cardinal contained himself in the audience, but, going out literally suffocated with the rage he had suppressed. The bad blood his bad heart had been so long making rushed to his head, and he died on his return home. Men laughed, and proposed that all the widows he had deprived of a maintenance should combine to follow *his* bier. It was said boys hissed as that bier passed. Now a splendid suit of lace being for sale in a shop of the Corso, everybody says: "Have you been to look at the lace of Cardinal Massimo, who died of rage, because he could no longer devour the public goods." And this is the last echo of *his* requiem.

The Pope is anxious to have at least well-intentioned men in places of power. Men of much ability, it would seem, are not to be had; his last Prime Minister was a man said to have energy, good dispositions, but no thinking power. The Cardinal Bofondi,[3] whom he has taken now, is said to be a man of scarce any ability, there being few among the new Councilors the public can name as fitted for important trust; in consolation we must remember that the Chancellor Oxenstiern[4] found nothing more worthy of remark to show his son than by how little wisdom the world could be governed. We must hope these men of straw will serve as thatch to keep out the rain, and not be exposed to the assaults of a devouring flame.

Yet that hour may not be distant. The disturbances of the first of January here were answered by similar excitements in Leghorn and Genoa, produced by the same hidden and malignant foe. At the same time the Austrian Government in Milan organized an attempt to rouse the people to revolt, with a view to arrests and other measures calculated to stifle the spirit of independence they know to be latent there.[5] In this iniquitous attempt they murdered eighty

[3] José Bofondi (1795–1867) became a cardinal in 1846. In 1848 he joined the group of prelates invited to advise the pope on civil reforms (*Encyclopedia universal ilustrada europeo-americana*, 60 vols. [Madrid: Espasa-Calpe, 1926]).

[4] Axel, count of Oxenstiern (1583–1654), was a counselor to Gustavus Adolphus, king of Sweden. While in that position, he wrote a constitution for Sweden. He told his son: "You will find out, my son, with how little wisdom the world is governed" (Zorzi 122).

[5] Fuller refers to the "tobacco riots" in Milan. Since tobacco was an Austrian monopoly, the citizens of Lombardy attempted a boycott of tobacco, which was surprisingly successful.

persons, yet the citizens, on their guard, refused them the hoped-for means of ruin, and they were forced to retractions as impudently vile as their attempts had been. The Viceroy proclaimed that "he hoped the people would confide in him *as* he did in them;" and no doubt they will. At Leghorn and Genoa, the wiles of the foe were baffled by the wisdom of popular leaders, as I trust they always will be, but it is needful daily to expect these nets laid in the path of the unwary.

Sicily is in full insurrection; and it is reported Naples, but not sure.[6] There was a report, day before yesterday, that the poor stupid King was already here, and had taken cheap chambers at the Hotel d'Allemagne, as indeed it is said he has always a turn for economy when he cannot live at the expense of his suffering people. Day before yesterday, every carriage that the people saw with a stupid-looking man in it they did not know, they looked to see if it was not the Royal runaway. But it was their wish was father to that thought, and it has not as yet taken body as fact. In like manner they report this week the death of Prince Metternich; but I believe it is not sure he is dead yet, only dying.[7] With him passes one great embodiment of ill to Europe. As for Louis Philippe, he seems reserved to give the world daily more signal proofs of his base apostasy to the cause that placed him on the throne, and that heartless selfishness of which his face alone bears witness to any one that has a mind to read it. How the French nation could look upon that face, while yet flushed with the hopes of the Three Days, and put him on the throne as representative of those hopes, I cannot conceive.[8] There is a story current in Italy that he is really the child of a man first a barber, afterward a police officer, and was substituted at nurse for the true heir of Orleans, and the vulgarity of form in his body of limbs, power of endurance, greed of gain, and hard cunning intellect, so unlike all traits of the weak but more "genteel" Bourbon race, might well lend plausibility to such a fable.

The Austrians retaliated by paying officers and others to smoke cigars and blow smoke in the faces of Italian men on the streets. When the Italian men responded to the insult, eighty of them were killed. Instead of stifling the "spirit of independence" that Fuller mentions, the citizens were stirred to stronger hatred of the Austrians (Deiss 108–09).

[6] On 12 January 1848 revolution broke out in Palermo, Sicily, and Ferdinand II, threatened with additional uprisings in Apulia, Basilicata, Calabria, and Naples, granted the people of his kingdom a popular constitution.

[7] Prince Clemens-Wenzel Lothar von Metternich (1773–1859), the Austrian statesman, was a symbol of the conservative order in Austria and Europe. He was forced to resign after the revolution in Vienna on 13 March 1848, but returned in September 1851 and lived the rest of his life in quiet retirement (Newman).

[8] Fuller refers to the three days in July 1830 during which the French people overthrew the Bourbon monarch, Charles X, in favor of Louis Philippe, the "Citizen King" (Robertson 12–13).

But to return to Rome, where I hear the Ave Maria just ringing; by the way, nobody pauses, nobody thinks, nobody prays.

"Ave Maria! 'tis the hour of prayer,
Ave Maria! 'tis the hour of love," &c.[9]

is but a figment of the poet's fancy.

To return to Rome: what a Rome!—the fortieth day of rain, and damp, and abominable reeking odors, such as blessed cities swept by the sea-breeze— bitter sometimes, yet indeed a friend—never know. It has been dark all day, though the lamp has only been lit half an hour. The music of the day has been, first the atrocious arias which last in the Corso till near noon, though certainly less in virulence on rainy days. Then came the wicked organ-grinder, who, apart from the horror of the noise, grinds exactly the same obsolete abominations as at home or in England—"The Copenhagen Waltz," "Home, sweet home," and all that! The cruel chance that both an English my-lady and a Councilor from one of the Provinces live opposite keeps him constantly before my window, hoping baiocchi [10]—forgetful that Marszas got something very different to punish the noise *he* made. Within, the three pet-dogs of my landlady, bereft of their walk, unable to employ their miserable legs and eyes—exercise themselves by a continual barking, which is answered by all the dogs in the neighborhood. An urchin returning from the laundress, delighted with the symphony, lays down his white bundle in the gutter, seats himself on the curb-stone and attempts an imitation of the music of cats as a tribute to the concert. The door-bell rings, *Chi è?* "Who is it?" cries the handmaid, with unweariable senselessness, as if any one would answer *Rogue* or *Enemy,* instead of the traditional *Amico, Friends.* May it be, perchance, a letter, news of home, or some of the many friends who have neglected so long to write, or some ray of hope to break the clouds of the difficult Future. Far from it.—Enter a man poisoning me at once with the smell of the worst possible cigars, not to be driven out, insisting I shall look upon frightful, ill-cut cameos, and worse-designed mosaics, made by some friend of his, who works in a chamber and will sell *so* cheap. Man of ill-odors and meanest smile! I am no Countess to be fooled by you. For dogs they were not even— dog-cheap.

A faint and misty gleam of sun greeted the day on which there is the feast to the Bambino, the most venerated doll of Rome. This is the famous image of the infant Jesus, reputed to be made of wood from a tree of Palestine, and

[9] Byron, *Don Juan,* canto 3, 103, lines 1–2 (*The Works of Byron* 6:178).
[10] Riches or wealth

which, being taken away from its present abode—the Church of Ara Cœli [11]—
returned by itself, making the bells ring as it sought admittance at the door. It
is this which is carried in extreme cases to the bedside of the sick. It has received
more splendid gifts than any other idol. An orphan by my side, now struggling with difficulties, showed me on its breast a splendid jewel, which a doting
grandmother thought more likely to benefit her soul if given to the Bambino,
than if turned into money to give her grandchildren education and prospects in
life. The same old lady left her vineyard, not to these children, but to her confessor, a well-endowed Monsignor, who occasionally asks this youth, his god-
son, to dinner! Children, so placed, are not quite such devotees to Catholicism
as the new proselytes of America!—They are not so much patted on the head,
and things do not show to them under quite the same silver veil.

The Church of Ara Cœli is on or near the site of the temple of Capitoline
Jove, which certainly saw nothing more idolatrous than these ceremonies. For
about a week the Bambino is exhibited in an illuminated chapel, in the arms
of a splendidly dressed Madonna doll. Behind, a transparency represents the
shepherds, by moonlight, at the time the birth was announced, and, above,
God the Father, with many angels hailing the event. —A pretty part of this exhibition, which I was not so fortunate as to hit upon, though I went twice on
purpose, is the children making little speeches in honor of the occasion. Many
readers will remember some account of this in Andersen's "Improvisatore." [12]

The last time I went was the grand feast in honor of the Bambino. The
church was entirely full, mostly with contadini and the poorer people, absorbed
in their devotions: one man near me never raised his head or stirred from his
knees to see anything; he seemed in an anguish of prayer, whether from repentance or anxiety. I wished I could have hoped the ugly little doll could do him
any good. The noble stair which descends from the great door of this church
to the foot of the Capitol—a stair made from fragments of the old imperial
time—was flooded with people; the street below was a rapid river also, whose
waves were men. —The ceremonies began with splendid music from the organ,
pealing sweetly long and repeated invocations. As if answering to this call, the
world came in, many dignitaries, the Conservatori, [13] I think, (Conservatives are

[11] S. Maria d'Aracœli, the Church of the Altar of Heaven, is built on the site of the Capitoline Temple of Juno. The festival that Fuller describes begins on Christmas Day and lasts
until 6 January (Baedeker 2:137, 227).

[12] Hans Christian Andersen's *Improvisatore; or Life in Italy* was translated by Mary Howitt
in 1845.

[13] The Palace of the Conservatori, the town council, is near the church (Baedeker 2:230).
Fuller is punning on the meaning of "conservatori"—government officials—as preservers
of the status quo.

the same everywhere, official or no,) and did homage to the image; then men in white and gold, with the candles they are so fond here of burning by daylight, as if the poorest artificial were better than the greatest natural light, uplifted high above themselves the baby, with its gilded robes and crown, and made twice the tour of the church, passing twice the column lettered from the home of Augustus, while the band played—what? the Hymn to Pius IX. and the "Sons of Rome awake!" Never was a crueler comment upon the irreconcilableness of these two things. Rome seeks to reconcile Reform and Priestcraft.

But their eyes are shut that they see not. Oh awake, indeed, Romans! and you will see that the Christ who is to save men is no wooden dingy effigy of by-gone superstitions, but such as art has seen Him in your better mood—a Child, living, full of love, prophetic of a boundless Future—a Man acquainted with all sorrows that rend the heart of all, but only loving Man, with sympathy and faith death cannot quench—*that* Christ lives or is sought; burn your doll of wood.

How any one can remain a Catholic—I mean who has ever been aroused to think, and is not biased by the partialities of childish years—after seeing Catholicism here in Italy I cannot conceive. There was ever a soul in the religion while the blood of its martyrs was yet fresh upon the ground, but that soul was always too much encumbered with the remains of Pagan habits and customs: that soul is now quite fled elsewhere, and in the splendid catafalque, watched by so many white and red-robed, snuff-taking, sly-eyed men, would they let it be opened, nothing would be found but bones! [14]

Then the College for propagating all this, the most venerable Propaganda, has given its exhibition in honor of the feast of the Kings Magi, wise men of the East, I was there one day. In conformity with the general spirit of Rome, strangely inconsistent in a country where the Madonna is far more frequently and devoutly worshiped than God or Christ, in a city where at least as many female saints and martyrs are venerated as male; there was no good place for women to sit. All the good seats were for the men in the area below, but in the gallery windows, and from the organ-loft, a few women were allowed to peep at what was going on. I was one of these exceptional characters. The exercises were in all the different languages under the sun. It would have been exceedingly interesting to hear them, one after the other, each in its peculiar cadence

[14] Catholic readers of the *Tribune* took offense at Fuller's anti-Catholicism, and Greeley felt called upon to admit that his correspondent was "ultra-Protestant," but he added that indeed the Jesuits were guilty of denying liberty to the Italian people (*New-York Daily Tribune*, 24 February 1848, p. 1:2). Bishop Hughes of New York City was particularly upset about the *Tribune*'s coverage of Italian affairs (Marraro 58–60).

and inflection, but much of the individual expression was taken away by that
general false academic tone which is sure to pervade such exhibitions where
young men speak who have as yet nothing to say. It would have been different
indeed if we could have heard natives of all those countries, who were animated
by real feelings, real wants. Still it was interesting, particularly the language
and music of Kurdistan and the full-grown beauty of the Greek after the ruder
dialects. Among those who appeared to the best advantage were several blacks,
and the majesty of the Latin hexameters was confided to a full-blooded Guinea
negro, who acquitted himself better than any other I heard. I observed, too,
the perfectly gentlemanly appearance of these young men, and that they had
nothing of that Cuffy swagger by which those freed from a servile state try to
cover a painful consciousness of their position in our country. Their air was self-
possessed, quiet and free beyond that of most of the lily-livered.

January 22—2 o'clock P.M.

Pour, pour, pour again, dark as night—many people coming in to see me
because they don't know what to do with themselves.[15] I am very glad to see
them for the same reason; this atmosphere is so heavy I seem to carry the weight
of the world on my head and feel unfitted for every exertion. As to eating, that is
a bygone thing; wine, coffee, meat, I have resigned; vegetables are few and hard
to have, except horrible cabbage, in which the Romans delight. A little rice
still remains, which I take with pleasure, remembering it growing in the rich
fields of Lombardy, so green and full of glorious light. That light fell still more
beautiful on the tall plantations of hemp, but it is dangerous just at present to
think of what is made from hemp.

This week all the animals are being blessed, and they get a gratuitous baptism, too, the while. The lambs one morning were taken out to the church of

[15] Among her friends at this time were Story, an amateur painter and sculptor, and his
wife Emelyn Eldridge Story (1820–94) (*DAB*). William Story went to Italy in 1847 to study
sculpture. Although the Storys had known Fuller in Boston, they were not friendly until
they encountered one another in Rome. Emelyn Story recalled that Fuller seemed quite different in Rome than she had been in New England: "Margaret suffered from ill health this
winter, and she afterwards attributed it mainly to the fact, that she had not the sun. As
soon as she heard of our arrival, she stretched forth a friendly, cordial hand, and greeted
us most warmly. She gave us great assistance in our search for convenient lodgings, and we
were soon happily established near her. Our intercourse was henceforth most frequent and
intimate, and knew no cloud nor coldness. Daily we were much with her, and daily we felt
more sensible of the worth and value of our friend. To me she seemed so unlike what I had
thought her to be in America, that I continually said, 'How have I misjudged you,—you
are not at all such a person as I took you to be' " (*Memoirs* 2:282–83).

St. Agnes for this purpose. The little companion of my travels,[16] if he sees this letter, will remember how often we saw her with her lamb in pictures. The horses are being blessed by St. Antonio, and under his harmonizing influence are afterward driven through the city, twelve and even twenty in hand. They are harnessed into light wagons, and men run beside them to guard against accident, in case the good influence of the Saint should fail.

This morning came the details of infamous attempts by the Austrian Police to exasperate the students of Pavia. The way is to send persons to smoke cigars in forbidden places who insult those who are obliged to tell them to desist. These traps seem particularly shocking when laid for fiery and sensitive young men. They succeeded: the students were lured into combat and a number left dead and wounded on both sides. The University is shut up; the inhabitants of Pavia and Milan have put on mourning; even at the theater they wear it. The Milanese will not walk in that quarter where the blood of their fellow-citizens has been so wantonly shed. They have demanded a legal investigation of the conduct of the officials.

At Piacenza similar attempts have been made to excite the Italians by smoking in their faces and crying, 'Long live the Emperor.' It is a worthy homage to pay to the Austrian Crown, the offering of cigars and blood: Faugh! this offence is rank; it reeks to Heaven.[17]

This morning authentic news is received from Naples. The King, when assured by his own brother that Sicily was in a state of irresistible revolt, and that even the women quelled the troops—showering on them stones, furniture, boiling oil, such means of warfare as the household may easily furnish to a thoughtful matron—had, first, a stroke of apoplexy, from which the loss of a good deal of bad blood relieved him. His mind, apparently, having become clearer thereby, he has offered his subjects an amnesty and terms of reform, which, it is hoped, will arrive before his troops have begun to bombard the cities in obedience to earlier orders.

Comes also to-day the news that the French Chamber of Peers propose an Address to the King, echoing back all the falsehoods of his speech, including those upon reform, and the enormous one that "the peace of Europe is now assured." But that some members have worthily opposed it and spoken truth in an honorable manner.

---

[16] Fuller refers to Edward Spring, the son of Marcus and Rebecca Spring, whose company she had enjoyed for nearly a year of traveling in Europe.

[17] Fuller here misquotes Shakespeare, *Hamlet* III.iii.36: "O, my offence is rank, it smells to heaven."

Also that the infamous sacrifice of the poor little Queen of Spain puts on more tragic colors; that it is pretended she has epilepsy, and she is to be made to renounce the throne, which, indeed, has been a terrific curse to her; and Heaven and Earth have looked calmly on, while the King of France has managed all this with the most unnatural of mothers.[18]

January 27

This morning comes the plan of the Address of the Chamber of Deputies to the King: it contains some passages that are keenest satire upon him, as also some remarks have been made, some words of truth spoken in the Chamber of Peers, that must have given him some twinges of nervous shame as he read. M. Guizot's speech on the affairs of Switzerland shows his usual shabbiness and falsehood; surely never Prime Minister stood in so mean a position as he: one like Metternich seems noble and manly in comparison; for if there is a cruel, atheistical, treacherous policy, there needs not at least continual evasion to avoid declaring in words what is so glaringly manifest in fact.

There is news that the revolution has now broken out in Naples: that neither Sicilians nor Neapolitans will trust the King, but demand his abdication; and that his bad demon, Coclo,[19] has fled, carrying two hundred thousand ducats of gold. But in particulars these news is not sure, though, no doubt, there is truth at the bottom.

Aggressions on the part of the Austrians continue in the North. The advocates Tommaseo, and Manin (a light thus reflected on the name of the last Doge), having dared to protest formally the necessity of Reform, are thrown into prison.[20] Every day the cloud swells, and the next fortnight is likely to bring important material for the record of   ★

---

[18] Cristina, queen-mother of the seventeen-year-old Isabel II of Spain, had conspired with King Louis Philippe of France to marry Isabel to Don Francisco de Asís, a man of ignoble character and feeble constitution. They regarded it as certain that Isabel would bear him no children, and that Louis Philippe's son, the duc de Montpensier, would sit on the throne of Spain as the consort of María Luisa Fernanda. In July 1850 the queen gave birth to a child of doubtful paternity and its survival would have been fatal to the Montpensier succession; the death of the boy was attributed to foul play in which Isabel's mother and sister were alleged to have been concerned (*Cambridge Modern History* 11:555–57).

[19] Monsignor Celestino Cocle was the Confessor to Ferdinand II, reviving the old practice of the father confessor from the Spanish court. He was dismissed in 1848 by the liberal leaders and exiled to Malta (Zorzi 123).

[20] Niccolò Tommaseo (1802–74) was a poet and patriot who was arrested in 1848 with Daniele Manin, a Venetian leader. When they were liberated from prison, Tommaseo served as minister of public education and ambassador to France in the government of the short-lived Venetian Republic, headed by Manin (*New Cambridge Modern History* 10:396; Bondanella).

Dispatch 23

THE SPRINGTIME REVOLUTIONS OF '48

ROME, 29th March, 1848 [1]

It is long since I have written; my health entirely gave way beneath the Roman Winter. The rain was constant, commonly falling in torrents from the 16th December to the 19th March. Nothing could surpass the dirt, the gloom, the desolation of Rome. Let no one fancy he has seen her who comes here only in the Winter. It is an immense mistake to do so. I cannot sufficiently rejoice that I did not first see Italy in the Winter.

The climate of Rome at this time of extreme damp I have found equally exasperating and weakening. I have had constant nervous headache without strength to bear it, nightly fever, want of appetite. Some constitutions bear it better, but the complaint of weakness and extreme dejection of spirits is general among foreigners in the wet season. The English say they become acclimated in two or three years and cease to suffer, though never so strong as at home.

Now this long dark dream—to me the most idle and most suffering season of my life—seems past. [2] The Italian heavens wear again their deep blue; the sun shines gloriously; the melancholy lustres are stealing again over the Campagna, and hundreds of larks sing unwearied above its ruins.

Nature seems in sympathy with the great events that are transpiring; with the emotions which are swelling the hearts of men. The morning sun is greeted by the trumpets of the Roman Legions marching out once more, but now not to oppress but to defend. The stars look down on their jubilees over the good news which nightly reaches them from their brothers of Lombardy. [3] This week has been one of nobler, sweeter feeling of a better hope and faith than Rome in her greatest days ever knew. How much has happened since I wrote!—First,

[1] First published as "Things and Thoughts in Europe. No. XXIII" in *New-York Daily Tribune*, 4 May 1848, p. 1:1–3.

[2] Fuller would not, of course, explain that the main reason for her illness was the first few months of her pregnancy, which she kept secret from family and friends.

[3] Milan had just experienced her "Five Glorious Days." The revolution began on the morning of 18 March, and after five days of furious street fighting during which the Milanese used barricades and homemade weapons to combat the 18,000 to 20,000 Austrian troops, the Austrian general Radetzky abandoned the city. On 22 March his army retreated to the Quadrilateralo, a district between the mountains and the sea. On this same day, Venice staged its successful revolution, forcing the governor and military commandant to evacuate the town and the surrounding forts (*Cambridge Modern History* 11:81–82).

the victorious resistance of Sicily and the revolution of Naples. This has led us yet only to half measures, but even these have been of great use to the progress of Italy. The Neapolitans will, probably, have to get rid at last of the stupid crowned head who is at present their puppet, but their bearing with him has led to the wiser sovereigns granting these Constitutions, which, if eventually inadequate to the wants of Italy, will be so useful, are so needed, to educate her to seek better, completer forms of administration.

In the midst of all this serious work came the play of Carnival, in which there was much less interest felt than usual, but enough to dazzle and captivate a stranger. One thing, however, had been omitted in the description of the Roman Carnival; *i.e.* that it rains every day. Almost every day came on violent rain just as the tide of gay masks was fairly engaged in the Corso. This would have been well worth bearing once or twice for the sake of seeing the admirable good humor of this people. Those who had laid out all their savings in the gayest, thinnest dresses, on carriages and chairs for the Corso, and found themselves suddenly drenched, their finery spoiled, and obliged to ride and sit shivering all the afternoon. But they never murmured, never scolded, never stopped throwing their flowers. Their strength of constitution is wonderful. While I, in my shawl and boa, was coughing at the open window from the moment I inhaled the wet sepulchral air, the servant girls of the house had taken off their woolen gowns, and arrayed in white muslins and roses, sat in the drenched street beneath the drenching rain, quite happy, and have suffered nothing in consequence.

The Romans renounced the *moccaletti,* [4] ostensibly as an expression of sympathy for the sufferings of the Milanese, but really because, at that time, there was great disturbance about the Jesuits, and the Government feared that difficulties would arise in the excitement of the evening. But, since, we have had this

---

[4] Story was quite taken with the *moccoletti*, the feast of the tapers that ends the Roman Carnival. He explains what Fuller had observed: "Thousands of little waxen tapers then flutter about like living things, dancing along balconies and open windows, quivering up and down the entire length of the Corso, flickering from carriage to carriage, flying backwards and forwards at the ends of long *canne*, and pursued by flapping handkerchiefs that seek to extinguish them. A soft yellow light glows over the brown palace façades, gleaming on the window-panes, and illuminating below a sea of merry faces. Up the Corso, far as the eye can reach, the *moccoletti* sparkle like swarms of brilliant fire-flies. The street resounds with a tumultuous cry of *'Ecco il moccolo—moccolo,'* as the little tapers are brandished and shaken in the air, and the loud jeers of *'Senza moccolo—senza moccolo,'* as dexterous hands and lips suddenly extinguish them. The scene is always gay; but the wild, glad exultation of the spectacle in 1848, when the news of Italian victories came in from Lombardy, and the people, waving their *moccoletti,* poured into the Corso, cheering and singing their national songs, surpassed for enthusiasm anything I ever saw" (2:552–53).

entertainment in honor of the Revolutions of France and Austria, and nothing could be more beautiful. The fun usually consists in all the people blowing one another's lights out; we had not this; all the little tapers were left to blaze, and the long Corso swarmed with tall fire-flies.—Lights crept out over the surface of all the houses, and such merry little twinkling lights, laughing and flickering with each slightest movement of those who held them. Up and down the Corso, they twinkled, they swarmed, they streamed, while a surge of gay triumphant sound ebbed and flowed beneath that glittering surface. Here and there danced men carrying aloft *moccoli,* and clanking chains, emblem of the tyrannic power now vanquished by the people. The people, sweet and noble, who, in the intoxication of their joy, were guilty of no rude or unkindly word or act, and who, no signal being given as usual for the termination of their diversion, closed, of their own accord and with one consent, singing the hymns for Pio, by nine o'clock, and retired peacefully to their homes, to dream of hopes they yet scarce understand.

This happened last week. The news of the dethronement of Louis Philippe reached us just after the close of the Carnival. It was just a year from my leaving Paris.[5] I did not think, as I looked with such disgust on the empire of sham he had established in France, and saw the soul of the people imprisoned and held fast as in an iron vice, that it would burst its chains so soon. Whatever be the result, France has done gloriously; she has declared that she will not be satisfied with pretexts while there are facts in the world—that to stop her march is a vain attempt, though the onward path be dangerous and difficult. It is vain to cry Peace, peace, when there is no peace. The news from France, in these days, sounds ominous, though still vague; it would appear that the political is being merged in the social struggle: it is well; whatever blood is to be shed, whatever altars cast down. Those tremendous problems MUST be solved, whatever be the cost! That cost cannot fail to break many a bank, many a heart in Europe, before the good can bud again out of a mighty corruption. To you, people of America, it may perhaps be given to look on and learn in time for a preventive wisdom. You may learn the real meaning of the words FRATERNITY, EQUALITY: you may, despite the apes of the Past, who strive to tutor you, learn the needs of a true Democracy. You may in time learn to reverence, learn to guard, the true aristocracy of a nation, the only really noble—the LABORING CLASSES.[6]

[5] On 22–24 February the French workers, joined by students and members of the bourgeoisie, especially urban artisans, overthrew the monarchy of Louis Philippe and proclaimed France a republic. A provisional government was established with the poet-statesman Alphonse de Lamartine at its head.

[6] In Paris communist and socialist ideas had become familiar to the working classes and contributed to the prevailing social unrest. *The Communist Manifesto,* which appeared in Feb-

And Metternich, too, is crushed; the seed of the Woman has had his foot on the serpent. I have seen the Austrian arms dragged through the streets of Rome and burned in the Piazza del Popolo. —The Italians embraced one another and cried *Miracolo, Providenza!* the modern Tribune Ciceraucchio fed the flame with faggots; Adam Mickiewicz, the great Poet of Poland, long exiled from his country or the hopes of a country, looked on, while Polish women, exiled too, or who, perhaps, like one nun who is here, had been daily scourged by the orders of a tyrant, brought little pieces that had been scattered in the street and threw into the flames—an offering received by the Italians with loud plaudits.[7] It was a transport of the people, who found no way to vent their joy, but the symbol, the poesy, natural to the Italian mind; the ever-too-wise "upper classes" regret it, and the Germans choose to resent as an insult to Germany; but it was nothing of the kind; the insult was to the prisons of Spielberg, to those who commanded the massacres of Milan; a base tyranny little congenial to the native German heart, as the true Germans of Germany are at this moment showing by their struggles, by their resolves.

When the double-headed eagle was pulled down from above the lofty portal of the Palazzo di Venezia, the people placed there in its stead one of white and gold inscribed with the name ALTA ITALIA, and quick upon the emblem followed the news that Milan was fighting against her tyrants—that Venice had driven them out and freed from their prisons the courageous Protestants in favor of truth, Tommaseo and Manin—that Manin, descendant of the last Doge, had raised the Republican banner on the Place St. Mark—and that Modena, that Parma, were driving out the unfeeling and imbecile creatures who had mocked Heaven and Man by the pretence of Government there.

With indescribable rapture these news were received in Rome. Men were seen dancing, women weeping with joy along the street. The youth rushed to enrol themselves in regiments to go to the frontier. In the Colosseum their names were received. Father Gavazzi,[8] a truly patriotic monk, gave them the

---

ruary 1848, was just one of many calls for the overthrow of existing social conditions in Europe. During her stay in Paris in the winter of 1846–47, Fuller encountered socialist revolutionary thought at first hand, but several years before, she had gotten an early sense of it. In the summer of 1845 she translated a letter from the Paris correspondent of the *Deutsche Schnellpost,* a German immigrants' newspaper, which discussed Marx and ended with a long quotation from Engels's *Condition of the Working Class in England.* According to Chevigny, who sees Fuller becoming more Marxist in Europe, "this is surely among the very earliest notices of Marx and Engels in America" (294).

[7] On 14 March 1848 Fuller wrote Emerson that Mickiewicz "is with me here, and will remain some time" (Hudspeth 5:55).

[8] Alessandro Gavazzi (1809–89) a priest born at Bologna, became a Barnabite monk and a supporter of Pius IX. After the fall of Rome in 1849, he escaped to England and founded the (Protestant) Italian Free Church (*Chambers's Biographical Dictionary*).

cross to carry on a new, a better, because defensive crusade. Sterbini, long exiled, addressed them; he said, "Romans, do you wish to go; do you wish to go with all your hearts? If so, you *may,* and those who do not wish to go themselves may give money. To those who will go, the government gives bread and fifteen baiocchi a day." The people cried "We too wish to go, but we do not wish so much; the Government is very poor; we can live on a paul[9] a day." The princes answered by giving, one sixty thousand, others twenty, fifteen, ten thousand dollars. The people answered by giving at the benches which are opened in the piazzas literally everything; street-peddlers gave the gains of each day; women gave every ornament—from the splendid necklace and bracelet down to the poorest bit of coral; servant girls gave five pauls, two pauls, even half a paul, if they had no more; a man all in rags gave two pauls; "it is," said he, "all I have." "Then," said Torlonia, "take from me this dollar;" the man of rags thanked him warmly and handed that also to the bench, which refused to receive it. "No! *that* must stay with you," shouted all present. These are the people whom the traveler accuses of being unable to rise above selfish considerations. Nation, rich and glorious by nature as ever, capable, like all nations, all men, of being degraded by slavery, capable as are few nations, few men, of kindling into pure flame at the touch of a ray from the Sun of Truth, of Life.

The two or three days that followed, the troops were marching about by detachments, followed always by the people, to Ponte Malle, often farther. The women wept; for the habits of the Romans are so domestic, that it seemed a great thing to have their sons and lovers gone even for a few months. The English—or, at least those of the illiberal, bristling nature—too often met here, which casts out its porcupine quills against everything like enthusiasm (of the more generous Saxon blood I know some noble examples,) laughed at all this. They have said that this people would not fight; when the Sicilians, men and women, did so nobly they said, "Oh! the Sicilians are quite unlike the Italians; you will see when the struggle comes on in Lombardy, they cannot resist the Austrian force a moment." I said, "That force is only physical; do not you think a sentiment can sustain them?" They reply, "All stuff and poetry; it will fade the moment their blood flows." When news came that the Milanese, men and women, fight as the Sicilians did, they said, "Well, the Lombards are a better race, but these Romans are good for nothing; it is a farce for a Roman to try to walk even; they never walk a mile; they will not be able to support the first day's march of thirty miles, and not to have their usual minestra to eat either." Now the troops were not willing to wait for the Government to make the necessary arrangements for their march, so at the first night's station—Monterose—they

---

[9] The baiocchi was the smallest unit of money minted in the Papal States. The paul was a silver coin, originally minted by Pope Paul III. Both coins were worth very little.

did *not* find food or bedding, yet the second night, at Civita Castellana, they were so well alive as to remain dancing and vivaing Pio Nino in the piazza till after midnight. No, Messieurs, Soul is not quite nothing, if Matter be a clog upon its transports.

The Americans show a better, warmer feeling than they did; the meeting in New-York was of use in instructing the Americans abroad! The dinner given here on Washington's birthday, was marked by fine expressions of sentiment and a display of talent unusual on such occasions. There was a poem from Mr. Story of Boston, which gave great pleasure; a speech by Mr. Hillard, said to be very good, and one by Mr. Hedge of Bangor, exceedingly admired for the felicity of thought and image and the finished beauty of style.[10]

Next week we shall have more news, and I shall try to write and mention also some interesting things want of time obliges me to omit in this letter.[11] I annex a poem of Cranch's, descriptive of a picture he sends to Mr. Ogden Haggerty of your City, interesting in itself and not irrelevant to this present communication:

THE CASTLE OF THE COLONNAS.

BY C. P. CRANCH.

High on a rugged mountain, gray and old,
Gray like the rocks themselves—where heat and cold
For centuries with the battlements have striven,
As Man did once—its walls all bare and riven,
The castle stands—a mass of frowning stone,
With dark-green vines and ivy over-grown,
Through the gray rifts the deep Italian day
Smiles as it ever smiles on all decay.
Here in the olden days of feudal might
The proud Colonna donned his armor bright
And strode upon the ramparts, to survey
The vassal plains that far beneath him lay,
And mustering his brave knights, held them intent
To guard each oft-assaulted battlement.
Here bristling up the steep and narrow path

---

[10] Although Fuller apparently did not attend this dinner, her friends were clearly leaders. She saw the Storys virtually every day; George Stillman Hillard, who was Charles Sumner's law partner, was an old friend, and Frederic Henry Hedge (1805–90) was the Unitarian clergyman whose name was attached to Hedge's Club, known also as the Transcendental Club, the group of New England intellectuals with whom Fuller associated during her years in Boston (*DAB*).

[11] The rest of this paragraph and the poem are omitted in *AHA*.

Host after host came flaming in fierce wrath.
Through the bright day and through the starlit night
Thundered the tempest of the bloody fight;
And those far Volscian mounta'ns, soft and blue,
Smiled through their purple haze, as now they do
On the deep stillness of this peaceful day,—
When nought is heard save—faint and far away,
Down by the vineyards green—the shepherd's song
Floating the vale and mountain side along;
Or cawing rooks that clamor hour by hour
Sailing around the Ruin's topmost tower.

Up the gray rocks no more the files advance;
No more the battle stern, the wild romance.
Peace hath her victories now, perchance as famed
As those in olden time the Warrior claimed.
All Italy hath breathed a freer air
Since good Mastai fills Saint Peter's chair:
More mildly seems to bend the Summer sky
It's infinite dome of blue; the morning's eye
Opens more hopefully, and evening closes
With tinted clouds like dropping leaves of roses,
Over the Roman streets and shrines and fountains,
O'er the Campagna and the purple mountains
Love, Freedom, Truth may yet extend their wing,
And all be realized that poets sing.

When great Colonna, driven from his home,
Landless, and stripped of all, went forth to roam,
"Where is thy fortress now?" they asked. With pride,
His hand upon his heart, the chief replied
" 'Tis here!"—And thou around whose onward course
Threaten the legions of tyrannic force,
Sovereign whom God hath surely blest and sent
To be of future good His instrument,
Though all desert thee in thine hour of need,
And leave thee houseless on the rocks to bleed,
Let thy soul's watchword be a truer light
Than even his who ruled by fear and might.
Thy Heart thy Fortress! An unfading youth
Shall yearly crown its battlements of truth.

In the bright panoply of God encased
No years shall molder and no tyrant waste.
No Ruin of the Past that heart shall be,
But a great Beacon-tower for the good and free.

Rome, February, 1848.

———— April 1.

Yesterday I passed at Ostia and Castle Fusano. A million birds sang; the woods teemed with blossoms: the sod grew green hourly over the graves of the mighty Past; the surf rushed in on a fair shore; the Tiber majestically retreated to carry inland her share from the treasures of the deep; the sea breezes burnt my face, but revived my heart; I felt the calm of thought, the sublime hopes of the Future, Nature, Man—so great, though so little—so dear, though incomplete.[12] Returning to Rome, I find the news, pronounced official, that the viceroy Ranieri has capitulated at Verona; that Italy is free, independent, and One.[13] I trust this will prove no April foolery, no premature news; it seems too good, too speedy a realization of hope, to have come on earth, and can only be answered in the words of the proclamation made yesterday by Pius IX.:

"The events which these two months past have seen rush after one another in so rapid succession, are no human work. Woe to him who in this wind, which shakes and tears up alike the lofty cedars and humble shrubs, hears not the voice of God! Woe to human pride, if to the fault or merit of any man whatsoever it refer these wonderful changes, instead of adoring the mysterious designs of Providence." ★

---

[12] Castle Fusano, a seventeenth-century villa, is two miles south of Ostia, near Italy's west coast. Fuller's biographer Madeleine B. Stern believes that "Margaret Fuller and Giovanni Ossoli were married in a civil ceremony of April 4, 1848, in one of the towns near Rome." She bases this conjecture on the fact that "April 4 seems to have been an anniversary for the Ossolis. Their letters of April 3 and 4, 1849, express keen regret that they cannot be together on the fourth and hope that the next year will bring them better luck on that day" (430).

[13] Archduke Rainier, the Hapsburg viceroy of Lombardy and Venetia, was outmaneuvered by Manin, who established a civic guard on March 22 (Fejtö ix).

Dispatch 24

NOBLE SENTIMENT AND
THE LOSS OF THE POPE

ROME, 19th April, 1848[1]

In closing my last, I hoped to have some decisive intelligence to impart by this time, as to the fortunes of Italy. But though everything, so far, turns in her favor, there has been no decisive battle, no final stroke. It pleases me much, as the news comes from day to day, that I passed so leisurely last Summer over that part of Lombardy, now occupied by the opposing forces, that I have in my mind the faces both of the Lombard and Austrian leaders. A number of the present members of the Provisional Government of Milan I knew while there; they are men of twenty-eight and thirty, much more advanced in thought than the Moderates of Rome, Naples, Tuscany, who are too much fettered by a bygone state of things, and not on a par in thought, knowledge, preparation for the great Future, with the rest of the civilized world at this moment. The papers that emanate from the Milanese Government are far superior in tone to any that have been uttered by the other States. Their protest in favor of their rights, their letters to the Germans at large and the countries under the dominion of Austria, are full of nobleness and thoughts sufficiently great for the use of the coming age. The latter I translate, thinking they may not in other form reach America.

THE PROVISIONAL GOVERNMENT OF MILAN TO THE GERMAN NATION.
We hail you as brothers, valiant, learned, generous Germans:
This salutation from a people just risen after a terrible struggle to self-consciousness and to the exercise of its rights ought deeply to move your magnamimous hearts.
We deem ourselves worthy to utter that great word, BROTHERHOOD, which effaces among nations the traditions of all ancient hate, and we proffer it over the new-made graves of our fellow-citizens who have fought and died to give us the right to proffer it without fear or shame.
We call brothers all nations who believe and hope in the improvement of the human family, and seek the occasion to further it—but you, especially, we call brothers; you Germans, with whom we have in common so many noble sympathies, the love of the arts and higher studies, the

[1] First published as "Things and Thoughts in Europe. No. XXIV" in *New-York Daily Tribune*, 15 June 1848, p. 1:1–5.

delight of noble contemplation, with whom also we have much correspondence in our civil destinies.

With you are of first importance the interests of the great country,
Germany—with us those of the great country, Italy.

We were induced to rise in arms against Austria, (we mean not the
People but the Government of Austria,) not only by the need of redeeming
ourselves from the shame and grief of thirty-one years of the most abject
despotism, but by a deliberate resolve to take our place upon the plane of
nations, to unite with our brothers of the Peninsula, and take rank with
them under the great banner raised by Pius IX, on which is written, THE
INDEPENDENCE OF ITALY.

Can you blame us, independent Germans? In blaming us, you would
sink beneath your history, beneath your most honored and recent declarations.

We have chased the Austrian from our soil; we shall give ourselves no
repose till we have chased him from all parts of Italy. To this enterprise we
are all sworn; for this fights our army enrolled in every part of the Peninsula, an army of brothers led by the King of Sardinia, who prides himself
on being the sword of Italy.

And the Austrian is not more our enemy than yours.

The Austrian—we speak still of the Government and not of the
People—has always denied and contradicted the interests of the whole
German nation at the head of an assemblage of races, differing in language, in customs, in institutions. When it was in his power to have
corrected the errors of time and a dynastic policy, by assuming the high
mission of uniting them by great moral interests, he preferred to arm one
against the other and to corrupt them all.

Fearing every noble instinct, hostile to every grand idea, devoted to
the material interests of an oligarchy of princes spoiled by a senseless education, of ministers who had sold their consciences, of speculators who
subjected and sacrificed everything to gold, the only aim of such a Government was to sow division everywhere.—What wonder if everywhere
in Italy as in Germany it reaps harvests of hate and ignominy. Yes, of hate!
To this the Austrian has condemned us, to know hate and its deep sorrows.
But we are absolved in the sight of God and by the insults which have
been heaped upon us for so many years, the unwearied efforts to debase
us, the destruction of our villages, the cold-blooded slaughter of our aged
people, our priests, our women, our children. And you—you should be
the first to absolve us, you, virtuous among the Germans, who certainly
have shared our indignation when a venal and lying press accused us of

being enemies of your great and generous nation, and we could not answer and were constrained to devour in silence the shame of an accusation which wounded us to the heart.

We honor you, Germans; we pant to give you glorious evidence of this. And, as a prelude to the friendly relations we hope to form with your Governments, we seek to alleviate as much as possible the pains of captivity to some officers and soldiers belonging to various States of the Germanic Confederation, who fought in the Austrian army. These we wish to send back to you, and are occupied by seeking the means to effect this purpose. We honor you so much that we believe you capable of preferring to the bonds of race and language the sacred titles of misfortune and of right.

Ah! answer to our appeal, valiant, wise and generous Germans; clasp the hand which we offer you with the heart of a brother and friend; hasten to disavow every appearance of complicity with a Government which the massacres of Gallicia and Lombardy have blotted from the list of civilized and Christian Governments.—It would be a beautiful thing for you to give this example which will be new in history and worthy of these miraculous times, the example of a strong and generous people casting aside other sympathies, other interests, to answer the invitation of a regenerate people, to cheer it in its new career, obedient to the great principles of Justice, of Humanity, of Civil and Christian Brotherhood.

THE PROVISIONAL GOVERNMENT OF MILAN TO THE NATIONS SUBJECT TO THE RULE OF THE HOUSE OF AUSTRIA.

From your lands have come three armies which have brought war into ours; your speech is spoken by those hostile bands who come to us with fire and sword; nevertheless we come to you as to brothers.

The war which we combat is not your war; you are not our enemies: you are only instruments in the hand of our foe, and this foe, brothers, is common to us all.

Before God, before men, solemnly we declare it; our only enemy is the Government of Austria.

And that Government, which for so many years has labored to cancel, in the races it has subdued, every vestige of nationality, which takes no heed of their wants or prayers, bent only on serving miserable interests and more miserable pride, fermenting always antipathies conformably with the ancient maxim of tyrants, *divide and govern,* this Government has constituted itself the adversary of every generous thought, the ally and patron of all ignoble causes, the Government declared by the whole civilized world paymaster of the executioners of Gallicia.

This Government, after having pertinaciously resisted the legal expression of moderate desires—after having defied with ludicrous hauteur the opinion of Europe, has found itself in its metropolis too weak to resist an insurrection of students, and has yielded—has yielded, making an assignment on time, and throwing you, brothers, as an alms-gift to the importunate beggar, the promise of institutions which, in these days, are held essential conditions of life for a civilized nation.

But you have not confided in this promise; for the youth of Vienna, which feels the inspiring breath of this miraculous time, is impelled on the path of progress; and therefore the Austrian Government, uncertain of itself and of your dispositions, took its old part of standing still to wait for events, in the hope of turning them to its own profit.

In the midst of this it received the news of our glorious Revolution, and it thought to have found in this the best way to escape from its embarrassment. First it concealed that news; then made them known piece-meal and disfigured by hypocrisy and hatred. We were a handfull of rebels thirsting for German blood.—We make a war of stilettos, we wish the destruction of all Germany. But for us answers the admiration of all Italy, of all Europe, even the evidence of your own people whom we are constrained to hold prisoners or hostages, who will unanimously avow that we have shown heroic courage in the fight, heroic moderation in victory.

Yes! we have risen as one man against the Austrian Government to become again a nation, to make common cause with our Italian brothers, and the arms which we have assumed for so great an object we shall not lay down till we have attained it. Assailed by a brutal executor of brutal orders, we have combatted in a just war; betrayed, a price set on our heads, wounded in the most vital parts, we have not transgressed the bounds of legitimate defence. The murders, the depredations of the hostile band, irritated against us by most wicked arts, have excited our horror, but never a reprisal. The soldier, his arms once laid down, was for us only an unfortunate.

But behold how the Austrian Government provokes you against us, and bids you come against us as a crusade; a crusade! The parody would be ludicrous if it were not so cruel. A crusade against a people which, in the name of Christ, under a banner blessed by the Vicar of Christ and revered by all the nations, fights to secure its indefeasible rights.

Oh! if you form against us this crusade,—we have already shown the world what a people can do to reconquer its liberty, its independence; we will show, also, what it can do to preserve them. If, almost unarmed, we have put to flight an army inured to war, (surely, brothers, that army wanted faith in the cause for which it fought,) can we fear that our courage will grow faint after our triumph, and when aided by all our brothers of Italy? Let the Austrian Government send against us its threatened battalions, they will find in our breasts a barrier more insuperable than the Alps. Everything will be a weapon to us; from every villa, from every field, from every hedge will issue defenders of the national cause; women and children will fight like men; men will centuple their strength, their courage; and we will all perish amid the ruins of our city, before receiving a foreign rule into this land which at last we call ours.

But this must not be, you, our brothers, must not permit it to be; your honor, your interests do not permit it. Will you fight in a cause which you must feel to be absurd and wicked? You sink to the condition of hirelings, and do you not believe that the Austrian Government, should it conquer us and Italy, would turn against you the arms you had furnished for the conquest? Do you not believe it would act as after the struggle with Napoleon? And are you not terrified by the idea of finding yourself in conflict with all civilized Europe, and constrained to receive, to feast as your ally, the Autocrat of Russia, that perpetual terror to the improvement and independence of Europe. It is not possible for the house of Lorraine to forget its traditions; it is not possible that it should resign itself to live tranquil in the atmosphere of Liberty. You can only constrain it by sustaining yourself, with the Germanic and Sclavonian nationalities, and with this Italy, which longs only to see the nations harmonize with that resolve which she has finally taken that she may never more be torn in pieces.

Think of us, brothers; this is for you and for us, a question of life and of death; it is a question on which depends, perhaps, the peace of Europe.

For ourselves, we have already weighed the chances of the struggle, and subordinated them all to this final resolution, that we will be free and independent with our brothers of Italy.

We hope that our words will induce you to calm counsels; if not, you will find us on the field of battle generous and loyal enemies, as now we profess ourselves your generous and loyal brothers.

Signed:	CASATI, President,	BORROMEO,
	DURINI,	P. LITTA,
	STRIGELLI,	GUILINI,
	BERETTA,	GUERRIERI,
	GRAPPI,	PORRO,

TURRONI,	MORRONI,
REZZONICO,	AB. ANELLI,
CARBONERA.	CORRENTI, SEC. GEN.

These are the names of men whose hearts glow with that generous ardor the noble product of difficult times. Into their hearts flows wisdom from on high—thoughts great, generous, brotherly. They may not all remain true to this high vocation, but, at any rate, they will have lived a period of true life. I knew some of these men when in Lombardy, of old aristocratic families, with all the refinement of inheritance and education; they are thoroughly pervaded by principles of a genuine Democracy of brotherhood and justice. In the flower of their age, they have before them a long career of the noblest usefulness, if this era follows up its present promise, and they are faithful to their present creed, and ready to improve and extend it.

Every day produces these remarkable documents. So many years as we have been suffocated and poisoned by the atmosphere of falsehood in official papers, how refreshing is the tone of noble sentiment in Lamartine![2] What a real wisdom and pure dignity in the letter of Béranger![3] *He* was always absolutely true; an oasis in the pestilential desert of Humbug; but the present time allowed him a fine occasion.

The Poles have also made noble manifestations. Their great poet, Adam Mickiewicz, has been here to enrol the Italian Poles, publish the declaration of faith in which they hope to re-enter and re-establish their country, and receive the Pope's benediction on their banner.

In their declaration of faith are found these three articles:

"Every one of the nation a citizen—every citizen equal in rights and before authority.

"To Israel, our elder brother, respect, brotherhood, aid on the way to his eternal and terrestrial good, entire equality in political and civil rights.

"To the companion of life, Woman, brotherhood, citizenship, entire equality of rights."

This last expression of just thought the Poles ought to initiate, for what

[2] Alphonse-Marie-Louis de Prat de Lamartine (1790–1869) was an important French romantic poet and orator. His *Histoire des Girondins* (1847) committed him to the republican cause, and during the February French revolution he assumed the leadership of the Provisional Government. As writer and public figure, he exerted a great influence upon the writers of the American renaissance (see Reynolds 18–24 and passim).

[3] Fuller had met Béranger in Paris and was quite impressed with this poet who was engaged in the struggle for liberty.

other nation has had such truly heroic women? Women indeed—not children, servants or playthings.

Mickiewicz, with the squadron that accompanied him from Rome, was received with the greatest enthusiasm at Florence. Deputations from the Clubs and journals went to his hotel and escorted him to the Piazza del Gran Duca, where, amid an immense concourse of people, some good speeches were made. A Florentine, with a generous forgetfulness of national vanity, addressed him as the "Dante of Poland, who, more fortunte than the great bard and seer of Italy, was likely to return to his country to reap the harvest of the seed he had sown."

"O, Dante of Poland! who, like our Alighieri, hast received from Heaven sovereign genius, divine song—but from earth sufferings and exile: more happy than our Alighieri, thou hast reacquired a country; already thou art meditating on the sacred harp the patriotic hymn of restoration and of victory. The Pilgrims of Poland are become the warriors of their nation.
"Long live Poland and the brotherhood of nations!"

When this address was finished, the great Poet appeared on the balcony to answer. The people received him with a tumult of applause, followed by a profound silence, as they anxiously awaited his voice, which began as follows: (Those who are acquainted with the powerful eloquence, the magnetism of Mickiewicz as an orator, will not be surprised at the effect produced by this speech, though delivered in a foreign language. It is the force of truth, the great vitality of his presence, that loads his words with such electric power.)

"PEOPLE OF TUSCANY: Friends! Brothers! We receive your shouts of sympathy in the name of Poland, not for us, but for our country. Our country, though distant, claims from you this sympathy by its long martyrdom. The glory of Poland, its only glory, truly Christian, is to have suffered more than all the nations. In other countries the goodness, the generosity of heart of some sovereigns protected the people: as yours has enjoyed the dawn of the era now coming, under the protection of your excellent Prince. [Viva Leopold II.!] But conquered Poland, slave and victim of sovereigns who were her sworn enemies and executioners; Poland, abandoned by the Governments and the Nations, lay in agony on her solitary Golgotha. She was believed slain, dead, buried. "We have slain her," shouted the despots, "she is dead!" [No, no; long live Poland!] The dead cannot rise again, replied the diplomatists; we may now be tranquil. [A universal shudder of feeling in the crowd.] There came a moment in which the world doubted of the Mercy and Justice of the Omnipotent. There was a moment in which the nations thought that the Earth might be forever abandoned by God, and condemned to the rule of the Demon, its ancient lord. The nations forgot that Jesus Christ came down from Heaven to give Liberty and Peace to the Earth. The nations had forgotten all this. But God is just. The voice of Pius IX. roused Italy. [Long live Pius IX!] The people of Paris has driven out the great traitor against the cause of the Nations. [Bravo! Viva the people of Paris!] Very soon will be heard the voice of Poland; Poland will rise again! [Yes, yes, Poland will rise again!] Poland will call to life all the Sclavonic races: the Croats, the Dalmatians, the Bohemians, the Moravians, the Illyrians. These will form the bulwark against the tyrant of the North. [Great applause.] They will close forever the way against the Barbarians of the North—destroyers of Liberty and of Civilization. Poland is called to do more yet; Poland, as crucified nation, is risen again and called to serve her sister nations. The will of God is that Christianity should become in Poland, and through Poland elsewhere, no more a dead letter of the law, but the living law of States and civil associations. [Great applause.] That Christianity should be manifested by acts, the sacrifices of generosity and of liberality. This Christianity is not new to you, Florentines, your ancient Republic knew and has acted from it; it is time that the same spirit make to itself a larger sphere. The will of God is that the nations should act toward one another as neighbors, as brothers, [a tumult of applause;] and you, Tuscans, have to-day done an act of Christian brotherhood. Receiving thus foreign, un-known pilgrims, who go to defy the greatest powers of the earth, you have in us saluted only what is in us of spiritual and immortal—our Faith and our Patriotism. [Applause.] We thank you, and we will now go into the church to thank God."

"All the people then followed the Poles to the Church of Santa Croce, where was sung the *Benedictus Dominus,* and amid the memorials of the greatness of Italy collected in that temple, was forged more strongly the chain of sympathy, and of union, between two nations, sisters in misfortunes and in glory."

This speech and its reception, literally translated from the journal of the day, show how pleasant it is on great occasions to be brought in contact with this people, so full of natural eloquence and of lively sensibility to what is great and beautiful.

It is a glorious time for the exiles who return and reap even a momentary fruit of their long sorrows. Mazzini, too, has been able to return from his seven-teen years' exile, when there was no hour, night or day, that the thought of Italy was banished from his heart—no possible effort that he did not make to achieve the emancipation of his people, and with it the progress of mankind. He returns, like Wordsworth's great man "to see what he foresaw."[4] He will see his predictions accomplishing yet for a long time, for Mazzini has a mind far in advance of his times in general and his nature in particular—a mind that will be best revered and understood when the "illustrious Gioberti" shall be remembered as a pompous verbose charlatan, with just talent enough to catch the echo from the advancing wave of his day, but without any true sight of the wants of man at this epoch. And yet Mazzini sees not all: he aims at political emancipation; but he sees not, perhaps would deny, the bearing of some events, which even now begin to work their way. Of this more anon, but not to-day nor in the small print of *The Tribune*. Suffice it to say, I allude to that of which the cry of Communism, the systems of Fourier, &c. are but forerunners. Mazzini sees already—at Milan, where he is, he has probably this day received the intelligence of the accomplishment of his foresight, implied in his letter to the Pope, which angered Italy by what was thought its tone of irreverence and doubt some six months since.

To-day is the 7th May, for I had thrown aside this letter, begun the 19th April, from a sense that there was something coming that would supersede what was then, to say. This something has appeared in a form that will cause deep sadness to good hearts everywhere. Good and loving hearts that long for a human form which they can revere, will be unprepared and for a time must suffer much from the final dereliction of Pius IX. to the cause of Freedom, Progress, and of War.[5] He was a fair image, and men went nigh to idolize it; this they can do no more though they may be able to find the excuse for his feebleness, love his good heart no less than before, and draw instruction from the causes that have produced his failure, more valuable than his success would have been.

Pius IX. no one can doubt, who has looked on him, has a good and pure heart; but it needed also not only a strong but a great mind—

[4] In November 1848 Fuller paraphrased this section in a letter to an unknown recipient: "Mazzini has returned from his seventeen years' exile, 'to see what he foresaw.' He has a mind far in advance of his times, and yet Mazzini sees not all." Mazzini arrived in Milan on 7 April 1848; Fuller paraphrases Wordsworth's "The Character of the Happy Warrior" (Hudspeth 5:154–55; *William Wordsworth: The Poems* 1:663).

[5] On April 29 Pius IX issued an allocution that put an end to hopes for a republic that he would head: he disavowed the war against Austria. In so doing, the pope ended his brief career as a political leader and caused unrest in Rome which Fuller witnessed first hand (Hudspeth 5:65).

"To *comprehend his trust,* and to the same
Keep faithful with a singleness of aim." [6]

A highly esteemed friend in the United States wrote to express distaste at some observations in a letter of mine to *The Tribune* on first seeing the Pontiff a year ago, observing "To say that he had not the expression of great intellect was *uncalled for.*" Alas! far from it; it was an observation that rose inevitably on knowing something of the task before Pius IX. and the hopes he had excited. The problem he had to solve was one of such difficulty that only one of those minds, the rare product of ages for the redemption of mankind, could be equal to its solution; the question that inevitably rose on seeing was, "Is he such an one?" The answer was immediately negative. But at the same time, he had such an aspect of true benevolence and piety that a hope arose that Heaven would act through him and impel him to measures wise beyond his knowledge.

This hope was confirmed by the calmness he showed at the time of the conspiracy of July and the occupation of Ferrara by the Austrians. Tales were told of simple wisdom, of instinct which he obeyed in opposition to the counsels of all his Cardinals. Everything went on well for a time.

But tokens of indubitable weakness were shown by the Pope in early acts of the Winter, in the removal of a censor from the suggestion of others, in his speech to the Consistory, in his answer to the first address of the Council. In these he declared that, when there was conflict between the priest and the man, he always meant to be the priest, and that he preferred the wisdom of the Past to that of the Future.

Still, times went on bending his predeterminations to the call of the moment. He *acted* wiselier than he intended, as for instance, three weeks after declaring he would not give a constitution to his people he gave it; a sop to Cerberus indeed, a poor vamped-up thing that will by-and-by have to give place to something more legitimate, but which served its purpose at the time as a declaration of rights for the people. When the news of the Revolution of Vienna arrived, the Pope himself cried Viva Pio IX. and this ebullition of truth in one so humble, though opposed to his formal declarations, was received by his people with that immediate assent which truth commands.

The Revolution of Lombardy followed. The troops of the line were sent to that portion; the volunteers rushed to accompany them. In the streets of Rome was read the proclamation of Charles Albert in which he styles himself the servant of Italy and of Pius IX. The priests preached the war, and justly, as a crusade; the Pope blessed their banners. Nobody dreamed, or had cause to dream,

[6] Fuller again quotes Wordsworth's "The Character of the Happy Warrior." The lines are: "Who comprehends his trust, and to the same / Keeps faithful with a singleness of aim."

that these movements had not his full sympathy, and his name was in every form invoked as the chosen instrument of God to inspire Italy to throw off the oppressive yoke of the foreigner and recover her rights in the civilized world.

At the same time, however, the Pope was seen to act with great blindness in the affair of the Jesuits. The other States of Italy drove them out by main force, resolved not to number in the midst of the war a foe and spy in the camp. Rome wished to do the same, but the Pope rose in their defence. He talked as if they were assailed as a *religious* body, when he could not fail, like everybody else, to be aware that they were dreaded and hated solely as agents of despotism. He demanded they should be assailed only by legal means, when none such were available. The end was in half measures, always the worst possible. He would not entirely yield, and the People would not at all. The Order was ostensibly dissolved; but great part of the Jesuits really remain here in disguise, a constant source of irritation and mischief, which, if still greater difficulties had not arisen, would of itself have created enough. Meanwhile, in the earnestness of the clergy about the pretended loss of the head of St. Andrew, in the ceremonies of the holy week, which at this juncture excited no real interest, was much matter for thought to the calm observer as to the restlessness of the new wine, the old bottles being heard to crack on every side and hour by hour.

Thus went on from day to day affairs; the Pope kissing the foot of the brazen Jupiter and blessing palms of straw at St. Peter's; the *Circalo Romano* erecting itself into a kind of Jacobin Club, dictating programmes for an Italian Diet general, and choosing committees to provide for the expenses of the war. The Civic Guard arresting people who tried to make mobs as if famishing, and being searched were found well provided both with arms and money: the Ministry at their wits' end, with their trunks packed up ready to be off at a moment's warning, when the report, it is not yet known whether true or false, that one of the Roman Civic Guard, a well known artist engaged in the war of Lombardy, had been taken and hung by the Austrians as a brigand, roused the people to a sense of the position of their friends, and they went to the Pope to demand that he should take a decisive stand and declare war against the Austrians.

The Pope summoned a consistory; the people waited anxiously, for expressions of his were reported as if the troops ought not to have thought of leaving the frontier, while every man, woman and child in Rome knew, and every letter and bulletin declared, that all their thought was to render active aid to the cause of Italian independence. This anxious doubt, however, had not prepared at all for the excess to which they were to be disappointed.

The speech of the Pope declared that he had never any thought of the great results that had followed his actions; that he had only intended local reforms, such as had previously been suggested by the potentates of Europe; that he regretted the *mis*use that had been made of his name; and wound up by lamenting over the war—dear to every Italian heart as the best and holiest cause in which for ages they had been called to embark their hopes—as if it was something offensive to the spirit of religion, and which he would fain see hushed up, and its motives smoothed out and ironed over.

A momentary stupefaction received this astounding performance, succeeded by a passion of indignation, in which the words *traitor* and *imbecile* were associated with the name that had been so dear to his people. This again yielded to a settled grief; they felt that he was betrayed but no traitor; timid and weak, but still a sovereign they had adored, and a man who had brought them much good, which could not be quite destroyed by his wishing to disown it. Even of this they had no time to stop and think; the necessity was too imminent of obviating the worst consequences of this ill; and the first thought was to prevent the news leaving Rome to dishearten the Provinces and Army before they had tried to induce the Pontiff to wiser resolves, or, if this could not be, to supersede his power.

I cannot repress my admiration at the gentleness, clearness and good sense with which the Roman people acted under these most difficult circumstances. It was astonishing to see the clear understanding which animated the crowd as one man, and the decision with which they acted to effect their purpose. Wonderfully has this people been developed within a year!

The Pope, besieged by deputations, who mildly but firmly showed him that if he persisted the temporal power must be placed in other hands, his ears filled with the reports of Cardinals, "such venerable persons," as he pathetically styles them, would not yield in spirit, though compelled to in act. After two days' struggle he was obliged to place the power in the hands of the persons most opposed to him, and nominally acquiesce in their proceedings, while in his second Proclamation, very touching from the sweetness of its tone, he shows a fixed misintelligence of the cause at issue, which leaves no hope of his ever again being more than a name or an effigy in their affairs.

His people were much affected and entirely laid aside their anger, but they would not be blinded as to the truth. While gladly returning to their accustomed habits of affectionate homage toward the Pontiff, their unanimous sense and resolve is thus expressed in an able pamphlet of the day, such as in every respect would have been deemed impossible to the Rome of 1847:

"From the last allocution of Pius result two facts of extreme gravity. The entire separation between the spiritual and temporal power and the express refusal of the Pontiff to be Chief of an Italian Republic. But far from drawing hence reason for discouragement and grief, who looks well at the destiny of Italy may bless Providence which breaks or changes the instrument when the work is completed, and by secret and inscrutable ways conducts us to the fulfillment of our desires and of our hopes.

"If Pius IX. refuses, not therefore has the Italian people renounced. Nothing remains to the free people of Italy except to unite in one Constitutional Kingdom, founded on the largest basis, and if the chief who, by our Assemblies, shall be called to the highest honor, either declines or does not answer worthily, the people will take care of itself.

"Italians! down with all emblems of private and partial interests. Let us unite under one single banner, the tricolor, and if he who has carried it bravely thus far lets it fall from his hand, we will take it one from the other, twenty-four millions of us, and, till the last of us shall have perished on the banner of our redemption, the stranger shall not return into Italy.

"Viva Italy! viva the Italian people!"

These events make indeed a crisis. The work began by Napoleon is finished. There will never more be really a Pope, but only the effigy or simulacrum of one.

The loss of Pius IX. is for the moment a great one. His name had real moral weight; was a trumpet appeal to sentiment. It is not the same with any man that is left. There is not one that can be truly a leader in the Roman Dominion, not one who has even great intellectual weight.

The responsibility of events now lies wholly with the People and that wave of Thought which has begun to pervade them. Sovereigns and Statesmen will go where they are carried; it is probable influence will be changed continually from hand to hand, and Government become, to all intents and purposes, representative. Italy needs now quite to throw out her stupid King of Naples, who hangs like a dead weight on her movements. The King of Sardinia and the Grand Duke of Tuscany will be trusted while they keep their present course; but who can feel sure of any sovereign, now that Louis Philippe has shown himself so mad and Pius IX. so blind? It seems as if Fate was at work to bewilder and cast down the dignities of the world and democratize Society at a blow.

In Rome there is now no anchor except the good sense of the people. It seems impossible that collision should not arise between him who retains the name but not the place of Sovereign, and the Provisional Government which calls itself a Ministry. The Count Mamiani, its new head, is a man of reputation as a writer, but untried as yet as a leader or a statesman.[7] Should agitations arise, the Pope can no longer calm them by one of his fatherly looks.

[7] Terenzio Mamiani (1799–1885), a philosopher and teacher, had been living in exile since 1831. The pope allowed him to return in 1847 and asked him to lead the government on 2 May. He held office only briefly, resigning on 19 July when Austria invaded Ferrara (Hudspeth 5:70).

All lies in the Future; and our best hope must be that the Power which has begun so great a work will find due means to end it, and make the year 1850 a year of true jubilee to Italy; a year not merely of pomps and tributes, but of recognized rights and intelligent joys; a year of real peace: peace, founded not on compromise and the lying etiquettes of diplomacy, but on Truth and Justice.

Then this sad disappointment in Pius IX. may be forgotten, or while all that was lovely and generous in his life is prized and reverenced, may be drawn from his errors deep instruction as to the inevitable dangers of a priestly or princely environment, and a higher knowledge may elevate a nobler commonwealth than the world has yet known.

Hoping this era, I remain at present here.—Should my hopes be dashed to the ground, it will not change my faith, but the struggle for its manifestation is to me of vital interest. My friends write to urge my return; they talk of our country as the land of the Future. It is so, but that spirit which made it all it is of value in my eyes, which gave all of hope with which I can sympathize for that Future, is more alive here at present than in America. My country is at present spoiled by prosperity, stupid with the lust of gain, soiled by crime in its willing perpetuation of Slavery, shamed by an unjust war, noble sentiment much forgotten even by individuals, the aims of politicians selfish or petty, the literature frivolous and venal. In Europe, amid the teachings of adversity a nobler spirit is struggling—a spirit which cheers and animates mine. I hear earnest words of pure faith and love. I see deeds of brotherhood. This is what makes *my* America. I do not deeply distrust my country. She is not dead, but in my time she sleepeth, and the spirit of our fathers flames no more, but lies hid beneath the ashes. It will not be so long; bodies cannot live when the soul gets too overgrown with gluttony and falsehood. But it is not the making a President out of the Mexican War that would make me wish to come back.[8] Here things are before my eyes worth recording, and, if I cannot help this work, I would gladly be its historian.   ★

May 13.

Returning from a little tour in the Alban Mount, where everything looks so glorious this glorious Spring, I find a temporary quiet.[9] The Pope's brothers

[8] The Mexican War ended on 2 February 1848. General Zachary Taylor, who had gained fame and popularity with his victories at the battles of Palo Alto, Monterrey, and Buena Vista, would run for president on the Whig ticket and be elected, as Fuller here foresees.

[9] Fuller and Ossoli took a brief tour of the hills near Rome before Fuller had to leave Rome for the countryside. Because Ossoli could not leave his position in the Civic Guard, he could not accompany her. At this point, Fuller clearly feared discovery of her pregnancy and wished to avoid detection. She had not told her family and friends and continued to write to them of her illness, the hardship of her life, and, increasingly, her sense that she would soon die (Deiss 140–41).

have come to sympathize with him; the crowd sighs over what he has done, presents him with great bouquets of flowers, and reads anxiously the news from the North and the proclamations of the new Ministry. Meanwhile the nightingales sing; every tree and plant is in flower, and the sun and moon shine as if Paradise were already reëstablished on earth. I go to one of the villas to dream it is so, beneath the pale light of a   ★

Dispatch 25

THE SUMMER OF '48

ROME, December 2, 1848 [1]

Messrs. Greeley & McElrath:

Easy is the descent to ill.

I have not written for six months, and within that time what changes have taken place on this side "the great water." Changes of how great dramatic interest historically—of bearing infinitely important ideally. [2]

I wrote last when Pius IX. had taken the first stride on the downward road. He had proclaimed himself the foe of farther Reform measures, when he implied that Italian independence was not important in his eyes, when he abandoned the crowd of heroic youth who had gone to the field with his benediction, to some of whom his own hand had given crosses. All the Popes, his predecessors, had meddled with, most frequently instigated, war; now came one who must carry out, literally, the doctrines of the Prince of Peace, when the war was not for mercy, or the aggrandizement of individuals, but to redeem national, to redeem human, rights from the grasp of foreign oppression.

I said some cried "traitor," some "imbecile," some "wept," but in the minds of all, I believe, at that time grief was finally predominant. They could no longer depend on him they had thought their best friend. They had lost their father.

Meanwhile his people would not submit to the inaction he urged. They saw it was not only ruinous to themselves, but base and treacherous to the rest of Italy. They said to the Pope, "This cannot be; you must follow up the pledges you have given, or, if you will not act to redeem them, you must have a Ministry that will." The Pope, after he had once declared to the contrary, ought to

---

[1] First published as "Things and Thoughts in Europe. No. XXV" in *New-York Daily Tribune*, 19 January 1849, p. 1:1–3.

[2] During the six months, Fuller had experienced her removal to Aquila and then Rieti, and the difficult last months of her pregnancy. Her child, Angelo Eugenio Filippo Ossoli, was born on 5 September 1848. She returned to Rome in early November.

have persisted. He ought to have said, "I cannot thus belie myself, I cannot put my name to acts I have just declared to be against my conscience."

The Ministers of the people ought to have seen that the position they assumed was utterly untenable; that they could not advance with an enemy in the background cutting off all supplies. But some patriotism, and some vanity exhilarated them, and the Pope, having weakly yielded, they unwisely began their impossible task. Mamiani, their chief, I esteem a man, under all circumstances, unequal to such a position—a man of rhetoric, merely. But no man could have acted, unless the Pope had resigned his temporal power, the Cardinals been put under sufficient check, and the Jesuits and emissaries of Austria driven from their lurking-places.

A sad scene began. The Pope—shut up more and more in his palace, the crowd of selfish and insidious advisers darkening round, enslaved by a confessor—he who might have been the liberator of suffering Europe, permitted the most infamous treacheries to be practiced in his name. Private letters were written to the foreign powers denying the acts he outwardly sanctioned; the hopes of the people were evaded or dallied with; the Chamber of Deputies permitted to talk and pass measures which they never could get funds to put into execution; legions to form and maneuver, but never to have the arms and clothing they needed. Again and again the people went to the Pope for satisfaction. They got only—benediction.

Thus plotted and thus worked the scarlet men of sin, playing the hopes of Italy off and on, while *their* hope was of the miserable defeat consummated by a still worse traitor at Milan on the 6th August.[3] But, indeed, what could be expected from the "SWORD OF PIUS IX." when Pius IX. himself had thus failed to his high vocation. The King of Naples bombarded his city and set on the lazzaroni to rob and murder the subjects he had deluded by his pretended gift of the Constitution.[4] Pius proclaimed that he longed to embrace *all* the Princes of Italy. He talked of peace when all knew for a great part of the Italians there was no longer hope of peace except in the sepulchre, or Freedom.

[3] Fuller refers here to King Charles Albert's evacuation of Milan, which he had promised to defend. His Piedmontese troops had been completely defeated by the Austrians at Custozza on 23 July, and he retreated to Milan. The king then withdrew his troops to Piedmont, leaving the city at the mercy of the Austrians who entered it on 5 August 1848, inflicting severe reprisals. The capitulation of Milan so enraged its citizens that they tried to assassinate Charles Albert, accusing him of treachery (Fejtö 129).

[4] Ferdinand II abruptly ceased his support of the war against Austria following the pope's speech of 29 April announcing he was not in favour of the war. Seizing as his excuse current disorders caused by agents provocateurs, the king dismissed his parliament, ordered his army to sack Naples, and recalled his seven thousand troops from the north (Berkeley 3: 272–74, 279–80; Fejtö 129).

The taunting manifestoes of Welden are a sufficient comment on the conduct of the Pope.[5] "As the Government of His Holiness is too weak to control his subjects"—"As, singularly enough, a great number of Romans are found fighting against us, contrary to the *expressed* will of their Prince,"—such were the excuses for invasions of the Pontifical dominions and robbery and insult by which they were accompanied. Such invasions, it was said, made His Holiness very indignant; he remonstrated against these; but we find no word of remonstrance against the tyranny of the King of Naples—no word of sympathy for the victims of Lombardy, the sufferings of Verona, Vicenza, Padua, Mantua, Venice. In the affairs of Europe there are continued signs of the plan of the retrograde party to effect similar demonstrations in different places at the same hour. The 15th May was one of these marked days.[6] On that day the King of Naples made use of the insurrection he had contrived to excite to massacre his people, and find an excuse for recalling his troops from Lombardy. The same day a similar crisis was hoped in Rome from the declarations of the Pope, but that did not work at the moment exactly as the foes of enfranchisement hoped.

However, the wounds were cruel enough. The Roman volunteers received the astounding news that they were not to expect protection or countenance from their Prince; all the army stood aghast that they were no longer to fight in the name of Pio. It had been so dear, so sweet to love and reverence really the Head of their Church, so inspiring to find their religion for once in accordance with the aspirations of the soul. They were to be deprived, too, of the aid of the disciplined Neapolitan troops and their artillery, on which they had counted. How cunningly all this was contrived to cause dissension and dismay may easily be seen.

The Neapolitan General Pepe nobly refused to obey, and called on the troops to remain with him.[7] They wavered; but they are a pampered army, personally much attached to the King, who pays them well and indulges them at the expense of his people, that they may be his support against that people when in a throe of Nature it rises and strives for its rights. For the same reason, the sentiment of patriotism was little diffused among them in comparison with the other troops. And the alternative presented was one in which it required a very clear sense of higher duty to act against habit. Generally, afer wavering a while,

[5] Austrian field marshal Graf Weldon's job during the campaign in Piedmont late in April was to maintain communications from Trent to Verona and thus maintain Radetzky's link to Austria (Berkeley 3:98–200).

[6] On 15 May there were riots in Vienna (after which Emperor Ferdinand granted universal suffrage) and demonstrations in Paris advocating Polish independence (Fejtö x).

[7] General Guglielmo Pepe, a liberal Neapolitan, was an ardent supporter of the revolution (Berkeley 2:270, 284).

they obeyed and returned. The Roman States which had received them with so many testimonials of affection and honor, were not slack to show a correspondent aversion and contempt on their retreat. The towns would not suffer their passage; the hamlets were unwilling to serve them even with fire and water. They were filled at once with shame and rage; one officer killed himself, unable to bear it; in the unreflecting minds of the soldiers, hate sprung up for the rest of Italy, and especially Rome, which will make them admirable tools of tyranny in case of civil war.

This was the first great calamity of the war. But apart from the treachery of the King of Naples and the dereliction of the Pope, it was impossible it should end thoroughly well. The people were in earnest, and have shown themselves so; brave, and able to bear privation. No one should dare, after the proofs of the Summer, to reiterate the taunt, so unfriendly frequent on foreign lips at the beginning of the contest, that the Italian can boast, shout, and fling garlands, but not *act*. The Italian always showed himself a noble and a brave, even in foreign service, and is doubly so in the cause of his country. But efficient heads were wanting. The Princes were not in earnest; they were looking at expediency. The Grand Duke, timid and prudent, wanted to do what was safest for Tuscany; his Ministry, *"Moderate"* and prudent, would have liked to win a great prize at small risk. They went no farther than the people pulled them. The King of Sardinia had taken the first bold step, and the idea that treachery on his part was premeditated cannot be sustained; it arises from the extraordinary aspect of his measures, and the knowledge that he is not incapable of treachery, as he proved in early youth.[8] But now it was only his selfishness that worked to the same results. He fought and planned, not for Italy but the house of Savoy, which his Balbis and Giobertis[9] had so long been prophesying was

[8] Fuller refers to Charles Albert's behavior during the Piedmontese revolution of 1821. Though seemingly sympathetic with a group of young aristocrats of liberal persuasion, Charles Albert turned upon them when they staged a revolution and forced the abdication of his father, Victor Emmanuel I. As regent, Charles Albert refused to lead a war against Austria and secretly prepared a counterrevolution with such troops as had remained loyal (*Dictionary of Modern Italian History,* ed. Frank J. Coppa [Westport, Conn.: Greenwood Press, 1985], 75–76).

[9] Cesare Balbo and Abbé Vincenzo Gioberti (1801–52) represented the moderates who favored uniting Italy by federation. Gioberti, a distinguished philosopher, had published *Del primato morale e civile degli Italiani* in 1843. The *Primato* was enormously influential on Pius IX, as was Balbo's book *Delle speranze d'Italia,* also published in 1843. Gioberti's plan, which Mazzini opposed, specifically called for the pope to be the president of a confederation of Italian states. Balbo considered Gioberti his master, but Balbo's scheme claimed the leadership of the confederation for Piedmont, and he left the question of the presidency of the confederation open (Berkeley 1:44–50, 187–92; 2:xix–xx; Maurice 120–25).

to reign supreme in the new great Era of Italy. These prophecies he more than half believed, because they chimed with his ambitious wishes; but he had not soul enough to realize them; he trusted only in his disciplined troops; he had not nobleness enough to believe he might rely at all on the sentiment of the people. For his troops he dared not have good Generals; conscious of meanness and timidity, he shrank from the approach of able and earnest men; he was only afraid they would, in helping Italy, take her and themselves out of his guardianship. Antonini was insulted,[10] Garibaldi rejected; other experienced leaders, who had rushed to Italy at the first trumpet-sound, could never get employment from him.[11] As to his generalship, it was entirely inadequate, even if he had made use of the first favorable moments. But his first thought was not to strike a blow at the Austrians before they recovered from the discomfiture of Milan, but to use the panic and need of his assistance to induce Lombardy and Venice to annex themselves to his kingdom. He did not even wish seriously to get the better till this was done, and when this was done, it was too late. The Austrian army was recruited, the Generals had recovered their spirits, and were burning to retrieve and avenge their past defeat. The conduct of Charles Albert had been shamefully evasive in the first months. The account given by Franzini,[12] when challenged in the Chamber of Deputies at Turin, might be summed up thus: "Why, gentlemen, what would you have? Every one knows that the army is in excellent condition, and eager for action. They are often reviewed, hear speeches, and sometimes get medals. We take places always, if it is not difficult. I myself was present once when the troops advanced; our men behaved gallantly, and had the advantage in the first skirmish, but afterward the enemy pointed on us artillery from the hights, and naturally, we retired. But as to supposing that his Majesty Charles Albert is indifferent to the success of Italy in the war, that is absurd. He is the Sword of Italy; he is the most magnanimous of Princes! he is seriously occupied about the war; many a day I have been called into his tent to talk it over, before he was up in the morning!"

[10] Giacomo Antonini (1792–1854) was a solid member of Mazzini's National Association in 1848, which arose in Italy to unite some five hundred men of diverse nationalities (Zorzi 187).

[11] Giuseppe Garibaldi (1807–82) had been a member of Mazzini's Young Italy in his youth and was forced into exile in 1834, going to South America where he earned fame as a military commander defending Montevideo against the Argentinians. He left Montevideo on 15 April 1848 and landed at Nice on 23 June. Though rejected by Charles Albert as a suitable military leader, he fought with the Milanese against Austria in the summer of 1848. In 1849 he would organize the defense of the Roman Republic against the French.

[12] Antonio Franzini (1788–1860) had served in Napoleon's armies as an artillery officer for five years. He was Charles Albert's minister of war in 1848 (Zorzi 187; Berkeley 3:46).

Sad was it that the heroic Milan, the heroic Venice, the heroic Sicily, should lean on such a reed as this, and by hurried acts, equally unworthy as unwise, sully the glory of their shields. Some names, indeed, stand out quite free from this blame. Mazzini, who kept up a combat against folly and cowardice, of day by day and hour by hour, with almost supernatural strength, warned the people constantly of the evils which their advisers were drawing upon them. He was heard then only by a few, but in this "Italia del Popolo" may be found many prophecies exactly fulfilled, as those of "the golden-haired love of Phœbus" during the struggles of Illium. He himself, in the last sad days of Milan, compared his lot to that of Cassandra.[13] At all events, his hands are pure from all that ill. What could be done to arouse Lombardy he did, but the "Moderate" party unable to wean themselves from old habits, the pupils of the wordy Gioberti thought there could be no safety unless under the mantle of a Prince. They did not foresee that he would run away and throw that mantle on the ground.

Tommaseo and Manin also were clear in their aversion to these measures; and with them, as with all who were resolute in principle at that time, a great influence has followed.

It is said Charles Albert feels bitterly the imputations on his courage, and says they are most ungrateful when he has exposed the lives of himself and his sons in the combat. Indeed, there ought to be made a distinction between personal and mental courage. The former Charles Albert may possess, may have too much, of what this still aristocratic world calls "the feelings of a gentleman" to shun exposing himself to a chance shot now and then. And entire want of mental courage he has shown. His decisive battle was made so by giving up the moment Fortune turned against him. It is shameful to hear so many say this result was inevitable, just because the material advantages were in favor of the Austrians. Pray, was never a battle won against material odds? It is precisely such that a good leader, a noble man, may expect to win. Were the Austrians driven out of Milan because the Milanese had that advantage? The Austrian would again have suffered repulse from them, but for the baseness of this man, on whom they had been cajoled into relying: a baseness that deserves the pillory; and on a pillory will the "magnanimous," as he was meanly called in face of the crimes of his youth and the timid selfishness of his middle age, stand in the sight of posterity. He made use of his power only to betray Milan; he took from the citizens all means of defence, and then gave them up to the spoiler; he promised to defend them "to the last drop of his blood," and sold them the

[13] Cassandra's fate was that no one believed her dire prophecies even though they were accurate. In Greek myth Phoebus Apollo gave her the gift of prophecy to woo her; later, when thwarted, he decreed no one should believe her.

next minute; even the paltry terms he made he has not seen maintained. Had the people slain him in their rage, he well deserved it at their hands; and all his conduct since had confirmed that sudden verdict of passion.

Of all this great drama I have much to write, but elsewhere, in a more full form, and where I can duly sketch the portraits of actors little known in America. The materials are over-rich. I have bought my right in them by much sympathetic suffering; yet, amid the blood and tears of Italy, 't is joy to see some glorious new births.—the Italians are getting cured of mean adulation and hasty boasts; they are learning to prize and seek realities; the effigies of straw are getting knocked down, and living, growing men, take their places. Italy is being educated for the Future: her leaders are learning that the time is past for trust in Princes and precedents—that there is no hope except in Truth and God; her lower people are learning to shout less and think more.

Though my thoughts have been much with the public in this struggle for life, I have been away from it during the Summer months, in the quiet valleys, on the lonely mountains. There, personally undisturbed, I have seen the glorious Italian Summer wax and wane: the Summer of Southern Italy, which I did not see last year. On the mountains it was not too hot for me, and I enjoyed the great luxuriance of vegetation. I had the advantage of having visited the scene of the war minutely last Summer, so that, in mind, I could follow every step of the campaign; while around me were the glorious reliques of old times, the crumbling theater or temple of the Roman day; the bird's-nest village of the Middle Ages—on its purple hight shone the sun and moon of Italy in changeless lustre. It was great pleasure to me to watch the gradual growth and change of the seasons, so different from ours. Last year I had not leisure for this quiet acquaintance. Now I saw the fields first dressed in their carpets of grain, enameled richly with the red poppy and blue corn-flower—in that sunshine how resplendent! Then swelled the fig, the grape, the olive, the almond; and my food was of these products of this rich clime. For near three months I had grapes every day; the last four weeks enough daily for two persons for a cent! Exquisite salad for two persons' dinner and supper, a cent. All other products of the region in the same proportion. One who keeps still in Italy, and lives as the people do, may really have much simple luxury for very little money; though both travel and, to the inexperienced foreigner, life in the cities are expensive.   ★

Dispatch 26

REVOLUTION IN ROME

ROME, December 2, 1848 [1]

Messrs. Greeley & McElrath:

Not till I saw the snow on the mountains grow rosy in the Autumn sunset did I turn my steps again toward Rome. I was very ready to return. After three or four years of constant excitement this six months of seclusion had been welcome; but now I felt the need of meeting other eyes beside those, so bright and so shallow, of the Italian peasant. Indeed, I left what was most precious that I could not take with me; still it was a compensation that I was again to see Rome.[2] Rome that almost killed me with her cold breath of last Winter, yet still with that cold breath whispered a tale of import so divine. Rome so beautiful, so great; her presence stupifies, and one has to withdraw to prize the treasures she has given. City of the Soul! yes, it is *that;* the very dust magnetizes you, and thousand spells have been chaining you in every careless, every murmuring moment. Yes! Rome, however seen, thou must be still adored; and every hour of absence or presence must deepen love with one who has known what it is to repose in thy arms.

Repose! for whatever be the revolutions, tumults, panics, hopes of the present day, still the temper of life here is Repose. The great Past enfolds us, and the emotions of the moment cannot here importantly disturb that impression. From the wild shout and throng of the streets the setting sun recalls us as it rests on a hundred domes and temples—rests on the Campagna, whose grass is rooted in departed human greatness. Burial-place so full of spirit that Death itself seems no longer cold; oh let me rest here, too! Rest, here, seems possible; meseems myriad lives still linger here, awaiting some one great summons.

The rivers had burst their bounds, and beneath the moon the fields round Rome lay, one sheet of silver.[3] Entering the gate while the baggage was under

---

[1] First published as "Things and Thoughts in Europe. No. XXVI" in *New-York Daily Tribune,* 26 January 1849, p. 1:1–4.

[2] Fuller refers to her son; she had not yet written to her family and friends of his birth.

[3] In a long letter to her mother, dated 16 November 1848, Fuller described her arrival in Rome, which was made difficult because of the flooding she describes here: "As we approached the Tiber, the towers and domes of Rome could be seen, like a cloud lying low on the horizon. The road and the meadows, alike under water, lay between us and it, one sheet of silver. The horses entered; they behaved nobly; we proceeded, every moment uncertain if the water would not become deep; but the scene was beautiful, and I enjoyed it highly" (Hudspeth 5:48–49). The Tiber flooded frequently until embankments were constructed in the late nineteenth century.

examination I walked to the gate of a villa. Far stretched its overarching shrubberies, its deep-green bowers; two statues with foot advanced and uplifted finger, seemed to greet me; it was near the scene of great revels, great splendors in the old time; there lay the gardens of Sallust, where were combined palace, theater, library, bath and villa. Strange things have happened now, the most attractive part of which—the secret heart—lies buried or has fled to animate other forms: for of that part historians have rarely given a hint, more than they do now of the truest life of our day, that refuses to be embodied by the pen; it craves forms more mutable, more eloquent than the pen can give.

I found Rome empty of foreigners: most of the English have fled in affright—the Germans and French are wanted at home—the Czar has recalled many of his younger subjects; he does not like the schooling they get here.[4] That large part of the population which lives by the visits of foreigners was suffering very much—trade, industry, for every reason, stagnant. The people were every moment becoming more exasperated by the impudent measures of the Minister Rossi, and their mortification at seeing Rome represented and betrayed by a foreigner.[5] And what foreigner? A pupil of Guizot and Louis Philippe. The news had just reached them of the bombardment and storm of Vienna. Zucchi, the Minister-of-War, left Rome to put down over-free manifestations in the Provinces, and impede the entrance of the troops of the Patriot Chief, Garibaldi, into Bologna.[6] From the Provinces came soldiery, called by Rossi to keep order at the opening of the Chamber of Deputies. He reviewed them in the face of the Civic Guard; the Press began to be restrained; men were arbitrarily seized and sent out of the kingdom; the public indignation rose to its hight; the cup overflowed.

The 15th was a beautiful day and I had gone out for a long walk. Returning

---

[4] The depopulation of Rome made it possible for Fuller to locate inexpensive accommodations, very important to her at this time because of her very slender means. She found a large, sunny room on the upper story of 60 Piazza Barberini, which she rented by the month. From one side, she could see the Barberini Palace and the pope's gardens, from the other the piazza and the Street of the Four Fountains (Stern 442).

[5] Pellegrino Rossi (1787–1848), a lawyer and professor, was an Italian political exile naturalized in France whom Guizot appointed the French ambassador to Rome in 1845. He had become a friend and advisor to the pope, who appointed him prime minister of the Papal States on 16 September 1848. Though a brilliant statesman, he was disliked and distrusted by many in Rome who considered him arrogant and retrogressive (Robertson 363–64; Hudspeth 5:50).

[6] General Carlo Zucchi had unsuccessfully led a troup of rebels against the Austrians in March 1831 and had been imprisoned (*New Cambridge Modern History* 10:554–55). Zucchi had been involved in the defense of Palmanova against the Austrians and accepted an invitation from Rossi to maintain order in the Papal army (Berkeley 3:400).

at night, the old Padrona met me with her usual smile a little clouded, "Do you know," said she, "that the Minister Rossi has been killed?"[7]

"Killed!"

"Yes—with a thrust in the back. A wicked man, surely, but is that the way to punish CHRISTIANS?"[8]

"I cannot," observed a Philosopher, "sympathize under any circumstances with so immoral a deed; but surely the manner of doing it was *grandiose*."

The people at large was not so refined in their comments as either the Padrona or the Philosopher; but soldiers and populace alike ran up and down singing "Blessed the hand that rids the earth of a tyrant."

"Certainly, the manner *was* grandiose."

The Chamber was awaiting the entrance of Rossi. Had he lived to enter, he would have found the Assembly, without a single exception, ranged upon the Opposition benches. His carriage approached, attended by a howling, hissing multitude. He smiled, affected unconcern, but must have felt relieved when his horses entered the courtyard gate of the *Cancelleria*.[9] He did not know he was entering the place of his execution. The horses stopped; he alighted in the midst of a crowd; it jostled him as if for the purpose of insult; he turned abruptly and received as he did so the fatal blow. It was dealt by a resolute, perhaps experienced, hand; he fell and spoke no word more.

The crowd, as if all previously acquainted with the plan, as no doubt most of them were, issued quietly from the gate and passed through the outside crowd—its members, among whom was he who dealt the blow, dispersing in all directions.—For two or three minutes this outside crowd did not know that anything special had happened.—When they did, the news was at the moment received in silence. The soldiers in whom Rossi had trusted, whom he had hoped to flatter and bribe, stood at their posts and said not a word.—Neither they nor any one asked "Who did this? Where is he gone?"[10] The sense of the people certainly was that it was an act of summary justice on an offender whom the laws could not reach, but they felt it to be indecent to shout or exult on the spot where he was breathing his last. Rome, so long supposed the Capi-

[7] No Roman said *murdered* [Fuller's note].

[8] Arthur Fuller changed this phrase to read "to punish even the wicked?" in *AHA*.

[9] The Palazzo della Cancelleria was built in the fifteenth century. The gate to the courtyard was added by Domenico Fontana (Baedeker 2:218).

[10] Apparently the murderer was Luigi Brunetti, the oldest son of Ciceruacchio, acting at the instigation of the politician Sterbini and with the cooperation of a group of volunteers returned from the Lombard campaign, known as the Reduci. An associate of theirs named Grandoni was unjustly condemned for the murder in May 1854 and died in prison a month later (Trevelyan 80–81).

tal of Christendom, certainly took a very pagan view of this act, and the piece represented on the occasion at the theaters was "The Death of Nero."

The next morning I went to the church of St. Andrea della Valle, where was to be performed a funeral service, with fine music, in honor of the victims of Vienna; for this they do here for the victims all round—"victims of Milan," "victims of Paris," "victims of Naples," and now "victims of Vienna." But to-day I found the church closed, the service put off—Rome was thinking about her own victims.

I passed into the church of *San Luigi dei Francesi*. The Republican flag was flying at the door; the young Sacristan said the fine musical service which this church gave formerly on St. Philip's day, in honor of Louis Philippe, would now be transferred to the Republican Anniversary, the 25th of February. I looked at the monument Chateaubriand erected when here, to a poor girl, who died last of her family, having seen all the others perish round her.[11] I entered the Domenichino Chapel, and gazed anew on those magnificent representations of the Life and Death of St. Cecilia. She and St. Agnes are my favorite saints. I love to think of those angel visits which her husband knew by the fragrance of roses and lilies left behind in the apartment. I love to think of his visit to the Catacombs, and all that followed. In this picture St. Cecilia, as she stretches out her arms toward the suffering multitude, seems as if an immortal fount of purest love sprung from her heart. She gives very strongly the sense of an inexhaustible love—the only love that is much worth thinking about.

Leaving the church I passed along, toward the *Piazza del Popolo,* "Yellow Tiber rose," but not high enough to cause "distress," as he does when in a swelling mood rather than "mantle" it. I heard the drums beating, and, entering the Piazza, I found the troops of the line already assembled, and the Civic Guard marching in by platoons; each *battaglione* saluted as it entered by trumpets and a fine strain from the hand of the Carbineers.

I climbed the Pincian to see better. There is no place so fine for anything of this kind as the Piazza del Popolo, it is so full of light, so fair and grand, the obelisk and fountain make so fine a center to all kinds of groups.

The object of the present meeting was for the Civic Guard and troops of the line to give pledges of sympathy preparatory to going to the Quirinal to demand a change of Ministry and of measures. The flag of the Union was placed in front of the obelisk; all present saluted it; some officials made addresses; the trumpets sounded, and all moved toward the Quirinal.

[11] Vicomte François-Auguste-René de Chateaubriand (1768–1848), an important precursor of romanticism, won fame with *Le Génie du christianisme* (1802) *(OCFL).*

Nothing could be gentler than the disposition of the crowd. They were resolved to be played with no longer, but no threat was heard or thought.—They believed that the Court would be convinced by the fate of Rossi that the retrograde movement it had attempted was impracticable. They knew the retrogade party were panic-struck, and hoped to use the occasion to free the Pope from their meshes. All felt that Pius IX. had fallen irrevocably from his high place of the friend of Progress and father of Italy: but still he was personally beloved, and still his name, so often shouted in hope and joy, had not quite lost its *prestige*.

I returned to the house, which is very near the Quirinal. On one side I could see the Palace and gardens of the Pope, on the other the Piazza Barberini and street of the Four Fountains. Presently I saw the carriage of Prince Barberini drive hurriedly into his court-yard gate, the footman signing to close it, a discharge of firearms was heard, and the drums of the Civic Guard beat to arms.[12]

The Padrona ran up and down crying with every round of shot, "Jesu Maria, they are killing the Pope! O! poor Holy Father—Tita, Tita, (out of the window to her husband,) what *is* the matter?"

The lord of creation disdained to reply.

"Oh! Signora, pray, pray, ask Tita what is the matter?" I did so. "I don't know, Signora; nobody knows."

"Why don't you go on the mount and see?"

"It would be an imprudence, Signora; nobody will go."

I was just thinking to go myself when I saw a poor man borne by, badly wounded, and heard that the Swiss were firing on the people. Their doing so was the cause of whatever violence there was, and it was not much.

The people had assembled, as usual, at the Quirinal, only with more form and solemnity than usual. They had taken with them several of the Chamber of Deputies, and they sent an embassy, headed by Galetti,[13] who had been in the late Ministry, to state their wishes. They received a peremptory negative.

---

[12] Fuller wrote her mother a detailed account of this scene: "To-day, all the troops and the people united and went to the Quirinal to demand a change of measures. They found the Swiss Guard drawn out, and the Pope dared not show himself. They attempted to force the door of his palace, to enter his presence, and the guard fired. I saw a man borne by wounded. The drum beat to call out the National Guard. The carriage of Prince Barberini [Francesco-Maria Barberini-Colona (1772–1853)] has returned with its frightened inmates and liveried retinue, and they have suddenly barred up the court-yard gate" (Hudspeth 5:49–50).

[13] Giuseppe Galletti (1798–1873), a Bolognese lawyer who was serving a life sentence for his revolutionary activities in 1844, was freed by Pius IX in the general amnesty of 1846. Galletti was made minister of the interior by the pope in 1848 and, after the pope's flight, worked to organize the election of a constituent assembly for the entire country (Berkeley 2:39; Hearder 108, 109; Zorzi 207).

They then insisted on seeing the Pope, and pressed on the palace. The Swiss became alarmed, and fired from the windows, from the roof. They did this, it is said, without orders, but who could, at the time, suppose that? If it had been planned to exasperate the people to blood, what more could have been done? As it was, very little was shed; but the Pope, no doubt, felt great panic. He heard the report of fire-arms—heard that they tried to burn a door of the palace. I would lay my life that he could have shown himself without the slightest danger; nay, that the habitual respect for his presence would have prevailed, and hushed all tumult. He did not think so, and to still it once more degraded himself and injured his people, by making promises he did not mean to keep.

He protests now against those promises as extorted by violence, a strange plea, indeed, for the representative of St. Peter!

Rome is all full of effigies of those over whom violence had no power. There is an early Pope about to be thrown into the Tiber; violence had no power to make him say what he did not mean. Delicate girls, men in the prime of hope and pride of power—they were all alike about that. They could be done to death in boiling oil, roasted on coals, or cut to pieces; but they could not say what they did not mean. These formed the true Church; it was these who had power to disseminate the religion of Him, the Prince of Peace, who died a bloody death of torture between sinners, because He never could say what He did not mean.

A little church outside the gate of St. Sebastian commemorates this affecting tradition of the Church; Peter, alarmed at the persecution of the Christians, had gone forth to fly, when in this spot he saw a bright figure in his path and recognized his Master traveling toward Rome.

"Lord," he said, "whither goest thou?"

"I go," replied Jesus, "to die, with my people."

Peter comprehended the reproof. He felt that he must not a fourth time deny his Master, yet hope for salvation. He returned to Rome to offer his life in attestation of his faith.

The Roman Catholic Church has risen a monument to the memory of such facts. And has the present Head of that Church quite failed to understand their monition?

Not all the Popes have so failed, though the majority have been intriguing, ambitious men of the world. But even the mob of Rome—and in Rome there *is* a true mob of unheeding cabbage-sellers, who never had a thought before beyond contriving how to satisfy their animal instincts for the day—said, on hearing the protest, "There was another Pius, not long since, who talked in a very different style. When the French threatened him, he said, 'You may do with me as you see fit, but I cannot consent to act against my convictions.'"

In fact, the only dignified course for the Pope to pursue was to resign his temporal power. He could no longer hold it on his own terms; but to that he clung; and the counselors around him were men to wish him to regard *that* as the first of duties. When the question was of waging war for the independence of Italy, they regarded him solely the head of the Church; but when the demand was to satisfy the wants of his people, and ecclesiastical goods were threatened with taxes, then he was the Prince of the State, bound to maintain all the selfish prerogative of by-gone days for the benefit of his successors. Poor Pope! how has his mind been torn to pieces in these later days. It moves compassion. There can be no doubt that all his natural impulses are generous and kind, and in a more private station he would have died beloved and honored; but to this he was unequal; he has suffered bad men to surround; and by their misrepresentations and insidious suggestions, at last entirely to cloud his mind. I believe he really thinks now the Progress movement tends to anarchy, blood, all that looked worst in the first French Revolution. However that may be I cannot forgive him some of the circumstances of this flight.[14] To fly to Naples to throw himself in the arms of the bombarding monarch, blessing him and thanking his soldiery for preserving that part of Italy from anarchy—to protest that all his promises at Rome were null and void, when he thought himself in safety to choose a commission for governing in his absence, composed of men of princely blood, but as to character so null that everybody laughed and said he chose those who could best be spared if they were killed; (but they all ran away directly;) when Rome was thus left without any Government, to refuse to see any deputation, even the Senator of Rome, whom he had so gladly sanctioned,— these are the acts either of a fool or a foe. They are not his acts, to be sure, but he is responsible, he lets them stand as such in the face of the world, and weeps and prays for their success.

No more of him! His day is over. He has been made, it seems unconsciously, an instrument of good his regrets cannot destroy. Nor can he be made so important an instrument of ill. These acts have not had the effect the foes of freedom hoped. Rome remained quite cool and composed; all felt that they had not demanded more than was their duty to demand, and were willing to accept what might follow. In a few days all began to say, "Well, who would have thought it? The Pope, the Cardinals, the Princes are gone, and Rome is perfectly tranquil, and one does not miss anything, except that there are not so many rich carriages and liveries."

The Pope may regret too late that he ever gave the people a chance to make this reflection. Yet the best fruits of the movement may not ripen for long. It is one which requires radical measures, clear-sighted, resolute men: these last, as

[14] The pope fled, disguised as an ordinary priest, on 24 November 1848.

yet, do not show themselves in Rome. The new Tuscan Ministry has three men of superior force in various ways: Montanelli, Guerrazzi, D'Aguila; such are not as yet to be found in Rome.[15]

But should she fall this time, (and she must either advance with decision and force, or fall—since to stand still is impossible,) the people have learned much; ignorance and servility of thought are lessened—the way is paving for final triumph.

And my country, what does she? You have chosen a new President from a Slave State, representative of the Mexican War. But he seems to be honest, a man that can be esteemed, and is one really known to the people; which is a step upward after having sunk last time to choosing a mere tool of party.[16]

Pray send here a good Ambassador—one that has experience of foreign life, that he may act with good judgment; and, if possible, a man that has knowledge and views which extend beyond the cause of party politics in the United States; a man of unity in principles, but capable of understanding variety in forms. And send a man capable to prize the luxury of living in, or knowing Rome: it is one that should not be thrown away on a person who cannot prize or use it. Another century, and I might ask to be made Ambassador myself ('tis true, like other Ambassadors, I would employ clerks to do the most of the duty,) but woman's day has not come yet. They hold their clubs in Paris, but even George Sand will not act with women as they are. They say she pleads they are too mean, too treacherous. She should not abandon them for that, which is not nature but misfortune. How much I shall have to say on that subject if I live, which I hope I shall not,[17] for I am very tired of the battle with giant wrongs, and would like to have some one younger and stronger arise to say what ought to be said, still more to do what ought to be done. Enough! if I felt these things in privileged America, the cries of mothers and wives beaten at night by sons and husbands for their diversion after drinking, as I have repeatedly heard them these past months, the excuse for falsehood, "I *dare not* tell my husband, he would be ready to kill me," have sharpened my perception as to the ills of

---

[15] Giuseppe Montanelli (1813–62) and Francesco Domenico Guerrazzi (1804–73) were actively working for a constituent assembly in Tuscany (Berkeley 3:407). The third man Fuller refers to is probably their colleague Mariano d'Ayala (1807–77) (Zorzi 208).

[16] General Zachary Taylor, a Virginian, had just been elected president of the United States on the Whig ticket. The *Tribune* under Greeley's editorship was, of course, a Whig newspaper. The outgoing president, James K. Polk, a "dark horse" candidate at the 1844 Democratic convention, had gained the nomination due to then-President Martin Van Buren's opposition to the annexation of Texas. The militantly nationalistic Polk narrowly defeated the Whig candidate Henry Clay, who also opposed the annexation of Texas (*OCAL*).

[17] Arthur Fuller changed this phrase to "if I live which I desire not" in *AHA*.

Woman's condition and remedies that must be applied. Had I but genius, had I but energy, to tell what I know as it ought to be told! God grant them me, or some other more worthy woman, I pray.[18]

But the hour of sending to the post approaches, and I must leave these great matters for some practical details. I wish to observe to my friends and all others, whom it may concern, that a banking-house here having taken Mr. Hooker, an American, into partnership, some facilities are presented for intercourse with Rome, which they may value.[19] Mr. Hooker undertakes to have pictures copied, and to purchase those little objects of virtu peculiar to Rome, for those who cannot come themselves, as I suppose few would wish to at this time. He has the advantage of a general acquaintance with the artist to be employed, and an experience, that, no doubt, would enable him to do all this with better advantage than any stranger can for himself. It is also an excellent house to have to do with in money matters, reasonable, exact, and where none of the petty trickery or neglect so common at Torlonia's need be apprehended. They have now made arrangements with Livingston, Wells & Co. for the transmission of letters. Many addressed to me have been lost, I know not how; and I should like my friends to send to me when they can through this channel. Men who feel able can pay their letters through in this way, which has been impossible before. I have received many letters marked *paid through,* and I fear my friends in America have often paid what was quite useless, as no arrangements had been made for forwarding the letters post-paid to Rome. Those who write now can pay their letters to Florence, if they have friends there, through *Livingston, Wells & Co.* to care *Maquay, Pakenham & Co. Florence.* To us of Rome they can be sent through the same, to care of *Pakenham, Hooker & Co. Rome.*

Those of our friends, (I speak of the poor artists as well as myself,) who cannot afford to pay, should at least forbear to write on thick paper and under an envelop, the unnecessary use of which doubles the expense of the letter. I am surprised to find even those who have been abroad so negligent in these respects. I might have bought all the books of reference I needed, and have been obliged to do without money that could have been saved by attention from my friends to these particulars.

Write us two, three, four sheets if you will, on this paper, without crossing. Then if one pays a couple of dollars for a letter, at least one has something for the money: and letters are too important to happiness; we cannot afford to be

[18] The following three paragraphs are omitted from *AHA.*

[19] A constant source of irritation to Fuller was the difficulty of getting her mail regularly. She continually wrote sets of instructions to her correspondents about where and how to send letters. James Clinton Hooker (1818–94), of Vermont, was associated with the banking firm of Maquay, Packenham in Rome (Hudspeth 5:76).

without knowledge of your thoughts, your lives; but it is hard, in people who can scarcely find bread, to pay for coarse paper and an envelop the price of a beautiful engraving, and know at the same time that they are doomed to leave Rome unable to carry away a single copy of what they have most loved here, for possession or for gift. So write, dear friends, much and often, but dont ruin us for nothing.

Don Tirlone, the *Punch* of Rome, has just come in. This number represents the Fortress of Gaeta; outside hangs a cage containing a parrot (Pappagallo), the plump body of the bird is surmounted by a noble large head with benign face and Papal head-dress. He sits on the perch now with folded wings, but the cage door, in likeness of a loggia, shows there is convenience to come forth for the purposes of benediction, when wanted. Outside, the King of Naples, dressed as Harlequin, plays the organ for instruction of the bird (unhappy penitent, doomed to penance,) and grinning with sharp teeth observes: "He speaks in my way now." In the background a young Republican holds ready the match for a barrel of gunpowder, but looks at his watch waiting the moment to ignite it.

A happy New-Year to my country! may she be worthy of the privileges she possesses, while others are lavishing their blood to win them—that is all that need be wished for her at present.   ★

Dispatch 27

REPUBLICAN ROME

ROME, Evening of Feb. 20, 1849 [1]

It is said you cannot thoroughly know anything till you have both summered and wintered it; but more than one Summer and Winter of experience seems to be needed for Rome. How I fretted last Winter, during the three months' rain and the sepulchral chill, and far worse than sepulchral odors which accompanied it! I thought it was the invariable Roman Winter, and that I should never be able to stay here another such, so took my room only by the month, thinking to fly so soon as the rain set in. And lo! it has never rained at all; but there has been glorious Sun and Moon, unstained by cloud, always, and these last days have been as warm as May—the days of the Carnival, for I have just come in from seeing the *Moccoletti.* [2]

The Republican Carnival has not been as splendid as the Papal; the absence of Dukes and Princes being felt in the way of coaches and rich dresses; there

---

[1] First published as "Things and Thoughts in Europe. No. XXVII" in *New-York Daily Tribune,* 31 March 1849, p. 1:2–4.

[2] See Dispatch 23, n.4.

are also fewer foreigners than usual, many having feared to assist at this most peaceful of revolutions. But, if less splendid, it was not less gay; the costumes were many and fanciful—flowers, smiles and fun abundant.

This is the first time of my seeing the true *Moccoletti*; last year in one of the first triumphs of Democracy, they did not blow out the lights, thus turning it into an illumination. The effect of the swarms of lights, little and large, thus in motion all over the fronts of the houses and up and down the Corso was exceedingly pretty and fairy-like, but that did not make up for the loss of that wild, innocent gayety of which this people alone is capable after childhood, and which never shines out so much as on this occasion. It is astonishing the variety of tones, the lively satire and taunt of which the words *Senza Moccolo—senza mo,* are susceptible from their tongues. It is the best parody on the life of the "respectable" world that can be imagined. A ragamuffin with a little piece of candle, not even lighted, thrusts it in your face with an air of far greater superiority than he can wear who, dressed in gold and velvet, erect in his carriage, holds aloft his light on a tall pole. In vain his security; while he looks down on the crowd to taunt the wretches *senza mo,* a weak female hand from a chamber window blots out his pretensions by one flirt of an old handkerchief.

Many handsome women, otherwise dressed in white, wore the red liberty cap,[3] and the noble though somewhat coarse Roman outline beneath this brilliant red, by the changeful glow of million lights, made a fine effect. Men looked *too* vulgar in the liberty cap.

How I mourn that my little companion E. never saw these things that would have given him such store of enchanting reminiscences for all his after years.[4] I miss him always on such occasions; formerly it was through him that I enjoyed them. —He had the child's heart, had the susceptible fancy, and, naturally, a fine discerning sense for whatever is individual or peculiar.

I missed him much at the Fair of St. Eustachio.[5] Thus, like the Carnival, was last year entirely spoiled by constant rain. I never saw it at all before. It comes in the first days, or rather nights, of January. All the quarter of St. Eustachio is turned into one toy-shop, the stalls are set out in the street and brightly lighted

[3] Fuller is reporting on the revival of the brimless, canonical cap, worn as a symbol of liberty during the French Revolution.

[4] Fuller is thinking again of Edward Spring, the oldest child of Marcus and Rebecca Spring.

[5] The church of S. Eustachio in Platana dates from the fourth century; it is in the Via degli Staderari. St. Eustace, who became a Christian after seeing a vision of Christ while hunting near Tivoli, was a military hero in Hadrian's army and was put to death for refusing to offer a sacrifice to Jupiter after a victory (Masson 163).

up. These are full of cheap toys—prices varying from half a cent up to twenty cents; the dolls, which are dressed as husband and wife, or sometimes grouped in families, are the most grotesque rag-babies that can be imagined. Among the toys are great quantities of whistles, tin trumpets and little tamborines; of these every man, woman and child has bought one and is using it to make a noise. This extempore concert begins about ten o'clock and lasts till midnight; the delight of the numerous children that form part of the orchestra, the good-humored familiarity without the least touch of rudeness in the crowd, the lively effect of the light upon the toys, and the jumping, shouting figures that exhibit them, make this the pleasantest Saturnalia. Had you only been there, E., to guide me by the hand, blowing the trumpet for both, and spying out a hundred queer things in nooks that entirely escape me!

The Roman still plays amid his serious affairs, and very serious have they been this past Winter. The Roman legions went out singing and dancing to fight in Lombardy, and they fought no less bravely for that. When I wrote last, the Pope had fled, guided, he says, "by the hand of Providence"—Italy deems by the hand of Austria—to Gaeta. He had already soiled his white robes, and defamed himself forever, by heaping benedictions on the King of Naples and the bands of mercenaries whom he employs to murder his subjects on the least sign of restlessness in their most painful position. Most cowardly had been the conduct of his making promises he never meant to keep, stealing away by night in the coach of a foreign diplomatist, protesting that what he had done was null because he had acted under fear, as if such a protest could avail to one who boasts himself representative of Christ and his apostles, guardian of the legacy of the martyrs. He selected a band of most incapable men to face the danger he had feared for himself; most of these followed his example and fled. Rome sought an interview with him, to see if reconciliation were possible; he refused to receive her messengers. His wicked advisers calculated upon great confusion and distress as inevitable on the dilemma; but, for once, the hope of the bad heart was doomed to immediate disappointment. Rome coolly said, "If you desert me— if you will not hear me—I must act for myself." She threw herself into the arms of a few men who had courage and calmness for this crisis; they bade her think upon what was to be done, meanwhile avoiding every excess that could give a color to calumny and revenge; the people, with admirable good sense, comprehended and followed up this advice. Never was Rome so truly tranquil, so nearly free from gross ill as this Winter. A few words of brotherly admonition have been more powerful than all the spies, dungeons and scaffolds of Gregory.

"The hand of the Omnipotent works for us," observed an old man whom I saw in the street selling cigars the evening before the opening of the Constitutional Assembly. He was struck by the radiant beauty of the night. The old people observe that there never has been such a Winter since that of the establishment by the French of the Republic.

May the omens speed well! A host of enemies without are ready to levy war against this long-suffering people, to rivet anew their chains. Still there is now an obvious tide throughout Europe toward a better order of things, and a wave of it may bear Italy onward to the shore.

The revolution, like all genuine ones, has been instinctive, its results unexpected and surprising to the greater part of those who achieved them. The waters that had flowed so secretly beneath the crust of habit that many never heard their murmur, unless in dreams, have suddenly burst to light in full and beautiful jets; all rush to drink the pure and living draught.

As in the time of Jesus, the multitude has been long enslaved beneath a cumbrous ritual, their minds designedly darkened by those who should have enlightened them, brutified, corrupted amid monstrous contradictions and abuses; yet the moment they hear a word correspondent to the original nature, "Yes, it is true," they cry. "It is spoken with authority. Yes, it ought to be so. Priests ought to be better and wiser than other men; if they were they would not need pomp and temporal power to command respect. Yes, it is true; we ought not to lie; we ought not try to impose upon one another. We should rather our children would work honestly for their bread than get it by cheating, begging, or the prostitution of their mothers. It would be better to act worthily and kindly, probably would please God more than the kissing of reliques. We have long darkly felt that these things were so; *now* we know it."

The unreality of relation between the people and the hierarchy was obvious instantly upon the flight of Pio. He made an immense mistake then, and he made it because neither he nor his Cardinals were aware of the unreality. They did not know that, great as is the force of habit, truth *only* is imperishable. The people had abhorred Gregory, had adored Pio, upon whom they looked as a savior, as a liberator; finding themselves deceived, a mourning-veil had overshadowed their love; still, had Pio remained here, and had courage to show himself on agitating occasions, his position as Pope before whom they had been bred to bow, his aspect, which had once seemed to them full of blessing and promise, like that of an angel, would have still retained power. Probably the temporal dominion of the Papacy would not have been broken up. He fled; the people felt contempt for his want of force and truth. He wrote to reproach them with ingratitude; they were indignant. What had they to be grateful for? a Constitution to which he had not kept true an instant; the institution of the National Guard, which he had begun to neutralize; benedictions, followed by such actions as the desertion of the poorer volunteers in the war for Italian independence. Still, the people were not quite alienated from Pio. They felt sure that his heart was, in substance, good and kindly, though the habits of the priest and the arts of his counselors had led him so egregiously to falsify its dictates and forget the vocation with which he had been called. Many hoped he would see his mistake and return to be at one with the people. Among the more ignorant, there was a superstitious notion that he would return in the night of 5th January. There were many bets that he would be found in the palace of the Quirinal the morning of the 6th. All these lingering feelings were finally extinguished by the advice of excommunication. As this may not have reached America, I subjoin a translation. Here I was obliged to make use of a manuscript copy; all the printed ones were at once destroyed. It is probably the last document of the kind the world will see:

PIUS PAPA IX.

To our most Beloved Subjects:

From this pacific abode to which it has pleased Divine Providence to conduct us, and whence we can freely manifest our sentiments and our will, we have waited for testimonies of remorse from our misguided children for the sacrileges and misdeeds committed against persons attached to our service, among whom some have been slain, others outraged in the most barbarous manner, as well as for those against our residence and our person. But we have seen nothing except a sterile invitation to return to our capital, but unaccompanied by a word of condemnation for those crimes or the least guaranty for our security against the frauds and violences of that same company of furious men which still tyrannizes with a barbarous despotism over Rome and the States of the Church. We also waited expecting that the protests and orders we have uttered would recall to the duties of fidelity and subjection those who have despised and trampled upon them in the very capital of our States. But, instead of this, a new and more monstrous act of undisguised felony and of actual rebellion by them audaciously committed, has filled the measure of our affliction, and excited at the same time our just indignation, as it will afflict the Church Universal. We speak of that act, in every respect detestable, by which has been pretended to intimate the convocation of a so-called General National Assembly of the Roman States, by a decree of the 29th December past to establish new political forms for the Pontifical dominion. Adding thus iniquity to iniquity, the authors and favorers of the demagogical anarchy strive to destroy the temporal authority of the Roman Pontiff over the dominions of Holy Church, however irrefragibly established through the most ancient and solid rights, and venerated,

recognized and sustained by all the nations, supposing and making others
believe that his sovereign power can be subject to controversy or depend
on the caprices of the factious. We shall spare our dignity the humiliation
of dwelling on all that is monstrous contained in that act, abominable
through the absurdity of its origin, no less than the illegality of its form
and the impiety of its scope; but it appertains to the apostolic authority,
with which, however unworthy, we are invested, and to the responsibility
which binds us by the most sacred oaths in the sight of the Omnipotent,
not only to protest in the most energetic and efficacious manner against
that same act, but to condemn it in the face of the Universe as an enormous and sacrilegious crime, against our independence and sovereignty,
meriting the chastisements threatened by divine and human laws. We
are persuaded that on receiving the impudent invitation, you remained
full of holy indignation, and will have rejected far from you a so guilty
and shameful provocation, notwithstanding, so that none of you may say
that he has been deluded by fallacious seductions, and by the preachers
of subversive doctrines, or ignorant of what is contriving by the foes of
all order, all law, all right, true liberty and your happiness, we to day
again raise and spread abroad our voice so that you may be more certain
of the absoluteness with which we prohibit men of whatever class and
condition from taking any part in the meetings, which those persons
may dare to call for the nomination of individuals to be sent to the condemned Assembly. At the same time we recall to you how this absolute
prohibition is sanctioned by the decrees of our Predecessors and of the
Councils, especially of the Sacred Council General of Trent, Sect. XXII,
Chap. 11, in which the Church has fulminated many times her censures,
and especially the greater excommunication, as incurred without fail by
any declaration of whomsoever may dare to become guilty of whatsoever
attempt against the temporal sovereignty of the Supreme Pontiff, such
as we declare to have been already unhappily incurred by all those who
have given aid to the above-named act and others preceding, intended
to prejudice the same sovereignty, and in other modes and under false
pretexts have perturbed, violated, and usurped our authority. Yet, though
we feel ourselves obliged by conscience to guard the sacred deposit of the
patrimony of the Spouse of Jesus Christ confided to our care by use of the
sword of such severity given to us for that purpose, we cannot therefore
forget that we are on earth the representative of him who in exercise of his
justice does not forget mercy. Raising, therefore, our hands to Heaven,
while we to it recommend a cause which is indeed more its than ours,
and while anew we declare ourselves ready, with the aid of its powerful

grace to drink even to the dregs, for the defence and glory of the Catholic Church, the cup of persecution which He first wished to drink for the salvation of the same, we shall not desist from supplicating Him benignly to hear the fervent prayers which day and night we unceasingly offer for the salvation of the misguided. No day certainly could be more joyful for us than that in which it shall be granted to see return into the fold of the Lord those our sons from whom now we derive so much bitterness and so great tribulations. The hope of enjoying soon the happiness of such a day, is strengthened in us by the reflection that universal are the prayers which, united to ours, ascend to the throne of Divine Mercy from the lips and the heart of the faithful throughout the Catholic world, urging it continually to change the hearts of sinners and reconduct them into the paths of truth and of justice.

Gaeta, 6th January, 1849.

Its silliness, its bigotry, its ungenerous tone excited a simultaneous movement in the population.[6] The procession which carried it, mumbling chants, for deposit in places provided for lowest uses, and then taking from the doors of the hatters' shops the cardinals' hats, threw them into the Tiber, was a real and general expression of popular disgust. From that hour the power of the Scarlet Hierarchy fell to rise no more. No authority can survive a universal movement of derision. From that hour tongues and pens were loosed, the leaven of Machiavellism which still polluted the productions of the more liberal disappeared, and people talked as they felt, just as those of us who do not will to be slaves can in America.

"Jesus," cried an orator, "bade them feed his lambs. If they have done so, it has been to rob their fleece and drink their blood."

"Why," said another, "have we been so long deaf to the saying that the temporal dominion of the Church was like a thorn in the wound of Italy, which shall never be healed till that thorn is extracted?"

And then, without passion, all felt that the temporal dominion was in fact

[6] In her diary for 6 January, Fuller describes the controversy that surrounded this document: "Instead of the pope comes from him an excommunication against those engaged in the movements of the 15th and 16th of November and in the changes to which they led and are leading *in somma,* against the major part of Romans in this city or in the provinces. I have not yet seen the document but it is said to be worded in all the most foolish phrases of ancient superstition. The people received it with jeers, tore it at once from the walls and yesterday (Saturday) evening carried it in procession through the Corso round a candle's end, the only light of the procession. They ran along giggling and mumbling in imitation of priestly chants detachments occasionally digressing to throw copies into some privy. Such is the finale of St. Peterdom" (Rostenberg 213).

accomplished of itself, and that it only remained to organize another form of government. ★

Dispatch 28

THE UNCERTAIN FUTURE

The League between the Italian States, the Diet which was to establish it, had been the thought of Gioberti, had found its instrument at Rome in Mamiani.[2] Its Deputies were to be named by Princes or Parliaments, their mandate to be limited by the then institutions of the several States, measures of mutual security and some modifications in the way of reform would be the utmost that could be hoped from it. The scope of this party did not go beyond more vigorous prosecution of the War for Independence, and the establishment of good Institutions for the several Principalities on a basis of assimilation.

Mazzini, the great radical thinker of Italy, was on the contrary persuaded that Unity not union was necessary to this country. He had taken for his motto GOD AND THE PEOPLE, and believed in no other powers. He wished an Italian Constitutional Assembly, selected directly by the People, and furnished with an unlimited mandate to decide what form was now required by the needs of the Peninsula. His own wishes, certainly, aimed at the Republic; but the decision remained with the Representatives of the People.

The thought of Gioberti had been at first the popular one, as he, in fact, was the seer of the so-called Moderate party. For myself I always looked upon him as entirely a charlatan, who covered his want of all real force by the thickest embroidered mantle of words. Still, for a time, he corresponded with the wants of the Italian mind. He assailed the Jesuits, and was of real use by embodying the distrust and aversion that brooded in the minds of men against these most insidious and inveterate foes to liberty and progress. This triumph, at least, he may boast: that sect has been obliged to yield; its extinction seems impossible, of such life-giving power was the fiery will of Loyola. In the *Primato* he had embodied the lingering hope of the Catholic Church; Pio IX. had answered to the appeal, had answered only to show its futility. He had run through Italy as courier for Charles Albert, when the so basely styled Magnanimous entered,

[1] First published as "Things and Thoughts in Europe. No. XXVIII" in *New-York Daily Tribune*, 4 April 1849, p. 1:1–3.

[2] As head of the Papal States government, Mamiani, a Giobertian moderate, had tried unsuccessfully to establish the pope as a constitutional monarch (Berkeley 3:3, 334–35).

pretending to save her from the stranger, really hoping to take her for himself. His own cowardice and treachery neutralized the hope, and Charles Albert, abject in his disgrace, took a retrograde Ministry. This the country would not suffer, and obliged him after a while to reassume at least the position of a year since by taking Gioberti for his Premier. But it soon became evident that the Ministry of Charles Albert was in the same position as had been that of Pio IX. The hand was powerless when the head was indisposed. Meantime the thought of Mazzini had echoed through Tuscany from the revered lips of Montanelli;[3] it reached the Roman States, and, though at first propagated by foreign impulse, yet, as soon as understood, was welcomed as congenial. Montanelli had nobly said, addressing Florence, "We could not regret that the realization of this project should take place in a sister city, still more illustrious than ours." The Romans took him at his word; the Constitutional Assembly for the Roman States was elected with a double mandate, that the Deputies might sit in the Constitutional Assembly for all Italy whenever the other Provinces could send theirs. They were elected by universal suffrage. Those who listened to Jesuits and Moderates predicted that the project would fail of itself. The people were too ignorant to make use of the liberty of suffrage.

But ravens now-a-days are not the true prophetic birds. The Roman Eagle recommences her flight, and it is from its direction only that the High Priest may draw his augury. The people is certainly as ignorant as centuries of the worst government, the neglect of popular education, the enslavement of speech and the Press, could make it; yet it has an instinct to recognize measures that are good for it. A few weeks' schooling at some popular meetings, the clubs, the conversations of the National Guards in their quarters or on patrol, was sufficient to concert measures so well that the people voted in larger proportion than at contested elections in our country, and made a very good choice.

The opening of the Constitutional Assembly gave occasion for a fine procession. All the troops in Rome defiled from the Campidoglio; among them many bear the marks of suffering from the Lombard war. The banners of Sicily, Venice and Bologna waved proudly; that of Naples was veiled with crape. I was in a balcony in the Piazza Di Venezia; the Palazzo Di Venezia, that sternest feudal pile, so long the headquarters of Austrian machinations, seemed to frown as the bands each in passing struck up the *Marseillaise*. The nephew of Napoleon[4] and

---

[3] Montanelli, a professor of commercial law at the University of Pisa, founded the Fratelli Italiani (a society for the promotion of unity) in 1843 and helped write the Manifesto of Rimini in 1845. He founded a clandestine newspaper in Tuscany and at this time was a staunch supporter of Mazzini (Berkeley 2:128; Maurice 138).

[4] Carlo Luciano Bonaparte, prince of Canino and Musignano (1803–57). In her journal,

Garibaldi, the hero of Montevideo, walked together, as Deputies. The Deputies, a grave band, mostly advocates or other professional men, walked without other badge of distinction than the tricolored scarf. I remembered the entrance of the Deputies to the Council only fourteen months ago, in the magnificent carriages lent by the Princes for the occasion; they too were mostly Nobles and their liveried attendants followed, carrying their scutcheons. Princes and Counselors have both fled or sunk into nothingness: in those Counselors was no Counsel. —Will it be found in the present? Let us hope it! What we see to-day has much more the air of reality than all that parade of scutcheons, or the pomp of dress and retinue with which the Ecclesiastical Court was wont to amuse the people.

A few days after followed the proclamation of the Republic.[5] An immense crowd of people surrounded the *Palazzo della Cancelleria,* within whose court-yard Rossi fell, while the debate was going on within. At one o'clock in the morning of the 9th February, the Republic was resolved upon and the crowd rushed away to ring all the bells.

Early next morning I rose and went forth to seek the Republic. Over the Quirinal I went, through the Forum to the Capitol. There was nothing to be seen except the magnificent calm emperor, the tamers of horses, the fountain, the trophies, the lions, as usual; among the marbles for living figures, a few dirty, bold women, and Murillo boys in the sun just as usual. I passed into the Corso; there were men in the liberty cap; of course the lowest and vilest had been the first to assume it; all the horrible beggars persecuting as impudently as usual. I met some English; all their comfort was, "It would not last a month."— "They hoped to see all those fellows shot yet."—The English clergyman; more mild and legal, only hopes to see them (as the Ministry, Deputies, &c.) *hung.*

Mr. Carlyle would be delighted with his countrymen. They are entirely ready and anxious to see a Cromwell for Italy.[6] They, too, think it is no matter what

---

Fuller recorded notes about this event on 5 February 1849: "Day of the inauguration of the Constituente Romana which it is hoped may lead to the Constituente Italiana. . . . Arm in arm with foolish Bonaparte walked Garibaldi. Why? The fine array of troops and beautiful order of the procession was calculated to have a great effect on the people" (Rostenberg 216–17).

   [5] On 8 February 1849.

   [6] At this point in his career, Carlyle was a reactionary; as Emerson put it in his journal, "Carlyle is no idealist in opinions, but a protectionist in political economy, aristocrat in politics, epicure in diet, goes for murder, money, punishment by death, & all the pretty slavery, & all the pretty abominations, tempering them with epigrams" (*The Journals and Miscellaneous Notebooks of Ralph Waldo Emerson,* vol. 10, ed. Merton M. Sealts, Jr. [Cambridge: Harvard University Press, 1973], 551). In *Oliver Cromwell's Letters and Speeches* (1845), Carlyle praised Cromwell as a "Puritan hero, God-sent to save England, grappling 'like a giant, face

happens in "the back parlor," when the people starve. What signifies that, if there is "order" in the front? How dare they make a noise to disturb us yawning at billards!

I met an American. He "had no confidence in the Republic." Why? Because he "had no confidence in the People." Why? Because "they were not like *our* People." Ah! Jonathan and John—excuse me, but I must say the Italian has a decided advantage over you in the power of quickly feeling generous sympathy, as well as some other things which I have not time now to particularize. *Mais nous nous reverrons.* I have memoranda from you both in my note-book.

At last the procession mounts the Campidoglio. It is all dressed with banners. The tricolor surmounts the Palace of the Senator; the Senator himself has fled. The Deputies mount the steps, and one of them reads, in a clear, friendly voice, the following words:

FUNDAMENTAL DECREE OF THE CONSTITUTIONAL ASSEMBLY OF ROME.

ARTICLE I. The Papacy has fallen in fact and in right from the temporal Government of the Roman State.

ART. II. The Roman Pontifex shall have all the necessary guaranties for independence in the exercise of his spiritual power.

ART. III. The form of Government of the Roman State shall be a pure Democracy, and will take the glorious name of Roman Republic.

ART. IV. The Roman Republic will have with the rest of Italy the relations exacted by a common nationality.

Between each of these expressive sentences the speaker paused; the great bell of the Capitol gave forth its solemn melodies; the cannon answered; while the crowd shouted, *viva la Republica! viva Italia!*

The imposing grandeur of the spectacle to me gave new force to the thought that already swelled my heart; my nerves thrilled, and I longed to see in some answering glance a spark of Rienzi,[7] a little of that soul which made my country what she is. The American at my side remained impassive.[8] Receiving all his

---

to face, heart to heart, with the naked truth of things' " (*OCEL*). Fuller reviewed Carlyle's *Cromwell* book in the *Daily Tribune*, 19 December 1845, p. 1:4.

[7] Cola di Rienzo, or Rienzi (1331–54), proclaimed himself tribune of Rome in 1347 and tried to restore the Roman Republic. He won the support of the people for lowering taxes and instituting other reforms, but was later forced out of power by Pope Clement VI. After a period of exile, he returned to Italy in 1354 and tried again to establish himself as a senator and ruler. He was killed in a revolt on 8 October 1854 (*The Cambridge Medieval History* [New York: Macmillan, 1932], 7:53–54).

[8] Probably Thomas Hicks, who was in Rome during the winter of 1849 and returned to the United States later in the year. Fuller had written to Caroline Sturgis (now Tappan) that

birthright from a triumph of Democracy, he was quite indifferent to this manifestation on this consecrated spot. Passing the Winter in Rome to study Art, he was insensible to the artistic beauty of the scene—insensible to this new life of that spirit from which all the forms he gazes at in galleries emanated. He "did not see the *use* of these popular demonstrations."

Again, I must mention a remark of his as a specimen of the ignorance in which Americans usually remain during their flighty visits to these scenes, where they associate only with one another. And I do it the rather as this seemed a really thoughtful, intelligent man; no vain, vulgar trifler. He said—

"*The people* seem only to be looking on; they take no part."

"What people?" said I.

"Why, these round us; there is no other people."

There are a few beggars, errand-boys and nurse-maids.

"The others are only soldiers."

"Soldiers! The Civic Guard; all the decent men in Rome."

Thus it is that the American, on many points, becomes more ignorant for coming abroad, because he attaches some value to his crude impressions and frequent blunders. It is not thus that any seed-corn can be gathered from foreign gardens. Without modest scrutiny, patient study and observation, he spends his money and goes home with a new coat perhaps, but a mind befooled rather than instructed. It is necessary to speak the languages of these countries and know personally some of their inhabitants in order to form any accurate impressions.

The flight of the Grand Duke of Tuscany followed. In imitation of his great exemplar he promised and smiled to the last, deceiving Montanelli, the pure and sincere, at the very moment he was about to enter his carriage, into the belief that he persevered in his assent to the liberal movement. His position was certainly very difficult, but he might have left it like a gentleman, like a man of honor.'T was pity to destroy so lightly the good opinion the Tuscans had of him. Now Tuscany meditates union with Rome.

Meanwhile, Charles Albert is filled with alarm. He is indeed betwixt two fires. Gioberti has published one of his prolix, weak addresses, in which he says that in the beginning of every revolution you must fix a limit beyond which you will not go; that, for himself, he has done it—others are surpassing his mark and he will not go any farther. Of the want of thought, of insight to historic and all other truths which distinguishes the "illustrious Gioberti," this

"Hicks is going home this summer, you must see him. He is the only American with whom I have been intimate; at first I was not intellectual enough for him; but we were always becoming intimate" (Hudspeth 5:199).

assumption is a specimen. But it makes no difference; he and his Prince must go sooner or later, if the movement continues, nor is there any prospect of its being stayed unless by foreign intervention. This the Pope has not yet, it is believed, solicited, but there is little reason to hope he will be spared that crowning disgrace. He has already consented to the incitement of civil war. Should an intervention be solicited, all depends on France. Will she basely forfeit every pledge and every duty, to say nothing of her true interest? It seems that her President stands doubtful, intending to do what is for *his* particular interest;[9] but if his interest proves opposed to the republican principle, will France suffer herself again to be hoodwinked and enslaved? It is impossible to know, she has already shown such devotion to the mere prestige of a name.

On England no dependence can be placed. She is guided by no great idea; her Parliamentary leaders sneer at sentimental policy, and the "jargon" of ideas. She will act, as always, for her own interest; and the interest of her present Government is becoming more and more the crushing of the democratic tendency. They are obliged to do it at home both in the back and the front parlor; it would not be decent as yet to have a Spielberg just at home for obstreperous patriots, but England has so many ships, it is just as easy to transport them to a safe distance. Then the Church of England, so long an enemy to the Church of Rome, feels a decided interest with it on the subject of temporal possessions. The rich English traveler, fearing to see the Prince Borghese stripped of one of his palaces for a hospital or some such low use, thinks of his own twenty-mile park and the crowded village of beggars at its gate, and muses: "I hope to see them all shot yet, these rascally republicans."

How I wish my country would show some noble sympathy when an experience so like her own is going on. Politically she cannot interfere; but formerly when Greece and Poland were struggling, they were at least aided by private contributions. Italy, naturally so rich, but long racked and impoverished by her oppressors, greatly needs money to arm and clothe her troops. Some token of sympathy, too, from America would be so welcome to her now. If there were a circle of persons inclined to trust such to me, I might venture to promise the trust should be used to the advantage of Italy. It would make me proud to have my country show a religious faith in the progress of ideas, and make some small sacrifice of its own great resources in aid of a sister cause, now.

But I must close this letter, which it would be easy to swell to a volume from the material in my mind. One or two traits of the hour I must note. Mazzarelli, chief of the present Ministry, was a prelate, and named spontaneously by the

[9] Louis-Napoleon Bonaparte had won the French presidential election on 10 December 1848.

Pope before his flight. He has shown entire and frank intrepidity. He has laid aside the title of Monsignor, and appears before the world as a layman.

Nothing can be more tranquil than has been the state of Rome all Winter. Every wile has been used by the obscurantists to excite the people, but their confidence in their leaders could not be broken. A little mutiny in the troops, stimulated by letters from their old leaders, was quelled in a moment. The day after the proclamation of the Republic, some zealous ignoramuses insulted the carriages that appeared with servants in livery. The Ministry published a grave admonition, that democracy meant liberty, not license, and that he who infringed upon an innocent freedom of action in others must be declared traitor to his country. Every act of the kind ceased instantly. An intimation that it was better not to throw large comfits or oranges during the Carnival, as injuries have thus been sometimes caused, was obeyed with equal docility.

On Sunday last placards affixed in the high places summoned the city to invest Giuseppe Mazzini with the rights of a Roman Citizen. I have not yet heard the result. The Pope made Rossi a Roman Citizen; he was suffered to retain that title only one day. It was given him 14th Nov. he died the 15th. Mazzini enters Rome at any rate for the first time in his life as deputy to the Constitutional Assembly; it would be a noble poetic justice, if he could enter also a Roman Citizen.

24th.—The Austrians have invaded Ferrara, taken $200,000 and six hostages and retired. This step is no doubt intended to determine whether France will resent the insult, or whether she will betray Italy. It shows also the assurance of the Austrian that the Pope will approve of an armed intervention. Probably before I write again these matters will reach some decided crisis.   ★

Dispatch 29

KINGS, REPUBLICANS, AND AMERICAN ARTISTS

ROME, March 20, 1849[1]

The Roman Republic moves on better than could have been expected. There are great difficulties about money, necessarily, as the Government, so beset with difficulties and dangers, cannot command confidence in that respect. The solid coin has crept out of the country or lies hid, and in the use of paper there are the corresponding difficulties. But the poor, always the chief sufferers from such

[1] First published as "Things and Thoughts in Europe. No. XXIX" in *New-York Daily Tribune,* 16 May 1849, p. 1:1–5.

a state of things, are wonderfully patient, and I doubt not that the new form, if Italy could be left to itself, would be settled for the advantage of all. Tuscany would soon be united with Rome, and to the Republic of Central Italy, no longer broken asunder by petty restrictions and sacrificed to the interests of a few persons, would come that prosperity natural to a region so favored by Nature.

Could Italy be left alone! but treacherous, selfish men at home strive to betray, and foes threaten her from without on every side. Even France, her natural ally, promises to prove foolishly and basely faithless. The dereliction from principle of her Government seems certain, and thus far the nation, despite the remonstrance of a few worthy men, gives no sign of effective protest. There would be little hope for Italy, were not the thrones of her foes in a tottering state, their action liable at every moment to be distracted by domestic difficulties. The Austrian Government seems as destitute of support from the nation as is possible for a Government to be, and the army is no longer what it was, being made up so largely of new recruits. The Croats are uncertain in their adhesion, the war in Hungary likely to give them much to do, and if the Russian is called in, the rest of Europe becomes hostile. All these circumstances give Italy a chance she otherwise could not have; she is in great measure disfurnished of arms and money; her King in the South is a bloody, angry, well-armed foe; her King in the North, a proved traitor. Charles Albert has now declared war because he could not do otherwise; but his sympathies are in fact all against Liberty; the splendid lure that he might become King of Italy glitters no more; the Republicans are in the ascendant, and he may well doubt, should the stranger be driven out, whether Piedmont could escape the contagion. Now, his people insisting on war, he has the air of making it with a good grace, but should he be worsted, probably he will know some loop-hole by which to steal out. The rat will steal out and leave the lions in the trap.

The "illustrious Gioberti" has fallen—fallen forever from his high scaffold of words. His demerits were too unmistakable for rhetoric to hide. That he sympathized with the Pope rather than the Roman people, and could not endure to see him stripped of his temporal power, no one could blame in the author of the *"Primato."* That he refused the Italian General Assembly, if it was to be based on the so-called Montanelli system[2] instead of his own, might be conviction or it might be littleness and vanity. But that he privily planned, without even adherence of the council of Ministers, an armed intervention of the Piedmontese

---

[2] Professor Montanelli, who had been imprisoned by the Austrians, had been allowed to return to Tuscany, where he devised a plan for a constituent assembly that would include all of Italy (Maurice 419).

troops in Tuscany, thus willing to cause civil war, and, at this great moment, to see Italian blood shed by Italian hands, was treachery. I think, indeed, he has been probably made the scape-goat in that affair; that Charles Albert planned the measure, and finding himself unable to carry it out, in consequence of the vigilance and indignant opposition of the Chamber of Deputies, was somewhat consoled by making it an occasion to victimize the "Illustrious," whom four weeks before the people had forced him to accept as his Minister.

Now the name of Gioberti is erased from the corners of the streets to which it was affixed a year ago; he is stripped of all his honorary degrees, and proclaimed an unworthy son of the country. Mazzini is the idol of the people. "Soon to be hunted out," sneered the skeptical American. Possibly yes! for no man is secure of his palm till the fight is over. The civic wreath may be knocked from his head a hundred times in the ardor of the contest. No matter, if he can always keep the forehead pure and lofty, as will Mazzini.

In thinking of Mazzini, I always remember Petrarch's invocation to Rienzi.[3] Mazzini comes at a riper period in the world's history, with the same energy of soul, but of purer temper and more enlarged views to answer them.

I do not know whether I mentioned a kind of poetical correspondence about Mazzini and Rossi. Rossi was also an exile for liberal principles, but he did not value his birthright; he alienated it, and as a French citizen became Peer of France and Representative of Louis Philippe in Italy. When, with the fatuity of those whom the gods have doomed to perish, Pius IX. took the representative of the fallen Guizot policy for his Minister, he made him a Roman citizen. He was proclaimed such the 14th of November. On the 15th he perished before he could enter the parliament he had called. He fell at the door of the Cancelleria when it was sitting.

Mazzini, in his exile, remained absolutely devoted to his native country. Because, though feeling as few can, that the interests of humanity in all nations are identical, he felt also that, born of a race so suffering, so much needing devotion and energy, his first duty was to that. The only powers he acknowledged were *God and the People,* the special scope of his acts the unity and independence of

[3] Fuller refers to Petrarch's letter to Francesco Calvo da Napoli, apostolic prothonotary for Clement VI and Innocent VI from 1347 to 1359. In this letter, Petrarch warmly defends Cola di Rienzo, who was brought to Avignon for judgment by the Papal Court. In defending Rienzo, Petrarch celebrates the autonomy of the Roman people and, in a passage that must have reminded Fuller of Mazzini, exclaims, "A crime worthy of the cross and vultures, that a Roman citizen should grieve to see his land, the rightful mistress of all others, enslaved to the basest of men!" (*Letters on Familiar Matters,* vol. 2, book 13, letter 6, trans. Aldo S. Bernardo [Baltimore: Johns Hopkins University Press, 1982], 196; Kenelon Foster, *Petrarch: Poet and Humanist* [Edinburgh: Edinburgh University Press, 1984], 14; Morris Bishop, trans., *Letters from Petrarch* [Bloomington: Indiana University Press, 1966], 116).

Italy. Rome was the theme of his thoughts, but, very early exiled, he had never seen that home to which all the orphans of the soul so naturally turn. Now he entered it as a Roman citizen, elected representative of the people by universal suffrage. His motto, *Dio e Popolo,* is put upon the coin with the Roman eagle; unhappily this first-issued coin is of brass, or else of silver, with much alloy. *Dii, avertite omen,* [4] and may peaceful days turn it all to pure gold!

On his first entrance to the house Mazzini, received with fervent applause and summoned to take his place beside the President, spoke as follows:

"It is from me, colleagues, that should come these tokens of applause, these tokens of affection, because the little good I have not done, but tried to do, has come to me from Rome. Rome was always a sort of talisman for me; a youth, I studied the history of Italy, and found while all the other nations were born, grew up, played their part in the world, then fell to re-appear no more in the same power, a single city was privileged by God to die only to rise again greater than before, to fulfill a mission greater than the first. I saw the Rome of the Empire extend her conquests from the confines of Africa to the confines of Asia. I saw Rome perish, crushed by the barbarians, by those whom even yet the world calls barbarians. I saw her rise again after having chased away these same barbarians, reviving in its sepulchre the germ of Civilization. I saw her rise more great for conquest, not with arms, but with words—rise in the name of the Popes to repeat her grand mission. I said in my heart, the city which, alone in the world, has had two grand lives, one greater than the other, will have a third. After the Rome which wrought by conquest of arms, the Rome which wrought by conquest of words, must come a third which shall work by virtue of example. After the Rome of the Emperors—after the Rome of the Popes, will come the Rome of the People. The Rome of the People is arisen; do not salute with applauses, but let us rejoice together! I cannot promise anything for myself, except concurrence in all you shall do for the good of Rome, of Italy, of Mankind. Perhaps we shall have to pass through great crises; perhaps we shall have to fight a sacred battle against the only enemy that threatens us, Austria. We will fight it, and we will conquer. I hope, please God, that foreigners may not be able to say any more that which so many of them repeat to-day, speaking of our affairs, that the light which comes from Rome is only an *ignis fatuus* wandering among the tombs; the world shall see that it is a starry light, eternal, pure and resplendent as those we look up to in the Heavens!"

---

[4] The Italian motto is: "God and the People." The Latin is: "Oh gods, turn aside the omen."

On a later day he spoke more fully of the difficulties that threaten at home the young Republic, and said:

> "Let us not hear of right, of left, of center; these terms express the three powers in a constitutional monarchy; for us they have no meaning; the only divisions for us are of Republicans or non-Republicans—or of sincere men and temporizing men. Let us not hear so much of the Republicans of to-day and of yesterday; I am a Republican of twenty years' standing. Entertaining such hopes for Italy, when many excellent, many sincere men held them as Utopian, shall I denounce these men because they are now convinced of their practicability?"

This last I quote from memory. In hearing the gentle tone of remonstrance with those of more petty mind, or influenced by the passions of the partisan, I was forcibly reminded of the parable by Jesus of the Vineyard and the discontent of the laborers that those who came at the eleventh hour "received also a penny."[5] Mazzini also is content that all should fare alike as brethren, if only they will come into the vineyard. He is not an orator, but the simple conversational tone of his address is in refreshing contrast with the boyish rhetoric and academic swell common to Italian speakers in the present unfledged state. As they have freer use of the power of debate they will become more simple and manly. The speech of Mazzini is laden with mind—it goes straight to the mark by the shortest path and moves without effort from the irresistible impression of deep conviction and fidelity in the speaker. Mazzini is a man of genius, an elevated thinker, but the most powerful and first impression from his presence must always be of the religion of his soul, of his *virtue,* both in the modern and antique sense of that word.[6]

If clearness of right, if energy, if indefatigable perseverance, can steer the ship through this dangerous pass, it will be done. He said "we will conquer;" whether Rome will this time is not to me certain, but such men as Mazzini conquer always—conquer in defeat. Yet Heaven grant that no more blood, no more corruption of priestly government, be for Italy. It could only be for once more, for the strength of her present impulse would not fail to triumph at last; but even one more trial seems too intolerably much when I think of the holocaust of broken hearts, baffled lives, that must attend it.

[5] Matthew 20:1–16.

[6] Fuller had written to Mazzini on March 3 to offer a "tribute of affection" (Hudspeth 5: 196–97). In a long letter to Caroline Sturgis Tappan, Fuller combined additional information about her son, Nino, with some details about her great affection for Mazzini (Hudspeth 5:207–11).

But enough of politics for the present; this letter goes by private hand, and as news, will be superseded before it can arrive.

Let me rather take the opportunity to say some things that I have let lie by, while writing of political events. Especially of our Artists I wish to say something. I know many of them, if not all, and see with pleasure our young country so fairly represented.

Among the painters I saw of Brown only two or three pictures at the exhibition in Florence; they were coarse, flashy things.[7] I was told he could do better, but a man who indulges himself with such coarse sale-work, cannot surely do well at any time.

The merits of Terry and Freeman are not my merits; they are beside both favorites in our country, and have a sufficient number of pictures there for every one to judge.[8] I am no connoisseur as regards the technical merits of paintings; it is only poetic invention, or a tender feeling of nature which captivates me.

Terry loves grace, and consciously works from the model. The result is a pleasing transposition of the hues of this clime. But the design of the picture is never original, nor is it laden with any message from the heart. Of Freeman I know less; as the two or three pictures of his that I have seen never interested me. I have not visited his studio.

Of Hicks I think very highly.[9] He is a man of ideas, an original observer, and with a poetic heart. His system of coloring is derived from a thoughtful study, not a mere imitation of nature, and shows the fineness of his organization. Struggling unaided to pursue the expensive studies of his art, he has had only a small studio, and received only orders for little cabinet pictures. —Could he carry out adequately his ideas, in him would be found the treasure of genius. He has made the drawings for a large picture of many figures; the design is original and noble, the grouping highly effective. Could he paint this picture I believe it would be a real boon to the lovers of Art, the lovers of Truth. I hope

[7] Henry Kirke Brown (1814–86), a sculptor and portrait painter, lived in Europe from 1844 to 1848 (Groce).

[8] James Edward Freeman (1808–84) was a genre and portrait painter who settled in Italy in the late 1830s. From 1840 to 1849 he was the American consul at Ancona, though he resided in Rome and performed his duties by proxy (Groce).

[9] Fuller had been very friendly with Hicks during his stay in Rome. She wrote to Samuel G. Ward to encourage him to visit Hicks in New York, where Hicks had returned in the fall of 1849: "When you are in N.Y. do me the pleasure of visiting the studio of Hicks and seeing him, if you can. I have loved him very much; we have been very intimate; I should like to have you see him; perhaps an acquaintance will spring up; in his soul is real greatness; his life has been a battle but waged on his side with great calmness" (Hudspeth 5:279). After returning to the United States, Hicks became a prosperous portraitist (Chevigny 424).

very much that when he returns to the United States, some competent patron of art—one of the few who has mind as well as purse, will see the drawings and order the picture. Otherwise he cannot paint it, as the expenses attendant on models for so many figures, &c. are great, and the time demanded could not otherwise be taken from the claims of the day.

Among landscape painters Cropsey and Cranch have the true artist spirit. In faculties, each has what the other wants. Cropsey is a reverent and careful student of nature in detail; it is no pedantry, but a true love he has, and his pictures are full of little gentle signs of intimacy. They please and touch, but yet, in poetic feeling of the heart of nature, he is not equal to Cranch, who produces fine effects by means more superficial, and, on examination, less satisfactory. Each might take somewhat from the other to advantage, could he do it without diminishing his own original dower. Both are artists of high promise, and deserve to be loved and cherished by a country which may, without presumption, hope to carry landscape painting to a pitch of excellence unreached before. For the historical painter, the position with us is, for many reasons, not favorable, but there is no bar in the way of the landscape painter, and fate, bestowing such a prodigality of subject, seems to give us a hint not to be mistaken. I think the love of landscape painting is genuine in our nation, and as it is a branch of art where achievement has been comparatively low, we may not unreasonably suppose it has been left for us. I trust it will be undertaken in the highest spirit.— Nature, it seems to me, reveals herself more freely in our land; she is true, virgin and confiding—she smiles upon the vision of a true Endymion. I hope to see not only copies upon canvas of our magnificent scenes, but a transfusion of the spirit which is their divinity.

Then why should the American landscape-painter come to Italy?—cry many. I think, myself, he ought not to stay here very long. Yet a few years' study is precious, for here Nature herself has worked with Man, as if she wanted to help him in the composition of pictures. The ruins of Italy, in their varied relations with vegetation and the heavens, make speeches from every stone for the instruction of the artist; the greatest variety here is found with the greatest harmony; to know how this union may be accomplished is a main secret of art, and though the coloring is not the same, yet he who has the key to its mysteries of beauty is the more initiated to the same in other climates, and will easily attune afresh his more instructed eye and mind to the contemplation of that which molded his childhood.

I may observe of the two artists I have named, that Cranch has entered more into the spirit of Italian landscape, while Cropsey is still more distinguished on subjects such as he first loved. He seemed to find the Scotch lake and mountain scenery very congenial; his sketches and pictures taken from a short residence there are impressive. Perhaps a melancholy or tender subject suits him best; something rich, bold and mellow is more adapted to call out the genius of Cranch.

Among the Sculptors new names rise up to show that this is decidedly a province for hope in America. I look upon this as the natural talent of an American, and have no doubt that glories will be displayed by our sculptors unknown to classic art. The facts of our history, ideal and social, will be grand and of new import; it is perfectly natural to the American to mold in clay and carve in stone. The permanence of material and solid relief in the forms correspond to the positiveness of his nature better than the mere ephemeral and even tricky methods of the painter—to his need of motion and action, better than the chambered scribbling of the poet. He will thus record his best experiences, and these records will adorn the noble structures that must naturally arise for the public uses of our society.

It is particularly gratifying to see men that might amass far more money and attain more temporary power in other parts, despise those lower lures too powerful in our country, and aim only at excellence in the expression of thought. Among these I may mention Story and Mozier.[10] Story has made in Florence the model for a statue of his father. This I have not seen, but two statuettes that he modeled here from the "Fisher" of Goethe pleased me extremely. The languid, meditative revery of the boy, the morbid tenderness of his nature, is most happily expressed in the first, as is the fascinated surrender to the syren murmur of the flood in the second. He has taken the moment

"Half drew she him; half sank he in," [11] &c.

---

[10] Joseph Mozier (1812–70) was a successful merchant in New York, who abandoned his business career in 1845 and went to Italy to become a sculptor (Groce). He was exceptionally kind to Fuller during her sickness in Florence in the summer of 1847 but gossiped maliciously about her and Ossoli to Nathaniel Hawthorne some eleven years later, provoking an infamous entry in Hawthorne's Italian notebooks. According to Hawthorne, Mozier said that Ossoli was a handsome man but "destitute of manners" and "half an idiot." He also said that Fuller, before her return to America, "had quite lost all power of literary production" and that her manuscript "History of the Roman Revolution . . . never had existence." This information led Hawthorne to declare, "There appears to have been a total collapse in poor Margaret, morally and intellectually" and to comment on "her strange, heavy, unpliable, and, in many respects, defective and evil nature" (Chevigny 416–19; Nathaniel Hawthorne, *The French and Italian Notebooks,* ed. Thomas Woodson [Columbus: Ohio State University Press, 1980], 155–56).

[11] Another translation of this part of Goethe's "The Fisherman" reads: "She spoke to him, she sang to him; / The fellow, done for then, / Half yielded too as half she drew, / Was never seen again" (Goethe, *Selected Poems,* ed. Christopher Middleton [Boston: Suhrkamp / Insel, 1983], 75).

I hope some one will give him an order to make them in marble. Mozier seemed to have an immediate success. The fidelity and spirit of his portrait-busts could be appreciated by every one; for an ideal head of Pocahontas too, he had at once orders for many copies. It was not an Indian head, but in the union of sweetness and strength with a princelike, childlike dignity, very happily expressive of his idea of her character. I think he has modeled a Rebecca at the Well, but this I did not see.

These have already a firm hold on the affections of our people; every American who comes to Italy visits their studios, and speaks of them with pride, as indeed they well may, in comparing them with artists of other nations. It will not be long before you see Greenough's group; it is in spirit a pendent to Cooper's novels. I confess I wish he had availed himself of the opportunity to immortalize the real noble Indian in marble. This is only the man of the woods—no Metamora, no Uncas.[12] But the group should be very instructive to our people.

You seem as crazy about Powers's Greek Slave as the Florentines were about Cimabue's Madonnas, in which we still see the spark of genius, but not fanned to its full flame.[13] If your enthusiasm be as genuine as that of the lively Florentines, we will not quarrel with it; but I am afraid a great part is drawing-room raptures and newspaper echoes. Genuine enthusiasm, however crude the state of mind from which it springs, always elevates, always educates, but in the same proportion talking and writing for effect stultifies and debases. I shall not judge the adorers of the Greek Slave, but only observe that they have not kept in reserve any higher admiration for works even now extant, which are, in comparison with that statue, what that statue is compared with any weeping marble on a common monument.

I consider the Slave as a form of simple and sweet beauty, but that neither as an ideal expression or a specimen of plastic power is it transcendent. Powers stands far higher in his busts than in any ideal statue. His conception of what is individual in character is clear and just; his power of execution almost unrivaled; but he has had a lifetime of discipline for the bust, while his studies on the human body are comparatively limited; nor is his treatment of it free and masterly. To me, his conception of subject is not striking: I do not consider him rich in artistic thought.

[12] Fuller refers to heroic portrayals of Native Americans. Metamora was another name for King Philip (?–1676), chief of the Wampanoag tribe of the Plymouth colony from 1662. The actor Edwin Forrest starred in the popular romantic tragedy about him by J. A. Stone, revised by R. M. Bird, entitled *Metamora* (1836) (*OCAL*). Uncas (1600–1683) was chief of the Mohigan tribe and appears as a heroic figure in Cooper's Leatherstocking tales.

[13] Powers's *The Greek Slave* was exhibited at the Great Exhibition in 1851 and became one of the most talked about statues in the nineteenth century (*OCA*).

He, no less than Greenough and Crawford, would feel it a rich reward for many labors, and a happy climax to their honors to make an equestrian statue of Washington for our country. I wish they might all do it, as each would show a different kind of excellence. To present the man on horseback, the wise centaur, the tamer of horses, may well be deemed a highest achievement of modern as it was of ancient art. The study of the anatomy and action of the horse, so rich in suggestions, is naturally most desirable to the artist; happy he who, obliged by the brevity of life and the limitations of fortune, to make his studies conform to his "orders," finds himself justified by a national behest in entering on this department.

At home one gets callous about the character of Washington, from a long experience of 4th of July bombast in his praise. But seeing the struggles of other nations, and the deficiencies of the leaders who try to sustain them, the heart is again stimulated and puts forth buds of praise. One appreciates the wonderful combination of events and influences that gave our independence so healthy a birth, and the almost miraculous merits of the men who tended its first motions. In the combination of excellences needed at such a period with the purity and modesty which dignify the private man in the humblest station, Washington as yet stands alone. No country has ever had such a good future; no other is so happy as to have a pattern of spotless worth which will remain in her latest day venerable as now.

Surely then that form should be immortalized in material solid as its fame; and, happily for the artist, that form was of natural beauty and dignity, and he who places him on horseback simply represents his habitual existence. Everything concurs to make an equestrian statue of Washington desirable.

The dignified way to manage that affair would be to have a Committee chosen of impartial judges, men who would look only to the merits of the work and the interests of the country, unbiased by any personal interest in favor of some one artist. It is said it is impossible to find such a one, but I cannot believe it. Let there be put aside the mean squabbles and jealousies, the vulgar pushing of unworthy friends, with which, unhappily, the artist's career seems more rife than any other, and a fair concurrence established; let each artist offer his design for an equestrian statue of Washington, and let the best have the preference.

Mr. Crawford has made a design which he takes with him to America, and which, I hope, will be generally seen. He has represented Washington in his actual dress; a figure of Fame, winged, presents the laurel and civic wreath; his gesture declines them; he seems to say, "For me the deed is enough—I need no badge, no outward token in reward."

This group has no insipid allegorical air, as might be supposed; and its composition is very graceful, simple, and harmonious. The costume is very happily managed. The angel figure is draped, and with the Liberty cap, which as a badge both of ancient and modern times, seems to connect the two figures, and in an artistic point of view balances well the cocked hat; there is a similar harmony between the angel's wings and the extremities of the horse. The action of the winged figure induces a natural and spirited action of the horse and rider. I thought of Goethe's remark, that a fine work of art will always have, at a distance, where its details cannot be discerned, a beautiful effect, as of architectural ornament, and that this excellence the groups of Raphael share with the antique. He would have been pleased with the beautiful balance of forms in this group, with the freedom with which light and air play in and out, the management of the whole being clear and satisfactory at the first glance. But one should go into a great number of studies, as you can in Rome or Florence, and see the abundance of heavy and inharmonious designs to appreciate the merits of this; anything really good seems so simple and so a matter of course to the unpracticed observer.

Some say the Americans will not want a group, but just the fact; the portrait of Washington riding straight onward like Marcus Aurelius, or making an address, or lifting his sword. I do not know about that—it is a matter of feeling. This winged figure not only gives a poetic sense to the group, but a natural support and occasion for action to the horse and rider. Uncle Sam must send Major Downing [14] to look at it, and then, if he wants other designs, let him establish a concurrence, as I have said, and choose what is best. I am not particularly attached to Mr. Greenough, Mr. Powers or Mr. Crawford. I admire various excellencies in the works of each, and should be glad if each received an order for an equestrian statue. Nor is there any reason why they should not. There is money enough in the country, and the more good things there are for the people to see freely in open daylight the better. That makes artists germinate.

I love the artists, though I cannot speak of their works in a way to content their friends or even themselves, often. Who can, that has a standard of excellence in the mind and a delicate conscience in the use of words? My highest tribute is meager of superlatives in comparison with the hackneyed puffs with which artists submit to be besmeared. Submit, alas! often they court them, rather. I do not expect any kindness from my contemporaries. I know that what is to me justice and honor is to them only a hateful coldness. Still I love them, I wish for their good, I feel deeply for their sufferings, annoyances, privations, and would lessen them if I could. I have thought it might perhaps be of use to

[14] Major Jack Downing is the pseudonym of Seba Smith (1792–1868). Fuller alludes to Major Downing's penchant for commenting on current events with a shrewdness that belies his rustic simplicity. *The Life and Writings of Major Jack Downing* appeared in 1834 (*OCAL*).

publish some account of the expenses of the artist. There is a general impression that the artist lives very cheaply in Italy. This is a mistake. Italy, compared with America, is not so very cheap, except for those who have iron constitutions to endure bad food, eaten in bad air, damp and dirty lodgings. The expenses, even in Florence, of a simple but clean and wholesome life, are little less than in New-York. The great difference is for people that are rich. An Englishman of rank and fortune does not need the same amount of luxury as at home to be on a footing with the nobles of Italy. The Broadway merchant would find his display of mahogany and carpets thrown away in a country where a higher kind of ornament is the only one available. But poor people who can, at any rate, buy only the necessaries of life, will find them in the Italian cities, where all sellers live by cheating foreigners, very little cheaper than in America.

The patron of Art in America, ignorant of these facts, and not knowing the great expenses which attend the study of Art and the production of its wonders, are often guilty of most undesigned cruelty, and do things which it would grieve their hearts to have done, if they only knew the facts. They have read essays on the uses of adversity in developing genius, and they are not sufficiently afraid to administer a dose of adversity beyond what the forces of the patient can bear. Laudanum in drops is useful as a medicine, but a cup-full kills downright.

Beside this romantic idea about letting artists suffer to develop their genius, the American Mæcenas is not sufficiently aware of the expenses attendant on producing the work he wants. He does not consider that the painter, the sculptor, must be paid for the time he spends in designing and molding, no less than in painting and carving; that he must have his bread and sleeping-house, his workhouse or studio, his marbles and colors; the sculptor his workmen; so that if the price be paid he asks, a modest and delicate man very commonly receives *no* guerdon for his thought—the real essence of the work—except the luxury of seeing it embodied which he could not otherwise have afforded. The American Mæcenas often pushes the price down, not from want of generosity, but from a habit of making what are called good bargains—*i.e.* bargains for one's own advantage at the expense of a poorer brother. Those who call these good do not believe that

"Mankind is one,
And beats with one great heart."

They have not read the life of Jesus Christ.

Then the American Mæcenas sometimes, after ordering a work, has been known to change his mind when the statue is already modeled. It is the American who does these things, because an American, who either from taste or vanity buys a picture, is often quite uneducated as to the arts and cannot understand why a little picture or figure costs so much money. The Englishman or Frenchman, of a suitable position to seek these adornments for his house, usually understands better than the visitor of Powers who, on hearing the price of the Proserpine, wonderingly asked, "Isn't statuary riz lately?" Queen Victoria of England, and her Albert, it is said, use their royal privilege to get works of art at a price below their value, but their subjects would be ashamed to do so.

To supply means of judging to the American merchant, (full of kindness and honorable sympathy as beneath the crust he so often is) who wants pictures and statues not merely from ostentation, but as means of delight and improvement to himself and his friends, who has a soul to respect the genius and desire the happiness of the artist, and who, if he errs, does so from ignorance of the circumstances, I give the following memorandum, made at my desire by an artist, my neighbor:

The rent of a suitable studio for modeling in clay and executing statues in marble may be estimated at $200 a year.

The best journeyman carver in marble at Rome receives $60 a month. Models are paid $1 a day. The cost of marble varies according to the size of the block, being generally sold by the cubic palm, a square of 9 inches English. As a general guide regarding the prices established among the higher sculptors of Rome I may mention that for a statue of life-size the demand is from $1,000 to $5,000, varying according to the composition of the figure and the number of accessories.

It is a common belief in the United States that a student of art can live in Italy and pursue his studies on an income of $300 or $400 a year. This is a lamentable error; the Russian Government allows its pensioners $700, which is scarcely sufficient. $1000 per annum should be placed at the disposal of every young artist leaving our country for Europe.

Let it be remembered, in addition to considerations inevitable from this memorandum, that you may, in your work of art, for years and months of uncheered and difficult waiting on the part of the artist, after he has gone through the earlier stages of an education, too largely based and of aim too high to finish in this world.

The Prussian artist here on my left hand, learned not only his art, but reading and writing, after he was thirty. A farmer's son, he was allowed no freedom to learn anything till the death of the head of the house left him a beggar, but set him free; on foot he walked hundreds of miles to Berlin, attracted by his first works some attention, and received some assistance in money, earned more by invention of a plowshare, walked to Rome, struggled through every privation, and has now a reputation which has secured him the means of putting his thoughts into marble. True, at 49 years of age he is still severely poor; he cannot marry because he cannot maintain a family; but he is cheerful, because he can work in his own way, trusts with childlike reliance in God, and is still sustained by the vigorous health he won laboring in his father's fields. Not every man could continue to work, circumstanced as he is, at the end of the half century. For him the only sad thing in my mind is that his works are not worth working, though of merit in composition and execution, yet ideally a product of the galvanized piety of the German school, more mutton-like than lamb-like to my unchurched eyes.

You are likely to have a work by the great master of that school, Overbeck, to look at in the United States, Mr. Perkins of Boston, who knows how to spend his money with equal generosity and discretion, having bought his *Wise and Foolish Virgins*. It will be precious to the country from great artistic merits. As to the spirit, "blessed are the poor in spirit." That kind of severity is, perhaps has become, the nature of Overbeck. He seems like a monk, but a really pious and pure one.—This spirit is not what I seek; I deem it too narrow for our day, but being deeply sincere in him, its expression is at times also deeply touching.— Barrabbas borne in triumph, and the child Jesus who, playing with his father's tools, has made himself a cross, are subjects best adapted for expression of this spirit. I have written too carelessly—much writing hath made me mad of late. Forgive if the "style be not neat, terse, and sparkling," if there be nought of the "thrilling," if the sentences seem not "written with a diamond pen," like all else that is published in America. Sometime I must try to do better. For this time

"Forgive my faults; forgive my virtues too."

21st.—Day before yesterday was the feast of St. Joseph.[15] He is supposed to have acquired a fondness for fried rice-cakes, during his residence in Egypt. Many are eaten in the open street, in arbors made for the occasion. One was made beneath my window, on Piazza Barberini. All day and the evening men cleanly dressed in white aprons and liberty caps, quite new, of fine, red cloth, were frying them for crowds of laughing, gesticulating customers. It rained a little, and they held an umbrella over the frying-pan, but not over themselves. The arbor is still there, and little children are playing in and out of it; one still lesser runs in its leading strings, followed by the bold, gay nurse, to the brink of the fountain after its orange which has rolled before it. Tenerani's workmen are coming out of his studio, the priests are coming home from Ponta Pio, the

[15] The Feast of St. Joseph, celebrated on 19 March, was introduced in Rome by Pope Sixtus IV in 1479 (*NCE*).

contadini beginning to play at *mora,* for the setting sun has just lit up the magnificent range of windows in Palazzo Barberini, and then faded tenderly, sadly
away, and the mellow bells have chimed the Ave Maria.[16]

Rome looks as Roman, that is to say, as tranquil as ever, despite the trouble
that tugs at her heart-strings. There is a report that Mazzini is to be made Dicta-
tor, as Manin is in Venice, for a short time, so as to provide hastily and energeti-
cally for the war. Ave Maria Santissima! when thou didst gaze on thy babe with
such infinite hope, thou didst not dream that so many ages after blood would
be shed and curses uttered in his name. Madonna Addolorata! hadst thou not
hoped peace and good will would spring from his bloody woes, couldst thou
have borne these hours at the foot of the cross. O Stella! woman's heart of love,
send yet a ray of pure light on this troubled deep!   ★

Dispatch 30

A R R I V A L   O F   T H E   F R E N C H

ROME, 6th May, 1849 [1]

I write you from barricaded Rome. The Mother of Nations is now at bay against
them all.[2]

---

[16] The *contadini* were peasants, working men, or farm workers. *Morra* (or *mora*) is an old
game, popular with the contadini. Fuller was not the only American visitor to Italy in the
nineteenth century to be struck by its pervasiveness. According to Story, the game was so
absorbing that beggars would play away their earnings; the usual stakes were, however, a
bottle of wine. He describes it thus: "Two persons place themselves opposite each other,
holding their right hands closed before them. They then simultaneously and with a sudden
gesture throw out their hands, some of the fingers being extended, and others shut up on
the palm,—each calling out in a loud voice, at the same moment, the number he guesses
the fingers extended by himself and his adversary to make. If neither cry out aright, or if
both cry out aright, nothing is gained or lost; but if only one guess the true number, he wins
a point. Thus, if one throw out four fingers and the other two, he who cries out six makes
a point, unless the other cry out the same number. The points are generally five, though
sometimes they are doubled; and as they are made, they are marked by the left hand, which
during the whole game is held stiffly in the air at about the shoulders' height, one finger
being extended for every point. When the *partito* is won, the winner cries out *'Fatto!'* or
'Guadagnato!' or *'Vinto!'* or else strikes his hands across each other in sign of triumph. This
last sign is also used when Double *Morra* is played, to indicate that five points are made" (1:
119–24).

[1] First published as "Undaunted Rome" in *New-York Daily Tribune,* 5 June 1849, p. 2:3.
Arthur Fuller did not include this letter in *AHA.*

[2] Fuller had just returned to Rome after spending the end of March and most of April in
Rieti with her son (see her letters to Ossoli in Hudspeth 5:218–26).

Rome was suffering before. The misfortunes of other regions of Italy, the defeat at *Novara,* preconcerted in hope to strike the last blow at Italian independence, the surrender and painful condition of Genoa, the money difficulties—insuperable, unless the Government could secure confidence abroad as well as at home—prevented her people from finding that foot-hold for which they were ready.[3] The vacillations of France agitated them, still they could not seriously believe she would ever act the part she has.[4] We must say France, because, though many honorable men have washed their hands of all share in the perfidy, the Assembly voted funds to sustain the expedition to Cività Vecchia, and the Nation, the Army have remained quiescent.

No one was, no one could be, deceived as to the scope of this expedition. It was intended to restore the Pope to the temporal sovereignty, from which the People, by the use of suffrage, had deposed him. No doubt the French, in case of success, proposed to temper the triumph of Austria and Naples, and stipulate for conditions that might soothe the Romans and make their act less odious. Also they were probably deceived by the representations of Gaeta, and believed that a large party, which had been intimidated by the republicans, would declare in favor of the Pope when they found themselves likely to be sustained. But this last pretext may in no way avail them. They landed at Cività Vecchia, and no one declared for the Pope. They marched on Rome. Placards were affixed within the walls by hands unknown, calling upon the Papal party to rise within the town. Not a soul stirred. The French had no excuse left for pretending to believe that the present Government was not entirely acceptable to the people. Notwithstanding, they assail the gates, they fire upon St. Peter's, and their balls pierced the Vatican. They were repulsed as they deserved, retired in quick and shameful defeat, as surely the brave French soldiery could not, if they had not been demoralized by a sense of what an infamous course they were pursuing. France, eager to destroy the last hope of Italian emancipation, France the alguazil[5] of Austria, the soldiers of republican France, firing upon republican Rome! If there be angel as well as demon powers that interfere

---

[3] On 23 March Radetzky and the Austrian army defeated Charles Albert at Novara; Charles Albert was forced to abdicate (Fejtö xii).

[4] On 31 March the French Chamber of Deputies authorized an invasion of Italy. The French general Nicolas Charles Victor Oudinot arrived at Cività Vecchia on 24 April, pretending to be on a mission to save Italy from the Austrians. On 30 April the French attacked the Roman defenses outside the city and were defeated by Garibaldi. A truce was declared. In the meantime, Ferdinand II had crossed the border with 9000 troops, and Garibaldi moved to attack the Neapolitans, who were forced back across their own borders and were defeated on 19 May (Fejtö xii; Hudspeth 5:227, 230).

[5] Police officer

in the affairs of men, those bullets could scarcely fail to be turned back against
their own breasts. Yet Roman blood has flowed also; I saw how it stained the
walls of the Vatican Gardens on the 30th April[6]—the first anniversary of the
appearance of Pius IX's too famous encyclic letter. Shall he, shall any Pope ever
again walk peacefully in these gardens. Impossible! The temporal sovereignty
of the Popes was gone, by their shameless, merciless measures taken to restore
it. The spiritual dominion falls too into irrevocable ruin.

What may be the issue, at this moment we cannot guess. The French have
retired to Città Vecchia, but whether to re-embark or to await re-inforcements
we know not. The Neapolitan force has halted within a few miles of the walls;
it is not large, and they are undoubtedly surprised at the discomfiture of the
French. Perhaps they wait for the Austrians, but we do not yet hear that these
have entered Romana.[7] Meanwhile Rome is strongly barricaded, and, though
she cannot stand always against a world in arms, she means at least to try. Mazzini is at her head; she has now a guide "who understands his faith," and all there
is of noble spirit will show itself. We all feel very sad, because the idea of bombs
barbarously thrown in, and street-fight in Rome is peculiarly dreadful. Apart
from all the blood and anguish inevitable at such times, the glories of Art may
perish, and mankind be forever despoiled of the most beautiful inheritance. Yet
I would defend Rome to the last moment. She must not be false to the higher
hope that has dawned upon her. She must not fall back again into servility and
corruption. And no one is willing. The interference of the French has roused the
weakest to resistance. "From the Austrians, from the Neapolitans," they cried,
"we expected this; but from the French, it is too infamous, it cannot be borne,"
and they all ran to arms and fought nobly.

The Americans here are not in a pleasant situation. Mr. Cass, the Chargé of
the United States, stays here without recognizing the Government.[8] Of course,
he holds no position at the present moment that can enable him to act for us.
Beside, it gives us pain that our country, whose policy it justly is to avoid physical interference with the affairs of Europe, should not use a moral influence.

---

[6] Fuller wrote an essay about this, which appeared as "Recollections of the Vatican,"
United States Magazine and Democratic Review, 27 (July 1850): 64–71.

[7] The province of Romagna, also known as the Legations, historically had opposed the
rule of the popes and was shortly to be occupied by the Austrians (Derek Beales, *The Risorgimento and the Unification of Italy* [New York: Barnes and Noble, 1971], 23, 45, 59, 65).

[8] Lewis Cass, Jr. (1813?–78), was the American chargé d'affaires to the Papal States.
He had become a close friend of Fuller's at this time (Hudspeth 5:13, 228). Cass was sent
to Rome in January 1849 with instructions from the secretary of state not to deliver his
credentials either to the minister of foreign affairs of Pope Pius IX, or to the revolutionary government, until he should receive further instructions from the State Department
(Marraro 26).

Rome has, as we did, thrown off a Government no longer tolerable; she has made use of the suffrage to form another; she stands on the same basis as ourselves. Mr. Rush did us great honor by his ready recognition of a principle as represented by the French Provisional Government;[9] had Mr. Cass been empowered to do the same, our country would have acted nobly, and all that is most truly American in America would have spoken to sustain the sickened hopes of European democracy. But of this more when I write next. Who knows what I may have to tell another week?   ★

Dispatch 31

BETWEEN THE HEAVES OF STORM

ROME, May 27, 1849[1]

I have suspended writing in the expectation of some decisive event, but none such comes yet. The French, entangled in a web of falsehood, abashed by a defeat that Oudinot has vainly tried to gloss over, the expedition disowned by all honorable men at home, disappointed by Gaeta, because it dares not go the length the Papal infatuation demands, knows not what to do. The Neapolitans have been decidedly driven back, the last time in a most shameful rout; the King flying in front into their own borders. We have heard for several days that the Austrians were advancing, but they come not. They also, it is probable, meet with unexpected embarrassments. They find that the sincere movement of the Italian people is very unlike that of troops commanded by princes and generals who never wished to conquer and were always waiting to betray. Then their troubles at home are constantly increasing, and, should the Russian intervention quell them to-day, it is only to raise a storm far more terrible to-morrow.[2]

The struggle is now fairly, thoroughly commenced between the principle of

[9] Richard Rush (1780–1859), a lawyer, diplomat, and statesman, was appointed ambassador to France on 3 March 1847 by President Polk. Rush witnessed the February revolution and, without waiting for instructions from Washington, formally recognized the new republic (*DAB*).

[1] First published as "Things and Thoughts in Europe. No. XXX" in *New-York Daily Tribune*, 23 June 1849, p. 1:2–4.

[2] A series of events had taken place since Fuller's twenty-ninth dispatch. On 30 April 1849 the first encounter between French and Italian armies took place outside Città Vecchia and the French were driven back. Garibaldi then defeated the Neapolitans at Velletri. Throughout May, the Austrian army advanced and besieged Ancona. Pius IX remained in Gaeta, where he had taken refuge. The Russians, fearing the further spread of revolution in Europe, were prepared to bring pressure to bear on Austria to preserve the status quo (Hearder 118).

Democracy and the old powers, no longer legitimate. That struggle may last fifty years, and the earth be watered with the blood and tears of more than one generation, but the result is sure. All Europe, including Great Britain, where the most bitter resistance of all will be made, is to be under Republican Government in the next century.

'God works in a mysterious way.'[3]

Every struggle made by the old tyrannies, all their Jesuitical deceptions, their rapacity, their imprisonments and executions of the most generous men, only sow more Hydra teeth; the crop shoots up daily more and more plenteous.[4]

When I first arrived in Italy, the vast majority of this people had no wish beyond limited monarchies, constitutional governments. They still respected the famous names of the nobility; they despised the priests, but were still fondly attached to the dogmas and ritual of the Roman Catholic Church. It required King Bomba, it required the triple treachery of Charles Albert, it required Pio IX. and the 'illustrious Gioberti,' it required the naturally kind-hearted, but, from the necessity of his position, cowardly and false Leopold of Tuscany, it required the vagabond "serene" meannesses of Parma and Modena, the "fatherly" Radetzky, and finally the imbecile Louis Bonaparte, "would-be Emperor of France," to convince this people that no transition is possible between the old and the new. *The work is done;* the revolution in Italy is now radical, nor can it stop till Italy become independent and united as a republic. Protestant she already is. The memory of saints and martyrs may continue to be revered, the ideal of Woman to be adored under the name of Maria. —Christ will now begin to be a little thought of; *his* idea was always kept carefully out of sight under the old regime; all the worship was for Madonna and Saints, who were to be well paid for interceding for sinners. An example which might make men cease to be such was no way to be coveted. Now the New Testament has been translated into Italian; copies are already dispersed far and wide; men calling

[3] William Cowper, "Light Shining Out of Darkness," line 1: "God moves in a mysterious way" (*The Poems of William Cowper,* vol. 1, ed. John D. Baird and Charles Ryskamp [Oxford: Oxford University Press, 1974], 174).

[4] Fuller may have two myths in mind. In the Greek myth about Hercules, the Hydra is a dragon (or in some versions, a water snake) that has many heads. As Hercules chops off one head, two grow in its place. Hercules defeats the monster by chopping off the center head and burying it. The more likely reference is to book 3 of Ovid's *Metamorphoses,* in which Cadmus kills a serpent and, according to the directions of Pallas, buries the teeth. As soon as the seeds are buried, warriors appear as if sprung from the ground and begin a fierce battle. The survivors found a new state (Harry Thurston Peck, ed., *Harper's Dictionary of Classical Literature and Antiquities* [New York: American Book Co., 1923]).

themselves Christians will no longer be left entirely ignorant of the precepts and life of Jesus.

The people of Rome have burnt the Cardinals' carriages. They took the confessionals out of the churches, and made mock confessions in the piazzas, the scope of which was, "I have sinned, father, so and so." "Well, my son, how much will you pay to the church for absolution?" Afterward the people thought of burning the confessionals or using them for barricades, but at the request of the Triumvirate they desisted, and even put them back into the churches.[5] But it was from no reaction of feeling that they stopped short, only from respect for the government. The "Tartuffe" of Molière has been translated into Italian, and was last night performed with great applause at the Valle.[6] Can all this be forgotten? Never! Should guns and bayonets replace the Pope on the throne, he will find its foundations, once deep as modern civilization, now so undermined that it falls with the least awkward movement.

But I cannot believe he will be replaced there. France alone could consummate that crime, that for her cruelest, most infamous treason. The Elections in France will decide. In three or four days we shall know whether the French nation at large be guilty or no—whether it be the will of the Nation to aid or strive to ruin a Government founded precisely on the same basis as their own.

I do not dare to trust that people. The peasant is yet very ignorant. The suffering workman is frightened as he thinks of the punishments that ensued on the insurrections of May and June. The man of property is full of horror, at the brotherly scope of Socialism. The aristocrat dreams of the guillotine always when he hears speak of the people. The influence of the Jesuits is still immense in France. Both in France and England the grossest falsehoods have been circulated with unwearied diligence about the state of things in Italy. An amusing specimen of what is still done in this line I find just now in a foreign journal, where it says there are red flags on all the houses of Rome, meaning to imply that the Romans are athirst for blood. Now, the fact is, that these flags are put up at the entrance of those streets where there is no barricade, as a signal to coachmen and horsemen that they can pass freely. There is one on the house where I am, in which is no person but myself who thirst for peace, and the *padrone* who thirsts for money.

Meanwhile the French troops are encamped at a little distance from Rome. Some attempts at fair and equal treaty when their desire to occupy Rome was

[5] Rome at this time was governed by the triumvirate of Mazzini, Aurelio Saffi, and Carlo Armellini, but Mazzini was de facto head of state.

[6] Story considered the Valle one of the better theaters in Rome, where "the drama is played by an excellent company" (1:210).

firmly resisted, Oudinot describes in his dispatches as a readiness for *submission*.
Having tried in vain to gain this point, he has sent to France for fresh orders.
These will be decided by the turn the election takes. Meanwhile the French
troops are much exposed to the Roman force where they are. Should the Austrians come up, what will they do? Will they shamelessly fraternize with them,
after pretending and proclaiming that they came here as a check upon their
aggressions? Will they oppose them in defence of Rome with which they are
at war?

Ah! the way of falsehood, the way of treachery, how dark—how full of pit-
falls and traps! Heaven defend from it all who are not yet engaged therein!

War near at hand seems to me even more dreadful than I had fancied it. True!
it tries men's souls, lays bare selfishness in undeniable deformity. Here, it has
produced much fruit of noble sentiment, noble act; but still it breeds vice, too,
drunkenness, mental dissipation, tears asunder the tenderest ties, lavishes the
productions of earth for which her starving poor stretch out their hands in vain,
in the most unprofitable manner. And the ruin that ensues, how terrible. Let
those who have ever passed happy days in Rome grieve to hear that the beautiful plantations of *Villa Borghese*—that chief delight and refreshment of citizens,
foreigners, and little children, are laid low, as far as the obelisk.[7] The fountain,
singing alone amid the fallen groves, cannot be seen and heard without tears; it
seems like some innocent infant calling and crowing amid dead bodies on a field
which battle has strewn with the bodies of those that once cherished it. Also,
the plantations of *Villa Salvage* on the Tiber, the beautiful avenue on the way
from St. John Lateran to *La Maria Maggiore,* the trees of the Forum are fallen.
Rome is shorn of the locks which lent grace to her venerable brow. She looks
desolate, profaned. I feel what I never expected to, as if I might by and by be
willing to leave Rome.

Then I have, for the first time, seen what wounded men suffer.[8] The night
of the 30th April I passed in the hospital, and saw the terrible agonies of those
dying or who needed amputation, felt their mental pains, and longing for the
loved ones who were away,—for many of these were Lombards, who had come
from the field of Novara to fight upon a fairer chance—many were students
of the University, who had enlisted and threw themselves into the front of the
engagement. (N.B.—The impudent falsehoods of the French general's dis-

---

[7] The Villa Borghese, one of the Roman park villas, consists of formal gardens, plots
of trees, and a variety of buildings, including the Borghese Gallery (Masson 217–18). The
park lies adjacent to the Piazza del Popolo, which has an obelisk and fountain at its center.

[8] By this time, Fuller had accepted the position of *regolatrice,* or director, of the Hospital
of the Fate Bene Fratelli, offered to her by Princess Christina Trivulzio di Belgiojoso.

patches are incredible. The French were never decoyed on in any way. They were received with every possible mark of hostility. They were defeated in open field, the Garibaldi legion rushing out to them, and though they suffered much from the walls, they sustained themselves nowhere. —They never put up a white flag till they wished to surrender. The vanity that strives to cover over these facts is unworthy men. The only excuse for the impudent conduct of the expedition is that they were deceived, not by the Romans here, but by the priests of Gaeta leading them to expect action in their favor within the walls. These priests themselves were deluded by their hopes and old habits of mind. The troops did not fight well, and Gen. Oudinot abandoned his wounded without proper care. All this says nothing against French valor, proved by ages of glory, beyond the doubt of their worst foes. They were demoralized because they fought in so bad a cause, and there was no sincere ardor or clear hope in any breast.)

But to return to the hospitals: these were put in order, and have been kept so by the Princess Belgiojoso.[9] The Princess was born of one of the noblest families of the Milanese, a descendant of the great Trivulzio, and inherited a large fortune. Very early she compromised it in liberal movements, and, on their failure, was obliged to fly to Paris, where for a time she maintained herself by writing, and I think by painting also. A Princess so placed naturally excited great interest, and she drew around her a little court of celebrated men. After recovering her fortune, she still lived in Paris, distinguished for her talents and munificence, both toward literary men and her exiled countrymen. Later, on her estate, called Locate, between Pavia and Milan, she had made experiments in the Socialist direction with fine judgment and success. Association for education, for labor, for transaction of household affairs, had been carried on for several years; she had spared no devotion of time and money to this object, loved and was much beloved by those objects of her care, and said she hoped to die there. All is now despoiled and broken up, though it may be hoped that some seeds of peaceful reform have been sown which will spring to light when least expected. The Princess returned to Italy in 1847–48, full of hope in Pius IX and Charles Albert. She showed her usual energy and truly princely heart, sustaining, at her own expense, a company of soldiers and a journal up to the last sad betrayal of Milan, August 6. These days undeceived all the people, but few of the noblesse; she was one of the few with mind strong enough to understand the lesson, and is now warmly interested in the Republican movement. From

[9] Fuller had written her brother, Richard, on 8 February 1848 that she intended to write about the princess in the *Tribune* (Hudspeth 5:52). Deiss has called the princess "a sophisticated, aristocratic, strangely beautiful, European Margaret Fuller . . . . She was the fantasy Margaret Fuller of the real Margaret Fuller" (120).

Milan she went to France, but, finding it impossible to effect anything serious there in behalf of Italy, returned, and has been in Rome about two months. Since leaving Milan she receives no income, her possessions being in the grasp of Radetsky, and cannot know when, if ever, she will again. But as she worked so largely and well with money, so can she without. She published an invitation to the Roman women to make lint and bandages and offer their services to the wounded; she put the hospitals in order; the central one, Trinita de Pellegrini, (once the abode where the Pilgrims were received during Holy week, and where foreigners were entertained by seeing their feet washed by the noble dames and dignitaries of Rome,) she has remained day and night since the wounded were first there, on the 30th of April. Some money she procured at first by going through Rome, accompanied by two other ladies veiled, to beg it. Afterward the voluntary contributions were generous; among the rest, I am proud to say, the Americans in Rome gave $250, of which a handsome portion came from Mr. Brown, the Consul.

I value this mark of sympathy more because of irritation and surprise occasioned here by the position of Mr. Cass, the Envoy. It is most unfortunate that we should have an envoy here for the first time, just to offend and disappoint the Romans. When all the other ambassadors are at Gaeta ours is in Rome, as if by his presence to discountenance the Republican Government which he does not recognize. Mr. Cass, it seems, is limited by his instructions not to recognize the Government till sure it can be sustained. Now, it seems to me the only dignified ground for our Government, the only legitimate ground for any Republican Government, is to recognize for any nation the Government chosen by itself. The suffrage had been correct here, and the proportion of votes to the whole population was much larger, it was said, by Americans here, than it is in our country at the time of contested elections. It had elected an Assembly, that Assembly had appointed, to meet the exigencies of this time, the Triumvirate. If any misrepresentations have induced America to believe, as France affects to have believed, that so large a vote could have been obtained by moral intimidation, the present unanimity of the population in resisting such immense odds, and the enthusiasm of their every expression in favor of the present Government, puts the matter beyond a doubt. The Roman people claims once more to have a national existence. It declines farther serfdom to an ecclesiastical court. It claims liberty of conscience, of action and of thought. Should it fall from its present position, it will not be from internal dissent, but from foreign oppression.

Since this is the case, surely our country, if no other, is bound to recognize the present Government *so long as it can sustain itself*. This position is that to which we have a right: being such, it is no matter how it is viewed by others.

But I dare assert it is the only respectable one for our country, in the eyes of the Emperor of Russia himself.

The first best occasion is past, when Mr. Cass might, had he been empowered to act as Mr. Rush did in France, have morally strengthened the staggering Republic, which would have found sympathy where alone it is of permanent value on the basis of principle. Had it been in vain, what then? America would have acted honorably; as to his being compromised thereby with the Papal Government, that fear is idle. Pope and Cardinals have great hopes from America; the giant influence there is kept up with the greatest care; the number of Catholic writers in the United States, too, carefully counted. Had our Republican Government acknowledged this Republican Government, the Papal Camarilla [10] would have respected us more, but not loved us less, for have we not the loaves and fishes to give as well as the precious souls to be saved? Ah! here, indeed, America might go straight forward with much to-be-deprecated impunity. Bishop Hughes himself need not be anxious. [11] The first best occasion has passed, and the unrecognized, unrecognizing Envoy has given offense and not comfort, by a presence that seemed constantly to say, I do not think you can sustain yourselves. It has wounded both the heart and the pride of Rome. Some of the lowest people have asked me, "Is it not true that your country had a war to become free?"—"Yes." "Then why do they not feel for us?" Yet even now it is not too late. If America would only hail triumphant, if she would not sustain injured Rome, that would be something. "Can you suppose Rome will triumph," you say, "without money, and against so potent a league of foes?" I am not sure, but I hope, for I believe something in the heart of a people when fairly awakened. I have also a lurking confidence in what our fathers spoke of so constantly, a providential order of things, by which brute force and selfish enterprises are sometimes set at nought by aid which seems to descend from a higher sphere. Even old Pagans believed in that, you know, and I was born in America, Christianized by the Puritans—America, freed by eight years' patient

[10] In the sense Fuller uses the term here, a *camarilla* is an unflattering name for a close adviser of the pope. It implies that the adviser molds policies to benefit himself.

[11] Bishop John Joseph Hughes (1797–1864) worked throughout his life for the development of the Roman Catholic church in America. He traveled frequently in Europe to recruit priests and nuns and became well known for his fight against the Public School Society and for the establishment of Catholic schools (*DAB*). He was an avid supporter of Pius IX, and in response to the Roman revolution, he claimed that the republicans had established "a reign of terror over the Roman people." Hughes took particular offense at the *Tribune*'s coverage and declared, "And this is the phalanx recognized by Mr Greeley as the Roman republic! Yet no ambassador from foreign countries has recognised such a republic, except it be the female plenipotentiary who furnishes the Tribune with diplomatic correspondence" (*New York Herald*, 27 June 1849, p. 2).

suffering, poverty and struggle—America, so cheered in dark days by one spark of sympathy from a foreign shore—America, first "recognized" by Lafayette. I saw him in traversing our country, then great, rich, and free. Millions of men who owed in part their happiness to what, no doubt, was once sneered at as romantic sympathy, threw garlands on his path. It is natural that I should have some faith.[12]

Send, dear America, a talisman to thy ambassadors, precious beyond all that boasted gold of California. Let it loose his tongue to cry "Long live the Republic, and may God bless the cause of the People, the brotherhood of nations and of men—the equality of rights for all." *Viva America!*

Hail to my country! May she live a free, a glorious, a loving life, and not perish, like the old dominions, from the leprosy of selfishness.   ★

Evening.

I am alone in the ghostly silence of a great house, not long since full of gay faces and echoing with gay voices, now deserted by every one but me—for almost all foreigners are gone now, driven by force either of the Summer heats or the foe. I hear all the Spaniards are going now, that twenty-one have taken passports to-day; why that is, I do not know.

I shall not go till the last moment; my only fear is of France. I cannot think in any case there would be found men willing to damn themselves to latest posterity by bombarding Rome. Other cities they may, careless of destroying the innocent and helpless, the babe and old grandsire who cannot war against them. But Rome, precious inheritance of mankind, will they run the risk of marring their shrined treasures? Would they dare do it?

Two of the balls that struck St. Peter's have been sent to Pio IX. by his children, who find themselves so much less "beloved" than were the Austrians.

These two days, days of solemn festivity in the kalends of the Church, have been duly kept, and the population looks cheerful as it swarms through the streets. The order of Rome, thronged as it is with troops, is amazing. I go from one end to the other, and where the poorest and most barbarous of the population (barbarously ignorant, I mean) alone and on foot. My friends send out their little children alone with their nurses. The amount of crime is almost nothing, what it was. The Roman, no longer pent in ignorance and crouching beneath espionage, no longer stabs in the dark. His energies have true vent; his better feelings are roused; he has thrown aside the stiletto. The power here is indeed miraculous, since no doubt still lurk within the walls many who are eager to incite brawls, if only to give an excuse for slander.

---

[12] Fuller had probably seen General Lafayette (1757–1834) in Cambridge, Massachusetts, during his celebrated tour of the United States in 1824.

To-day I suppose twelve thousand Austrians marched into Florence. The Florentines have humbled and disgraced themselves in vain. They recalled the Grand Duke to ward off the entrance of the Austrians, but in vain went the deputation to Gaeta (in an American steamer!). Leopold was afraid to come till his dear cousins of Austria had put everything in perfect order; then the Austrians entered to take Leghorn, but the Florentines still kept on imploring they would not come there; Florence was as subdued, as good as possible already; they have had the answer they deserved. Now they crown their work by giving over Guerrazzi and Petracci to be tried by an Austrian Court Martial.[13] Truly the cup of shame brims over.

I have been out on the *loggia* to look over the city. All sleeps with that peculiar air of serene majesty known to this city only.—This city that has grown, not out of the necessities of commerce nor the luxuries of wealth, but first out of heroism, then out of faith. Swelling domes, roofs softly tinted with yellow moss—what deep meaning, what deep repose, in your faintly seen outline!

The young Moon climbs among clouds—the clouds of a departing thunderstorm. Tender, smiling Moon! can it be that thy full orb may look down on a smoking, smoldering Rome, and see her best blood run along the stones without one in the world to defend, one to aid—scarce one to cry out a tardy "Shame?" We will wait, whisper the nations, and see if they can bear it. Rack them well to see if they are brave. *If they can do without us,* we will help them. Is it thus ye would be served in your turn? Beware!   ★

Dispatch 32

NEGOTIATIONS AND BETRAYAL

ROME, June 10, 1849[1]

Messrs. Greeley & McElrath:

What shall I write of Rome in these sad but glorious days? Plain facts are the best; for my feelings I could not find fit words.

When I last wrote the second act of the French comedy[2] was being played.

In the first, the French Government affected to consult the Assembly. The Assembly, or a majority of the Assembly, affect to believe the pretext it gave and voted funds for 12,000 men to go to Cività Vecchia. Arriving there, Oudi-

---

[13] Francesco Domenico Guerrazzi, a confirmed revolutionary, had become one of the triumvirs of the Florentine republic in October 1848 (Berkeley 390; *New Cambridge Modern History* 10:408).

[1] First published as "Things and Thoughts in Europe. No. XXXII" in the *New-York Daily Tribune*, 24 July 1849, p. 1:2–4.

[2] In *AHA* Arthur Fuller substituted the term "farce."

not proclaimed that he had come as a friend and brother. He was received as such. Immediately he took possession of the town, disarmed the Roman troops and published a manifesto in direct opposition to his first.

He sends to Rome that he is coming there as a friend; receives the answer that he is not wanted and cannot be trusted. This answer he chooses to consider as coming from a minority and advances on Rome. The pretended majority on which he counts never shows itself by a single motion within the walls. He makes an assault and is defeated. On this subject his dispatches to his Government are full of falsehoods that would disgrace the lowest pick-pocket, falsehoods which it is impossible he should not know to be such.[3] The Assembly passes a vote of blame. M. Louis Bonaparte writes a letter of compliment and assurance that this course of violence shall be sustained. In conformity with this promise 12,000 more troops are sent. This time it is not thought necessary to consult the Assembly.

SECOND ACT.

Now appears in Rome M. Ferdinand Lesseps, Envoy, &c. of the French Government. He declares himself clothed with full powers to treat with Rome.[4] He cannot conceal his surprise at all he sees there, at the ability with which preparations have been made for defense, at the patriotic enthusiasm which pervaded the population. Nevertheless, in beginning his game of treaty-making he was not ashamed to insist on the French occupying the city. Again and again repulsed, he again and again returned to the charge on this point. And here I shall translate the letter addressed to him by the Triumvirate, both for its perfect candor of statement and to give an idea of the sweet and noble temper with which these treacherous aggressions have been met:

[3] Oudinot, in his dispatch to the French Assembly, described the firing under the walls of the Vatican as a "reconnaissance," failed to mention the battle outside the gates in which Garibaldi routed the French, and summed up by declaring that "this affair of April 30 is one of the most brilliant in which the French troops have taken part since our great wars" (Trevelyan 146).

[4] Ferdinand-Marie, viscomte de Lesseps (1805–94), was a diplomat and financier who built the Suez Canal. He was sent to Rome as minister pleni-potentiary to negotiate an agreement with the republican government on 15 May 1849. Despite Fuller's opinion, Lesseps apparently was acting in good faith in his efforts to make a compromise. However, Oudinot and Louis-Napoleon did not intend for the Roman Republic to survive, and they did not pay attention to Lesseps's information about the "patriotic enthusiasm" that Fuller mentions here (Hudspeth 5:230; Newman). On 8 May, the same day the French minister for foreign affairs charged Lesseps with his mission, Louis-Napoleon wrote to Oudinot, "Our military honour is at stake, I will not suffer it to be compromised. You may rely on being reinforced" (Trevelyan 145–46).

NOTE OF THE TRIUMVIRS TO MONSIEUR LESSEPS,
May 25, 1849.

We have had the honor, Monsieur, to furnish you, in our note of the 16th, with some information as to the unanimous consent which was given to the formation of the Government of the Roman Republic. We, to-day, would speak to you of the actual question, such as it is debated in fact, if not by right, between the French Government and ours. You will allow us to do it with the frankness demanded by the urgency of the situation, as well as the sympathy which ought to govern all relations between France and Italy. Our diplomacy is the truth, and the character given to your mission is a guarantee that the best possible interpretation will be given to what we shall say to you.

With your permission we return for an instant, to the source of the present situation.

In consequence of conferences and arrangements which took place without the Government of the Roman Republic ever being called on to take part, it was sometime since decided by the Catholic Powers; 1st, That a modification should take place in the Government and institutions of the Roman States; 2d, That this modification should have for basis the return of Pius IX, not as Pope, for to that no obstacle is interposed by us, but as temporal sovereign; 3d, That if, to attain that aim, a continuous intervention was judged necessary, that intervention should take place.

We are willing to admit that while for some of the contracting Governments the only motive was the hope of a general restoration and absolute return to the treaties of 1815, the French Government was drawn into this agreement only in consequence of erroneous information tending systematically to depict the Roman States as given up to anarchy and governed by terror exercised in the name of an audacious minority. We know also that in the modification proposed the French Government intended to represent an influence more or less liberal, opposed to the absolutist programme of Austria and of Naples.—It does none the less remain true that under the Apostolic or Constitutional form, with or without liberal guarantees to the Roman people, the dominant thought in all the negotiations to which we allude has been some sort of return toward the past, a compromise between the Roman people and Pius IX considered as a temporal prince.

We cannot dissemble to ourselves, Monsieur, that the French expedition has been planned and executed under the inspiration of this thought. Its object was, on one side, to throw the sword of France into the bal-

ance of negotiations which were to be opened at Rome, on the other to
guarantee the Roman people from the excess of retrogade, but always on
condition that it should submit to constitutional monarchy in favor of the
Holy Father. This is assured to us partly from informations which we believe we possess as to the concert with Austria, from the proclamations of
General Oudinot, from the formal declarations made by successive envoys
to the Triumvirate, from the silence obstinately maintained always when
we have sought to approach the political question and obtain a formal
declaration of the fact proved in our note of the 16th that the institutions
by which the Roman people are governed at this moment are the free
and spontaneous expression of the wish of the people inviolable when
legally interrogated. For the rest, the vote of the French Assembly sustains
implicitly the fact that we affirm.

In presence of such a situation, under the menace of an inadmissible
compromise, and of negotiations which the state of our people no way provoked, our part, Monsieur, could not be doubtful. To resist,—we owed
this to our country, to France, to all Europe. We ought, in fulfillment of a
mandate, loyally given, loyally accepted, to maintain to our country the
inviolability, so far as that was possible to us, of its territory, and of the
institutions decreed by all the powers, by all the elements, of the State.
We ought to conquer the time needed for appeal from France ill-informed
to France better-informed, to save the sister Republic the disgrace and
the remorse which must be hers if, rashly led on by bad suggestions from
without, she became, before she was aware, accomplice of an act of violence to which we can find no parallel without going back to the first
partition of Poland in 1772.—We owed to Europe to maintain, as far as
we could, the fundamental principles of all international life, the independence of each people in all that concerns its internal administration. We
say it without pride, for if it is with enthusiasm that we resist the attempts
of the Neapolitan monarchy and of Austria, our eternal enemy, it is with
profound grief that we are ourselves constrained to contend with the arms
of France; we believe in following this line of conduct to have deserved
well, not only of our country, but of all the people of Europe and of France
herself.

We come to the actual question. You know, Monsieur, the events which
have followed the French intervention. Our territory has been invaded by
the King of Naples.

Four thousand Spaniards were to embark on the 17th for invasion of
this country. The Austrians having surmounted the heroic resistance of
Bologna have advanced into Romagna, are now marching on Ancona.

We have beaten and driven out of our territory the forces of the King of Naples. We believe we should do the same by the Austrian forces if the attitude of the French here did not fetter our action.

We are sorry to say it, but France must be informed that the expedition of Città Vecchia, said to be planned for protection, costs us very dear. Of all the interventions with which it is hoped to overwhelm us, that of the French has been the most perilous. Against the soldiers of Austria and the King of Naples we can fight, for God protects a good cause. But we *do not wish to fight* against the French. We are toward them in a state not of war but of simple defense. But this position, the only one we wish to take wherever we meet France, has for us all the inconveniences without any of the favorable chances of war.

The French expedition has, from the first, forced us to concentrate our troops, thus leaving our frontier open to Austrian invasion, Bologna and the cities of Romagna unsustained. The Austrians have profited by this. After eight days of heroic resistance by the population Bologna was forced to yield. We had bought in France arms for our defense. Of these ten thousand fusils have been detained between Marseilles and Città Vecchia. These are in your hands. Thus with a single blow you deprive us of ten thousand soldiers. In every armed man is a soldier against the Austrians.

Your forces are disposed around our walls as if for a siege. They remain there without avowed aim or programme. They have forced us to keep the city in a state of defense which weighs upon our finances. They force us to keep here a body of troops who might be saving our cities from the occupation and ravages of the Austrians. They hinder our circulation, our provisions, our couriers. They keep minds in a state of excitement and distrust which might, if our population were less good and devoted, lead to sinister results. They do *not* engender anarchy nor reaction, for both are impossible at Rome, but they sow the seed of irritation against France and it is a misfortune for us who were accustomed to love and hope in her.

We are besieged, Monsieur, besieged by France, in the name of a protective mission, while some leagues off the King of Naples, flying, carries off our hostages, and the Austrian slays our brothers.

You have presented propositions. Those propositions have been declared inadmissible by the Assembly. To-day you add a fourth to the three already rejected.—This says that France will protect from foreign invasion all that part of our territory that may be occupied by her troops. You must yourself feel that this changes nothing in our position.

The parts of the territory occupied by your troops are in fact protected; but if only for the present, to what are they reduced? and if it is for the future, have we no other way to protect our territory than by giving it up entirely to you?

The root of the question is not true. It is in the occupation of Rome. This demand has constantly stood first in your list of propositions. Now we have had the honor to say to you, Monsieur, that is impossible. The people will never consent to it. If the occupation of Rome has for its aim only to protect it, the people thank you, but tell you at the same time that, able to defend Rome by its own forces, it would be dishonored even in your eyes by declaring itself insufficient, and needing the aid of some regiments of French soldiers. If the occupation has otherwise a political object, which God forbid, the people, which has given itself freely these institutions, cannot suffer it. Rome is its Capital, its Palladium, its Sacred City. It knows very well that apart from its principles, apart from its honor, there is civil war at the end of such an occupation. It is filled with distrust by your persistence. It foresees, once the troops admitted, changes in men and in intentions which would be fatal to its liberty. It knows that, in presence of foreign bayonets, the independence of its Assembly, of its Government, would be a vain word.—It has always Città Vecchia before its eyes.

On this point be sure its will is irrevocable. It will be massacred from barricade to barricade, before it will surrender. Can the soldiers of France wish to massacre a brother people whom they came to protect, because it does not wish to surrender to them its Capital?

There are for France only three parts to take in the Roman States. She ought to declare herself for us, against us, or neuter. To declare herself for us would be to recognize our Republic and fight side by side with us against the Austrians.

To declare against us is to crush without motive the liberty, the national life, of a friendly people, and fight side by side with the Austrians.

France *cannot* do that. She *will* not risk a European War to depress us her ally. Let her, then, rest neuter in this conflict between us and our enemies; only yesterday we hoped more from her, but to-day we demand only this.

The occupation of Città Vecchia is a fact accomplished; let it go. France thinks that, in the present state of things, she ought not to remain distant from the field of battle. She thinks that, vanquishers or vanquished, we may have need of her moderative action and of her protection. We do not think so; but we will not react against her. Let her keep Città Vecchia. Let her even extend her encampments, if the numbers of her troops require it in the healthy regions of Città Vecchia and Viterbo. Let her then wait the issue of the combats about to take place. All facilities will be offered her, every proof of frank and cordial sympathy given; her officers can visit Rome; her soldiers have all the solace possible. But let her neutrality be sincere and without *arrière-pensée*. Let her declare herself in explicit terms. Let her leave us free to use all our forces. Let her restore our arms. Let her not by her cruisers drive back from our ports the men who come to our aid from other parts of Italy. Let her, above all, withdraw from before our walls, and let even the appearance of hostility cease between two nations who, later, undoubtedly, are destined to unite in the same international faith, as now they have adopted the same form of Government.

In his answer, Lesseps appears moved by this statement, and particularly expresses himself thus:

"One point appears above all to occupy you; it is the thought that we wish forcibly to impose upon you the obligation of receiving us as friends. FRIENDSHIP AND VIOLENCE ARE INCOMPATIBLE. Thus it would be IN-CONSEQUENT on our part to begin by firing our cannon upon you to make you natural protectors, SUCH A CONTRADICTION ENTERS NEITHER INTO MY INTENTIONS, NOR THOSE OF THE GOVERNMENT OF THE FRENCH REPUBLIC, NOR OF OUR ARMY AND ITS HONORABLE CHIEF."

These words were written at the headquarters of Oudinot, and of course seen and approved by him. At the same time, in private conversation, "the honorable chief" would swear he would occupy Rome by "one means or another." A few days after, Lesseps consented to conditions such as the Romans would tolerate. He no longer insisted on occupying Rome, but would content himself with good positions in the country.—Oudinot protested that the Plenipotentiary had "exceeded his powers"—that he should not obey—that the Armistice was at an end, and he should attack Rome on Monday. It was then Friday.—He proposed to leave these two days for the few foreigners that remained to get out of town. Mr. Lesseps went off to Paris, in great seeming indignation, to get *his* treaty ratified. Of course we could not hear from him for eight or ten days. Meanwhile, the *honorable* chief, alike in all his conduct, attacked on Sunday instead of Monday. The attack began before sunrise and lasted all day. I saw it from my window, which, though distant, commands the Gate St. Pancrazio.[5]

---

[5] Oudinot's rationalization for his deception was that in his notice to the defenders of Rome he said he would not attack "the place" until Monday, the 4th of June, and that he privately interpreted the word *place* to exclude the Roman outposts (Trevelyan 162). Fuller wrote Emelyn Story: "On Sunday, from our loggia, I witnessed a terrible, a real battle. It began at four in the morning; it lasted to the last gleam of light. The musket-fire was almost

Why the whole force was bent on that part, I do not know. If they could take it, the town would be cannonaded and the barricades useless; but it is the same with the Pincian Gate. Small parties made feints in two other directions, but they were at once repelled. The French fought with great bravery, and this time it is said with beautiful skill and order, sheltering themselves in their advance by moveable barricades. The Italians fought like lions, and no inch of ground was gained by the assailant. The loss of the French is said to be very great: it could not be otherwise. Six or seven hundred Italians are dead or wounded, among them were many officers, those of Garibaldi especially, who are much exposed by their daring bravery, and whose red tunic makes them the natural mark of the enemy. It seems to me great folly to wear such a dress amid the dark uniforms, but Garibaldi has always done it. He has now been wounded twice here and seventeen times in Ancona.

All this week I have been much at the Hospitals where are these noble sufferers. They are full of enthusiasm; this time was no treason, no Vicenza, no Novara, no Milan. They had not been given up by wicked chiefs at the moment they were shedding their blood and they had conquered. All were only anxious to get out again and be at their posts. They seemed to feel that those who died so gloriously were fortunate; perhaps they were, for if Rome is obliged to yield, and how can she stand always unaided against the four powers? where shall these noble youths fly? They are the flower of the Italian youth, especially among the Lombards are some of the finest young men I have ever seen. If Rome falls, if Venice falls, there is no spot of Italian earth where they can abide more, and certainly no Italian will wish to take refuge in France. Truly you said, Mr. Lesseps, "Violence and friendship are incompatible."

A military funeral of the officer Ramorino[6] was sadly picturesque and affecting. The white-robed priests went before the body singing, while his brothers in arms bore the lighted tapers. His horse followed, saddled and bridled. The horse hung his head and stepped dejectedly; he felt there was something strange and gloomy going on—felt that his master was laid low. Ramorino left a wife and children. A great proportion of those who run those risks are, happily, alone. Parents weep, but will not suffer long, their grief is not like that of widows and children.

Since the 3d we have only cannonade and skirmishes. The French are at

---

unintermitted; the roll of the cannon, especially from St. Angelo, most majestic. As all passed at Porta San Pancrazio and Villa Pamfili, I saw the smoke of every discharge, the flash of the bayonets; with a glass could see the men" (Hudspeth 5:238).

[6] General Gerolamo Ramorino (1792–1849) had been court-marshaled and condemned to death on 22 May 1849 for his disobedience to military orders that enabled Radetzky and the Austrians to win the battle at Novara in March 1849 (*Grande dizionario enciclopedico Utet*).

their trenches, but cannot advance much; they are too much molested from the walls. The Romans have made one very successful sortie. The French availed themselves of a violent thunder-storm, when the walls were left more thinly guarded, to try to scale them, but were immediately driven back. It was thought by many that they never would be willing to throw bombs and shells into Rome, but they do whenever they can. That generous hope and faith in them as republicans and brothers, which put the best construction on their actions and believed in their truth, as far as possible, is now destroyed. The Government is false, and the people do not resist; the General is false, and the soldiers obey.

Meanwhile, frightful sacrifices are being made by Rome. All her glorious oaks, all her gardens of delight, her casinos, full of the monuments of genius and taste, are perishing in the defense. The houses, the trees which had been spared at gate St. Pancrazio, all afforded shelter to the foe, and caused so much loss of life, that the Romans have now fully acquiesced in destruction agonizing to witness. Villa Borghese is finally laid waste, the villa of Raphael has perished, the trees are all cut down at Villa Albani, and the house, that most beautiful ornament of Rome, must, I suppose, go too. The stately marble forms are already driven from their place in that portico where Winkelmann sat and walked with such delight.[7] Villa Salvaze is burnt, with all its fine frescoes, and that bank of the Tiber, shorn of its lovely plantations.

Rome will never recover the cruel ravage of these days, perhaps only just begun. I had often thought of living a few months near St. Peter's that I might go as much as I liked to the Church and the Museum, have Villa Doria Pamfili and Monte Mario within the compass of a walk. It is not easy to find lodgings there, as it is a quarter foreigners never inhabit, but walking about to see what pleasant places there were, I had fixed my eye on a clean simple house near Ponte St. Angelo. It bore on a tablet that it was the property of Angela ———— *libera,* its little balconies with their old wooden rails, full of flowers in humble earthen vases, the many bird cages, the air of domestic quiet, and comfort marked it as the home of some vestal or widow, some lone woman, whose heart was centered in the ordinary and simplest pleasures of a home. I saw also she was one of the most limited income, and I thought "she will not refuse to let me a room for a few months, as I shall be as quiet as herself, and sympathize about the flowers and birds." Now the Villa Pamfili is all laid waste. The French encamp on Monte Mario, what they have done there is not known yet. The cannonade reverberates all day under the dome of St. Peter's, and the house

---

[7] Johann Joachim Winckelmann (1717–68), an art historian and archaeologist, went to Rome in 1755 (*OCA*).

of poor Angela is leveled with the ground. I hope her birds and the white pea-
cocks of the Vatican gardens are in safety—but who cares for gentle, harmless
creatures now?

I have been often interrupted while writing this letter, and suppose it is confused as well as incomplete. I hope my next may tell of something decisive one
way or the other. News is not yet come from Lesseps, but the conduct of Oudinot, and the formation of the new French Ministry give reason to hope no good.
Many seem resolved to force back Pius IX. among his bleeding flock, into the
city ruined by him, where he cannot remain, and if he come all this struggle
and sorrow is to be borne over again. Mazzini stands firm as a rock. I know not
whether he hopes for a successful issue, but he *believes* in a God bound to protect
men who do what they deem their duty. Yet how long, O Lord, shall the few
trample on the many?

POSTSCRIPT.—I am surprised to see the air of perfect good faith with which
articles from the London *Times,* upon the revolutionary movements, are copied
into our papers. There exists not in Europe a paper more violently opposed
to the cause of freedom than the *Times,* and neither its leaders nor its foreign
correspondence are to be depended upon.[8] It is said to receive money from Austria. I know not whether this be true, or whether it be merely subservient to
the aristocratical feeling of England, which is far more opposed to Republican
movements than is that of Russia; for in England fear embitters hate. It is droll
to remember our reading in the class-book,

"Ay, down to the dust with them, slaves as they are."

To think how bitter the English were on the Italians who succumbed, and see
how they hate those who resist; and their cowardice here in Italy, is ludicrous. It
is they who run away at the least intimation of danger—it is they who invent all
the "fe, fo, fum" stories about Italy,—it is they who write to the *Times* and elsewhere that they dare not for their lives stay in Rome, where I, a woman, walk
everywhere alone, and all the little children do the same, with their nurses.
More of this anon.   ★

---

[8] Trevelyan confirms Fuller's opinion. He writes, "The 'Times' correspondent remained
within the French lines, and his thirst for blood could not be satisfied by Oudinot's tardy
and comparatively humane operations. The sneers of the great newspaper at the 'degenerate
remnant of the Roman people,' who 'will believe they are heroes,' revealed that remarkable
form of pride in British institutions which used to consider it an insult to ourselves that any
other race should aspire to progress and freedom" (110).

Dispatch 33

ROME UNDER SIEGE

ROME, June 21, 1849 [1]

Messrs. Greeley & McElrath:

It is now two weeks since the first attack of Oudinot, and as yet we hear nothing decisive from Paris. I know not yet what news may have come last night, but by the morning's mail we did not even receive notice that Lesseps was arrived in Paris.

Whether Lesseps was consciously the servant of all these base intrigues time will show. His conduct was boyish and foolish, if it was not treacherous. The only object seemed to be to create panic, to agitate, to take possession of Rome somehow, though what to do with it, if they could get it, the French Government would hardly know.

Pius IX. in his Allocution of the last 29th April has explained himself fully. He has disavowed every liberal act which ever seemed to emanate from him, with the exception of the Amnesty. He has shamelessly recalled his refusal to let Austrian blood be shed while Roman flows daily at his request. He has implicitly declared that his future government, could he return, would be absolute despotism, has dispelled the last lingering illusion of those still anxious to apologize for him as only a prisoner now in the hands of the Cardinals and the King of Naples. The last frail link is broken that bound to him the people of Rome, and could the French restore him, they must frankly avow themselves, abandon entirely and fully the position they took in February, 1848, and declare themselves the allies of Austria and of Russia.

Meanwhile they persevere in the Jesuitical policy that has already disgraced and is to ruin them. After a week of vain assaults Oudinot sent to Rome the following letter, which I translate, as well as the answers it elicited:

LETTER OF GEN. OUDINOT,
Intended for the Roman Constituent Assembly, the Triumvirate, the Generalissimo, and the Commander-in-Chief of the National Guard.

SIGR. GENERAL: The events of war have, as you know, conducted the French army to the gates of Rome.

Should the entrance into the city remain closed against us, I should see myself constrained to employ immediately all the means of action that France has placed in my hands.

---

[1] First published as "Things and Thoughts in Europe. No. XXXI" in *New-York Daily Tribune*, 23 July 1849, p. 1:2–4.

Before having recourse to such terrible necessity, I think it my duty to make a last appeal to a people that cannot have toward France sentiments of hostility.

The Roman army wishes, no doubt, equally with myself, to spare bloody ruin to the Capital of the Christian world.

With this conviction, I pray you, Sigr. General, to give the inclosed proclamation the most speedy publicity. If twelve hours after this dispatch shall have been delivered to you, an answer corresponding to the honor and the intentions of France shall not have reached me, I shall be constrained to give the forcible attack. Accept, &c.

VILLA PAMFILI, 12th June, 1849.—5 P.M.

(He was in fact at Villa Santucci, much further out, but would not be content without falsifying his date as well as all his statements.)

PROCLAMATION.

INHABITANTS OF ROME: We did not come to bring you war. We came to sustain among you order, with liberty. The intentions of our Government have been misunderstood. The labors of the siege have conducted us under your walls. Till now we have wished every now and then to answer the fire of your batteries. We approach these last moments when the necessities of war burst out in terrible calamities. Spare them to a city full of so many glorious memories.

If you persist in repelling us, on you alone will fall the responsibility of irreparable disasters.

The following are the answers of the various functionaries to whom this letter was sent:

ANSWER OF THE ASSEMBLY.

GENERAL: The Roman Constitutional Assembly informs you, in reply to your dispatch of yesterday, that having concluded a Convention from the 31st May, 1849, with M. de Lesseps, Minister Plenipotentiary of the French Republic, a Convention which we confirmed soon after your protest, it must consider that Convention obligatory for both parties, and indeed the safeguard of the rights of nations until it has been ratified or declined by the Government of France. Therefore the Assembly must regard as a violation of that Convention every hostile act of the French army since the above named 31st May, and all others that shall take place before the resolution of your Government can be made known, and before the expiration of the time agreed upon for the armistice. You demand, General, an answer correspondent to the intentions and power of France.

Nothing could be more conformable to the intentions and power of France than to cease a flagrant violation of the rights of nations.

Whatever may be the results of such violation, the people of Rome are not responsible for them. It is strong in the right, decided to maintain the conventions which attach it to your nation; only it finds itself constrained by the necessity of self-defense to repel unjust aggressions. Accept, &c., for the Assembly the President, GALLETTI.

Secretaries, FABRETTI, PANNACCHI, COCCHI.

ANSWER OF THE COMMANDER IN CHIEF OF THE NATIONAL GUARD.

GENERAL—The treaty, of which we await the ratification, assures this tranquil city from every disaster.

The National Guard, destined to maintain order, has the duty of seconding the resolutions of the Government; willingly and zealously it fulfills this duty, not caring for annoyance and fatigue.

The National Guard showed very lately when it escorted the prisoners sent back to you, its sympathy for France, but it shows also on every occasion a supreme regard for its own dignity, for the honor of Rome.

Every misfortune to the capital of the Catholic world, to the monumental city, must be attributed not to the pacific citizens constrained to defend themselves, but solely to its aggressors.

Accept, &c. STURBINETTI.

General of the National Guard, Representative of the People.

ANSWER OF THE GENERALISSIMO.

CITIZEN GENERAL: A fatality leads to conflict between the armies of two Republics, whom a better destiny would have invited to combat against their common enemy—for the enemies of the one cannot fail to be also enemies of the other.

We are not deceived, and shall combat by every means in our power whomsoever assails our institutions, and only the brave are worthy to stand beside the French soldiers.

Reflecting that there is a state of life worse than death, if the war you wage should put us in that state, it will be better to close our eyes for ever than to see the interminable oppressions of our country. I wish you well and desire fraternity. ROSSELLI.

ANSWER OF THE TRIUMVIRATE.

We have the honor to transmit to you the answer of the Assembly.

We never break our promises. We have promised to defend, in execution of orders, from the Assembly and People of Rome, the banner of the

Republic, the honor of the country and the sanctity of the Capital of the Christian world; this promise we shall maintain. Accept, &c.

The Triumvirs,

ARMELLINI.

MAZZINI.

SAFFI.

Observe the miserable evasion of this missive of Oudinot. "The fortune of war has conducted us." What war! He pretended to come as a friend, a protector; is enraged only because, after his deceits at Città Vecchia, Rome will not trust him within her walls. For this he daily sacrifices hundreds of lives. "The Roman People cannot be hostile to the French!" No, indeed; they were not disposed to be so. They had been stirred to emulation by the example of France. They had warmly hoped in her as their true ally. It required all that Oudinot has done to turn their faith to contempt and aversion.

Cowardly man! He knows now that he comes upon a city which wishes to receive him only as a friend, and he cries, "With my cannon—with my bombs, I will compel you to let me betray you."

The conduct of France—infamous enough before—looks tenfold blacker now that while the so-called Plenipotentiary is absent with the treaty to be ratified, her army daily assails Rome—assails in vain. After receiving these answers to his letter and proclamation, Oudinot turned all the force of his cannonade to make a breach, and began, what no one, even in these days, has believed possible, the bombardment of Rome.[2]

Yes! the French, who pretend to be the advanced guard of civilization, are bombarding Rome. They dare take the risk of destroying the richest bequests made to man by the great Past. Nay, they seem to do it in an especially barbarous manner. It was thought they would avoid, as much as possible, the hospitals for the wounded, marked to their view by the black banner, and the sides where are the most precious monuments; but several bombs have fallen on the chief hospital, and the Capitol evidently is especially aimed at. They made a

---

[2] During the month of June, Fuller had lived in great anxiety and fear about the safety of Ossoli, her child, and herself. In her letters to friends, she speaks constantly of the terrors of Rome under siege. She had given the Storys the details of the birth of Angelino and asked them to take care of him in the event of her death (Hudspeth 5:236). She wrote to Emerson of the new routine in her life: "Since the 30th April, I go almost daily to the hospitals, and, though I have suffered,—for I had no idea before, how terrible gunshot-wounds and wound-fever are,—yet I have taken pleasure, and great pleasure, in being with the men; there is scarcely one who is not moved by a noble spirit. Many, especially among the Lombards, are the flower of the Italian youth. When they begin to get better, I carry them books, and flowers; they read, and we talk" (Hudspeth 5:239).

breach in the wall,[3] but it was immediately filled up with a barricade, and all the week they have been repulsed in every attempt they made to gain ground, though with considerable loss of life on our side; on theirs it must be great, but how great we cannot know.

Ponte Malle, the scene of Raphael's fresco of a battle, in the Vatican, saw again a fierce struggle last Friday. More than fifty were brought wounded into Rome.

But wounds and assaults only fire more and more the courage of her defenders. They feel the justice of their cause, and the peculiar iniquity of this aggression. In proportion as there seems little aid to be hoped from man they seem to claim it from God. The noblest sentiments are heard from every lip, and, thus far, their acts amply correspond. The eve of the bombardment one or two officers went round with a fine band. It played in the piazzas the Marseillaise and Roman marches, and when the people were thus assembled they were told of the proclamation, and asked how they felt. Many shouted loudly, *Guerra, viva la repubblica Romana!* Afterward, bands of young men went round singing the chorus,

> "Vogliamo sempre quella,
> Vogliamo Libertà."

("We want always one thing; we want Liberty.") Guitars played, and some danced. When the bombs began to come, one of the Trasteverines, those noble images of the old Roman race, redeemed her claim to that descent by seizing one and extinguishing the match. She received a medal and a reward in money. A soldier did the same at Palazzo Spada, where is the statue of Pompey, at whose base great Caesar fell. He was promoted. Immediately the people were seized with emulation; armed with pans of wet clay they ran wherever the bombs fell, to extinguish them. Women collect the balls from the hostile cannon and carry them to ours. As very little injury has come to life in this way, the people cry, "Madonna protects us against the bombs; she wills not for Rome to be destroyed."

Meanwhile many poor people are driven from their homes, and provisions are growing very dear. The heats are now terrible for us, and must be far more so for the French. It is said a vast number are ill of fever; indeed it cannot be otherwise. Oudinot himself has it, and perhaps this is one explanation of the mixture of violence and weakness in his actions.

---

[3] Extensive efforts were made to seal off the city of Rome from the French. The existing walls were reinforced with barricades and brigades of soldiers were established at all of the most sensitive areas (Maurice 473–88).

He must be deeply ashamed at the poor result to his bad acts, that at the end of two weeks and so much bravado, he has done nothing to Rome, unless intercept provisions, kill some of her brave youth, and injure churches which should be sacred to him as to us. St Maria Trastevere, that ancient church so full of precious remains, and which had an air of mild repose more beautiful than almost any other, is said to have suffered particularly.[4]

As to the men who die, I share the impassioned sorrow of the Triumvirs. "O Frenchmen!" they wrote, "could you know what men you destroy. —*They* are no mercenaries, like those who fill your ranks, but the flower of the Italian youth, and the noblest souls of age. When you shall know of what minds you have robbed the world, how ought you to repent and mourn!"

This is especially true of the "Emigrant and Garibaldi legions." The misfortunes of North and South Italy, the conscription which compels to the service of tyranny all that remain, has driven from the Kingdom of Naples and from Lombardy all the brave and noble youth.[5] Many are in Venice or Rome, the forlorn hope of Italy. Radetzky, every day more cruel, now impresses aged men and the fathers of large families. He carries them with him in chains, determined, if he cannot have good troops to send into Hungary, at least to revenge himself on the unhappy Lombards.

Many of these young men, students from Pisa, Pavia, Padua and the Roman University, lie wounded in the hospitals, for naturally they rushed first in the combat. One kissed an arm which was cut off; another preserves pieces of bone which are being painfully extracted from his wound, as reliques of the best days of his life. —The older men, many of whom have been saddened by exile and disappointment, less glowing, are not less resolved. A spirit burns noble as ever animated the most precious facts we treasure from the heroic age. I suffer to see these temples of the soul thus broken, to see the fever-weary days and painful operations undergone by these noble men, these true priests of a higher hope, but I would not, for much, have missed seeing it at all. The memory will con-

---

[4] Fuller had written to Elizabeth Hoar that "the state of siege is very terrible, such continual alarms, then to hear the cannonade day and night and to know with every shot, some fellow man may be bleeding and dying. Sometimes I cannot sleep, sometimes I do again from sheer exhaustion. I did think, since this world was so full of ill, I was willing to see it all. I did not want to be cowardly and shut my eyes. Nor is this perpetual murder of men so bad as to see them indolently lying in the mud. The sad night is cheered by sparklings of pure fire. Yet it *is* very sad, and oh, Rome, *my* Rome, every day more and more desecrated! One of the most gentle hallowed haunts, La Maria di Trastevere, is I hear almost ruined by the bombs of day before yesterday. Almost nightly I see burning some fair cascine. Adieu, dear Lizzie, prize the thoughtful peace of Concord" (Hudspeth 5:241).

[5] The presence in Rome of revolutionaries who had fought unsuccessfully in the north against Austria was the basis for charges that "foreigners come from all parts of Italy" were oppressing the people of Rome (Trevelyan 107).

sole amid the spectacles of meanness, selfishness and faithlessness which life may yet have in store for the pilgrim.[6]

June 23.—Matters verge to a crisis. The French Government sustains Oudinot and disclaims Lesseps. Harmonious throughout, shameless in falsehood, it seems Oudinot knew that the mission of Lesseps was at an end, when he availed himself of his pacific promises to occupy Monte Mario.—When the Romans were anxious at seeing French troops move in that direction, Lesseps said it was only done to occupy them, and conjured the Romans to avoid all collision which might prevent his success with the Treaty. The sham treaty was concluded the 30th, a detachment of French having occupied Monte Mario the night of the 29th, Oudinot flies into a rage and refuses to sign; M. Lesseps goes off to Paris; meanwhile, the brave Oudinot attacks the 3d, after writing to the French Consul that he should not till the 4th, to leave time for the foreigners remaining to retire. He attacked in the night, was possessing himself of Villa Pamfili, as he had of Monte Mario, by treachery and surprise.

Meanwhile, M. Lesseps arrives in Paris, to find himself seemingly or really in great disgrace with the would-be Emperor and his cabinet.[7] To give reason for this, M. Drouyn de Lhuys,[8] who had publicly declared to the Assembly that M. Lesseps had no instructions except from the report of the sitting of 7th May, shamefully publishes a letter of special instructions, hemming him in on every side, which M. Lesseps, the "Plenipotentiary," dares not disown.

What are we to think of a great nation, whose leading men are such barefaced liars? M. Guizot finds his creed faithfully followed up.

The liberal party in France does what it can to wash its hands of this offense, but it seems too weak and unlikely to render effectual service at this crisis.[9]

---

[6] Despite these public, brave words, Fuller was suffering increasingly private distress over the events in Rome. To Ellen Fuller Channing, she wrote: "The world seems to go so strangely wrong! The bad side triumphs; the blood and tears of the generous flow in vain. I assist at many saddest scenes, and suffer for those whom I knew not before. Those whom I knew and loved,—who, if they had triumphed, would have opened for me an easier, broader, higher higher-mounting road,—are every day more and more involved in earthly ruin. Eternity is with us, but there is much darkness and bitterness in this portion of it. A baleful star rose on my birth, and its hostility, I fear, will never be disarmed while I walk below" (Hudspeth 5:242).

[7] Fuller's suspicions about Louis-Napoleon were well founded; in December 1851 he staged his coup d'état and in December 1852 made himself Emperor Napoleon III.

[8] Edouard Drouyn de Lhuys (1805–81), a diplomat and politician, was a protégé of Guizot. He was, for a short time, minister of foreign affairs, following Guizot's dismissal in 1848 (*Grande Larousse encyclopédique,* 20 vols. [Paris: Librairie Larousse, 1961]).

[9] Republicans and socialists in France were unanimously opposed to Louis-Napoleon's Italian policy, but the June 13 insurrections they staged to protest the siege of Rome were quickly suppressed, and harsh reprisals followed (Fejtö 103).

Venice, Rome, Ancona are the last strong holds of hope, and they cannot stand forever thus unsustained. Night before last a tremendous cannonade left no moment to sleep, even had the anxious hearts of mothers and wives been able to crave it. At morning a little detachment of French had entered by the breach of St. Pancrazio and entrenched itself in a vineyard.—Another has possession of Villa Poniatowski, close to Porta del Popolo, and attacks and alarms are hourly to be expected. I would like to see the final ones, dreadful as those hours may be, since now there seems no hope from delay. Men are daily slain, and this state of suspense is agonizing.

In the evening 'tis pretty, though a terror, to see the bombs, fiery meteors, springing from the horizon line upon their bright path to do their wicked message.'Twould not be so bad, meeems, to die of one of these, as wait to have every drop of pure blood, every child-like radiant hope, drained and driven from the heart by the betrayals of nations and of individuals, till at last the sickened eyes refuse more to open to that light which shines daily on such pits of iniquity. ★

Dispatch 34

BOMBARDMENT AND DEFEAT

ROME, July 6, 1849 [1]

If I mistake not, I closed my last letter just as the news arrived here that the attempt of the Democratic party in France to resist the infamous proceedings of the Government had failed, and thus Rome, as far as human calculation went, had not a hope for her liberties left. An inland city cannot long sustain a siege when there is no hope of aid. Then followed the news of the surrender of Ancona, and Rome found herself quite alone—for, though Venice continued to hold out, all communication was cut off.

The Republican troops, almost to a man, left Ancona, but a long march separated them from Rome.

The extreme heat of these days was far more fatal to the Romans than their assailants, for, as fast as the French troops sickened, their place was taken by fresh arrivals. Ours also not only sustained the exhausting service by day, but were harrassed at night by attacks, feigned or real.—These commonly began about 11 or 12 o'clock at night, just when all who meant to rest were fairly asleep. I can imagine the harassing effect upon the troops, from what I feel in my sheltered pavilion, in consequence of not knowing a quiet night's sleep for a month.

[1] First published as "Things and Thoughts in Europe. No. XXXIII" in *New-York Daily Tribune*, 11 August 1849, p. 2:5–7.

The bombardment became constantly more serious. The house where I live was filled as early as the 20th with persons obliged to fly from the *Piazza di Gesù,* where the fiery rain fell thickest. The night of the 21st–22d, we were all alarmed about 2 o'clock A.M. by a tremendous cannonade. It was the moment when the breach was finally made by which the French entered.—They rushed in, and, I grieve to say, that by the only instance of defection known in the course of the siege, those companies of the regiment Union, which had in charge a casino on that point, yielded to panic and abandoned it. The French immediately entered and intrenched themselves. That was the fatal hour for the city. Every day afterward, though obstinately resisted, they gained, till at last, their cannon being well placed, the city was entirely commanded from the Janiculum, and all thought of further resistance was idle.

This was true policy to avoid the street fight, in which the Italian, an unpracticed soldier, but full of feeling and sustained from the houses, would have been no match for their disciplined troops. After the 22d, the slaughter of the Romans became every day more fearful. Their defenses were knocked down by the heavy cannon of the French, and, entirely exposed in their valorous onsets, great numbers perished on the spot. Those who were brought into the Hospitals were generally grievously wounded, very commonly subjects for amputation. My heart bled daily more and more at these sights, and I could not feel much for myself, though now the balls and bombs began to fall round me also. The night of the 28th the effect was truly fearful, as they whizzed and burst near me. As many as 30 fell upon or near the *Hotel de Russie,* where Mr. Cass has his temporary abode. The roof of the studio in the pavilion, tenanted by Mr. Stermer, well known to the visitors of Rome, for his highly-finished cabinet pictures, was torn to pieces. I sat alone in my much-exposed apartment thinking "if one strikes me, I only hope it will kill me at once, and that God will transport my soul to some sphere where Virtue and Love are not tyrannized over by egotism and brute force, as in this." However, that night passed; the next, we had reason to expect a still more fiery salute to the Pincian, as here alone remained three or four pieces of cannon which could be used. But the morning of the 30th, in a contest at the foot of the Janiculum, the line, old Papal troops, naturally not in earnest like the free corps, refused to fight against odds so terrible, the heroic Manara[2] fell, with hundreds of his devoted Lombards. Garibaldi saw his best officers perish, and himself went in the afternoon to say to the Assembly that further resistance was unavailing.[3]

[2] Luciano Manara (1825–49), an aristocrat of Milan, had distinguished himself in the "Five Days" of street warfare that drove the Austrians from his city. In the spring of 1849 he led the Lombard brigade of six hundred volunteers to Rome and became an important officer under Garibaldi. He died at Villa Spada (Trevelyan 119; Zorzi 361).

[3] The Republic of Rome fell on 1 July 1849.

The Assembly sent to Oudinot, but he refused any conditions, refused even to guarantee a safe departure to Garibaldi, his brave foe. Notwithstanding, a great number of men left the other regiments to follow the leader, whose courage had captivated them and whose habit of superiority to difficulties commanded their entire confidence. Toward the evening of Monday, 2d July, it was known that the French were preparing to cross the river and take possession of all the city. I went into the Corso with some friends; it was filled with citizens and military, the carriage was stopped by the crowd near the Doria palace; the lancers of Garibaldi galloped along in full career, I longed for Sir Walter Scott to be on earth again, and see them; all are light, athletic, resolute figures, many of the forms of the finest manly beauty of the South, all sparkling with its genius and ennobled by the resolute spirit, ready to dare, to do, to die. We followed them to the piazza of St. John Lateran. Never have I seen a sight so beautiful, so romantic and so sad. Whoever knows Rome knows the peculiar solemn grandeur of that piazza, scene of the first triumph of Rienzi, the magnificence of the "mother of all churches," the Baptistery with its porphyry columns, the Santa Scala with its glittering mosaics of the early ages, the obelisk standing fairest of any of those most imposing monuments of Rome, the view through the gates of the Campagna, on that side so richly strewn with ruins. The sun was setting, the crescent moon rising, the flower of the Italian youth were marshaling in that solemn place. They had been driven from every other spot where they had offered their hearts as bulwarks of Italian Independence; in this last strong hold they had sacrificed hecatombs of their best and bravest in that cause; they must now go or remain prisoners and slaves. *Where* go, they knew not, for except distant Hungary there is not now a spot which would receive them, or where they can act as honor commands. They had all put on the beautiful dress of the Garibaldi legion, the tunic of bright red cloth, the Greek cap, or else round hat with Puritan plume, their long hair was blown back from resolute faces; all looked full of courage; they had counted the cost before they entered on this perilous struggle; they had weighed life and all its material advantages against Liberty, and made their election; they turned not back, nor flinched at this bitter crisis. I saw the wounded, all that could go, laden upon their baggage cars, some were already pale and fainting, still they wished to go. I saw many youths, born to rich inheritance, carrying in a handkerchief all their worldly goods; the women were ready, their eyes too were resolved, if sad. The wife of Garibaldi followed him horseback, he himself was distinguished by the white bournouse;[4] his look was entirely that of a hero of the middle ages, his face still young, for the excite-

---

[4] Garibaldi wore a white tunic, setting himself apart from the men of his legion, who wore red.

ments of his life, though so many, have all been youthful, and there is no fatigue upon his brow or cheek. Fall or stand, one sees in him a man engaged in the career for which he is adapted by nature. He went upon the parapet and looked upon the road with a spy-glass, and, no obstruction being in sight, he turned his face for a moment back upon Rome, then led the way through the gate. Hard was the heart, stony and seared the eye that had no tear for that moment. Go! fated, gallant band, and if God care not indeed for men as for the sparrows, most of ye go forth to perish.[5] And Rome, anew the Niobe! Must she lose also these beautiful and brave that promised her regeneration and would have given it, but for the perfidy, the overpowering force of the foreign intervention.

I know that many "respectable" gentlemen would be surprised to hear me speak in this way. Gentlemen who perform their "duties to society" by buying for themselves handsome clothes and furniture with the interest of their money, speak of Garibaldi and his men as "brigands" and "vagabonds." Such are they, doubtless, in the same sense as Jesus, Eneas and Moses were. To me men who can throw so slightly aside the ease of wealth, the joys of affection, for the sake of what they deem honor, in whatsoever form, are the "respectable." No doubt there are in these bands a number of men of lawless minds, and who follow this banner only because there is for them no other path. But the greater part are the noble youths who have fled from the Austrian conscription, or fly now from the renewal of the Papal suffocation, darkened by the French protection.

As for the protectors, they entirely threw aside the mask, as it was always supposed they would, the moment they had possession of Rome.

I do not know whether they were really so bewildered by their priestly coun-

---

[5] Garibaldi left Rome on 2 July 1849 with four thousand men. His goal was Venice. On the northward march, his troops covered more than five hundred miles, through mountainous terrain, with the Austrian, French, Spanish, and Neapolitan armies in pursuit. The hardships of the march and skirmishes with the enemy reduced his ranks, and on 31 July he reached the small republic of San Marino with 1,500 men. He there dissolved his army, and in the night with 250 of his staunchest followers slipped through the Austrian lines and set sail for Venice in thirteen fishing boats. On the night of 2 August the Austrian fleet captured eight of the boats, but Garibaldi with the other five made it ashore near Magnavacca. In the marshes of Comacchio he divided his men into two groups, the better to elude the Austrians, but one group was captured immediately and all of the men executed on the spot. Among those still with Garibaldi was his wife, Anita, who died on 4 August in a peasant's house where they had taken shelter in the swamps. Garibaldi then crossed the Apennines into Piedmont with one follower, Major Culiolo, and eventually made his way to London and then New York City. After ten years of exile, he returned to Italy and with his Thousand Redshirts united Italy under the rule of King Victor Emmanuel II (1820–78), Charles Albert's son (Andrea Viotti, *Garibaldi: The Revolutionary and His Men* [Dorset: Blandford Press, 1979], 68–69).

cilors as to imagine they would be well received in a city which they had bombarded, and where twelve hundred men were lying wounded by their assault. To say nothing of the justice or injustice of the matter, it could not be supposed that the Roman people, if it had any sense of dignity, would welcome them. However, I was not out, as what countenance I have I would not give on such an occasion; but an English lady, my friend, told me they seemed to look expectingly for the strong party of friends they had always pretended to have within the walls. The French officers looked up to the windows for ladies, and she being the only one they saw, saluted her. She made no reply. They then passed into the Corso. Many were assembled, the softer Romans being unable to control a curiosity the Milanese would have disclaimed, but preserving an icy silence. In an evil hour, a foolish priest dared to break it by the cry of *Viva Pio Nono.* The populace, roused to fury, rushed on him with their knives. He was much wounded; one or two others were killed in the rush. The people howled, then, and hissed at the French, who advancing their bayonets, and clearing the way before them, fortified themselves in the piazzas. Next day the French troops were marched to and fro through Rome to inspire awe into the people, but it has only created a disgust amounting to loathing, to see that, with such an imposing force, and in great part fresh, the French were not ashamed to use bombs also, and kill women and children in their beds. Oudinot, then, seeing the feeling of the people, and finding they pursued as a spy any man who so much as showed the way to his soldiers—that the Italians went out of the cafés if Frenchmen entered; in short, that the people regarded him and his followers in the same light as the Austrians, has declared the state of siege in Rome—the Press is stifled—everybody is to be in the house at 9½ P.M. and, whoever in any way insults his men, or puts any obstacle in their way, is to be shot.

The fruits of all this will be the same as elsewhere: temporary repression will sow the seeds of perpetual resistance; and never was Rome in so fair a way to be educated for the Republican form of Government as now.

Especially could nothing be more irritating for an Italian population, in the month of July, than to drive them to their homes at half-past nine. After the insupportable heat of the day, their only enjoyment and refreshment is found in evening walks, and chats together as they sit before their cafés, or in groups outside some friendly door. Now they must hurry home when the drum beats at 9 o'clock. They are forbidden to stand or sit in groups, and this by their bombarding *protector!* Comment is unnecessary.

French soldiers are daily missing; of some it is known that they have been killed by the Trasteverini for daring to make court to their women.—Of more than a hundred and fifty, it is only known that they cannot be found; and in two days of French "order" more acts of violence have been committed than in two months under the Triumvirate.

The French have taken up their quarters in the court-yards of the Quirinal and Venetian Palaces, which are full of the wounded, many of whom have
been driven well nigh mad, and their burning wounds exasperated by the sound
of their drums and trumpets—the constant sense of their insulting presence.
The wounded have been warned to leave the Quirinal at the end of eight days,
though there are many who cannot be moved from bed to bed without causing
them great anguish and peril, nor is it known that any other place has been provided as a hospital for them. At the palace of Venice the French have searched
for three emigrants that they wished to imprison, even in the apartments where
the wounded were lying; they ran their bayonets into the matresses; they have
taken for themselves beds given by the Romans to the hospital—not public
property, but private gift. The hospital of Santo Spirito was a Governmental
establishment and, in using a part of it for the wounded, its director, Mon-
signore, had been retained, because he had the reputation of being honest and
not illiberal. But as soon as the French entered he, with true priestly baseness,
sent away the women nurses, saying he had no longer money to pay them—
transported the wounded into a miserable, airless basement, that had before
been used as a granary and appropriated the good apartments to the use of the
French!

July 8.—The report of this morning is that the French yesterday violated
the domicile of our Consul, Mr. Brown, pretending to search for persons hidden there; that Mr. Brown, banner in one hand and sword in the other, repelled
the assault, and fairly drove them down stairs; that then he made them an appropriate speech, though in a mixed language of English, French and Italian;
that the crowd vehemently applauded Mr. Brown, who already was much liked
for the warm sympathy he had shown the Romans in their aspirations and their
distresses; that he then donned his uniform and went to Oudinot to make his
protest. How this was received I know not, but understand Mr. B. departed
with his family yesterday evening.

Will America look as coldly on the insult to herself as she has on the struggle
of this injured people?

To-day an edict is out to disarm the National Guard. The generous "protectors" wish to take all the trouble upon themselves. Rome is full of them; at every
step are met groups in the uniform of France, with faces bronzed in the African war,[6] and so stultified by a life without enthusiasm and without thought,
that I do not believe Napoleon would recognize them as French soldiers.—The
effect of their appearance compared with that of the Italian free corps is that

---

[6] Since 1830 the French had occupied Algiers. Their campaign to conquer northern Algeria lasted from 1834 until 1847, when they defeated the Algerian leader Abd al-Qadir. In
1848 Algeria was declared a French colony (*New Cambridge Modern History* 10:7, 424, 461).

of body as compared with spirit. It is easy to see how they could be used to purposes so contrary to the legitimate policy of France, for they do not look more intellectual, more fitted to have opinions of their own, than the Austrian soldiery.

July 10.—The plot thickens. The exact facts with regard to the invasion of Mr. Brown's house, I have not been able to ascertain. I suppose they will be published, as Oudinot has promised to satisfy Mr. Cass. I must add in reference to what I wrote sometime ago of the position of our envoy here, that the kind and sympathetic course of Mr. Cass toward the Republicans in these troubles, his very gentlemanly and courteous bearing, have from the minds of most removed all unpleasant feelings. They see that his position was very peculiar; sent to the Papal Government, finding here the Republican, and just at that moment violently assailed. Unless he had extraordinary powers he naturally felt obliged to communicate further with our Government before acknowledging this. I shall always regret, however, that he did not stand free to occupy the high position that belonged to the representative of the United States at that moment, and peculiarly because it was by a Republic that the Roman Republic was betrayed.—But, as I say, the plot thickens. Yesterday three families were carried to prison because a boy crowed like a cock at the French soldiery from the windows of the house they occupied. Another, because a man pursued took refuge in their court-yard. Yesterday, the city being most disarmed, came the edict to take down the arms of the Republic, "emblems of anarchy." But worst of all they have done is an edict commanding all foreigners who had been in the service of the Republican Government to leave Rome within twenty-four hours. This is the most infamous thing done yet, as it drives to desperation those who stayed because they had so many to go with and no place to go to, or because their relatives lie wounded here: no others wished to remain in Rome under present circumstances.

I am sick of breathing the same air with men capable of a part so utterly cruel and false. As soon as I can I shall take refuge in the mountains, if it be possible to find an obscure nook unpervaded by these convulsions.[7] Let not my friends be surprised if they do not hear from me for some time. I may not feel like writing. I have seen too much sorrow, and alas! without power to aid. It makes me sick to see the palaces and streets of Rome full of these injurious foreigners, and to see the already changed aspect of her population. The men of Rome had begun, filled with new hopes, to develop unknown energy—they walked quick, their

---

[7] In a letter of ca. 8 July 1849, Fuller wrote to Cass, asking for his assistance in providing the means for her to leave Rome. He was able to arrange a carriage and horses, and Fuller left Rome for Rieti and a reunion with her son shortly after 10 July (Hudspeth 5:243, 244).

eyes sparkled, they delighted in duty, in responsibility; in a year of such life their effeminacy would have been vanquished—now, dejectedly, unemployed, they lounge along the streets, feeling that all the implements of labor, all the ensigns of hope, have been snatched from them. Their hands fall slack, their eyes rove aimless, the beggars begin to swarm again, and the black ravens who delight in the night of ignorance, the slumber of sloth, as the only sureties for their rule, emerge daily more and more frequent from their hiding places.[8]

The following Address has been circulated from hand to hand:

TO THE PEOPLE OF ROME.

Misfortune, brothers, has fallen upon us anew. But it is trial of brief duration—it is the stone of the sepulcher which we shall throw away after three days, rising victorious and renewed, an immortal Nation. For with us are God and Justice—God and Justice, who cannot die, but always triumph, while Kings and Popes, once dead, revive no more.

As you have been great in the combat, be so in the days of sorrow— great in your conduct as citizens, of generous disdain, of sublime silence. Silence is the weapon we have now to use against the Cossacks of France and the Priests, their masters.

In the streets do not look at them; do not answer if they address you.

In the cafés, in the eating-houses, if they enter, rise and go out.

Let your windows remain closed as they pass.

Never attend their feasts, their parades.

The harmony of their musical bands be for you tones of slavery, and, when you hear them, fly.

Let the liberticide soldier be condemned to isolation; let him atone in solitude and contempt for having served priests and kings.

And you, Roman women—master-piece of God's work!—deign no look, no smile to those satellites of an abhorred Pope! Cursed be she who, before the odious satellites of Austria, forgets that she is Italian! Her name shall be published for the execration of all her people! And even the courtezans! let them show love for their country, and thus regain the dignity of citizens!

And our word of order, our cry of reunion and emancipation, be now and ever, VIVA LA REPUBLICA!

This incessant cry, which not even French slaves can dispute, shall pre-pare us to administer the bequest of our martyrs, shall be consoling dew to the immaculate and holy bones that repose, sublime holocaust of faith

---

[8] Fuller alludes to the Jesuits.

and of love, near our walls, and make doubly divine the Eternal City. In this cry we shall find ourselves always brothers, and we shall conquer. Viva Rome, the Capital of Italy! Viva the Italy of the People! Viva the Roman Republic!   A ROMAN.

Dated *Rome, July 4,* 1849.

For this day's anniversary, so joyously celebrated in our land, was that of the entrance of the French into Rome.

I know not whether the Romans will follow out this programme with constancy as the sterner Milanese have done. If they can, it will draw upon them endless persecutions, countless exactions, but at once educate and prove them worthy of a nobler life.

Yesterday I went over the scene of conflict. It was fearful even to *see* the casinos *Quattro Venti* and *Vascello* where the French and Romans had been several days so near one another, all shattered to pieces, with fragments of rich stucco and painting still sticking to rafters between the great holes made by the cannonade, and think that men had stayed and fought in them when only a mass of ruins. The French, indeed, were entirely sheltered the last days; to my unpracticed eyes the extent and thoroughness of their works seemed miraculous, and gave me first clear idea of the incompetency of the Italians to resist organized armies. I saw their commanders had not even known enough of the art of war to understand how the French were conducting the siege. —It is true their resources were at any rate inadequate to resistance; only continual sorties would have arrested the progress of the foe, and to make them and man the wall their forces were inadequate. I was struck more than ever by the heroic valor of *ours,* let me say, as I have said all along, for go where I may, a large part of my heart will ever remain in Italy. I hope her children will always acknowledge me as a sister, though I drew not my first breath here. A contadini showed me where thirty-seven braves are buried beneath a heap of wall that fell upon them in the shock of one cannonade. A marble nymph, with broken arm, looked sadly that way from her sun-dried fountain, some roses were blooming still, some red oleanders amid the ruin. The sun was casting its last light on the mountains on the tranquil, sad Campagna, that sees one leaf turned more in the book of Woe. This was in the Vascello. I then entered the French ground, all mapped and hollowed like a honey-comb. A pair of skeleton legs protruded from a bank of one barricade; lower a dog had scratched away its light covering of earth from the body of a man, and discovered it lying face upward all dressed; the dog stood gazing on it with an air of stupid amazement. I thought at that moment, recalling some letters received, "O men and women of America, spared these frightful sights, these sudden wrecks of every hope, what angel of Heaven do

you suppose has time to listen to your tales of morbid woe? If any find leisure
to work for men to-day, think you not they have enough to do to care for the
victims here."

I see you have meetings, where you speak of the Italians, the Hungarians. I
pray you *do something*; let it not end in a mere cry of sentiment. That is better
than to sneer at all that is liberal, like the English; than to talk of the holy
victims of patriotism as "anarchists" and "brigands,"—but it is not enough.
It ought not to content your consciences. Do you owe no tithe to Heaven for
the privileges it has showered on you, for whose achievement so many here suffer and perish daily? Deserve to retain them, by helping your fellow-men to
acquire them. Our Government must abstain from interference, but private
action is practicable, is due. For Italy, it is in this moment too late, but all that
helps Hungary helps her also, helps all who wish the freedom of men from an
hereditary yoke now become intolerable. Send money, send cheer—acknowledge as the legitimate leaders and rulers those men who represent the people,
who understand its wants, who are ready to die or to live for its good. Kossuth
I know not, but his people recognize him;[9] Manin I know not, but with what
firm nobleness, what persevering virtue, he has acted for Venice!—Mazzini I
know, the man and his acts, great, pure and constant,—a man to whom only
the next age can do justice, as it reaps the harvest of the seed he has sown in
this.[10]—Friends, countrymen, and lovers of virtue, lovers of freedom, lovers of
truth!—be on the alert; rest not supine in your easier lives, but remember

"Mankind is one,
And beats with one great heart."

[9] Kossuth delivered a fiery speech against Austrian hegemony in the Hungarian Diet
on 3 March 1848, which inflamed the students' demonstrations in Vienna and led to the
demand for a constitution from Emperor Ferdinand I. In October 1848 Kossuth and his
peoples' army drove Austrian imperial troops out of his country . Elected governor of the
newly proclaimed Hungarian Republic in April 1849, Kossuth fought with his countrymen
against overwhelming military odds; in August 1849 the republican forces were defeated by
the combined armies of Austria and Russia (Reynolds 154).

[10] After the French entered Rome and the fate of the republic was sealed, Mazzini
escaped to England. From London he planned new attempts at uprisings at Mantua in 1852,
at Milan in 1853, and at Genoa and Leghorn in 1857. With Kossuth he founded the Republican European Association and the Society of Friends of Italy. In 1861 he greeted the
news of the establishment of a unified kingdom of Italy with little joy; he continued to work
for a unified republic and refused a seat in the Italian parliament in protest. In 1870 he was
arrested and imprisoned at Gaeta. He died at Pisa on 10 March 1872 (*Chambers's Biographical
Dictionary*).

Dispatch 35

A R E T R O S P E C T

To write from Italy is now become a sorrowful business.[2] Yet I will send a few words, which may, at least, serve to contradict the falsehoods promulgated by the now enslaved and hireling press.

Order reigns—the same Order that reigned at Warsaw. Russian-Austrian clemency is yielded to those who remain to share it; those who would not, in honor could not, remain to live a lie all day, and weep alone at night, are sunk with cannon at the bottom of the sea—shot here and there, when caught, or driven from port to port, the noblest mendicants, except the Poles, the saddest exiles, since Troy fell. Yet triumph not, Oppressors! The exiles of Ilium founded a new world, and were the parents of all that is good on this very soil. He that had not where to lay His head,—His Apostles, driven from place to place even thus, scattered the seeds of doctrine, and conquered the world.

The French have not redeemed one pretext by which they painted over the ugly face of their perfidy. They have as yet obtained no guaranty whatever for the Roman People. Oudinot is put off with medals, flowery speeches, and visits to some shrine of Maria Santissima for whom he professes peculiar devotion. Meanwhile the priests rule, and as injudiciously as their worst foes could desire. Oudinot has only the consolation of uttering manifestoes, in which he proclaims that he has restored Order and Liberty. But the impudent falsehood of a man who pretends he has "put an end to the reign of terror," when Rome, even despoiled of all her brave youth, could hardly be kept down by main force when the discount was made on paper money, neither deceives himself nor the world. Facts are obstinate things. Oh Princes! Prelates! you may exile the brave; you may stifle them in prisons; you may invent crimes for them; you may talk of

---

[1] First published as "Italy" in *New-York Weekly Tribune,* 6 October 1849, p. 2:1–2. This letter was not included in *AHA.*

[2] Fuller had left Rome in mid-July and was living at Rieti with her son, whom she had found deathly ill. She had also just heard about the death of Pickie Greeley from his desolate father. In her letter of condolence to Greeley, Fuller told of leaving Rome and seeing her son again: "When at last we left, our dearest friends laid low, our fortunes finally ruined, and every hope for which we struggled, blighted, I hoped to find comfort in his smiles. I found him wasted to a skeleton; and it is only by a month of daily and hourly most anxious care (in which I was often assisted by memories of what Mrs. Greeley did for Pickie) that I have been able to restore him. But I hold him by a frail tenure; he has the tendency to cough by which I was brought so low" (Hudspeth 5:257).

your "adored Pontiff," while in the very presence of the French bayonets the crowd hooted and hissed at the first sound of the Hymn to Pius IX. but in the end the facts remain obstinately vital.

I see the charge of ingratitude is hackneyed in our country too, against this people. I utterly deny it. Is any one bound to be grateful for promises *unkept?* This people believed in Pius IX. as long as was possible. When he drew back from the war of Italian independence, and compromised all they held most dear, through the Summer of 1848; when he suffered the Ministry he had accepted, and every measure he promised to take, to be betrayed by the Cardinals—they still loved him; they believed him deceived by his counselors. All that was violent in the demonstration of the 16th November was incited by his wicked courtiers, who made the Swiss fire on the people. Even after he had fled, if he would have listened to any messengers, if he had not taken the absurd step of appointing to govern men who were utterly incompetent, and, no more than himself, dared face the difficulties of the situation, he could not have been deposed as yet from his temporal power. The people still clung to the idea that in heart he was good and fatherly; nothing but his sanction to the foreign intervention could have entirely alienated the heart of Italy and finally convinced the whole people that the temporal sovereignty of the Pope is inconsistent with the good of this country.

That intervention, the falsehood of France, the inertia of England, the entrance of Russia into Hungary—all these steps tracked in blood, which cause so much anguish at the moment, Democracy ought in fact to bless. They insure her triumphs—there is no possible compromise between her and the Old. The Roman Moderates will not again welcome a foreign help that abandons them to exile. Hungary will not again believe it is of use to appeal to England, and declare she only wanted to maintain her old privileges; she will know that Radical Reform is the only one possible in these desperate days. Heroic Venice, the land of Garibaldi, the unyielding mildness of Mazzini, will be remembered as possessing the only wisdom. Next time all the Kings have to fly from their thrones, they will know that to return is to undertake an insoluble problem, and that Governments cannot be sustained by conscription of the whole youth of a country to oppress their own fathers and mothers. All the more for what has happened in these sad days, will entire Europe, at the end of this century, be under Republican form of Government, and then Republics will never again elect as President any member of families formerly reigning. But enough of this for the present. I might give many details of the siege of Venice, now tending to a close, if not already closed by plague and famine—of the retreat of Garibaldi, worthy the pen of Xenophon. The French, refusing all terms to their valorous foe, cunningly evaded the ignominy of butchering him, by letting him go into the midst of the Austrian force. The Austrians, Spaniards and Neapolitans followed the little band a month, without ever hazarding an attack; their cowardice in face of a few resolved souls, scarcely less ludicrous than the bravado bulletins in which they uttered it. When Garibaldi at last reached the sea-shore, there were no means by which all his band could depart; he took with him those most compromised, and they embarked in poor fishing boats. The accounts of what followed are still so confused and uncertain I will not give them. I hope and think Garibaldi himself is in Venice, and that his wife, who accompanied and everywhere aided and sustained him amid all their terrible sufferings and fatigues, is alive and with him; though the "liberators" of Italy pleasantly proclaim her buried beneath the sands of the Pineta and add, "it is more likely she was his mistress than really his wife."

One word as to the triumphal entrées, joyous receptions of the foreign liberators, prelatic rulers, &c. I have seen *one* of them; it was managed thus: A message came that the force would enter the following day, and if the municipality valued their safety they would cut down the Liberty-tree before the entry, and have everything nicely ready for the comfort of the troops. The tree was cut down at night by half a dozen persons; the hosts of the locandas tried to feign sleep and avoid giving them drink after their midnight work, but they (the foes of anarchy!) threatened to break in and take it. *I heard them myself.* Next day entered the troops, the Pontifical arms were raised, a poor Caffi di *Progresso* shot. All the applause was from a few drunken peasants, though I saw several 'potent, grave and reverend seigniors' canvassing earnestly for more. No respectable *young* men were present. The foreign officers were disgusted, and freely said they had been entirely deceived as to the feeling of this people.

Another word as to the attempt made by Oudinot to prove that he never ran the risk of destroying the monuments of Rome. I see he feels far more sore under that accusation than that of betraying the Constitution, and I don't doubt he *was* checked in his operations during the siege by the fear. Nevertheless, if his bombs and shells did *not* effect important injury, it is not because they did not fall where they might. They fell in the Vatican quarter; often on the Quirinal, on the Capital, on the Pincian. I am eye-witness that they did.

The Wurtemburg Chargé d'Affaires has written a letter to flatter Oudinot, in which he retracts his share of the Consular protest on this subject, and says, as it was dangerous for him to go out during the siege, he had not an opportunity to know that the accounts of injury were exaggerated. I have felt more disgusted with this parasitical seconding of the calumnies against the patriot army of Rome than anything else I have seen. If this Chargé was such a coward, I wonder he is not ashamed to proclaim it. Priests were in danger: the people thought them spies; yet the acts of violence really committed against them were

few. Every one possible has now been raked up, as every old rag lost or mis-
laid in the occupation of huge monasteries as barracks has been put on the lists
of robberies; and let any one compare the lists of murders and robberies with
what has been said on that subject, and make his own inferences. As to not
being able to go out in safety, I reiterate what I have before said, and it ought to
be enough—I, a woman, walked alone at all hours, in all quarters of Rome; I
stood alone amid the throng of soldiers and of citizens; I took with me little girls
to help me at the hospitals, and their parents thought my protection sufficient;
I was at the gates, at the post-office, in the nearer quarters of Trastevere, in the
Vatican gardens—I never saw an act of violence, was never even jostled in the
excitement of the crowd; I do not believe ever people or soldiery showed a finer
spirit. I grant you, if I had cried *Viva Pio Nino!* or *Viva Napoleon!* it might have
angered them. As to robbery, even my friends the bankers, pale with anxiety
so many weeks, must confess that the Garibaldi "brigands" went away without
sacking any houses or touching their strong boxes, though surely these poor
desperadoes, many of them nobles who had given up their all for the cause, had
great need of a little help in retreat; yet I hope all the alarmists will have the
decency to confess how groundless all *that* talk was.

'Be thou as chaste as ice, as pure as snow, thou shalt not escape calumny,'
at least from contemporary tongues. But History does partial, God entire, justice. The voice of this age shall yet proclaim the names of some of these Patriots
whose inspiring soul was JOSEPH MAZZINI—men as nobly true to their convictions as any that have ever yet redeemed poor, stained Humanity. The Government of to-day has done all it could to degrade the title of Roman citizen by
conferring it on Oudinot and all his descendants, but they cannot destroy the
luster it gained from being awarded to the purest disinterested patriotism and
humanity, in the person of Mazzini.

Humbug shows itself now with a flare of departing light, and one grows
breathless at the impudence with which tyrants call on God to prosper their
bloody dealings, and Judases, instead of hanging themselves on the next tree,
parade themselves as liberators for having stifled the press, hunted true men
from their native sphere, and broken every pledge, verbally no less than spiri-
tually given; yet Truth is not dead, Honor yet glows in many breasts, and Falsehood cannot destroy immortal verities by its corrupt use of their names.

The fact that makes me saddest, is the desertion to which the wounded of
Rome were inevitably subjected. For their sakes, I wish there had been a capitulation. They were soon taken from the care of their countrymen and friends,
to be put under a Committee chosen by their foes. Many more must have died
than would under other circumstances, from painful excitement and cold care.
Those who recover—many mutilated, and not a few without the right arm—

will find themselves without resource. There was an infamous attempt to punish Princess Belgiojoso for her generous zeal in their behalf, by making her responsible for all the money that had been spent in the hospitals. She was willing to account for what had been spent under her signature, but that did not content those who had read her letters from Rome to the French journals; what had passed under *that signature* had offended too much. Happily, she was able to fly, and I believe English hospitality, which had suddenly shrunk, (*on dit*— at a hint from King Bomba,) was stretched so far as to admit her into Malta. Radetzky has excluded her from return to Lombardy, but the world is wide, though it is somewhat difficult to traverse it without money; and she, I fancy, had not carried away from Rome enough to purchase even the 'crust and hollow tree,' which are the richest portion of the lovers of Liberty in these days.[3]

Meanwhile the Italian sun shines gloriously, and the earth teems plenteous more than ever to feed the crowd of invaders that wound her bosom, and prevent her own children from perishing the while. For me as I heard the tramp of a great force come to keep down every throb of generous, spontaneous life, I shuddered at the sense of what existence is under such conditions, and felt for the first time joy over the noble men that have perished. Farewell.[4] ★

Dispatch 36

THE STATE OF ITALY

FLORENCE, Nov. 15, 1849[1]

The reception to-day of some "Tribunes" whets my blunted purpose to write. Amid the pains and disappointments with which the past months have been overflowing, it is refreshing to read how cordially America sympathized. She did not hug herself in selfish content with her more prosperous fortune; she glowed at the hope of relief for the suffering nations of Europe; she deeply mourned its overthrow; she is indignant at the treachery that consummated it. I love my country for the spirit she has shown; it proves that the lust of gold, her peculiar temptation, has not yet cankered her noble heart.

[3] Undaunted, the princess lived an active life until her death on 5 July 1871 (H. Remsen Whitehouse, *A Revolutionary Princess: Christina Belgiojoso-Trivulzio: Her Life and Times, 1808–1871* [London: T. Fisher-Unwin, 1907]).

[4] On the same day Fuller wrote this dispatch, she sent her mother the news that she had a son and a husband and that the three of them hoped to return to the United States in the summer (Hudspeth 5:259–62).

[1] First published as "Things and Thoughts in Europe. No. XXXV" in *New-York Daily Tribune,* 9 January 1850, p. 1:2–3.

And for the first time in my life I rejoice in the downfall of a fellow. I received from the family of Mr. Walsh kindness while in Paris, liked them, as I believe all Americans do, but I am glad to see punished in so signal an example a meanness and weakness too common to Americans abroad.[2] Too often I have had occasion to blush at their apostasy, their ingratitude to the principles, the institutions which have made them all of good they are. They disdain the "people," forgetting that if they have risen to peculiar privileges it was owing to freedom which kept the career open to talent; they stand cap in hand to the dignities of the old world and quote with contemptible delight opinions backed only by inherited rank. It is very painful to see how stupidly they abase themselves, apparently unhappy till they can present their breasts for a ribbon, forgetful that the same implies readiness of the forehead for the rod of the absolving priest, or of the back for the knout. The position of an American is so glorious, if he has simple good sense and manly dignity to uphold it, that it is lamentable indeed to see it thus forfeited on every-day occasions, but so signal a display as Mr. Walsh made in the late terrible conflict, covers his country with shame if it is not as signally reprobated. America is the star of hope to the enclaved nations, bitter indeed were the night of the world if that star were hid from its sight by foul vapors.

I have begun to write, yet little do I feel inclined; my mind, wearied with intense excitement of hope and fear, now for months past continually suffering from sympathy with the generous who suffer, needs repose. I take long walks into the country, I gaze on the beauty of nature, and seek thus to strengthen myself in the faith that the Power who delighted in these creations will not suffer his highest, ardent, aspiring, loving men, to live and die in vain; that immortal flowers bloom on the grave of all martyrs, and phoenix births rise from each noble sacrifice.[3] I look again upon art, and solace myself in its calm. Yet it is sad to think that the cloud which darkened even the soul of Michel Angelo is not lifted yet.

The state of Italy grows worse every day. You are aware that the Milanese

---

[2] Robert Walsh (1784–1859), a journalist and editor, established the *American Quarterly Review* in 1827. In 1837 he settled permanently in Paris and established an American salon; he became consul-general in 1844 and served until 1851 (*DAB*). Walsh had angered Americans in general and Fuller in particular with his accusations that Kossuth and the Hungarian revolution threatened the world with "barbarism and ruin"; Walsh intimated that Czar Nicholas of Russia was the man who could restore "political order and civilization." Such a position was at odds with the American government's support of the revolution in Hungary, and Walsh was severely castigated in the press (*New-York Daily Tribune*, 23 April 1850, p. 6:3).

[3] At this time Fuller was living in Florence. She and Ossoli spent much of their time sightseeing and visiting with various American and British friends, including the Brownings (Hudspeth 5:275, 279–80).

answered the amnesty of Radetzky by hisses, and on the occasion he applied
the bastinado to many persons, men and women; more than four hundred have
suffered it in Parma. A new conscription is to plunge Lombardy in yet deeper
affliction. In the kingdom of Naples, it is asserted, there are thirty thousand in
the prisons, and new arrests constantly made. In Rome a few Neapolitan refugees, who were foolish enough to believe the French would yield them some
protection, have been given back to King Bomba.[4] The situation of the French
in Rome is most humiliating, the object of contempt to all parties. New arrests
are constantly made there—the prelates tracking out their prey: now they are
beginning on those who had received the amnesty from Pio IX. It seems he cannot rest, or his wicked counsellors cannot rest, till he has recanted every good
thing he ever did. Alas! how these purple men of sin must sneer as they see such
men as De Tocqueville and Odilon Barrot cast down from the place where they
have sacrificed the fair fame they had acquired by years of action on the side of
liberality, of humanity.[5] How the Jesuits smile, with thin lips and eyes down-
dropped, and think how much better Ignatius knew the world than Jesus of
Nazareth.

By the way, an affecting incident took place at Rome, in the Church of St.
Ignatius, where they had solemnized the usual November service in honor of
the dead. As the service concluded, a deep voice sounded from the crowd the
words "Peace be with the souls of those who perished for their country!" and at
the same time a shower of roses and myrtles was thrown upon the catafalk, while
the crowd responded a fervent "Peace, Peace, Amen!" Every effort by the au-
thorities to discover the speaker was in vain. Be it observed, in this connection,
that all the French assurances of bringing to justice the slayer of Rossi seem to

---

[4] The 1849 reaction in Ferdinand's kingdom was indeed brutal. When the English statesman William E. Gladstone visited there in the winter of 1850–51, he was so disturbed that
he published two letters charging the Neapolitan government with the most odious crimes
against humanity. He related that citizens were searched, arrested, and imprisoned by the
thousands without specific charges being made and that once in the prisons they faced appalling conditions. The prisons were without light or ventilation and so filled with extreme
filth that the officers would not enter them. The sick had to come out in order to see their
physicians and men of high rank and great abilities were confined in small dungeons six feet
square, often far below the level of the surrounding sea. Gladstone quoted a sentence he
had heard repeatedly applied to the Neapolitan kingdom which he regarded as true: "The
negation of God was erected into a system of government" (Marraro 101–02).

[5] Alexis de Tocqueville (1805–59), the author of *Democracy in America* (1835, 1840),
served as a member of the Constituent Assembly and as minister of foreign affairs under the
premiership of Camille-Hyacinthe-Odilon Barrot (1791–1873) and the presidency of Louis-
Napoleon. Together Tocqueville and Barrot had the task of implementing the president's
unconstitutional intervention in Rome on behalf of the pope (Newman).

have ended in nothing. Have they, perhaps, discovered that he was in part an emissary of the Cardinals, as so many said at the time? I myself supposed it an act of popular vengeance, but many Romans thought it a trap of the Cardinals to ensnare Pope and People, as was the farce of conspiracy in July 1847.

Here in Tuscany the Government is become very unpopular; the Florentines regret their mean and cowardly abandonment of the liberal cause now it has led to the expensive maintenance of a large body of Austrians. It seems that only the rabble of boys in the streets, and the ladies of England associate with the Austrians. It is painful to see what a quantity of valuable objects the Austrian soldiers have to sell. Their depredations must have been very great. They have watches, many splendid women's jewels, chains, rings, brooches. It makes me sick when I think of the circumstances under which these came into their hands. The peasants of Tuscany so much under the influence of the priests, and who were really influenced to wish Leopold back, are enraged now that they are so heavily taxed. The priests here preach against Liberty; they quote the example of Jesus: He never, they say, rebelled against Cæsar; the only liberty he wished defended was liberty of the Church. This happened in a church of Florence, last week. The Pope's Nuncio wished to get the *"Statuto"*[6] prosecuted for impiety, because it spoke well of Gioberti and Father Ventura.[7] There is a partial liberty of the press, but it must every day be limited more and more by the action of Government. In Piedmont is still a struggle for Freedom; many refugees are there; the people shows itself undaunted by the great calamities past, and still anxious to throw what weight is left it on the liberal side. If it can keep or better this position, it will be a great thing for Italy in that new conflict which cannot be far distant, for the present state of things is one that cannot endure above two or three years, if so long—and aid the political education of the people meanwhile, every one eagerly seeking for what is printed in Piedmont. The King would, probably, be with Austria if he dared, but the Liberal party, though ill-organized at present, is earnest and powerful, and it will not be easy for him to evade it. The priesthood are in feverish struggle to crook back their flocks from the green field into the fold, but their zeal is indiscreet, not worthy

---

[6] The *Statuto,* proclaimed by Charles Albert on 4 March 1848, was a constitution that provided for the enfranchisement of a small part of the population of Piedmont-Sardinia. In addition, it declared the king as the holder of the throne "by the grace of God and by the will of the Nation." It could be amended by the two elected chambers and assented to by the king. The provisions of the Statuto, as vaguely defined as they were, did not impress the pope (*New Cambridge Modern History* 10:200–201).

[7] Father Ventura, a well-known preacher, believed that the Catholic church could be saved by the people through "agitazione amorosa" (loving agitation) with the pope. Like Gioberti, Father Ventura wanted the church reformed and liberalized (Berkeley 2:163–64).

the Jesuit skill of its directors. A little Socialist work, "Christ before a Council of War," was published in Genoa; the clergy preached against it—prosecuted it at law, but could not get it condemned, and lead to its being extensively read. Probably many pairs of eyes close sealed before, were thus opened in a direction that may lead to the redress of the frightful social ills of Europe, by a peaceful though radical revolution instead of bloody conflict. The Kings may find their thrones rather crumbling than tumbling; the priests may see the consecration wafer turn into bread to sustain the perishing millions even in their astonished hands. God grant it. Here lie my hopes now. I believed before I came to Europe in what is called Socialism, as the inevitable sequence to the tendencies and wants of the era, but I did not think these vast changes in modes of government, education and daily life, would be effected as rapidly as I now think they will, because they must.[8] The world can no longer stand without them.

Thus far had I written when an opportunity offering to send my letter, I break off now, knowing I shall every day become more ready and more worthy to resume upon the theme last opened with love to my country. O Lucifer, son of the morning, fall not this time from thy chariot, but herald in at last the long looked for, wept for, bled and starved for day of Peace and Good Will to men. ★

Dispatch 37

THE NEXT REVOLUTION

FLORENCE, Jan. 6, 1850[1]

Last winter began with meteors and the rose-colored Aurora Borealis. All the winter was steady sunshine, and the Spring that followed no less glorious, as if Nature rejoiced in and daily smiled upon the noble efforts and tender, generous impulses of the Italian people. This winter, Italy is shrouded with snow. Here in Florence the oil congeals in the closet beside the fire—the water in the chamber—just as in our country-houses of New-England, as yet uncomforted by furnaces. I was supposing this to be confined to colder Florence, but a letter, this day received, from Rome says the snow lies there two feet deep, and water freezes instantly if thrown upon the pavement. I hardly know how to be-

---

[8] On 12 December 1849 Fuller wrote to Marcus and Rebecca Spring: "I have become an enthusiastic Socialist; elsewhere is no comfort, no solution for the problems of the times" (Hudspeth 5:295).

[1] First published as "Italy" in *New-York Daily Tribune*, 13 February 1850, Supplement, p. 1:2–3. This dispatch was not included in *AHA*.

lieve it—I who never saw but one slight powdering of snow all my two Roman winters, scarce enough to cover a Canary bird's wing.

Thus Nature again sympathizes with this injured people, though, I fear me, many a houseless wanderer wishes she did not. For many want both bread, and any kind of shelter this winter, an extremity of physical deprivation that had seemed almost impossible in this richest land. It had seemed that Italians might be subjected to the extreme of mental and moral suffering, but that the common beggar's plea, "*I am hungry,*" must remain a mere poetic expression. 'Tis no longer so, for it proves possible for the wickedness of man to mar to an indefinite extent the benevolent designs of God. Yet, indeed, if indefinitely not infinitely. I feel now that we are to bless the very extremity of ill with which Italy is afflicted. The cure is sure, else death would follow.

The barbarities of reaction have reached their hight in the kingdom of Naples and Sicily. Bad government grows daily worse in the Roman dominions. The French have degraded themselves there enough to punish them even for the infamous treachery of which they were guilty. Their foolish national vanity, which prefers the honor of the uniform to the honor of the man, has received its due reward, in the numberless derisions and small insults it has received from a bitterer, blacker vice, the arrogance of the priests. President, envoys, ministers, officers, have all debased themselves; have told the most shameless lies; have bartered the fair fame slowly built up by many years of seeming consistency, for a few days of brief authority, in vain. Their schemes, thus far, have ended in disunion, and should they now win any point upon the right reverend cardinal vices, it is too late. The seeds for a vast harvest of hatreds and contempts are sown over every inch of Roman ground, nor can that malignant growth be extirpated, till the wishes of Heaven shall waft a fire that will burn down all, root and branch, and prepare the earth for an entirely new culture. The next revolution, here and elsewhere, will be radical. Not only Jesuitism must go, but the Roman Catholic religion must go. The Pope cannot retain even his spiritual power. The influence of the clergy is too perverting, too foreign to every hope of advancement and health. Not only the Austrian, and every potentate of foreign blood, must be deposed, but every man who assumes an arbitrary lordship over fellow man, must be driven out. It will be an uncompromising revolution. England cannot reason nor ratify nor criticize it—France cannot betray it—Germany cannot bungle it—Italy cannot bubble it away—Russia cannot stamp it down nor hide it in Siberia. The New Era is no longer an embryo; it is born; it begins to walk—this very year sees its first giant steps, and can no longer mistake its features. Men have long been talking of a transition state—it is over—the power of positive, determinate effort is begun. A faith is offered— men are everywhere embracing it; the film is hourly falling from their eyes and they see, not only near but far, duties worthy to be done. God be praised! It was a dark period of that sceptical endeavor and work, only worthy as helping to educate the next generation, was watered with much blood and tears. God be praised! that time is ended, and the noble band of teachers who have passed this last ordeal of the furnace and den of lions, are ready now to enter their followers for the elementary class.

At this moment all the worst men are in power, and the best betrayed and exiled. All the falsities, the abuses of the old political forms, the old social compact, seem confirmed. Yet it is not so: the struggle that is now to begin will be fearful, but even from the first hours not doubtful. Bodies rotten and trembling cannot long contend with swelling life. Tongue and hand cannot be permanently employed to keep down hearts. Sons cannot be long employed in the conscious enslavement of their sires, fathers of their children. That advent called EMMANUEL begins to be understood, and shall no more so foully be blasphemed. Men shall now be represented as souls, not hands and feet, and governed accordingly. A congress of great, pure, loving minds, and not a congress of selfish ambitions, shall preside. Do you laugh, Editor of the *"Times?"* (Times of the Iron Age.) Do you laugh, Roman Cardinal, as you shut the prison-door on woman weeping for her son martyred in the cause of his country? Do you laugh, Austrian officer, as you drill the Hungarian and Lombard youth to tremble at your baton? Soon you, all of you, shall *"believe* and tremble."

I take little interest now in what is going on here in Italy.[2] It is all leavened with the same leaven, and ferments to the same end. Tuscany is stupified. They are not discontented here, if they can fold the hands yet a little while to slumber. The Austrian tutelage is mild. In Lombardy and Venice they would gladly make it so, but the case is too difficult. The sick man tosses and tumbles. The so-called Italian moderates are fighting at last, (not battles, they have not energy for that,) but skirmishes in Piedmont. The result cannot be doubtful; we need not waste time and paper in predicting it.

Joy to those born in this day: In America is open to them the easy chance of a noble, peaceful growth, in Europe of a combat grand in its motives, and in

---

[2] Fuller was, at this time, busy with taking care of her son and planning her return to the United States. She wrote a number of letters to friends and family members in December, explaining that she and Ossoli would come to America together (see Hudspeth 5:286–307). She was, of course, saddened at the thought of leaving Italy; she wrote her mother: "Weary in spirit with the deep disappointments of the last year, I wish to dwell little on these things for the moment, but seek some consolation in the affections of my little boy is quite well now, and I often feel happy in seeing how joyous and full of activity he seems. Ossoli, too, feels happier here. The future is full of difficulties for us; but having settled our plans for the present we shall set it aside while we may" (Hudspeth 5:298).

its extent beyond what the world ever before so much as dreamed. Joy to them; and joy to those their heralds, who, if their path was desert, their work unfinished, and their heads in the power of a prostituted civilization, to throw as toys at the feet of flushed, triumphant wickedness, yet holy-hearted in unasking love, great and entire in their devotion, fall or fade, happy in the thought that there come after them greater than themselves, who may at last string the harp of the world to full concord, in glory to God in the highest, for peace and love from man to man is become the bond of life.   ★

EMENDATIONS

The texts of Fuller's dispatches are reprinted from their first appearances in the *New-York Tribune*, with the following emendations (page.line numbers refer to the present edition):

Dispatch 1

42.30	will increase] will
47.22	fable;] fable
48.1	Chantrey] Chartney

Dispatch 2

52.17	Edinburgh] Edinbugh
53.33	"Dion."] "Dn."
55.36	a posy] raposy
58.18	Force] Fore
58.20	Buttermere] Battermere
58.20	Crummock] Cromak

Dispatch 3

60.7	Crummock] Cromek
60.7	Buttermere] Battermer
60.19	successful] suceessful
61.8	Branksome] Branxholm

Dispatch 4

63.30	blood).] blood.

Dispatch 5

70.14	expected.] expected
72.9	convention] covention
72.19	not] *not*
74.11	Rowardennan] Rowardennen
74.16	for me] or me
75.21	Rowardennan] Rowardinnan
77.12	anguish and] anguish and and
77.16	majestic-looking] majestic looking

Dispatch 6

79.1	HELL'S GLEN] HELL GLEN
79.1	Loch Long] Loch Levy

Dispatch 8

89.11	felt.] felt
90.20	Moxon's] Moxen's
92.21	Suicides] Luicides

Dispatch 9

95.13	Canaletto] Canatello
99.31	exceeding] exceedng
100.2	Pistrucci] Pistracci
100.2	Mariotti] Mariatti

Dispatch 10

103.39	acting] actting
106.1	gypsy] gipsy
108.30	Cluny] Clugny
108.30	delightfully] delighfully

Dispatch 11

113.15	connoisseurs] connaisseurs
113.19	declares] declare
115.14	parts.] parts
116.16	Gardoni] Gardini
116.20	ray of] ray

Dispatch 12

119.13	just after] just before
120.9	purposes.] purposes
121.3	true,] true.
123.29	*Frères Chrétiens*] *Fréres Chrétiens*
124.5	*Crèche*] *Creche*

Dispatch 13

126.14	Cavaillé] Cavaille
128.17	*Crèches*] *Creches*
130.1	Cuma] Cama
130.1	Capri] Capré

Dispatch 14

135.4	Carracci] Caracci
135.8	Leonardo] Lionardo
135.12	connoisseurship] connaisseurship
135.14	frescoes] rescoes
136.4	pines] pineas
137.14	d'Azelgio] d'Azeglio
137.28	published] pubished
137.25–6	penitence.] penitence
138.15	Crèches] Creche
138.20–1	steam-engines,] steam-engines

Dispatch 15

143.13	Clotilda Tambroni] Matilda Tambreni

Dispatch 17

157.31	it.] it
157.37	Ferrara] Ferarra

Dispatch 18

162.39	connoisseurs] connaisseurs
165.16	insight into] insight to
165.29	spoliation] spollation

Dispatch 19

169.1	fleas] leas
171.26	dress,] dress.
172.32	it is] it
173.8	Sardinia has] Sardinia as
174.23	simpletons] simpleton
175.3	Tacitus, an] Tacitus,
175.6	Obscurantists] Oscurantists
175.8	Lombardo-Venetian] Lombardo-Venitian
176.4	sun] un

Dispatch 20

180.19	cadrò, ò cadrò] cadrè, da

Dispatch 21

184.20	Gesù] Gesei

187.22	Pope.] Pope
188.12	Ciceraucchio] Ciceronacchio
188.26	Ombrosi] Ombrossi
189.7	that has fallen] that fallen
192.2	summoning you.] summoning you
194.24	shall be,] shall
195.12	hierarchy] hierachy
196.6	work.] work
197.17	people;] people.

Dispatch 22

201.23	Oxenstiern] Oxensteirn
202.2	retractions] retractations
203.10	Corso] corso
203.23	*Chi è?*] *Chi.*
204.1	Ara] Ava
207.1	Agnes] Agnese
208.22	Tommaseo] Tomasco

Dispatch 23

212.3	Piazza del] Piazza
212.22	Tommaseo] Tommaso
214.9	Hillard] Hilliard

Dispatch 24

222.17	Béranger] Beranger
223.23	"PEOPLE] PEOPLE
225.4	has a] has
225.22	dereliction] direliction
227.21	*Circolo*] Circalo
227.40	such as] such
229.24	become,] become

Dispatch 25

236.15	Tommaseo] Tommasso

Dispatch 26

239.20	Garibaldi] Garribaldi
242.5	panic-struck] panic-stuck
245.2	Guerrazzi] Guerazzi

Dispatch 27

248.23	E.,] E.
251.29	capital of our] capital our

252.11   sacrilegious] sacriligious

Dispatch 28

255.29   Campidoglio] Campidaglio
255.32   Venezia] Venizia
255.32   Venezia] Venizia
257.10   Campidoglio] Campidaglio
258.22   to form any] to any

Dispatch 29

261.27   steal] stea
262.21   Italy.] Italy
265.13   connoisseur] connoiseur
269.32   fair] air
272.4   Isn't] Is'nt
273.34   Tenerani's] Tenenani's
274.1   *mora*] *moro*

Dispatch 30

275.2   Novara] Novera
275.9   Città] Civita
275.19   Città] Civita
276.9   Città] Civita
276.26   Chargé] Charge

Dispatch 31

277.15   because it] because i
278.17   Modena] Modina
278.18   Radetzky] Radetzsky
279.3   Cardinals'] Cardinal's
279.10   Molière] Moliere
279.15   there.] there
280.14   drunkenness] drunkeness
280.32   Novara] Novarra
281.15   Belgiojoso] Belgiojero
281.16   Trivulzio] Trivalzio
281.23   Pavia] Paia
281.31   heart,] heart
282.19   ambassadors] embassadors
285.4   steamer!).] steamer!
285.11   loggia] laggia

Dispatch 32

285.9   Guerrazzi] Guerazzi
286.9   pick-pocket,] pick-pocket

287.25   drawn] drawn;
288.9   16th that] 16th is that
289.5   Città] Civita
289.18   Città] Civita
290.18   Città] Civita
290.30   her] our
290.33   Città] Civita
290.38   Città] Civita
290.39   Città] Civita
292.26   Ramorino] Ramerion
292.30   Ramorino] Ramerino
293.24   Doria Pamfili] Pampili Doria

Dispatch 33

296.11   PAMFILI] PAMPILI
296.37   armistice] armstice
298.9   Città] Civita
299.24   Palazzo] Palazza
300.16   Radetzky] Radetsky
301.14   Pamfili] Pampli
301.22   we to] we

Dispatch 34

303.3   Gesù] Gesu
303.12   Janiculum] Janicular
303.32   Janiculum] Janicular
303.34   Manara] Marara
304.10   light,] light
305.10   intervention] inervention
306.38   Trasteverini] Trastevirini
310.32   leaf] eaf
311.14   send] send,
311.17   not,] not

Dispatch 35

315.2   barracks] barreks

INDEX